Teach Yourself

ARABIC

Teach Yourself

ARABIC

S.A. Rahman

GOODWORD

Dedicated to
my mother and father
who worked hard to make me what I am today.
I dedicate this book in all humanity.

First Published 2003
Reprinted 2015
© Goodword Books 2015

Goodword Books
A-21, Sector 4, Noida-201301, India
Tel. +91-8588822672, +91120-4314871
email: info@goodwordbooks.com
www.goodwordbooks.com

Goodword Books, Chennai
324, Triplicane High Road,
Triplicane, Chennai-600005
Tel. +9144-4352-4599
Mob. +91-9790853944, 9600105558
email: chennaigoodword@gmail.com

Goodword Books, Hyderabad
2-48/182, Plot No. 182, Street No. 22
Telecom Nagar Colony, Gachi Bawli
Hyderabad-500032
Tel. 04023000131, Mob. 07032641415
email: hyd.goodword@gmail.com

Islamic Vision Ltd.
426-434 Coventry Road, Small Heath
Birmingham B10 0UG, U.K.
Tel. 121-773-0137, Fax: 121-766-8577
e-mail: info@ipci-iv.co.uk, www.islamicvision.co.uk

IB Publisher Inc.
81 Bloomingdale Rd, Hicksville
NY 11801, USA
Tel. 516-933-1000, Fax: 516-933-1200
Toll Free: 1-888-560-3222
email: info@ibpublisher.com, www.ibpublisher.com

Printed in India

Contents

About the Book
List of Abbreviation
Names of Arabic Vowels
Names of Arabic Cases
Names of Arabic Tenses

6

8

من أراد أن يعمل كبيرا فى النحو
بعد كتاب سيبويه فليستحى

Introduction

India is a country where the tradition of Islam and Arabic studies stretches over centuries. There is no dearth of books on Islam, Arabic literature and other related subjects, Arabic language and its grammar. Whether it is a madrasah for religious studies or a school, college and University of modern education, the Arabic syllabi invariably include Arabic grammar. Indian scholars of the Arabic language have till date prepared a large number of books in an attempt to teach Arabic grammar in order to strengthen the foundations of the student of the Arabic language. Superficially and according to the abilities of the students some of the books have come to be known as good books and some others as bad books. However, I am of the conviction that no book on any subject and more so of the Arabic grammar should be compared with other books and classified as good or bad because every author prepares his book to the best of his information and ability and for a specific group of people with specific end in mind to achieve. Similarly no two persons or students will learn equally from the same book or the same teacher. Every author has his past experience in the field of the subject on the basis of which he builds up his book and every student has his own level of intellect and motivation to learn.

No single information can ordinarily be acquired from a single reading of a book and no single book can be read repeatedly due to monotony and boredom and hence he needs to read the same information encoded differently before it becomes a part and parcel of his acquisition.

It is more true of grammar of any language particularly for those who learn a foreign language in a foreign milieu through the grammar and not the grammar through the language like in the case of native languages.

Every author desires and tries to place his subject before readers in a way that he thinks is better and easy to comprehend and thus is created a corpus of reading material on the subject that provides choice to the readers and students.

In this book I have also tried to put things the way I think better and with my teaching experience spread over more than thirty long years. I believe that this book in hand will be of great utility for the students of the Arabic language anywhere and specially anywhere in India. I have employed the same method of placing things before the readers as I used in teaching my students in the classroom and since I had achieved good result with my students. Unlike many other books on Arabic grammar most favoured and popular with the students, I have written my own texts with specific grammar point in mind to teach through the lesson and precisely this is the reason that I could feed in the texts the grammar points I wanted and give maximum number of examples. It is of course not possible to write a lesson with only one grammar point, however, it is very much possible to teach only specific things through one lesson and indeed this is what I have tried to achieve. I think this could be possible for me because I have improvised texts for each lesson in preference to borrowing readymade texts from established writers of renown, or poetry, or the Quran and the Hadith of the prophet which is generally the case with a large number of books. I am fully aware that my improvised texts may not be very ornate and rhythmical as in some other books, however, I am confident that they are good enough to serve my end that is to make the readers and the students understand that they need to understand in an easy way and to achieve this end I am prepared to make any sacrifice.

In each lesson the text has been written and divided in lines in such a way that the meaning of the Arabic word, and phrase can be given just in front of it in order tc make the things easy for the readers and our success rate is quite high. It has also been attempted that only specific grammar point/s should be dealt with in each lesson and the readers should work to concentrate to deal only with that much.

As far as possible adequate explanation has been given with examples. At the end of each lesson a list of difficult words used in the lesson has also been provided with their meanings in English.

I have detailed major grammar points in thirty-five lessons and some essential points have been briefly summed up under "Arabic Grammar on Finger Tips". These include points which have either been discussed thoroughly in the lessons and I have mentioned them here just to serve as reminder while some minor points that do not merit detailed explanation but are considered vital, have been mentioned with adequate explanation and examples.

Through each book is complete in itself, however, no book is ever a final word on the subject. I believe that each book is complementary to the others on the subject as it provides another opportunity for the readers to compensate for what he or the authors might have missed in the others.

I have taken several books written on this topic of Arabic grammar as my model and tried to do this book in a different way—in a way that I considered better and closer to the ability of the students to understand.

It may be noted that I have basically prepared this book for the students who want to learn standard written Arabic outside its native milieu in most of the cases. I believe this book will be of great help for such people.

Before I finish I like to thank all those people who were in anyway helpful to me in preparing this small handbook of Arabic grammar and very specially Mr. Saniyasnain, the publisher of this book and who had actually prompted me to do this book about more than a year ago.

Finally, I thank God who gave me good health and ability to complete this work as best as I could.

(S.A. Rahman)

List of Abbreviations:

Adj.	Adjective
Adj. com	Adjective of comparative degree
Adj./Numeral	Adjective/ Numeral
Adj SF	Adjective Singular Feminine
Adj.SM	Adjective Singular Masculine
Adj./VN	Adjective / Verbal Noun
Adj.N.	Adjectival Noun
Adv.	Adverb
Adv of Time	Adverb of time
C N M	Collective Noun Masculine
e. g.	Exempli gratia/ for example
F D	Feminine Dual
i. e.	id est/ that is
M	Man/Men
W	Woman/Women
M D	Masculine Dual
N F	Noun Feminine
N M	Noun Masculine
N P P	Non-personal plural
N U	Noun of Unity
N U F	Noun of Unity Feminine
M F D	Masculine Feminine Dual
O. S.	One self
P	Plural
P. F.	Plural Feminine
Pl. non-personal	Plural non-personal
P M	Plural Masculine
P M & F/PMF	Plural Masculine & Feminine
P P	Past Participle/Passive Participle
PP/ SM	Past / Passive Participle / Singular Masculine
A P	Acive Participle

S M	Singular Masculine
S F	Singular Feminine
Prep.	Preposition
S M & F, SM/F	Singular Masculine & Feminine
V N/VNSM	Verbal Noun/Verbal Noun Singular Masculine
VN / Adj.	Verbal Noun/ Adjective

I P SMF	First Person Singular Masculine/ Feminine
I P D P M F	First Person Dual/ Plural Maculine / Feminine
II P SM	Second Person Singular Masculine
II P DM	Second Person Dual Masculine
II P PM	Second Person Plural Masculine
IIP SF	Second Person Singular Feminine
IIP DF	Second Person Dual Feminine
IIP PM	Second Person Plural Feminine
III PSM	Third Person Singular Masculine
IIIP DM	Third Person Dual Masculine
IIIP PM	Third Person Plural Masculine
IIIP SF	Third Person Singular Feminine
IIIP DF	Third Person Dual Feminine
IIIP PF	Third Person Plural Feminine

Explanation:

I Person	=	The person who speaks.
II Person	=	The person spoken to.
III Person	=	The Person spoken about.

Names of Arabic Vowels:

Fatḥah / fatḥah			ـَـ	فتحة
Kasrah/ kasrah			ـِـ	كسرة
Ḍammah/ ḍammah			ـُـ	ضَمَّة
Tanween/ tanween	ـٌـ	ـٍـ	ـًـ	تنوين

Sokoon/ sokoon	٥	سُكُون
Shaddah/ shaddah	ّ	شَدَّة
Shaddah with kasrah	ـِّ or ـّ	شَدَّة مَعَ الكَسْرَة
Shaddah with ḍammah	ـُّ	شَدَّة مَعَ الضَّمَّةُ
Shaddah with fatḥah	ـَّ	شَدَّة مَعَ الفتحة
Maddah	~	مَدَّة

(It is written above the initial alif only to elongate its sound)

Name Of Arabic Cases:

Terminal letter of a word indicates the case.

(1) When the last letter carries (single or double) ḍammah:

Nominative case   حالة الرفع/ مرفوع

(2) When the last letter carries (single or double) fatḥah:

Accusative Case   حَالة النصب/ منصوب

(3) When the last letter carries (single or double) kasrah:

Genitive case   حالة الجر/ مجرور

Names of Arabic Tenses:

Past Tense   الفعل الماضى

Present Tense   الفعل المضارع

Names of Arabic Moods:

When the last letter of a verb is silent i.e. it carries a sokoon:

Jussive mood   حالة الجزم/ مجزوم

When the last letter of a noun is silent i.e. it carries a sokoon:

A pocopate mood   حَالَة الجزم/ مجزوم

When the last letter of the verb/noun carries (single or double) *fatḥah*

Subjunctive mood   حالة النصب/ منصوب

LESSON – 1　　الدرس – ١

Arabic Alphabet　الابجدية العربية

ا　ب　ت　ث

ج　ح　خ　د

ذ　ر　ز　س

ش　ص　ض　ط

ظ　ع　غ　ف

ق　ك　ل　م

ن　ه　و　ى

ء　ة

Arabic is written and read from right to left. Hereunder are given (i) the Arabic letters in the top line and (ii) their approximate pronunciation (& their symbols in brackets) in the Roman letters in the second line.

(i) Read from right to left:

ث	ت	ب	ا
Thaa (TH)	Taa (T)	Baa (B)	Alif (A)
د	خ	ح	ج
Daal (D)	Khaa (KH)	Ḥaa (Ḥ)	Jeem (J)
س	ز	ر	ذ
Seen (S)	Zaa (Z)	Raa (R)	Dhaal (DH)
ط	ض	ص	ش
Ṭaa (Ṭ)	Ḍaa (Ḍ)	Ṣaa (Ṣ)	Sheen (SH)
ف	غ	ع	ظ
Faa (F)	Ghayn (GH)	'Ayn ('A)	Ẓaa (Ẓ)
م	ل	ك	ق
Meem (M)	Laam (L)	Kaaf (K)	Qaaf (Q)
ى	و	ﻩ/ﮬ	ن
Yaa (Y)	Waw (W)	Haa (H)	Noon (N)
		ة	ء
		Taa (Round) (T)	Hamza ('A)

Notes:

(1) There are twenty eight letters in the Arabic Alphabet.

Last two letters are in fact the variant forms of letters nos. 1 and 3 respectively. However, for our convenience we can consider them to be thirty letters. More so because these two letters i.e. Hamza and Round Taa play a distinctive role in the Arabic language in terms of Grammar and orthographic requirements and rules.

2. All Arabic letters are considered to be consonants. However, three letters i.e. Alif ١, Waw و, and Yaa ى , are also used as elongative vowels. Details regarding vowels and elongative vowels appear in lesson number 5 of this book.

3. Sound transcription of Arabic letters has been given in Roman letters for facilitating the process of learning the Arabic sounds. They should be treated as approximate sound equivalents and not the total equivalents.

4. Key to pronouncing peculiar Arabic sounds is given in lesson number 2.

Exercises:

(1) Read Arabic letters to acquaint yourself with their sounds (as explained in lesson no. 2) and independent shapes:

(2) Acquire Roman equivalents of Arabic letters as they are likely to occur elsewhere in this book.

LESSON – 2   الدرس—٢

Peculiar Arabic Sounds   الاصوات العربية الخاصة

Apart from the ordinary sounds available in the Indian languages specially in Hindi there are eleven sound in the Arabic language which may be termed as very peculiar of Arabic.

These sounds are as follows (Read from right to left):

ذ	خ	ح	ث
Dhaal	Khaa	Ḥaa	Thaa

ظ	ط	ض	ص
Ẓaa	Ṭaa	Ḍaa	Ṣaa

ق	غ	ع
Qaaf	Ghayn	'Ayn

In the following lines an attempt is made to guide the learners to say these sounds as close to the correct sounds as possible:

1. ث Thaa : It should be said like "th" in Elizabeth. To say this sound correctly one has to put the tip of the tongue on the inner edge of the upper teeth. Detach the tongue while saying the sound.

2. ح Ḥaa: Only your throat shall be functioning to say this sound. When you intend to say this sound your lower throat and uvula shall come very close leaving a negligible aperture between them for the air to pass out. Sound thus made will be heavy aspirate "Ḥ" and this is precisely what we know as Arabic Ḥaa.

3. خ Khaa: For saying this sound also only your throat functions. This sound may be equated with "ch" in LOCH of the Scotish Language. This sound is best produced when the throat is allowed to relax with the mouth open and the uvula hanging down hindering the free passage of the air. This sound may be compared with the snoring of a person when asleep.

4. ذ Dhaal: This sound can be said by putting the tip of the tongue on the inner side of the upper teeth. Detach the tongue when you intend to say the sound. This sound may be compared with soft "dh" sound as in DHOW.

5. ص Ṣaad: Give your tongue the Shape of a shallow bowl. Open your mouth moderately. Slowly close your mouth when you intend to say the sound. Your upper and lower teeth will join gently and the tip of the tongue shall touch the palate at the roots of the upper teeth while your lips will remain apart. This sound may be compared with the "s" sound as in BLAST.

6. ض Ḍaa: Shape of your tongue and other instructions remaining the same as in Ṣaa except only that the tip of the tongue shall join the palate at the roots of the upper teeth both before and after saying the sound. This sound may be compared with "d" as in DAD.

7. ط Ṭaa: Shape of the tongue remains the same as in the earlier two sounds. Put the tip of the tongue on the frontal palate. Detach the tongue as you release the sound. This sound may be compared with "t" as in FLAT.

8. ظ Ẓaa: Shape of the tongue remains the same as in the foregoing sound. However, here the tongue shall not touch the palate at all both before and after releasing the sound. Your tongue shall go very close to the frontal palate in preparation to say the sound. The tongue will have to be withdrawn when you intend to say the sound.

9. ع 'Ayn: Open your mouth at half its capacity. Stop the breath by lowering the root of the tongue inside the throat, thus narrowing the passage of the air. Slowly lift the root of the tongue and lower the uvula while releasing the sound. It may be remembered here that only the throat functions to say this sound.

10. غ Ghayn: Open your mouth at half its capacity. The softest part at the end of the palate and the uvula shall slowly come down as you prepare to say this sound. This sound is very close to "r" in the French language. It may also be compared with the strong gargling sound.

11. ق Qaaf: Stop the breath in the throat. Open your mouth moderately. Lower the uvula and lift the root of the tongue. Detach them as you say the sound.

Other sounds of the Arabic Language are available in almost all the Indian languages or otherwise they are easy to say.

Note: When given the physical apparition the sounds are technically known as letters.

Exercises:

1. Say all the Arabic sounds as many times as you can. Give special attention to such sounds which do not occur in Indian languages.
2. Repeat peculiar Arabic sounds till you are able to say them properly.

LESSON – 3

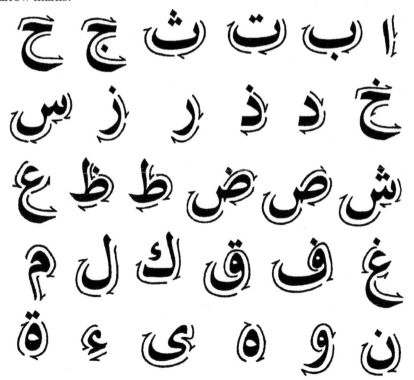 الدرس – ٣

How to write Arabic letters
كيف نكتب الحروف العربية

This lesson has been exclusively designed for giving the learners the right method of writing the Arabic letters.

It is essential keeping in view the fact that Arabic script itself poses a great challenge for a large majority of Indian students who want to learn the Arabic language.

I have shown here with arrow marks the directions which have to be followed strictly if one wants to master the Arabic script.

Read and write from right to left and only in the directions as shown by arrow marks:

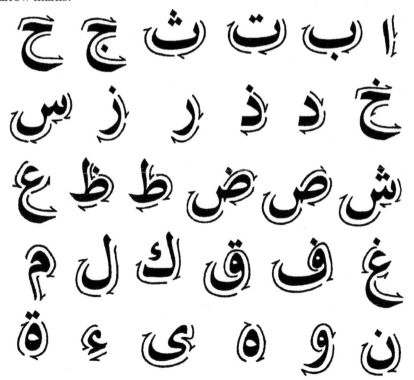

Notes:

1. Care should be taken to draw the proper shapes of the letters in the direction as indicated by arrow/s.

2. Right number of dots should be placed at the right places.

Exercises:

1. Write the shapes of the Arabic letters.

Note: It may be mentioned here that these shapes are known as the independent forms of the letters.

LESSON — 4

الدرس — ٤

Different Shapes Of Arabic Letters
مختلف اشكال حروف اللغة العربية

There are no capital letters in Arabic. Arabic words are obtained by joining these letters with one another. When we join Arabic letters together to obtain words they look to have assumed shapes different from their original independent shapes as per their placement in the words- in the beginning , in the middle and at the end.

Based on this premise we can say that Arabic letters can assume four different shapes. They are as follows:

1. Independent shapes
2. Initial shapes
3. Medial shapes
4. Terminal shapes

1. Independent shapes of letters have been shown in lesson No. 1. As would be evident from the word independent, each letter is written independent of the other i.e. one letter separate from the other.

2. By initial shapes of the letters it is intended to mean the shapes of the letters in the beginning of a word.

In this case only the commencing part of a letter is taken, or it might even be said that a miniature shape of a particular letter is used.

3. By medial shapes of the letters it is intended to mean the shapes of the letters somewhere between the first and the last letters of a word.

In this case also a miniature shape of the letter is used.

4. By terminal shapes of the letters it is intended to mean the shapes of the letters at the end of a word.

In this case the letter is drawn in its full shape. However, it is joined to its preceding letter and hence, it looks different from its independent shape.

Let us take for our example the letter Khaa خ and wirte it in its four forms as explained above in the following words:

Far khon   (young bird)   فَرْخٌ

The letter Khaa خ is written independently i. e. it is not joined to its preceding letter. It is the same as you have seen in the alphabetical table in lesson-1.

Khafeeron　　　　　　(watchman)　　　　　خَفِيْرٌ

Only the crown of the letter i. e. its initial part has been taken.

Makhfaron　　　　　　(guardroom)　　　　　مَخْفَرٌ

Only the crown of the letter with ligatures on both sides is used in this word.

Tafreekhon　　　　　　(incubation)　　　　　تَفْرِيْخٌ

The full form of the letter is used, however, here it is joined to its preceding letter. It is called the terminal attached shape.

In lesson no. 1, you have seen and practised the independent shapes of the Arabic letters. Hereunder we give the other three shapes of the Arabic letters. Alongside we also the give independent shapes of the letters for ready reference and comparison.

Terminal Shapes	Medial Shapes	Initial Shapes	Independent Shapes
ـا	ـا	ا	ا
ـب	ـبـ	بـ	ب
ـت	ـتـ	تـ	ت
ـث	ـثـ	ثـ	ث
ـج	ـجـ	جـ	ج
ـح	ـحـ	حـ	ح
ـخ	ـخـ	خـ	خ
ـد	ـد	د	د
ـذ	ـذ	ذ	ذ
ـر	ـر	ر	ر
ـز	ـز	ز	ز
ـس	ـسـ	سـ	س
ـش	ـشـ	شـ	ش
ـص	ـصـ	صـ	ص

ـط	ـطـ	طـ	ط
ـظ	ـظـ	ظـ	ظ
ـع	ـعـ	عـ	ع
ـغ	ـغـ	غـ	غ
ـف	ـفـ	فـ	ف
ـق	ـقـ	قـ	ق
ـك	ـكـ	كـ	ك
ـل	ـلـ	لـ	ل
ـم	ـمـ	مـ	م
ـن	ـنـ	نـ	ن
ـه	ـهـ / ـھـ	هـ	ه
ـو	ـو	و	و
ـي	ـيـ	يـ	ى

Keen and careful observation of different forms of Arabic letters shall reveal that barring a few letters the Arbic letters do not assume shapes really different from the original independent forms. It is however, the ligatures i.e. additional strokes drawn for joining letters in words which make them look different. It is very much true even of the English cursive writing. For example let us take the following two words:

cat / act

You can see in the above two words in cursive writing that component letters: c : a : t : do appear slightly different from their following typewritten forms:

cat : act

In the case of Arabic letters the change that occurs in cursive writing or running hand is slightly more or at least so it appears.

When joined together in words the Arabic stomached letters lose their stomachs in the beginning and in the middle. Only the crowns/initial portions of the letters or a representative tooth substitutes them in the said positions. They however retain their distinctive marks i.e. dots.

The letter Meem م when joined in the beginning or in the middle, loses its tail.

The letter 'Ayn ع and Ghayn غ are the only two letters in the Arabic alphabet which drastically change when joined in words. In the middle and at the end the crown assumes a triangular shape as it is given in the following: Ma'a (with) مَعَ

It is relevant to mention here that the following six letters are not joined with the letters that follow them. If any of these six letters occurs in the beginning or anywhere in the middle of a word we have to break the word at that stage and write the remainder part of the word afresh.

These six letters are as follows:

و	ز	ر	ذ	د	ا
Waw	Zaa	Raa	Dhaal	Daal	Alif

In brief we can say that the letters mentioned above can either be independent or terminal and when they occur in the beginning or somewhere in the middle of a word they should be treated as semi-terminals. For example:

Farkhon   فرخ   Waalidon   والد

(young bird)   (father)

Notes:

1.   Learners are advised to read this lesson carefully and practice sounds and shapes diligently.

2.   The letter Hamza ء is not at all joined. It may be written below or above Alif e. g. إ أ. It may be written on Waw and ى e.g. ؤ ئ. It may be written somewhere in the word on a tooth e.g. ـئـ. It may be written straight on the line ء.

3.   The Round Taa occurs only at the end of a noun. Noun ending with Round Taa is generally feminine singular . Counted few are singular msculine because they are specifically used for men. Occasionally some plural nouns can also terminate with round Taa. Learners will acquire this information in due course. It is written thus ة when it is terminal or independent. When it is joined to its preceding letter the shape appears thus ة .

Exercises:

1. Practice acquisition of sounds and shapes of Arabic letters.

Advice: Please seek learned help to achieve accuracy in pronunciation & writing.

LESSON — 5

الدرس — ٥

الحركات Vowels

There are two kinds of vowels in the Arabic language:

    i) Close Vowels

    ii) Long Vowels or Open Vowels

Names and usage of close vowels are as following:

a)   The first vowel is a small diagonal mark/ stroke above the letters.

Example:

تَ   بَ   اَ

Now we shall read the above mentioned letters as:

    "a" in attend

    "ba" in bandage

    "ta" in tanbark

This diagonal stroke is known in Arabic grammar terminology as fatḥah.

b)   The second close vowel is a diagonal stroke placed under a letter. It is called kasrah.

Example:

تِ   بِ   اِ

In this case we shall read the above metioned letters as:

    "i" in in

    "bi" in bin

    "ti" in tin

c)   Third close vowel is called ḍammah. It is an eyed coma placed always above the letters.

Example:

ثُ   بُ   اُ

Now we shall read these letters as follows:

"o" in oyster

"bo" in boil

"to" in toil

The vowels mentioned above may have to be written twice under or above the terminal letters of nouns and adjectives. In this case the sound of the concerned letter shall end in nunnation i.e. the sound of the concerned letter shall end in a strong "NOON" sound.

Example:

Now we shall read the above vowelled letters as:

"an" in anthrax

"ban" in bandy

"tan" in tandem

These diagonal strokes might occur under a terminal letter of nouns or adjectives.

Example:

These letters shall be read as:

"in" in inside

"bin" in dustbin

"tin" in tinker

Similarly two eyed comas might have to be written above the terminal letters of nouns and adjectives. In print we ordinarily see one right and the other inverse coma as shown below:

Example:

ﺕٌ   ﺏٌ   أً

In this case the terminal letters shall have to be read as:

"un" in munsif

"bun" in bundelkhand

"tun" in tundra

These three double vowels are known as:

    i) double *Fathah*

    ii) double *Kasrah*

    iii) double *Dammah*

The double *kasrah* and double *Dammah* are directly written under or above the letters as explained in the foregoing. However, in the case of double *fathah* one supportive Alif ١ is necessarily suffixed to the concerned terminal letter except the Round Taa and terminal Hamzah.

Example:

In the case of the Round Taa (Taa-e- Marboota in Grammar Terminology) the double *fathah* is directly placed above it and it does not need any supportive Alif.

Example:

ةً

Similarly double *fathah* is directly placed above the terminal Hamzah and placing Alif after it is a mistake.

Example:

ءً

Now let us take up the long or open vowels.

All the twenty eight letters of the Arabic alphabet (or say thirty) are consonants. However, three of them are used as long vowels also. They are:

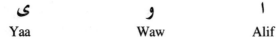

ى	و	١
Yaa	Waw	Alif

The first open vowel is a long "a" sound. It obtains when the Alif ١ is preceded by a letter bearing one fathah.

Example:

تَا   بَا

We shall read the above combinations as:

"ba" in bath or say baa

"ta" in talk or say taa

The second open vowel is a long "e" sound. It obtains when this elongative yaa ى is preceded by a letter bearing one kasrah.

Example:

تِى   بِى

We shall read the above combinations as:

"bee" in beef

"tee" in teeth

The third open vowel is a long "o" sound. It obtains when this elongative "Waw و is preceded by a letter bearing one *dammah*.

Example:

تُو   بُو

These combinations shall be read as:

"boo" in boon

"too" in tooth

Apart from the vowels mentioned above there are three more signs that fall under this category.

The first sign is a short zigzag stroke placed above consonant Alif ا to elongate the "a" sound as we would read double "aa" as in Baa. It is called Maddah and written thus:

آ

The second sign is a small stomached circle placed always above a letter. This is called sokoon or the silencing vowel. When this sign occurs above a letter it is required of a reader to make a brief pause there before proceeding to the next sound of a word composed of a few letters. It is written thus:

ث   بْ

Now we shall read them as:

"b" in obsolete

"t" in bat

The third singn is called shaddah. It is a three toothed sign placed always above a letter. It is used only where one and the same letter comes twice. In this case the letter is written only once bedecked with shaddah and read twice as per its vowel. It is written as follows:

حُبٌّ   حُبًّا   حُبٍّ

Now we shall read them as:

Hob-bun   Hob-ban   Hob-bin

It would be seen that double "ba" in the above combinations shall be read twice as "bb" in 'sub base'

Beside whatever has been said above about the vowels there are two dipthongs also in Arabic. Dipthong sounds occur in Arabic where a letter bearing *fathah* precedes Waw and Yaa with Sokoon.

Example:

أَىْ   أَوْ

Now these should be read as:

"ow" in owl

"y" in by

Note: When these vowels are placed on the terminal letters of the nouns, they indicate case. For example dammah-double or single—indicates that the noun is in the nominative case. Dammah at the terminal letter which indicates case is known in Arabic grammar as Raf'a. Similarly *fathah* at the terminal letter indicates that the noun is in the accusative case. This *fathah* is known as Nasb. The *kasrah* below the terminal letter of the noun is known as Jarr and the noun is considered to be in the genitive case. For details, please see lessons — 12 & 13

Exercises:

1. Read this lesson and the lessons preceding this thoroughly and practice well before proceeding any further.

LESSON — 6

الدرس — ٦

Words And Parts Of Speech

الكلمات و أقسام الكلام

A word is a combination of two or more letters which makes meaning.

Examples:

Hand	يَدٌ	} 1
Boy	وَلَدٌ	
New	جَدِيْدٌ	} 2
Old	قَدِيْمٌ	
This	هٰذَا	} 3
He	هُوَ	
In, Inside	فِيْ	} 4
With	مَعَ	
Infront of	أَمَامَ	} 5
Behind	وَرَاءَ	
He went	ذَهَبَ	} 6
He goes	يَذهَبُ	

A word may be a noun as in the case of the first two words;
it may be an adjective as in the case of the second two words;
it may be a pronoun as in the case of the third two words;
it may be a preposition as in the case of the fourth two words;
it may be an adverb as in the case of the fifth two words;
it may be a verb as in the case of the sixth two words.

When these words are arranged in a certain specified order they make
meaningful speech.

Broadly speaking we can divide the parts of speech into three groups of words. They are as follows:

1. Nouns   الاسماء
2. Verbs   الافعال
3. Particles i. e. Prepositions etc.   الحروف

Noun: It is a word which is used for naming a person, place, animal or thing.

Examples:

Person:

son/ boy	وَلَدٌ
daughter/girl	بِنتٌ
student	طَالِبٌ
worker	عَامِلٌ

Place:

garden	حَدِيْقَةٌ
airport	مَطَارٌ
house	بَيْتٌ
city	مَدِيْنَةٌ

Animal:

dog	كَلْبٌ
lion	أَسَدٌ
sparrow	عُصْفُوْرٌ
hen	دَجَاجَةٌ

Thing:

building	عِمَارَةٌ
table	طَاوِلَةٌ
book	كِتَابٌ
mountain	جَبَلٌ

Verb: It is a word which is used for meaning an action with involvement of time.

Examples:

(he) went	ذَهَبَ
(she) went	ذَهَبَتْ
(he) goes	يَذْهَبُ
(she) goes	تَذْهَبُ
(you) go	إِذْهَبْ
(you) don't go	لَا تَذْهَبْ

Particle: It is a word (preposition etc.)that is generally helpful in giving useful meaning to combination of words in a sentence.

Examples:

in	فِى
on	عَلَى
that	أَنْ

Note: Unless required otherwise under grammatical rules, all Arabic nouns terminate with double ḍammah.

Exercises:

1. Separate nouns, verbs and particles from the following list:

(they) went	ذَهَبُوْا
elephant	فِيْلٌ
behind	وَرَاءَ
aeroplane	طَائِرَةٌ
infront of	أَمَامَ
University	جَامِعَةٌ
(I) went	ذَهَبْتُ
hen	دَجَاجَةٌ
cock	دِيْكٌ
(I) go	أَذْهَبُ

school	مَدْرَسَةٌ
orchard	بُسْتَانٌ
with	مَعَ
teacher	مُدَرِّسٌ
college	كُلِّيَّةٌ
under	تَحْتَ
(we) went	ذَهَبْنَا
(we) go	نَذْهَبُ
airhostess	مُضِيفَةٌ
worker	عَامِلٌ
(they) go	يَذْهَبُونَ
woman	إِمْرَأَةٌ
man	رَجُلٌ
over (above)	فَوقَ
buffalo	جَامُوسَةٌ
scientist	عَالِمٌ
guard	حَارِسٌ
window	شُبَّاكٌ
glass, tumbler	كُوبٌ
girl	بِنْتٌ
pigeon	حَمَامٌ
pen	قَلَمٌ
shirt	قَمِيصٌ

2. Learn the vocabulary given in this lesson.
3. Write all the words given in this lesson.

LESSON—7   ٧ — الدرس

Moon And Sun Letters And The Definite Article
الحروف القمرية والشمسية واداة التعريف

The twenty eight letters of the Arabic Alphabet are divided into two groups.
They are:

     1. The Moon letters   الحروف القمرية

     2. The Sun letters   الحروف الشمسية

The Moon letters are as follows:

ف   غ   ع   خ   ح   ج   ب   ا

ى   و   ه   م   ك   ق

Remaining fourteen letters are known as the Sun letters . They are as
follows:

ش   س   ز   ر   ذ   د   ث   ت

ن   ل   ظ   ط   ض   ص

We divide the Arabic alphabet into these two groups for purposes of
grammar as detailed below:

All the Arabic nouns which end in nunnation i.e. with a strong "noon"
sound because of double *fatḥah* or double *kasrah* or double ḍammah, are
categorised as common nouns.

Example:

       a boy   وَلَدٌ وَلَداً وَلَدٍ

In this case "a boy" may be anyboy of whom you would be unable to
establish the identity. Such common or indefinite nouns will always end in
nunnation.

Where we want to specify and define the meaning of any noun we use the
definite article which is "the" in English.

The definite article of Arabic Al الـ is similarly used to restrict and define

the meaning of an ordinary i.e. a common noun and places it on par with
"proper noun". It is translated as "the" in English.

Function and utility of the Arabic definite article:

i)   When this Al ال is prefixed to a common noun, it renders it into a
     definite noun. For example when we prefix Al ال to:

وَلَدٍ   وَلَداً   وَلَدٌ

it would be written thus:

اَلْوَلَدِ   اَلْوَلَدَ   اَلْوَلَدُ

ii) The Arabic definite article does not allow double vowel at the terminal
     letter of the concerned noun. In other words we can say that when it
     comes to defining a common noun with the definite article they cease to
     have double vowels. Instead, they retain only single vowel of the
     respective category.

iii) When we prefix Al ال to a noun beginning with a Moon letter then the
     laam of the Arabic definite article is clearly pronounced.

Example:

وَلَدٌ   A boy

This noun begins with Waw و which is a moon letter. Now if we have to
prefix to it the Arabic definite article, we would write and read it as
follows:

The boy   Al wa la do   اَلْوَلَدُ

Here you would see that the laam sound of the Arabic definite article is
very clearly said and pronounced.

iv) When the Arabic definite article Alال is prefixed to nouns beginning
     with a Sun letter then the alif of this article is directly linked to the Sun
     letter and the laam is left unpronounced.

Example:

رَجُلٌ   A man

This noun begins with Raa ر which is a Sun letter. Now if we have to prefix
to it the Arabic definite article, we would write and read it as follows:

The man   Ar Rajolo   اَلرَّجُلُ

Here you would see that the laam sound of the Arabic definite article has disappeared and the alif has been directly linked to the initial Sun letter of the noun which is now doubly pronounced.

Exercises:

1. Write down all the Arabic common nouns you have known and then re-write them all with the defnite article as explained in the lesson.

2. Remove the definite article from the following nouns and re-write them all as common nouns with full vowel points.

The office	اَلْمَكْتَبُ	The house	اَلْبَيْتُ
The fan	اَلْمِرْوَحَةُ	The lamp	اَلْمِصْبَاحُ
The bed	اَلسَّرِيرُ	The car	اَلسَّيَّارَةُ
The teacher	اَلْمُدَرِّسُ	The student	اَلطَّالِبُ
The cow	اَلْبَقَرَةُ	The moon	اَلْقَمَرُ
The sun	اَلشَّمْسُ	The sparrow	اَلْعُصْفُورُ
The river	اَلنَّهْرُ	The dog	اَلْكَلْبُ
The train	اَلْقِطَارُ	The window	اَلشُّبَّاكُ
The ball	اَلْكُرَةُ	The playground	اَلْمَيْدَانُ
The dictionary	اَلْقَامُوسُ	The driver	اَلسَّائِقُ

3. Separate the above nouns as follows:

    i) Names of places
    ii) Names of persons
    iii) Names of things
    iv) Names of animals

LESSON — 8

الدرس — ٨

Nominal Sentence, Gender And Number

الجملة الاسمية والجنس و الصيغة العددية

The boy is sitting.	أَلْوَلَدُ جَالِسٌ.
The teacher (M) is present.	أَلْمُدَرِّسُ مَوْجُودٌ.
The book is new.	أَلْكِتَابُ جَدِيدٌ.
The pen is cheap.	أَلْقَلَمُ رَخِيصٌ.
The sparrow is beautiful.	أَلْعُصْفُورُ جَمِيلٌ.
The lion is sleeping.	أَلْأَسَدُ نَائِمٌ.
The girl is sitting.	أَلْبِنْتُ جَالِسَةٌ.
The lady teacher is present.	أَلْمُدَرِّسَةُ مَوْجُودَةٌ.
The notebook is new.	أَلْكُرَّاسَةُ جَدِيدَةٌ.
The table is durable.	أَلطَّاوِلَةُ مَتِينَةٌ.
The lioness is sleeping.	أَللَّبُؤَةُ نَائِمَةٌ.
The hen is beautiful.	أَلدَّجَاجَةُ جَمِيلَةٌ.
The boys are sitting.	أَلْأَوْلَادُ جَالِسُونَ.
The teachers (M) are present.	أَلْمُدَرِّسُونَ مَوجُودُونَ.
The books are new.	أَلْكُتُبُ جَدِيدَةٌ.
The pens are new.	أَلْأَقْلَامُ جَدِيدَةٌ.
The sparrows are beautiful.	أَلْعَصَافِيرُ جَمِيلَةٌ.
The lions are sleeping.	أَلْأُسُدُ نَائِمَةٌ.
The girls are sitting.	أَلْبَنَاتُ جَالِسَاتٌ.
The lady teachers are present.	أَلْمُدَرِّسَاتُ مَوْجُودَاتٌ.
The notebooks are new.	أَلْكُرَّاسَاتُ جَدِيدَةٌ.
The tables are durable.	أَلطَّاوِلَاتُ مَتِينَةٌ.
The lionesses are sleeping.	أَللَّبُؤَاتُ نَائِمَةٌ.
The hens are beautiful.	أَلدَّجَاجَاتُ جَمِيلَةٌ.

The boy is in the room.	اَلْوَلَدُ فِى الْغُرْفَةِ.
The girl student is in the room.	اَلطَّالِبَةُ فِى الْغُرْفَةِ.
The sparrow is in the cage.	اَلْعُصْفُورُ فِى الْقَفَصِ.
The lioness is in the jungle.	اللَّبُؤَةُ فِى الغَابَةِ.
The boystudents are in the room.	اَلطُّلَّابُ فِى الْغُرْفَةِ.
The sparrows are in the cage.	اَلْعَصَافِيْرُ فِى الْقَفَصِ.

Grammar   القواعد

There is no auxiliary verb in Arabic.

It is possible in Arabic to make a complete sentence with two nouns. These types of sentences are known as simple nominal sentences. Such sentences are always composed of two parts:

a) The first part is a noun about which some information is given. It is the subject which is knwon as Mubtada مُبْتَدا. The subject in Arabic can either be a pronoun or a proper noun or a common noun generally defined with the definite article Al الـ.

b) The second component of such a sentence is again a noun (adjectival, verbal etc). This part gives information about the noun of the first part. This is predicate which is known in Arabic as khabar خَبَر.

1. The pen is cheap.	١ . اَلْقَلمُ رَخِيصٌ.
2. The table is new.	٢ . اَلطَّاوِلَةُ جَدِيْدَةٌ
3. The boy is sitting.	٣ . الوَلَدُ جَالِسٌ
4. The girl is sitting.	٤ . اَلبِنْتُ جَالِسةٌ
5. The pens are cheap.	٥ .اَلْأَقلَامُ رَخِيصَةٌ
6. The tables are new.	٦ . اَلطَاوِلَاتُ جَدِيْدَةٌ
7. The boys are sitting.	٧ . اَلْأَولادُ جَالِسونَ
8. The girls are sitting.	٨ . البَنَاتُ جالساتٌ

While making these types of sentences, following things should be borne in mind:

i) if the subject is singular masculine then the predicate also will be singular masculine (see sentences 1 &3).

ii) if the subject is singular feminine then the predicate also will be singular feminine (see sentences 2 & 4).

iii) if the subject is plural masculine then the predicate will also be plural masculine (see sentence 7).

iv) if the subject is plural feminine then the predicate also will be plural feminine (see sentence 8).

v) if the subject is nonpersonal plural i.e. non-humanbeing then the predicate will be singular feminine irrespective of its gender (see sentences 5 & 6).

In other words we can say that the predicate will be in complete agreement with the subject—in number and gender. However, nonpersonal plural subject will take singular feminine predicate.

vi) in simple nominal setences, both the subject and the predicate will be in the nominative case i.e. the terminal letters of the two nouns will have dammah (or its substitute) like ون in جَالِسُونَ etc.

We should also know here that a preposition followed by a noun can also make predicate. However, in such cases the terminal letter of the noun occuring after the preposition will have kasrah. For example فى is a preposition meaning: in or inside:. Now we want to say that: The dog is in the house. We would say this in Arabic as follows:

$$اَلْكَلْبُ فِى الْبَيْتِ$$

You can see for yourself in the sentence above that the noun الْبَيْتِ has kasrah below the Taa ت which is the terminal letter in this case.

Genders:

Before proceeding any further I would like to explain one more thing. It is about the gender of the nouns. There are only two genders in Arabic as follows:

i) Masculine gender

ii) Feminine gender

There is no neutral gender in Arabic. A noun has to be necessarily either a masculine gender noun or a feminine gender noun.

All nouns in Arabic may be considered as masculine gender nouns unless they specifically mean a feminine/female e.g. اُمّ i. e. mother and بنت i. e. girl.

There are a few exceptions to this rule.

All such nouns which terminate with a round Taa ة, they are necessarily treated as the feminine gender nouns (with a few exceptions) . For example:

Chair	كراسَة
Table	طاولة
Girl student	طالبة

Number:

Arabic has three numbers i.e. (1) Singular or mofrad مفرَد, (2) dual or Mothannaa مثنّى, and (3) plural or Jam'a جمع. Henceforth in the lessons of this book we propose to mention plural & singular together as far as possible. Details regarding formation of plural & dual shall be discussed in lesson no. 18.

Exercises:

1) Read and write the sentences given in this lesson.

2) Read and write the following words:

sitting	جالِسٌ (جَالِسُونَ .p)	big	كَبِيْرٌ(كِبَارٌ .p)
absent	غَائِبٌ (غَائِبُونَ .p)	small	صَغِيْرٌ (صِغَارٌ .p)
open	مَفْتُوْحٌ	studious	مُجْتَهِدٌ (مُجْتَهِدُونَ .p)
writer	كَاتِبٌ (كَاتِبُونَ .p)	bag	حَقِيْبَةٌ (حَقَائِبُ .p)
clerk	كَاتِبٌ (كَتَبَةٌ .p)	fan	مِرْوَحَةٌ (مَرَاوِحُ .p)
busy	مَشْغُولٌ(مَشْغُولُونَ P)	lamp	مِصْبَاحٌ (مَصَابِيْحُ .p)
motor-car	سَيَّارَةٌ (سَيَّارَاتٌ .p)	officer	مُوَظَّفٌ (مُوَظَّفُونَ .p)
servant	خَادِمٌ (خَدَمٌ .p)	newspaper	جَرِيْدَةٌ (جَرَائِدُ .p)
aeroplane	طَائِرَةٌ(طَائِرَاتٌ .p)		

3) Make sentences from the following pairs as explained in the lesson:

lady teachers	مُدَرِّسَاتٌ (PF) ١.
present	مَوْجُوْدَاتٌ
airhostesses/waiteresses	مُضِيْفَاتٌ (PF) ٢.

standing	وَاقِفَاتٌ
students	٣. طُلَّابٌ (PM)
present	مَوجُودُونَ
officers; employees	٤. مُوَظَّفُونَ (PM)
absent	غَائِبُونَ
motorcars	٥. سَيَّارَاتٌ (Pl. nonpersonal)
new	جَدِيدَةٌ
elephants	٦. أَفْيَالٌ (Pl. nonpersonal)
big; huge	كَبِيرَةٌ
cat	٧. قِطَّةٌ (SF)
beautiful	جَمِيلَةٌ
city	٨. مَدِينَةٌ (SF)
old	قَدِيمَةٌ
pens	٩. أَقْلَامٌ (Pl. nonpersonal)
expensive	ثَمِينَةٌ
watchman	١٠. حَارِسٌ (SM)
active	نَشِيطٌ

4) Translate into English:

اَلْأُسْتَاذُ مَوْجُودٌ . اَلْأُسْتَاذُ مَوجُودٌ فِي الْفَصْلِ. اَلْأُسْتَاذُ وَاقِفْ. اَلْأُسْتَاذُ وَاقِفْ اَمَامَ السَّبُّورَةِ. اَلْكِتَابُ فِيْ يَدِ الْأُسْتَاذِ. اَلْكِتَابُ مَفْتُوحٌ. اَلْأُسْتَاذُ كَاتِبٌ عَلَى السَّبُّورَةِ بِالطَّبَاشِيرِ. اَلطُّلَّابُ جَالِسُوْنَ عَلَى الْكُرَاسِيِّ. اَلطُّلَّابُ كَاتِبُوْنَ فِي الْكُرَّاسَاتِ. اَلطَّالِبَاتُ جَالِسَاتٌ عَلَى الْكُرَاسِيِّ. اَلطَّالِبَاتُ كَاتِبَاتٌ فِى الْكُرَّاسَاتِ. اَلْغُرْفَةُ وَاسِعَةٌ وَ نَظِيفَةٌ.

Translate into Arabic:

(A) The College is big. The College is in the city. The College has many rooms. The rooms are big. The College has a library. The library is big. There are many books in the library.

(B) The school is small. The school is in the village. The school has many rooms. The rooms are small. The school has a library. The library is small. There are books in the library. The school has a playground. The playground is big. The school has a room for teachers. The room is big & beautiful.

Glossary: الكلمات العسيرة

College (P. كُلِّيَّات) (SF)	كُلِّيَّةٌ	Teacher, professor (P. أَسَاتِذَة)	أُسْتَاذٌ
City (p. مُدُنُ) (SF)	مَدِينَةٌ	Class, classroom (P فُصُولٌ) (SM)	فَصْلٌ
For (have/has) (Prep.)	لِ	Standing (P. وَاقِفُونَ) (SM)	وَاقِفٌ
Room (P. غُرَفٌ) (SF)	غُرْفَةٌ	Infront of, facing (Adv. of place)	أمامَ
A number/ many	عَدَدٌ	Black-board (P. سَبُّورَاتٌ) (SF)	سَبُّورَةٌ
A number of/many	عَدَدٌ مِنْ	Book (P. كُتُبٌ) (SM)	كِتَابٌ
Library (P. مَكْتَبَاتٌ) (SF)	مَكْتَبَةٌ	Hand (P. أَيْدٍ) (SF)	يَدٌ
School (P. مَدَارِسُ)(SF)	مَدْرَسَةٌ	Writing/writer (P. كَاتِبُونَ) (SM)	كَاتِبٌ
The school has	لِلْمَدْرَسَةِ	Big, spacious (Adj. SM)	وَاسِعٌ
Small (Adj. SM)	صَغِيرٌ	Clean (Adj. SM)	نَظِيفٌ
Big (Adj. SM)	كَبِيرٌ	Village (SM) (P. قُرًى)	قَرْيَةٌ
Beautiful (Adj. SM)	جَمِيلٌ	Ground, playground (SM)(مَيَادِينP)	مَيْدَانٌ

LESSON – 9

٩ – الدرس

The Pronouns

الضمائر

(A) The Nominative pronouns الضمائر المنفصلة

He is a boy.	هُوَ وَلَدٌ ۔
He is a man.	هُوَ رَجُلٌ ۔
They are boys.	هُمْ أَوْلَادٌ ۔
They are men.	هُمْ رِجَالٌ ۔
She is a cook.	هِيَ طَبَّاخَةٌ ۔
She is a student .	هِيَ طَالِبَةٌ ۔
They are (lady) cooks.	هُنَّ طَبَّاخَاتٌ ۔
They are (girl) students.	هُنَّ طَالِبَاتٌ ۔
You are (boy) student.	أَنْتَ طَالِبٌ ۔
You are a (man)grocer.	أَنْتَ بَقَّالٌ ۔
You are a (boy) students.	أَنْتُم طُلَّابٌ ۔
You are (men) grocers.	أَنْتُم بَقَّالُونَ ۔
You are a girl.	أَنْتِ بِنْتٌ ۔
You are a (lady) worker.	أَنْتِ عَامِلَةٌ ۔
You are girls.	أَنْتُنَّ بَنَاتٌ ۔
You are (lady) workers.	أَنْتُنَّ عَامِلَاتٌ ۔
I am a teacher.	أَنَا مُدَرِّسٌ ۔
I am a (lady) teacher.	أَنَا مُدَرِّسَةٌ ۔
We are (boy) students.	نَحْنُ طُلَّابٌ ۔
We are (girl) students.	نَحْنُ طَالِبَاتٌ ۔

Personal noun or pronoun is a word that replaces a proper noun i.e. a name or a noun. There are two kinds of these personal nouns:

a) Nominative pronouns الضمائر المنفصلة

b) Accusative and possessive pronouns الضمائر المتصلة

Nominative pronouns :

i) Third person   صيغة الغائب

He   هُوَ
She   هِيَ
They (PM)   هُمْ
They (PF)   هُنَّ

ii) Second Person   صيغة الحاضر

You (SM)   أَنْتَ
You (SF)   أَنْتِ
You (PM)   أَنْتُمْ
You (PF)   أَنْتُنَّ

iii) First Person   صيغة المتكلم

I (SM & F)   أَنَا
We (PM & F)   نَحْنُ

All nominative pronouns can be used as first part of simple nominal
sentences as has been shown in this lesson.

They are always written separately. That is precisely the reason that they are
called الضمائر المنفصلة or separately written pronouns.

Exercises:

1) Separate all the nominative pronouns i.e. personal nouns (of the
    nominative case) from the sentences given below and use them in
    phrases/ sentences of your own:

هَلْ أَنْتَ سَائِقٌ؟   هُوَ رَجُلٌ.
نَعَمْ، أَنَا سَائِقٌ.   هُوَ سَائِقٌ.
لَا، أَنَا أُسْتَاذٌ.   هُمْ رِجَالٌ.
هَلْ أَنْتُمْ ذَاهِبُوْنَ؟   هُمْ سَائِقُوْنَ.
نَعَمْ، نَحْنُ ذَاهِبُوْنَ اِلىَ الْجَامِعَة.   هِيَ بِنْتٌ.

هِيَ طَالِبَةٌ.   لَا، نَحْنُ قَادِمُوْنَ مِنَ الْمَكْتَبَةِ.

هُنَّ بَنَاتٌ.   مَنْ أَنتِ؟

هُنَّ طَالِبَاتٌ.   أنا خادمةٌ.

أَيْنَ أَنْتَ ذَاهِبٌ.   مَنْ أَنْتُنَّ؟

أَنَا ذَاهِبٌ الَى الْجَامِعَةِ.   نَحْنُ طَالِبَاتٌ.

مَا هٰذَا؟   هٰذَا كِتَابِى.

مَا ذَا فِىْ يَدِكَ؟   هٰذَا قَلَمٌ فِىْ يَدِى.

2) Use suitable pronoun with each of the following nouns to make meaningful sentences:

مُدَرِّسٌ	كَاتِبٌ	مَدْرَسَةٌ	اُمٌّ	أَبٌ	الف:
رَئِيسٌ	بَقَّالٌ	مُوَظَّفٌ	مُهَنْدِسٌ	طَالِبَةٌ	
	خَادِمٌ	طَبَّاخٌ	خَادِمَةٌ	عَالِمٌ	
مُدَرِّسُوْنَ	كَتَبَةٌ	مُدَرِّسَاتٌ	أُمَّهَاتٌ	آبَاءُ	ب:
رُؤُوسَاءُ	بَقَّالُونَ	مُوَظَّفُونَ	مُهَنْدِسُوْنَ	طَالِبَاتٌ	
	خَدَمٌ	طَبَّاخُونَ	خَادِمَاتٌ	عُلَمَاءُ	

(3) Translate into Arabic:

He is a teacher. He is a teacher in a school. She is a teacher. She is a teacher in a school. They are students. Are you also in the school? No, I am in the post office. Is he a worker in the school. Yes, he is a worker in this school. Are you also in this school. No, we are in an office.

LESSON – 10

الدرس — ١٠

The Pronouns

الضمائر

(B) The Possessive Pronouns or The Accusative/Genitive

الضمائر المتصلة

The boy's book is on the table.	كِتَابُ الْوَلَدِ عَلَى الطَّاوِلَةِ.
His book is new.	كِتَابُهُ جَدِيْدٌ.
His book is open.	كِتَابُهُ مَفْتُوحٌ.
He is a professor.	هُوَ أُسْتَاذٌ.
In his hand is a lighter.	فِىْ يَدِهِ وَلَّاعَةٌ.
(He has a lighter in his hand)	
His lighter is expensive.	وَلَّاعَتُهُ غَالِيَةٌ.
This is the girl's notebook.	هٰذِهِ كُرَّاسَةُ الْبِنْتِ.
Her notebook is on the table.	كُرَّاسَتُهَا عَلَى الطَّاوِلَةِ.
Their (men) books are on the table.	كُتُبُهُمْ عَلَى الطَّاوِلَةِ.
Their (women) notebooks are in the bags.	كُرَّاسَاتُهُنَّ فِى الْحَقَائِبِ.
Where is your (SM) bag?	أَيْنَ حَقِيْبَتُكَ؟
Are your (PM) bags in the room?	هَلْ حَقَائِبُكُمْ فِى الْغُرْفَةِ؟
Your (SF) pen is in my (SMF) hand.	قَلَمُكِ فِىْ يَدِى.
Are your (PF) pens in the bags.	هَلْ أَقْلَامُكُنَّ فِى الْحَقَائِبِ؟
My (SMF) car is infront of the office.	سَيَّارَتِىْ أَمَامَ الْمَكْتَبِ.
Our (PMF) friend is coming.	صَدِيْقُنَا قَادِمٌ.

Accusative/ genitive or possesive pronouns:

These pronouns are as follows:

i) Third person صيغة الغائب

Her, hers	هَا	His, of his	هُ
Their, Theirs (PF)	هُنَّ	Their, Theirs (PM)	هُمْ

ii) Second person صيغة الحاضر

Your, Yours (SF)	كِ	Your, Yours (SM)	كَ
Your, Yours (PF)	كُنَّ	Your, Yours (PM)	كُمْ

iii) First person صيغة المتكلم

Our, ours (PM&F)	نَا	My, mine (SM&F)	ىَ

The foregoing set of pronouns can be used to show possessor or they may be used after a preposition. They are also used as objects of the verbs.

They all have their fixed forms/sounds. Only هُمْ /هُ and هُنَّ are read as هِمْ/ هِ and هِنَّ wherever they are preceded by a *kasrah* or ى Yaa. Pronoun ى of first person singular meaning 'my/ mine' is ordinarily read as elongative ى with *kasrah* preceding it.

It may also be underlined here that these pronouns are joined to their preceding words/ letters wherever possible and hence comes the name الضمائر المتصلة.

Exercises:

1) Separate all the accusative/ genitive or possessive pronouns from the sentences given below and use them in phrases/ sentences of your own:

(a)

كِتَابُكَ	قَلَمُهُ	كِتَابُهَا	كِتَابُهُنَّ	كِتَابُكَ
كِتَابُكُمْ	كِتَابُكِ	كِتَابُكُنَّ	كِتَابِىْ	كِتَابُنَا

(b)

هٰذَا كِتَابُهُ۔ مَا هٰذَا فِىْ يَدِكَ؟	هٰذِهِ مَجَلَّتِى فِى يَدِىْ.
مَاذَلِكَ؟	ذَلِكَ قَلَمُكَ .
مَا ذَلِكَ فِىْ جَيْبِكَ؟	ذَلِكَ مِنْدِيْلٌ فِى جَيْبِى .
مَنْ فِىْ غُرْفَتِهِ؟	فِىْ غُرْفَتِهِ صَدِيْقُهُ
مَاذَا فِىْ يَدِهَا؟	فِىْ يَدِهَا مَجَلَّتُهَا.
هَلْ أَخُوْهُ غَائِبٌ؟	لَا، أَخُوْهُ حَاضِرٌ.

2) Use the following pronouns in sentences/ pharases:

كَ	هُنَّ	هُمْ	هَا	هُ
نَا	ىَ	كُنَّ	كُمْ	كِ

(3) Translate into Arabic:

He is Sameer. He has a family. His family is small. She is Rani. She is his wife. He is Nafe. He is his son. She is sameera. She is his daughter. Their house is big & beautiful. Who are you? I am Shyam. I am their cook. Who is she? She is Romila. She is their maidservant. Where is your house? My house is in R.K. Puram. We are Shuji, Sana & Sunaina. Our house is in Munirka.

Glossary	الكلمات العسيرة
Boy	وَلَدٌ (أُولادٌ PM)
Ban	رَجُلٌ (رِجَالٌ PM)
Cook	طَبَّاخٌ (طَبَّاخُونَ PM)
Lady cook	طَبَّاخَةٌ (طَبَّاخَاتٌ PF)
Boy student	طَالِبٌ (طُلَّابٌ PM)
Girl student	طَالِبَةٌ (طَالِبَاتٌ PF)
Grocer	بَقَّالٌ (بَقَّالُونَ PM)
Daughter/girl	بِنْتٌ (بَنَاتٌ PF)
Lady worker	عَامِلَةٌ (عَامِلَاتٌ PF)
Teacher	مُدَرِّسٌ (مُدَرِّسُونَ PM)
Lady teacher	مُدَرِّسَةٌ (مُدَرِّسَاتٌ PF)
Persent	حَاضِرٌ (حَاضِرُونَ PM)
Absent	غَائِبٌ (غَائِبُونَ PM)
Driver	سَائِقٌ (سَائِقُونَ PM)
It is an interrogative pronoun	هَلْ:

When used to open a sentence it suitably modifies the sentence into interrogative.

University	جَامِعَةٌ (SF) (جَامِعَاتٌ Pl. nonpersonal)
Going, goer	ذَاهِبٌ (ذَاهِبُونَ PM)
Coming, comer	قَادِمٌ (قَادِمُونَ PM)
Maidservant	خَادِمَةٌ (خَادِمَاتٌ PF)
Door	بَابٌ (SM) (أَبْوَابٌ Pl. nonpersonal)
Office	مَكْتَبٌ (SM) (مَكَاتِبُ Pl. nonpersonal)
Notebook	كُرَّاسَةٌ (SF) (كُرَّاسَاتٌ Pl. nonpersonal)
Book	كِتَابٌ (SM) (كُتُبٌ Pl. nonpersonal)
Chair	كُرْسِيٌّ (SM) (كَرَاسِيُّ Pl. nonpersonal)
Table	طَاوِلَةٌ (SF) (طَاوِلَاتٌ Pl. nonpersonal)
Engineer	مُهَنْدِسٌ (مُهَندِسُونَ PM)
Official/officer	مُوَظَّفٌ (مُوَظَّفُونَ PM)
Place of worship	مَعْبَدٌ (مَعَابِدُ Pl. nonpersonal)
President/chief/ head	رَئِيسٌ (رُؤَسَاءُ PM)
Lecture	مُحَاضَرَةٌ (SF) (مُحَاضَرَاتٌ Pl. nonpersonal)
College	كُلِّيَّةٌ (SF)(كُلِّيَّاتٌ Pl. nonpersonal)
Pen	قَلَمٌ(SM) (أَقْلَامٌ Pl. nonpersonal)
Lesson	دَرْسٌ(SM) (دُرُوسٌ Pl. nonpersonal)
Lighter	وَلَّاعَةٌ (SF) (وَلَّاعَاتٌ Pl. nonpersonal)
On	عَلَى(Prep.)
New	جَدِيدٌ(Adj.)
Open	مَفْتُوح (VN/Adj.)
Dear/ expensive	غَالِيَةٌ (Adj./SF)
Bag	حَقِيبَةٌ (SF) (حَقَائِبُ Pl. nonpersonal)

Room	غُرْفَةٌ (SF) (غُرَف Pl. nonpersonal)
Car	سَيَّارَةٌ (SF) (سَيَّاراتٌ Pl. nonpersonal)
Infront of	أمامَ (Adv. used as preposition.)
Friend	صَدِيقٌ (أَصدِقَاءُ PM)
Magazine	مَجَلَّةٌ (SF) (مَجَلَّاتٌ Pl. nonpersonal)
That	ذلِكَ (SM)
This	هذَا (SM)
Pocket	جَيْبٌ (SM) (جُيُوبٌ Pl. nonpersonal)
Hand-kerchief	مِنْدِيلٌ (SM) (مَنَادِيلُ Pl. nonpersonal)
Brother	أَخٌ (SM) (إخوانٌ .P)
(Boy's name) Sameer	سَمِيْر
Family	أُسْرَة (SF) (أُسَرٌ Pl. nonpersonal)
He has a family	لَهُ أُسْرَةَ
Rani (girl's name)	رَانِى
Small	صَغِيْرٌ (Adj. SM)
Big	كَبِيْرٌ (Adj. SM)
Beautiful	جَمِيْلٌ (Adj. SM)
Romila (girl's name)	رُوميلا
(Girl's name) Sameera	سَمِيْرة
House	بَيْتٌ (SM) (بُيُوتٌ Pl. nonpersonal)
Nafe (boy's name)	نَافِع
(Girl's name) Sunaina	سُنَيْنَا
Munirka (name of a locality)	مُنِيرْكَا
Son	إِبْنٌ (SM) (أَبْنَاءٌ .P)

LESSON – 11

الدرس – ١١

Demonstrative And Interrogative Pronouns

اسماء الاشارة و حروف الاستفهام

1. This is a boy.	١. هَذَا وَلَدٌ.
2. This is a lion .	٢. هَذَا اَسَدٌ.
3. This is a book.	٣. هَذَا كِتَابٌ.
4. This is a girl.	٤. هَذِهِ بِنْتٌ.
5. This is a lioness.	٥. هَذِهِ لَبُؤَةٌ.
6. This is a notebook.	٦. هَذِهِ كُرَّاسَةٌ.
7. These are boys.	٧. هَؤُلَاءِ اَوْلَادٌ.
8. These are girls.	٨. هَؤُلَاءِ بَنَاتٌ.
9. These are books.	٩. هَذِهِ كُتُبٌ.
10. These are lions.	١٠ هَذِهِ اُسُدٌ.
11. These are lionesses.	١١. هَذِهِ لَبُؤَاتٌ.
12. These are notebooks.	١٢. هَذِهِ كُرَّاسَاتٌ.
13. That is an officer.	١٣. ذَلِكَ مُوَظَّفٌ.
14. That is a chair.	١٤. ذَلِكَ كُرْسِيٌّ.
15. That is a dog.	١٥. ذَلِكَ كَلْبٌ.
16. That is a ladyteacher.	١٦. تِلْكَ مُدَرِّسَةٌ.
17. That is a table.	١٧. تِلْكَ طَاوِلَةٌ.
18. That is a bitch.	١٨. تِلْكَ كَلْبَةٌ.
19. Those are officers.	١٩. اُولَئِكَ مُوَظَّفُونَ.
20. Those are ladyteachers.	٢٠. اُولَئِكَ مُدَرِّسَاتٌ.
21. Those are chairs .	٢١. تِلْكَ كَرَاسِيٌّ.
22. Those are tables.	٢٢. تِلْكَ طَاوِلَاتٌ .
23. Those are dogs .	٢٣. تِلْكَ كِلَابٌ .
24. Those are bitches.	٢٤. تِلْكَ كَلْبَاتٌ .

25. This pen is new.   ٢٥. هَذَا القَلَمُ جَدِيْدٌ.

26. This man is an engineer.   ٢٦. هَذَا الرَّجُلُ مُهَنْدِسٌ.

27. This girl is a student.   ٢٧. هَذِهِ الْبِنْتُ طَالِبَةٌ.

28. These pens are new.   ٢٨. هَذِهِ الأَقْلَامُ جَدِيْدَةٌ.

29. These men are engineers.   ٢٩. هَؤُلَاءِ الرِّجَالُ مُهَنْدِسُوْنَ.

30. These girls are students.   ٣٠. هَؤُلَاءِ الْبَنَاتُ طَالِبَاتٌ.

31. That pen is old.   ٣١. ذَلِكَ الْقَلَمُ قَدِيْمٌ.

32. That man is hardworking.   ٣٢. ذَلِكَ الرَّجُلُ مُجْتَهِدٌ.

33. Those books are old.   ٣٣. تِلْكَ الْكُتُبُ قَدِيْمَةٌ

34. Those women are hardworking.   ٣٤. أُولَئِكَ النِّسَاءُ مُجْتَهِدَاتٌ.

35. Those men are engineers.   ٣٥. أُوْلَئِكَ الرِّجَالُ مُهَنْدِسُوْنَ.

Grammar:

Like any other language, Arabic also has a number of demonstrative pronouns to point to near and distant objects. They are used as follows:

a) Demonstrative pronouns for near objects:

This   (SM) هذا

It is used with all masculine nouns of singular order.

Example:

This is a man.   هَذَا رَجُلٌ.

This is a pen.   هَذَا قَلَمٌ.

This is an elephant.   هَذَا فِيْلٌ.

This   (SF) هَذِهِ

It is used with all feminine singular objects.

Example:

This is a girl.   هَذِهِ بِنْتٌ.

This is a car.   هَذِهِ سَيَّارَةٌ.

This is a cat.   هَذِهِ قِطَّةٌ.

These   (PM & F) هَؤُلَاءِ

It is used with the plurals of all feminine and masculine nouns that indicate personal nouns i.e. humanbeings.

Example:

| These are men. | هَوُّلَاءِ رِجَالٌ. |
| These are women. | هَوُّلَاءِ نِسَاءٌ. |

With the nonpersonal plurals (anything other than humanbeings), the singular feminine demonstrative pronoun is used i.e. هَذِهِ.

Example:

These are pens.	هَذِهِ اَقْلَامٌ.
These are elephants.	هَذِهِ اَفْيَالٌ.
These are motorcars.	هَذِهِ سَيَّارَاتٌ.
These are cats	هَذِهِ قِطَطٌ.

b) Demonstrative pronouns for distant objects:

| That | (SM) | ذَلِكَ |

It is used with all singular masculine objects.

Example:

That is a man.	ذَلِكَ رَجُلٌ.
That is a pen.	ذَلِكَ قَلَمٌ.
That is an elephant.	ذَلِكَ فِيْلٌ.
That	(SF)	تِلْكَ

It is used with all singular feminine objects.

Example:

That is a woman.	تِلْكَ اِمْرَأَةٌ.
That is a motorcar.	تِلْكَ سَيَّارَةٌ.
That is a cat.	تِلْكَ قِطَّةٌ.
Those	(PM & F)	أُوْلَئِكَ

It is used with the plurals of such feminine and masculine nouns which indicate only humanbeings.

Example:

Those are men	أُوْلَئِكَ رِجَالٌ .
Those are women	أُوْلَئِكَ نِسَاءٌ .

And with the plurals of feminine and masculine nonpersonal nouns, the singular feminine demonstrative pronoun is used.

Example:

Those are pens.	تِلَكَ أَقْلَامٌ .
Those are motorcars.	تِلْكَ سَيَّارَاتٌ .
Those are elephants .	تِلْكَ أَفْيَالٌ .
Those are cats.	تِلْكَ قِطَطٌ .

Interrogative pronouns:

أَ   هَلْ،   مَنْ،   مَا،

Maa i.e مَا is placed before a pronoun to ask a question, e. g. مَا هَذَا.

What is this?	مَا هَذَا؟
What is that?	مَا ذَلِكَ؟

It may be noted that مَا is used only for nonpersonal objects, whereas مَنْ is used to introduce a question for personal nouns e.g.مَنْ هَذَا الْوَلَدُ؟, who is this boy?, and مَنْ هُوَ i.e. who is he?, and مَنْ هِيَ i.e. who is she?

هَلْ & أَ i.e Hal & Hamza for interrogation have no meanings of their own. When they (anyone of them at one time) are placed before a sentence, they can give varied meanings like Is, are & am in question mood or do, does etc. in the beginning of the sentences in question mood, e.g.

Is he a boy?	هَلْ هُوَ وَلَدٌ؟
Are these boys?	هَلْ هَؤُلَاءِ أَوْلَادٌ؟

Hamza can replace هل fully and the meaning of the sentence remains the same as when هَلْ is used e.g.

Is he a boy?	أَهُوَ وَلَدٌ
Are these boys?	أَهَؤُلَاءِ أَوْلَادٌ

However it should he noted carefully that beside this use as above, Hamza is used for introducing negative interrogative sentences, e.g.

Is he not a boy?   أَمَا هُوَ وَلَدٌ؟

It is also used for introducing such interrogative questions where answer has to be fixed, e.g.

Is he a teacher or a worker?   أَهُوَ مُدَرِّسٌ أَمْ عَامِلٌ؟

In sum, هَلْ & أ can be used to replace each other in interrogative sentences where answers can be yes or no, while only Hamza أ can be used in negative interrogative and interrogative where answer has to be fixed and specified, and where in answer yes or no can not suffice.

Exercises:

1) Read every sentence of this lesson very carefully and write it for as many times as you can

2) Use all the nouns given below with appropriate demonstrative pronouns of near and distant objects:

Indian	(SM) هِنْدِيٌّ	Student	(SM) طَالِبٌ
Cock	(SM) دِيْكٌ	Orchard	(SM) بُسْتَانٌ
Garden	(SF) حَدِيْقَةٌ	Bed	(SM) سَرِيْرٌ
Indian	(SF) هِنْدِيَّةٌ	Girl-Student	(SF) طَالِبَةٌ
Newspaper	(SF) جَرِيْدَةٌ	Hen	(SF) دَجَاجَةٌ
Students	(PM) طُلَّابٌ	Magazine	(SF) مَجَلَّةٌ
Orchards	(NPP) * بَسَاتِيْنُ	Indians	(PM) هُنُوْدٌ
Beds	(NPP) سُرُرٌ	Cocks	(NPP) دُيُوْكٌ
Girl-students	(PF) طَالِبَاتٌ	Gardens	(NPP) * حَدَائِقُ
Newspapers	(NPP) * جَرَائِدُ	Indians	(PF) هِنْدِيَّاتٌ
		Magazines	(NPP) مَجَلَّاتٌ

3. Use interrogative pronouns appropriatiely in some of your sentences.

---

* Diptote i.e. the terminal letter can not allow nunnation.

4. Translate into Arabic:

This is a watch and that is a church.

This is a temple and that is a mosque.

This is a notebook and that is a book.

This is a house & that is a hut.

This is a radio & that is a television.

5. Translate into English:

أَ هَذَا كَلْبٌ أَمْ أَسَدٌ؟ هَذِهِ قِطَّةٌ وَ تِلْكَ عُصْفُورَةٌ . مَنْ هَؤُلَاءِ الْأَوْلَادُ؟ هَؤُلَاءِ الْأَوْلَادُ طُلَّابٌ فِى الْمَدْرَسَةِ. مَنْ هَذَا؟ هَذَا رَسَّامٌ وَذَلِكَ مِرْسَمٌ. أَ تِلْكَ بِنْتٌ؟ أَمَا هِيَ مَدْرَسَةٌ؟ بَلَى، هِيَ مَدْرَسَةٌ. أَمَا هُوَ طَالِبٌ؟ بَلَى، هُوَ مُدَرِّسٌ.

Note:

Yes   بَلَى

When the answer is affirmative to an interrogative negative.

Yes   نَعَمْ

This would also mean 'no' when the answer is negative to a negative interrogative as above, otherwise it is yes.

No   لَا

Glossary   الكلمات العسيرة

English	(P)	(S)
Hour/ watch	سَاعَاتٌ (P)	سَاعَةٌ (SF)
Church	كَنَائِسُ (P)	كَنِيسَةٌ (SF)
Place of worship	مَعَابِدُ (P)	مَعْبَدٌ (SM)
Copybook, notebook	كُرَّاسَاتٌ (P)	كُرَّاسَةٌ (SF)
Book	كُتُبٌ (P)	كِتَابٌ (SM)
House	بُيُوتٌ (P)	بَيْتٌ (SM)
Hut	أَكْوَاخٌ (P)	كُوخٌ (SM)
Radio	مَذَايِيعُ (P)	مِذْيَاعٌ (SM)
Television	تِلِفِزْيُونَاتٌ (P)	تِلِفِزْيُونٌ (SM)
Dog	كِلَابٌ (P)	كَلْبٌ (SM)
Bitch	كَلْبَاتٌ (P)	كَلْبَةٌ (SF)

Lion	أُسْدٌ (P) أُسُوْدٌ	أَسَدٌ (SM)
Cat	قِطَاتٌ (P)	قِطَّةٌ (SF)
Tomcat	قِطَطٌ(P)	قِطٌّ (SM)
Sparrow	عَصَافِيْرُ (P)	عُصْفُورَةٌ (SF)
Who	(interrogative—all persons & all numbers)	مَنْ
Boy	أَوْلَادٌ (P)	وَلَدٌ (SM)
Boy student	طُلَّابٌ (P)	طَالِبٌ (SM)
In		فِى (Prep)
School	مَدَارِسُ (P)	مَدْرَسَةٌ (SF)

What (interrogative—all nonpersonal nouns and all numbers)مَا

At places مَا is also used in the meaning of لَا i.e. no

Studio	مِرْسَمٌ (SM) مَرَاسِمُ (P)
Painter	رَسَّامٌ (SM) رَسَّامُونَ (P)
Girl	بِنْتٌ (SF) بَنَاتٌ (P)
Yes	نَعَمْ
No	لَا

١ It is an interrogative pronoun used as هَل

It also has some additional uses as explained in the lesson.

LESSON — 12

الدرس — ١٢

Proper Noun

اسم العلم

This is Shanker.	هَذَا شَنْكَر.
Shanker is a student in a school	شَنْكَر طَالِبٌ فِى مَدْرَسَةٍ
in Delhi.	فِى دِلْهِى.
Shanker has many friends	لِشَنْكَر اَصْدِقَاءُ كَثِيْرُونَ
in his school.	فِى مَدْرَسَتِهِ.
These are Nabeel, Mohammad	هَؤُلَاءِ نَبِيْل وَ مُحَمَّد
and Joseph.	وَجَوْزَف.
They are Shanker's friend.	هُمْ اَصْدِقَاءُ شَنْكَر.
Zainab also is a student	زَيْنَب اَيْضًا طَالِبَةٌ
in this school.	فِى هَذِهِ الْمَدْرَسَةِ.
These are Lali, Rani and Mamta.	هَؤُلَاءِ لَالِى وَ رَانِى وَ مَامْتَا.
They are Zainab's friends.	هُنَّ صَدِيْقَاتُ زَيْنَب.
Zainab has a good friend	لِزَيْنَب صَدِيْقَةٌ حَمِيْمَةٌ
in the city of Calcutta.	فَىْ مَدِيْنَةِ كَالْكُوتَا.

Grammar:

Proper noun is that specific name by which a certain person or place etc., is reffered to.

Example:

Nabeel	نَبِيْل	Mohammad	مُحَمَّد
Joseph	جَوزَف	Shanker	شَنْكَر
Delhi	دِلْهِى	Zainab (W)	زَيْنَب

| Lali (W) | لَالِى | Calcutta | كَالكُوتَا |
| Mamta (W) | مَامْتَا | Rani (W) | رَانِى |

It is relevant to tell here that: (i) All non-Arabic names irrespective of their gender, are treated in Arabic as diptotes i.e. they take only one dammah in the nominative case and one *fathah* in the remaining two cases.* However, for our convenience we can read, write and pronounce them as in the original languages without giving vowel marks to the last letter ii) All masculine Arabic names except those on the patterns of احمد and عمران are triptotes i.e they admit all the three cases as a normal noun.

Example:

Nominative case مُحَمَّدٌ Accusative case مُحَمَّدًا Genitive case مُحَمَّدٍ.

iii) Masculine names on the patterns of احمد and عمران, are diptotes.

Examples:

Nominative case   أَحْمَدُ

Accusative case   أَحْمَدَ

Gentitive case   أَحْمَدَ

iv) All feminine Arabic names are diptotes except هند.

Example:

Nominative case   زَيْنَبُ

Accusative case   زَيْنَبَ

Genitive case   زَيْنَبَ

---

* There are three cases in Arabic. They are: (1) Nominative case, (2) Accusative case and (3) Genitive case. Details follow in lessons 13 & 14.

However, those names which are bedecked with the definite article أل, they are generally treated as triptotes.

| Cairo | اَلْقَاهِرةُ |
| Medina | اَلْمَدِينَةُ |

vi) We do not prefix ال to the names of persons. However, some Arabic names do have Al ال as their integral part.

vii) Some names of places have Al ال and some others do not have. This has to be acquired slowly.

The name هِنْد in Arabic is treated as triptote:

Nominative case	هِنْدٌ (Hind)
Accusative case	هِنْدًا
Genitive case	هِنْدٍ

v) Names of places are generally diptotes :

Nominative case	مِصْرُ (Egypt)
Accusative case	مِصْرَ
Genitive case	مِصْرَ

Exercises:

1) Translate the following into English :

١. دِلْهِىْ مَدِينَةٌ فِىْ الْهِنْدِ.   ٢. زَيْنَب طَالِبَةٌ فِى الْكُلِّيَّةِ.

٣. مُحَمَّدٌ مُوَظَّفٌ فِى الْمَكْتَبِ.   ٤. هِنْدٌ مُدَرِّسَةٌ فِى الْجَامِعَةِ.

٥. هَلْ شَنْكَر اِبْنُكَ؟   ٦. هَلْ آشَا أُخْتُكَ؟

٧. هُوَ عَادِلٌ وَ اَنَا جَمِيْلٌ.   ٨. هَذَا السَّيِّدُ نَبِيْلٌ.

٩. هِيَ بِنْتٌ. اِسْمُهَا اَمِيْتَا. هِيَ أُخْتِى.   ١٠. هُوَ وَالِدِى. اِسْمُهُ عَزِيْزٌ.

2) Translate into Arabic:

1) That is a boy . He is my brother. His name is Ashok.

2) That girl is my sister. Her name is Usha.

3) He is Mr. Shamlal. He is an engineer.

4) His name is Mr. Adil. His pen is new.

5) Her name is Mrs. Lalima. She is a teacher.

6) What is her name? Is she your wife?

7) She is Miss Fatima. She is my sister.

8) Her name is Sunaina. She is my daughter.

9) Mr. Hari is a clerk in my office.

10) Is he your driver? What is his name?

3) Separate all the proper nouns in exercises. Nos: 1 and 2, and use them in sentences of your own.

Glossary: الكلمات العسيرة

India	اَلْهِنْدُ	City	مَدِينَةٌ (SF) مُدُنٌ (P)
And (conjunctive)	وَ	College	كُلِّيَّةٌ (SF) كُلِّيَّاتٌ (P)
Name	اِسْمٌ (SM) اَسْمَاءٌ (P)	Mr.	اَلسَّيِّدُ
		Is?	هَلْ

This word is an interrogative pronoun. When placed before positive sentences, it may be translated as; is ; are; am; in the simple nominal sentences and : do; does in the present indefinite and : did in the past indefinite and will, shall in future tense

Brother	(P)	اِخْوَةٌ	(SM)	اَخٌ
Sister	(P)	اَخَوَاتٌ	(SF)	اُخْتٌ
Engineer	(P)	مُهَنْدِسُونَ	(SM)	مُهَنْدِسٌ
Miss	(P)	اَلْاَوَانِسُ	(SF)	اَلْآنِسَةُ
Mrs.	(P)	اَلسَّيِّدَاتُ	(SF)	اَلسَّيِّدَةُ
Wife	(P)	زَوجَاتٌ	(SF)	زَوْجَةٌ
Clerk	(P)	كَتَبَةٌ	(SM)	كَاتِبٌ
Driver	(P)	سَائِقُونَ	(SM)	سَائِقٌ

Verb: Past Tense And Cases
الفعل: صيغة الماضي والحالات

This is Nabeel.	هَذَا نَبِيْل.
He is a student in the University.	هُوَ طَالِبٌ فِى الْجَامِعَةِ.
Nabeel went to the Univesity yesterday.	ذَهَبَ نَبِيْل إِلَى الْجَامِعَةِ أَمْسِ.
These are Adil, Shanker and Joseph.	هَؤُلَاءِ عَادِلٌ وَشَنْكَرُ وَ جَوْزَف.
Adil, Shanker and Joseph went	ذَهَبَ عَادِلٌ وَشَنْكَرُ وَ جَوْزَف
to the Univesity	إِلَى الْجَامِعَةِ
to attend the lessons (i.e. classes).	لِحُضُورِ الدُّرُوْسِ.
After attending the first lesson,	بَعْدَ حُضُوْرِ الدَّرْسِ الْأَوَّلِ
Adil, Shanker and Joseph left	خَرَجَ عَادِلٌ وَ شَنْكَرُ وَ جوزَف مِنَ
the class and they went	الْفَصْلِ وَذَهَبُوْا
to the canteen for drinking tea.	إِلَى الْمَطْعَمِ لِشُرْبِ الشَّايِ.
This is Hind.	هَذِهِ هِنْدٌ.
She is a student in the University.	هِيَ طَالِبَةٌ فِى الْجَامِعَةِ.
Hind went to the University yesterday.	ذَهَبَتْ هِنْدٌ إِلَى الْجَامِعَةِ أَمْسِ.
These are Zainab, Maria and Asha.	هَؤُلَاءِ زَيْنَبُ وَ مَارِيَا وَآشَا.
Zainab, Maria & Asha went	ذَهَبَتْ زَيْنَبُ وَ مَارِيَا وَآشَا
to the Univesity to attend the lessons.	إِلَى الْجَامِعَةِ لِحُضُوْرِ الدُّرُوْسِ.
After attending the first lesson,	بَعْدَ حُضُوْرِ الدَّرْسِ الْأَوَّلِ
Zainab, Maria & Asha left	خَرَجَتْ زَيْنَب وَمَارِيَا وَآشَا
the class and they went to the library.	مِنَ الْفَصْلِ وَذَهَبْنَ إِلَى الْمَكْتَبَةِ.
Who are you?	مَنْ أَنْتَ؟

I am Hamid. أَنَا حَامِدٌ.

I am a student in this University. أَنَا طَالِبٌ فِى هَذِهِ الْجَامِعَةِ.

Did you go to the University yesterday? هَلْ ذَهَبْتَ اِلىٰ الْجَامِعَةِ أمْسِ؟

Yes, I went to the University yesterday. نَعَمْ، ذَهَبْتُ اِلَى الْجَامِعَةِ أمْسِ.

And who are you? وَمَنْ أَنْتِ؟

I am Rani. أَنَا رَانِى.

I am also a student in this University. أَنَا طَالِبَةٌ أَيْضًا فِى هَذِهِ الْجَامِعَةِ.

Did you go to the University Yesterday? هَلْ ذَهَبْتِ اِلَى الْجَامِعَةِ اَمْسِ.

Yes, I went to the University yesterday. نَعَمْ، ذَهَبْتُ اِلَى الْجَامِعَةِ أمْسِ.

Nabeel, Shanker and Joseph, where نَبِيلٌ وَ شَنْكُرٌ وَ جُوزَفُ، أَيْنَ

did you go (in the) last week? ذَهَبْتُمْ فِى الأُسْبُوْعِ الْمَاضِى؟

We went to the bookfair ذَهَبْنَا اِلَى مَعْرِضِ الْكِتَابِ

(in the) last week. فِى الأُسْبُوْعِ الْمَاضِى.

And you, Asha, Zainab & Maria, وَأَنْتُنَّ، آشَا وَزَيْنَبُ وَ مَارِيَا،

did you go to the fair? هَلْ ذَهَبْتُنَّ اِلَى الْمَعْرِضِ؟

Yes, we also went to the fair. نَعَمْ، ذَهَبْنَا اَيْضًا اِلَى الْمَعْرِضِ.

Grammar:

Verb is that word which tells us about the happening of some action with reference to time.

Example:

The student went to his school. ذَهَبَ الطَّالِبُ اِلَى مَدْرَسَتِهِ.

In the sentence above the word ذَهَبَ 'went' tells us bout the happening of an action in the past and it is therefore, a verb. In Arabic there are only two tenses:

1. The Past Tense صيغة الماضى

2. The Present Tense صيغة المضارع

Other tenses e.g. past perfect and future etc. are formed from these two basic tenses by adding certain other words. We shall take up in this lesson the verb of the past tense and in the next lesson we shall deal with the verb of the present tense.

The past tense (verb):

The student went to his school.	ذَهَبَ الطَّالِبُ إِلَى مَدْرَسَتِهِ.
The Students went to their school.	ذَهَبَ الطُّلَّابُ إِلَى مَدْرَسَتِهِمْ.
The students went to their school.	اَلطُّلَّابُ ذَهَبُوا إِلَى مَدْرَسَتِهِمْ.
The girlstudent went to her school.	ذَهَبَتِ الطَّالِبَةُ إِلَى مَدْرَسَتِهَا.
The girlstudents went to their school.	ذَهَبَتْ الطَّالِبَاتُ إِلَى مَدْرَسَتِهِنَّ.
The girlstudents went to their school.	اَلطَّالِبَاتُ ذَهَبْنَ إِلَى مَدْرَسَتِهِنَّ.
Did you (SM) go to your school?	هَلْ ذَهَبْتَ إِلَى مَدْرَسَتِكَ؟
Yes, I went to my school.	نَعَمْ، ذَهَبْتُ إِلَى مَدْرَسَتِي.
Did you (PM) go to your school?	هَلْ ذَهَبْتُمْ إِلَى مَدْرَسَتِكُمْ؟
Yes, we went to our school.	نَعَمْ، ذَهَبْنَا إِلَى مَدْرَسَتِنَا.
Did you (SF) go to your school?	هَلْ ذَهَبْتِ إِلَى مَدْرَسَتِكِ؟
Yes, I went to my school.	نَعَمْ، ذَهَبْتُ إِلَى مَدْرَسَتِي.
Did you (PF) go to your school?	هَلْ ذَهَبْتُنَّ إِلَى مَدْرَسَتِكُنَّ؟
Yes, we went to our school.	نَعَمْ ذَهَبْنَا إِلَى مَدْرَسَتِنَا.

A large number of Arabic past tense verbs are composed of three letters. These three letters are called "root letters". Now by prefixing or interfixing one, two or more letters to these root letters we can make many more verbs with meanings akin to the original meanings in the majority of the cases.

The verb with three letters is called in Arabic الفعل المجرد i.e. the triliteral verb of the First Stem.

Other verbs which are formed by adding some other letters, are called الافعال المزيد فيها i.e. the derived verbs.

All Arabic verbs change according to the number and gender of the subject. It means that for third person singular masculine the verb has a form while for the third person singular feminine there is another form and so on. However, the first person singular of both the masculine and the feminine genders, has a common form of the verb. Similarly, the plural masculine and the plural feminine of the first person have a common form of the verb. These changing forms that obtain according to persons, numbers & genders, are called صَرْف i.e. conjugation. Let us take for example the verb:

(He went) ذَهَبَ

You should carefully examine the changing forms of this verb i.e. its conjugation so that it would be possible to conjugate other similar verbs.

III person masculine-feminine:

He went (SM)	ذَهَبَ
They went (PM)	ذَهَبُوا
She went (SF)	ذَهَبَتْ
They went (PF)	ذَهَبْنَ

II person masculine-feminine:

You went (SM)	ذَهَبْتَ
You went (PM)	ذَهَبْتُمْ
You went (SF)	ذَهَبْتِ
You went (PF)	ذَهَبْتُنَّ

l person masculine-feminine:

I went (SMF)	ذَهَبْتُ
We went (PMF)	ذَهَبْنَا

It is considered good in Arabic that the sentence should open with the verb. When the verb comes in the beginning of a sentence, it agrees with the subject only in gender. This rule applies to the third person nouns and the verbal forms for the second and the first person nouns always remain the same. The following examples shall further explain the rule:

وَلَدٌ i.e. boy is a singular masculine noun of the third person. Its plural is
أَوْلَادٌ i.e. boys:

ذَهَبَ الْوَلَدُ	The boy went
ذَهَبَ الْاَوْلَادُ	The boys went

In both the sentences given above the verb ذَهَبَ has come in the beginning
and it is precisely because of this reason that the verb agrees with its subject
only in gender and person. It does not agree with it here in number.
However, there might be occasions where you have to place the verb only
after the subject. In such cases the verb has to agree with its subject in
number also as you can see in the sentences below:

ذَهَبَ الْاَوْلَادُ اِلَى الْمَدْرَسَةِ
وَ جَلَسُوا فِى الْفَصْلِ.

The boys went to the school
and sat in the class.

In this sentence as would be clear, there are two verbs of which the second
has to be placed after the subject. The verb 'sat' therefore, agrees with its
subject in number also beside gender.

The same rule applies to the third person nouns of the feminine gender.

For example بِنْتٌ i.e. girl is a singular feminine noun of the third person. Its
plural would be بَنَاتٌ i.e. girls.

ذَهَبَتِ الْبِنْتُ	The girl went
ذَهَبَتِ الْبَنَاتُ	The girls went
اَلْبَنَاتُ ذَهَبْنَ	The girls went

Note: In the English language the verb is often refered to in its infinitive
form. However, in Arabic it is refered to in its past tense with its
root-letter. For example ذَ هَ بَ i.e. ذَهَبَ 'He went'. Taking these root
letters as the base, the verb is conjugated in the past and in the present
imperfect tenses. In the glossary henceforth, I propose to give past,
present and the infinitive forms of the verb with its meaning in the
English infinitve. For example:

ذَهَبَ / يَذْهَبُ / ذَهَابًا   to go

As explained earlier all the verbal forms for the second and the first person subjects are fixed and remain unchanged in all positions.

Examples:

I went	ذَهَبْتُ
I went	اَنَا ذَهَبْتُ
I went	ذَهَبْتُ اَنَا

In terms of their meanings the verbs may be divided into two categories. They are:

   1. The intransitive verb   الفعل اللازم

   2. The transitive verb   الفعل المتعدى

1. The intransitive verb is the one which takes only the subject and it does not at all require an object. The subject in Arabic is called اَلْفَاعِلُ and the object is called اَلْمَفْعُولُ.

Example of intransitive verb:

     The boy went   ذَهَبَ الْوَلَدُ

In Arabic the terminal letter of the subject i.e. الفاعل always takes *dammah* as would be amply evident from the example above. The noun functioning as subject is considered to be in the nominative case.

2. The meaning of the transitive verb extends to involve an object also beside the subject.

Example:

     The boy opened the book   فَتَحَ الْوَلَدُ الْكِتَابَ

The object is considered to be in the accusative case and in Arabic the terminal letter of the objectival noun is given *fathah*.

Beside these two cases there is one more grammatical case. It is known as the genitive case.

We have known earlier that if a noun is preceded by a preposition, then the terminal letter of this noun shall have *kasrah*.

Example:

     The boy went to the school.   ذَهَبَ الْوَلَدُ إِلَى الْمَدْرَسَةِ.

In the sentence above the noun اَلْمَدْرَسَةِ is preceded by إِلَى which is a preposition and thus it has a *kasrah*. Any noun that has a *kasrah* for this reason and any other grammatical reason, is considered to be in the genitive case.

In brief we can say that any noun for specific reasons can either be in the nominative case or in the accusative case or in the genitive case. In the nominative case the terminal letter of subject-noun will have *dammah*, single if it is a proper noun or any noun defined with the definite article and double if it is a common noun. In this case the *dammah* is known is رفع Raf'a. In the accusative case the terminal letter of the noun will have fathah, single and double as explained in the immediate preceding lines. The fathah indicating case terminal is known as Nasb. In the genitive case the terminal letter of the noun will have *kasrah*, single or double as per rule explained above. Here the kasrah is known as جر Jarr.

Exercises:

1) Conjugate the verbs given below and use them in sentence of your own. Remember the difference between the transitive verb and the intransitive verb. Also remember that the subject will take *dammah*, the object fathah and the noun after the preposition will take *kasrah*.

He wrote	كَتَبَ
He killed	قَتَلَ
He came	قَدِمَ
He sat	جَلَسَ

2) Translate into Arabic:

    (a) 1. The boy opened the book.

          2. The girl washed the clothes.

          3. The boys went to the garden.

          4. The girls washed their clothes.

          5. Shiela, did you go to Mumbai?

          6. Mr. Shanker, did you go to the garden?

          7. Did you all (men) go to the college?

          8. Did you all (womem) write your lessons?

9. Yes, we came to your house yesterday.

10. Yes, I sat on the chair.

(b) Mr. Rashid went to the market. He went on foot. He went to the butchers's shop. He bought some meat and returned to his hostel.

(c) Yesterday evening I visited my friend in his house. I sat with him in his drawing room. We drank tea. After that we left his house and went to the market. I bought books, notebooks and paper. I also bought apples, grapes, bananas and oranges. When I came back home, my wife saw my friend with me. She asked me: Who is he? I told her: He is my friend. His name is Shahid. When she saw these things in my hands, she asked me: what are these things in your hands? These are fruits and books, I told her.

3. Translate into English:

(a) ١. فَتَحَ الْفَرَّاشُ الْمَكْتَبَ.

٢. اَلطَّالِبَاتُ فَتَحْنَ كُتُبَهُنَّ.

٣. غَسَلَتِ الْخَادِمَةُ الْمَلَابِسَ.

٤. اَلطُّلَّابُ ذَهَبُوا اِلَى الْحَدِيقَةِ.

٥. اَلْحَارِسُ جَلَسَ عَلَى الْكُرْسِيِّ.

٦. شَرِبَ الْأُسْتَاذُ الْمَاءَ.

٧. هَلْ ذَهَبْتُمْ اِلَى السُّوْقِ اَمْسِ؟

٨. قَدِمْتُ مِنْ مُومباى هَذَا الصَّبَاحَ.

٩. هَلْ ذَهَبْتُنَّ اِلَى الْكُلِّيَّةِ فِى الْأُسْبُوعِ الْمَاضِى.

١٠. نَعَمْ، ذَهَبْنَا اِلَى الْكُلِّيَّةِ فِى الْأُسْبُوعِ الْمَاضِى.

(b) كَانَ الْيَوْمُ مَاطِرًا وَ بَارِدًا. وَعَادَ وَالِدِى مِنْ مَكْتَبِهِ فِى الْمَطَرِ. عِنْدَمَا وَصَلَ الْمَنْزِلَ كَانَ مُبْتَلًّا. غَيَّرَ وَالِدِى مَلَابِسَهُ وَ جَلَسَ فِى غُرْفَتِهِ. بَعْدَ وَقْتٍ قَلِيْلٍ شَكَا وَالِدِى عَنِ الْأَلَمِ فِى صَدْرِهِ. فَأَتَيْتُ بِالتَّاكْسِى وَ أَخَذْتُ وَالِدِى مَعِى وَذَهَبْتُ اِلَى الْمُسْتَشْفَى الْعَامِّ. كَانَ قِسْمُ الطَّوَارِئ مُزْدَحِمًا بِالنَّاسِ. جَلَسْنَا عَلَى دَكَّةٍ خَشَبِيَّةٍ فِى اِنْتِظَارِ نَوْبَتِنَا. شَرَحَ وَالِدِى حَالَتَهُ لِلدُّكْتُورِ. فَحَصَ الدُّكْتُورُ صَدْرَ وَالِدِى بِالسَّمَّاعَةِ وَسَأَلَهُ بَعْضَ الْأَسْئِلَةِ.

قَالَ الدُّكْتُور: أَنْتَ مُصَابٌ بِالْبَرْدِ الشَّدِيدِ لِأَنَّكَ بَقِيتَ فِى الْمَطَرِ لِوَقْتٍ طَوِيلٍ. مِنَ الضَّرُورِىّ بَقَاؤُكَ فِى الْمَنْزِلِ لِأُسْبُوعٍ. وَكَتَبْتُ لَكَ هَذَا الدَّوَاءَ لِثَلَاثَةِ أَيَّامٍ. أَخَذْتُ الرُّشْتَةَ مِنَ الدُّكْتُورِ وَ رَجَعْنَا لِلْمَنْزِلِ.

Glossary   الْكَلِمَاتُ الْعَسِيرَة

Peon ; attendant	(فَرَّاشُونَ p) (SM)	فَرَّاشٌ
He washed		غَسَلَ
Clothes	(P) مَلَابِسُ (SM)	مَلْبَسٌ
He drank		شَرِبَ
Water	(P) مِيَاةٌ (SM)	مَاءٌ
Mumbai	(Proper noun)	مُومْبَاى
Yesterday	(Adv. of time: it does not decline)	أَمْسِ
From	(Preposition)	مِنْ
Morning		صَبَاحٌ ⁄ صُبْحٌ
This morning		هَذَا الصَّبَاحَ ⁄ صَبَاحَ الْيَومِ
College	(P) كُلِّيَّاتٌ (SF)	كُلِّيَّةٌ
Week	(P) أَسَابِيعُ (SM)	أُسْبُوعٌ
Past, last		مَاضِى
Garden	(P) حَدَائِقُ (SF)	حَدِيقَةٌ
He wrote		كَتَبَ
He came		قَدِمَ
On	(Preposition)	عَلَى
On foot		عَلَى الْأَقْدَامِ

To	(Preposition) إِلَىٰ
He was	كَانَ
Rainy	(Adj. SM) مَاطِرٌ
Rain	(SM) مَطَرٌ أَمْطَارٌ (P)
When	(Adv. of time) عِنْدَمَا
He reached	وَصَلَ
House	(SM) مَنْزِلٌ مَنَازِلُ (P)
Wet, drenched	(Adj. SM) مُبْتَلٌّ
He changed	غَيَّرَ
After	(Adv. of time) بَعْدَ
Some, little	(Adj. SM) قَلِيْلٌ
He complained	شَكَا
About	(Prep.) عَنْ
Pain	(SM) أَلَمٌ آلَامٌ (P)
Chest	(SM) صَدْرٌ صُدُورٌ (P)
He came	أَتَى
He brought	أَتَى بِ
I brought taxi	أَتَيْتُ بِالتَّاكْسِى
With	(Preposition) مَعَ
With me	مَعِىَ
Hospital	(SM) مُسْتَشْفَى مُسْتَشْفَيَاتٌ (P)
General, public	(Adj. SM) عَامٌّ

Department	أَقْسَام (P) قِسْم (SM)
Emergency department	قِسْمُ الطَّوَارِى
Crowded	مُزْدَحِم (Adj. SM)
Bench	دَكَّات (P) دَكَّة (SF)
Wait, waiting	إِنْتِظَار (Infinitive/VN)
Turn	نَوْبَات (P) نَوْبَة (SF)
He explained	شَرَحَ
Condition, case	حَالَة (SF)
Doctor	دَكَاتِرَة (P) دُكْتُور (SM)
He examined, checked	فَحَصَ
He said	قَالَ
He took	أَخَذَ
I took	أَخَذْتُ
Stethoscope	سَمَّاعَات (P) سَمَّاعَة (SF)
He asked	سَأَلَ
He asked him	سَأَلَهُ
Some	بَعْض (Partitive Noun)
Hit	مُصَاب (past participle)
Cold	بَرْد (NM)
Caught bad cold	مُصَاب بِالْبَرْدِ الشَّدِيدِ
Because	لِأَنَّ (Causative)
He remained	بَقِىَ

You remained	بَقِيْتَ
Long	طَوِيْلٌ (Adj. SM)
Necessary/must	ضَرُوْرِيٌّ (Adj. SM)
Stay	بَقَاءٌ (NM)
Week	أَسَابِيْعُ (P) أُسْبُوْعٌ (SM)
Medicine	أَدْوِيَةٌ (P) دَوَاءٌ (SM)
Three	ثَلَاثَةٌ (Adj. N)
Day (of 24 hrs)	أَيَّامٌ (P) يَوْمٌ (SM)
He returned	رَجَعَ
Market, bazar	أَسْوَاقٌ (P) سُوْقٌ (SF)
Rashid/ Rasheed	رَشِيْدٌ (Male Name)
Butcher	جَزَّارُوْنَ (P) جَزَّارٌ (SM)
Shop, Showroom	مَحَلَّاتٌ (P) مَحَلٌّ (SM)
Shop	دَكَاكِيْنُ (P) دُكَّانٌ (SM)
He bought	إشترى
Meat	لُحُوْمٌ (P) لَحْمٌ (SM)
Hostel	دَاخِلِيَّةٌ (SF)
Evening	أَمْسِيَاتٌ (P) مَسَاءٌ (SM)
(In the) evening	مَسَاءً (Adv. of time)
He visited	زَارَ
I visited	زُرْتُ
Friend	صَدِيْقٌ SM (أَصْدِقَاءُ P)

Drawingroom	غُرْفَةُ الإسْتِقْبَالِ
To drink	شَرِبَ / يَشْرَبُ / شَرَاباً
Tea	شَاي (NM)
Paper	وَرَق (NM)
Apples	تُفَّاح (NM)
Grapes	عِنَبٌ (NM)
Banana	مَوْزٌ (NM)
Oranges	بُرْتُقَالٌ (NM)
Wife	زَوجَةٌ (SF) زَوجَاتٌ (P)
He saw	رَأى
She saw	رَأَتْ
I told her, I said to her	قُلْتُ لَها
Shahid	شَاهِدٌ (Male Name)
Hand	يَدٌ (SF) أيِدى (P)
She asked	سَألَتْ
Fruits	فَاكِهَةٌ (SF) فَوَاكِهُ (P)

LESSON — 14

الدرس — ١٤

Verb: Present Tense الفعل: صيغة المضارع

Who are you?	مَنْ أَنْتَ؟
I am a teacher.	أَنَا أُسْتَاذٌ.
What is your name?	مَا اسْمُكَ؟
My name is Mohammad.	اِسْمِى مُحَمَّدٌ.
Are you Indian?	هَلْ أَنْتَ هِنْدِيٌّ؟
Yes, I am Indian.	نَعَمْ، أَنَا هِنْدِيٌّ.
Who is he?	مَنْ هُوَ؟
He is my colleague.	هُوَ زَمِيلِى.
Where are you going now?	أَيْنَ تَذْهَبُ الآنَ؟
I am going to the University now.	أَذْهَبُ إِلَى الْجَامِعَةِ الآنَ.
Is your colleague also going to the University	هَلْ زَمِيلُكَ أَيْضًا يَذْهَبُ اِلَى الْجَامِعَةِ؟
Yes, he is also going to the University.	نَعَمْ، هُوَ أَيْضاً يَذْهَبُ إِلَى الْجَامِعَةِ.
Who are you?	مَنْ أَنْتِ؟
I am a (lady) teacher.	أَنَا مُدَرِّسَةٌ.
What is your name?	مَا اسْمُكِ؟
My name is Nihad.	اِسْمِى نِهَادُ.
Where do you work?	أَيْنَ تَعْمَلِينَ؟
I work in this University.	أَعْمَلُ فِىْ هَذِهِ الْجَامِعَةِ.
Where are you going now?	أَيْنَ تَذْهَبِينَ الآنَ؟
I am going to the hospital now.	أَذْهَبُ إِلَى الْمُسْتَشْفَىٰ الآنَ.

Who is he? — مَنْ هُوَ؟

He is our teacher. — هُوَ أُسْتَاذُنَا.

Does he go to the University everyday? — هَلْ هُوَ يَذْهَبُ إِلَى الْجَامِعَةِ كُلَّ يَوْمٍ؟

Yes, he goes to the University everyday. — نَعَمْ، هُوَ يَذْهَبُ إِلَى الْجَامِعَةِ كُلَّ يَوْمٍ.

Does Nihad also go to the University everyday? — هَلْ نِهَادُ أَيْضاً تَذْهَبُ إِلَى الْجَامِعَةِ كُلَّ يَوْمٍ؟

Yes, Nihad also goes to the University everyday. — نَعَمْ، نِهَادُ أَيْضًا تَذْهَبُ إِلَى الْجَامِعَةِ كُلَّ يَوْمٍ.

Are you (all) students in this University? — هَلْ أَنْتُم طُلَّابٌ فِى هَذِهِ الْجَامِعَةِ؟

Yes, we are (all) students in this University. — نَعَمْ، نَحْنُ طُلَّابٌ فِى هَذِهِ الْجَامِعَةِ.

And who are you (PF)? — وَمَنْ أَنْتُنَّ؟

We are (all) students in this University. — نَحْنُ طَالِبَاتٌ فِىْ هَذِهِ الْجَامِعَةِ.

Will you (all girls) go to the University next week? — هَلْ أَنْتُنَّ تَذْهَبْنَ إِلَى الْجَامِعَةِ فِى الْأُسْبُوعِ الْقَادِمِ؟

Yes, we will go to the University next week. — نَعَمْ، نَذْهَبُ إِلَى الْجَامِعَةِ فِى الْأُسْبُوعِ الْقَادِمِ.

Do the girl-students go to the University everyday. — هَلْ تَذْهَبُ الطَّالِبَاتُ إِلَى الْجَامِعَةِ كُلَّ يَوْمٍ؟

Yes, they go to the University everyday. — نَعَمْ، هُنَّ يَذْهَبْنَ إِلَى الْجَامِعَةِ كُلَّ يَوْمٍ.

Will these (boy) students go to the bookfair tomorrow? — هَلْ هَؤُلَاءِ الطُّلَّابُ يَذْهَبُونَ إِلَى مَعْرِضِ الْكِتَابِ غَدًا؟

Yes, they will go to the bookfair tomorrow. — نَعَمْ، هُمْ يَذْهَبُونَ إِلَى مَعْرِضِ الْكِتَابِ غَداً.

Grammar:

The Present tense verbs of Arabic are made from its past tense verbs by adding in the beginning and/ or at the end or both one or more of the following letters:

و ن ن ا ت ى

The Arabic present tense verb which is also known as the present imperfect, can normally be translated into English in three ways depending on the context:

1) In the present indicative/ imperfect

2) In the present continuous

3) In the future

We take the verb ذَهَبَ to explain our point further. This ذَهَبَ is a past tense verb meaning 'he went' as we have known in the preceding lesson. Its present form يَذْهَبُ can be rendered in three ways as follows:

He goes (present indicative/imperfect)	يَذْهَبُ
He is going now (present continuous)	يَذْهَبُ الآنَ
He will go tomorrow (future)	يَذْهَبُ غَداً

Now you should carefully examine the changing forms of this verb i.e. its conjugation so that in future you face no difficulty in conjugating other similar verbs.

III person masculine-feminine

He goes	يَذْهَبُ
They go (PM)	يَذْهَبُوْنَ
She goes	تَذْهَبُ
They go (PF)	يَذْهَبْنَ

II person masculine-feminine

You go (SM)	تَذْهَبُ
You go (PM)	تَذْهَبُونَ
You go (SF)	تَذْهَبِينَ
You go (PF)	تَذْهَبْنَ

I person masculine-feminine

I go (SMF)   اَذْهَبُ

We go (PMF)   نَذْهَبُ

It may be borne in mind that the verb of this present imperfect tense may also be translated in the present continuous and the future tenses depending on the context as explained earlier.

If the present imperfect verb is preceded by سَ or سَوفَ, then in that case the verb is necessarily in the future tense of English.

Example:

Will you (girls) go to the University?   هَلْ سَتَذْهَبْنَ إِلَى الْجَامِعَةِ؟

Yes, we will go to the University.   نَعَمْ، سَنَذْهَبُ اَلَى الْجَامِعَةِ؟

Theoretically, سَ defines the verb for the near future whereas سوف defines the verb for distant future. However, practically there is no difference between the two and both of them are equally used for defining the meaning of the present imperfect verb for future.

Similarly what applies to the placement of the past tense verb before and after the subject, applies to the present tense verb also. That is to say that the sentence should preferably be opened with the verb. In this case the verb agrees with its subject only in the gender. For example we would say:

The boy goes   يَذْهَبُ الْوَلَدُ

The boys go   يَذْهَبُ الاَوْلَادُ

In both these sentences the verb يَذْهَبُ is preceding the subject and therefore, it agrees with the subject only in gender. However, where the verb has to be placed after the subject the verb will have to agree with its subject in number also. For example we would say:

The boys go to the school   يَذْهَبُ الاَوْلَادُ إِلَى الْمَدْرَسَةِ

and sit in the class.   وَ يَجْلِسُونَ فِى الْفَصْلِ.

As you would find there are two verbs in this sentence. In this case the second verb has to be placed after its subject. Hence, it agrees with the subject in number also.

The same rule applies to the third person nouns of the feminine gender also.

Let us take for example the following sentences:

| The girl goes | تَذْهَبُ الْبِنْتُ |
| The girls go | تَذْهَبُ الْبَنَاتُ |

And where the verb has to come after the subject the verb will agree with the subject in number also. For example we would say:

| The girls go to the school | تَذْهَبُ الْبَنَاتُ اِلَى الْمَدْرَسَةِ |
| and sit in the class | وَ يَجْلِسْنَ فِى الْفَصْلِ |

However, the verbal forms for the first and the second person subjects are fixed and remain unchanged in all positions.

Examples:

I go	اَذْهَبُ
I go	اَذْهَبُ اَنَا
I go	اَنَا اَذْهَبُ
You (SM) go	تَذْهَبْ
You (PM) go	تَذْهَبُونَ
You (SF) go	تَذْهَبِيْنَ
You (PF) go	تَذْهَبْنَ

Exercises:

1. Conjugate in the present (Imperfect) tense all the verbs used in this lesson and make sentences from them.

2. Conjugate the following verbs in the present imperfect tense and use them in sentences of your own.

He plays	يَلْعَبُ
He eats	يَأْكُلُ
He takes	يَأْخُذُ
He rides/ boards	يَرْكَبُ
He helps	يَنْصُرُ

3. Translate the following into Arabic.

    1.   He will go to his office tomorrow.
    2.   She is writing a letter to her teacher.
    3.   They (M) will come to you in the next week.
    4.   They (F) are eating their lunch now.
    5.   Will you go (SM) to your college tomorrow?
    6.   Yes, I will go to my college tomorrow.
    7.   Do you (SF) read the newspaper in the morning?
    8.   Yes, I read the newspaper in the morning
    9.   Will you (PM) come to my house tomorrow in the morning?
    10. Yes, we will come to your house tomorrow in the morning.
    11. Do you (PF) eat meat?
    12. Yes, we eat meat.

(b) My friend Shahid came to me yesterday evening. I was very happy to
     see him. I revceived him with all cheerfulness and seated him in the
     drawingroom. Shahid asked me: Will you be busy during the next
     week? I said: yes, but why do you ask me this question? Shahid: I and
     Tara will go to Nainital during the next week. Will you accompany us?
     I said: It is a nice idea! Now-a-days it is hot in Delhi. It will be nice if
     we gc to Nainital. How long shall we stay in Nainital? Shahid: We will
     stay there for two weeks. I said: That is nice too! When we come back
     to Delhi after two weeks, it will not be very hot in Delhi. Shahid: Fine!
     then get ready to leave tomorrow morning. We shall go by bus.

4. Translate the following into English:

هَذَا الْوَلَدُ صَدِيقِى . هُوَ يَذْهَبُ إِلَى مَدْرَسَتِهِ كُلَّ يَومٍ فِى الصَّبَاحِ. لَهُ زُمَلَاءُ يَقْدَمُونَ إِلَى
الْمَدْرَسَةِ. اَلْبَنَاتُ اَيْضاً يَدْرُسْنَ فِى هَذِهِ الْمَدْرَسَةِ. هِىَ أُوشَا. هِىَ تَدْرُسُ فِى الصَّفِّ الْعَاشِرِ.
هَل أَنْتَ أَيْضاً تَدْرُسُ فِى هَذِهِ الْمَدْرَسَةِ يَاحَامِدُ؟ نَعَمْ، أَنَا اَيْضًا اَدْرُسُ فِى هَذِهِ الْمَدْرَسَةِ يَا
صَدِيقِى. وَهَؤُلَاءِ شَنْكُرُ وَ عَاقِلٌ وَ مَحْمُودٌ.

أَهْلًا بِكُمْ! هَلْ أَنْتُمْ أَيْضًا تَدْرُسُونَ فِى هَذِهِ الْمَدْرَسَةِ؟ نَعَمْ، نَحْنُ أَيْضًانَدْرُسُ فِى هَذِهِ
الْمَدْرَسَةِ. مَنْ هَؤُلَاءِ الْبَنَاتُ؟ هُنَّ آشَا وَ أُوْشَا وَ شَالُو. أَيْنَ تَدْرُسْنَ يَا بَنَاتُ؟ نَحْنُ أَيْضًا
نَدْرُسُ فِى هَذِهِ الْمَدْرَسَةِ.

Glossary	الكلمات العسيرة
Now	الآن(adverb of time)
Classmate	زَمِيل (SM) زُملاء (P)
University	جَامِعة (SF) جَامِعات (P)
Also	ايضا (Adverb of manner)
To work	عَمِلَ ⁄ يَعْمَلُ ⁄ عَمَلاً
Who	مَنْ (Interrogative pronoun)
Where	أَيْنَ (Interrogative pronoun)
Tomorrow	غَدًا (Adverb of time)
Hospital	مُسْتَشْفَى (SM) مُسْتَشْفَيَات (P)
Teacher / Professor	أُسْتَاذ (SM) أَسَاتِذَةُ (P)
Everyday	كُلَّ يَوْمٍ (Adverb of time)
(In the)next week	(فِى) الأُسْبُوعِ القَادِمِ
Fair, exhibiton	مَعْرِضٌ (SM) مَعَارِضُ (P)
To sit	جَلَسَ يَجْلِسُ ⁄ جُلُوسًا
Office	مَكْتَبٌ (SM) مَكَاتِبُ (P)
Letter/message	رِسَالَةٌ (SF) رَسَائِلُ (P)
Lunch	غَدَاءٌ
College	كُلِّيَّةٌ (SF) كُلِّيَّاتٌ(P)
In the morning	فِى الصَّبَاحِ
House	بَيْتٌ (SM)بُيُوتٌ(P)
Meat	لَحْمٌ (SM)لُحُومٌ (P)
Friend	صَدِيقٌ (SM) أَصْدِقَاءُ (P)
To come	قَدِمَ ⁄ يَقْدَمُ ⁄ قُدُومًا
To study	دَرَسَ ⁄ يَدْرُسُ ⁄ دَرْسًا
Class	صَفٌّ (SM) صُفُوفٌ (P)
Welcome	أَهْلاً بِكُمْ (greeting)

To see	رَأَى / يَرَى / رُؤْيَةً
To receive	إِسْتَقْبَلَ / يَسْتَقْبِلُ / إِسْتِقْبَالاً
Cheerfulness	بَشَاشَةٌ
To seat	أَجْلَسَ / يُجْلِسُ / إِجْلاسًا
Busy	مَشْغُولٌ (Past participle)
Why	لِمَاذَا (Interrogative)
Question	سُؤَالٌ (SM) (أَسْئِلَةٌP)
During	خِلالَ (Adv. of time)
To accompany	رَافَقَ / يُرَافِقُ / مُرَافَقَةً
Idea, thought	فِكْرَةٌ SF (فِكَرٌ P)
Nice idea	فِكْرَةٌ جَمِيلَةٌ
to return	رَجَعَ / يَرْجِعُ / رُجُوعاً
Calcutta	كَلْكَتَا
Wife	زَوْجَةٌ (SF) زَوْجَاتٌ (P)
To see (infinitive)	لِرُؤْيَةٍ
Son	إِبْنٌ (SM) أَبْنَاءٌ (P)
I have come	قَدْ + قَدِمْتُ
Child	طِفْلٌ (SM) أَطْفَالٌ (P)
To receive (infinitive)	لاِسْتِقْبَالِ
Here they are	هَا هُمْ هَؤُلاءِ
Hello	آلُو
Uncle	عَمٌّ (SM) عُمُومٌ (P) أَعْمَامٌ (P)
To live	سَكَنَ / يَسْكُنُ / سُكُوناً
Delhi	دِلْهِى
Daughter	بِنْتٌ (SF) بَنَاتٌ (P)
Who	مَنْ
O.K.	طَيِّبٌ
O.K.	حَسَنًا

Early	مُبَكِّراً
To answer	أَجَابَ ⁄ يُجِيْبُ ⁄ إِجَابَةً
To say	قَالَ ⁄ يَقُولُ ⁄ قَولاً
Alone	وَحْداً (وَحْدَه)
House	مَنْزِلٌ (SM) مَنَازِلُ (P)
To ask	سَأَلَ ⁄ يَسْأَلُ ⁄ سُؤَالاً
Zoo	حَدِيْقَةُ الْحَيَوَانَاتِ
Incidentally	بِالْمُنَاسَبَةِ
When	مَتَى
Market	سُوقٌ (SF) أَسْوَاقٌ (P)
To buy (infinitive)	لِشِرَاءٍ

LESSON – 15

الدرس—١٥

Simple Past Tense
الفعل الماضى البسيط

Ūse of the verb (Kaana) ie. (He) was (كان) استخدام الفعل

One day	ذَاتَ يَوْمٍ
in the morning	فِى الصَّبَاحِ
I went to the airport.	ذَهَبْتُ إِلَى الْمَطَارِ.
A friend of mine was coming	كَانَ صَدِيقٌ لِى قَادِمًا
from America.	مِنْ أَمْرِيكَا.
When I reached the airport	عِنْدَمَا وَصَلْتُ الْمَطَارَ
I saw many people .	رَأَيْتُ كَثِيرِينَ مِنَ النَّاسِ.
My friends Hameed, Joseph and	كَانَ أَصْدِقَائِى حَمِيدٌ وَجَوزِيف وَ
Kishan were already present there.	كِيشَانَ مَوْجُودِينَ هُنَاك مِنْ قَبْلُ.
They were standing infront of	هُمْ كَانُوا وَاقِفِينَ اَمَامَ
the glass facade.	الوَاجِهَةِ الزُّجَاجِيَّةِ.
I asked them:	فَسَأَلْتُهُمْ:
Where (were) Asha, Jamila and Elen?	أَيْنَ آشَا وَ جَمِيْلَةُوَ اَيْلَن؟
Hameed answered:	فَأَجَابَ حَمِيْد:
They were present here	كُنَّ مَوْجُودَاتٍ هِنَا
a little while ago.	قَبْلَ قَلِيْلٍ.
Now they have gone to the canteen.	ذَهَبْنَ الآنَ إِلَى الْمَطْعَمِ.
I asked Joseph:	سَأَلْتُ جَوزِيْف:
Where were you yesterday?	أَيْنَ كُنْتَ أَمْسِ؟
Joseph said:	قَالَ جَوزِيْف:
I was present in the school.	كُنْتُ مَوْجُودًا فِى الْمَدْرَسَةِ.

Asha came, and I asked her:	جَاءَتْ آشَا وَ سَأَلْتُهَا :
Where were You (O) Asha?	أَيْنَ كُنْتِ يَا آشَا؟
She said:	فَقَالَتْ :
I was sitting in the canteen	كُنْتُ جَالِسَةً فِى الْمَطْعَمِ
with Jameela & Elen.	مَعَ جَمِيْلَة وَ اَيْلَنَ.
The plane (ie. flight) was late.	كَانَتِ الطَّائِرَةُ مُتَأَخِّرَةً .
So we all went to the canteen.	فَذَهَبْنَا جَمِيْعًا اِلَى الْمَطْعَمِ.
We ate something and (we) drank tea.	أَكَلْنَا قَلِيْلًا وَ شَرِبْنَا الشَّاىَ.
After one hour we returned	بَعْدَ سَاعَةٍ عُدْنَا
to the waiting hall.	إِلَى قَاعَةِ الإِنْتِظَارِ
Our friend Shanker was present.	كَانَ صَدِيْقُنَا شَنْكَر مَوْجُوداً.
He saw us and asked us:	فَرَآنَا وَ سَأَلَنَا:
Where were you, O' Hameed, Joseph &	أَيْنَ كُنْتُمْ يَا حَمِيْدوَ جُوزِيْف وَ
Kishan?	كِيْشَان؟
We said:	قُلْنَا:
We were present here	كُنَّا مَوْجُودِيْنَ هُنَا
one hour before.	قَبْلَ سَاعَةٍ.
We did not eat anything	لَمْ نَاكُلْ شَيْئًا
in the morning.	فِى الصَّبَاحِ.
Therefore, we went to the canteen.	فَذَهَبْنَا إِلَى الْمَطْعَمِ.
And you (ladies),	وَاَنْتُنَّ،
where were you	أَيْنَ كُنْتُنَّ
O' Asha, Jameela and Elen?	يَا آشَاوَجَمِيْلَة وَاِيْلَنَ؟
We were also present here	كُنَّا أَيْضًا مَوْجُودَاتٍ هِنَا
an hour ago.	قَبْلَ ساعَةٍ
We also did not eat	نَحْنُ أَيْضاً لَمْ نَأْكُلَ
any thing in the morning.	شَيْئًا فِى الصَّبَاحِ.

Therefore, we went with Hameed,   فَذَهَبْنَا مَعَ حَمِيد

Joseph and Kishan to the canteen.   و جُوزِيْف وكِيْشَانَ إِلَى المَطْعَمْ.

The boy was sitting   كَانَ الوَلَدُ جالِساً

The boys were sitting   كَانَ الأوْلادُ جَالِسِيْنَ

The boys were sitting   اَلأولادُ كَانُوْا جَالِسِيْنَ

The girl was sitting   كَانَتِ البِنْتُ جَالِسَةً

The girls were sitting   كَانَتِ البَنَاتُ جَالِسَاتٍ

The girls were sitting   اَلبَنَاتُ كُنَّ جَالِسَاتٍ

You (SM) were sitting   كُنْتَ جَالِسًا

You (PM) were sitting   كُنْتُم جَالِسِيْنَ

You (SF) were sitting   كُنْتِ جَالِسَةً

You (PF) were sitting   كُنْتُنَّ جَالِسَاتٍ

I (SM) was sitting   كُنْتُ جَالِسًا

We (PM) were sitting   كُنَّا جَالِسِيْنَ

I (SF) was sitting   كُنْتُ جَالِسَةً

We (PF) were sitting   كُنَّا جَالِسَاتٍ

Grammar:

We have known that there is no equivalent of "is , are, am" in the Arabic language. We have also known that in the simple nominal sentences of the Arabic language المبتدا i.e. the subject should (normally*) be either a propernoun or a pronoun or any common noun defined with the definite article Al الـ and in the nominative case.

The predicate i.e. khabar in such sentences is a verbal or adjectival noun and that would also be in the nominative case.

---

* It may be undefined common noun also. In this case khabar will have precedence over Mobtada.

Example:

The boy is sitting   اَلْوَلَدُ جَالِسٌ

The girl is sitting   اَلْبِنْتُ جَالِسَةٌ

However, in the simple past tense we have to use one verb also. This verb is known as كان. In English it is translated as "was or were" depending on its form and the context.

We have known in lessons nos 13 & 14 dealing with the past and the present verbs that the Arabic verb is conjugated to agree with its subject in number, gender and person.

كان is an irregular verb in the sense that it has ا i.e. a weak letter occuring in the middle of this three lettered verb.

In the following is given the list of the changing forms of the verb كان for guidance. All the verbs matching the pattern of كان should be conjugated accordingly.

He was	كَانَ
They (PM) were	كَانُوْا
She was	كَانَتْ
They (PF) were	كُنَّ
You (SM) were	كُنْتَ
You (PM) were	كُنْتُم
You (SF) were	كُنْتِ
You (PF) were	كُنْتُنَّ
I (SMF) was	كُنْتُ
We (PMF) were	كُنَّا

Now, to change a simple nominal sentence into simple past tense we have to use an appropriate form of كان before or after the subject as per need. The Arabic verb كَانَ continues to allow ḍammah to the terminal letter of the اسم i.e. the subject. However, the predicate i.e. خبر will be given fatḥah. In other words we can say that the subject of كان will be in the nominative case and the predicate will be in the accusative case. For example:

The boy is sitting   اَلْوَلَدُ جَالِسٌ

It is a simple nominal sentence. However if we want to say:

The boy was sitting, then we would say in Arabic: كَانَ الْوَلَدُ جَالِسًا

It would be amply clear from the example that the verb كَانَ is in complete agreement with its subject which happens to be a singular masculine noun of third person. The noun اَلْوَلَدُ in the sentence above is the subject of كَانَ and therefore, it is in the nominative case with *dammah* i.e. raf'a at its terminal letter. The predicate 'sitting' i.e. جَالِسًا is in the accusative case with *fathah* i.e. nasb.

All (verbal*) nouns on the جَالِسٌ pattern are said to be singular and masculine. Such nouns can be changed into plural by suffixing to them ونَ in the nominative case. In this case the letter preceding و will have *dammah* and the ن *fathah*. For example the plural of جالس will be:

$$ جَالِسٌ + ونَ = جَالِسُونَ $$

In the accusative and the genitive cases the و is replaced by the ى and accordingly the letter preceding ى is given a *kasrah*. The ن letter however, retains its *fathah*. For example the plural of جَالِسٌ in the accusative and the genitive cases will be: جَالِسِينَ.

Singular masculine nouns of this pattern can be changed into feminine gender by suffixing to it the round Ta ة. For example:

$$ جَالِسٌ + ة = جَالِسَةٌ $$

The round Ta ة declines normally in different cases.

About the feminine plurals of these feminine singular verbal nouns, we have to drop the round Ta ة and replace it with ا and normal stretched ت . In the nominative case** this ت will have *dammah* and in the accusative and genitive cases** it will have *kasrah* only. For example:

$$ جَالِسَ ـة = جَالِس $$

---

* Verbal nouns are those which are derived from the verb.

** As explained earlier, the vowel i.e. حَرَكَة below or above the terminal letter of a noun indicates case and in this position they are technically termed as Raf'a for *dammah*, Nasb for Fathah and Jarr for Kasrah.

جَالِسٌ + اتٌ = جَالِسَاتٌ Nominative case

جَالِسٌ + اتٍ = جَالِسَاتٍ Accusative and Genitive cases

It should be borne in mind that all feminine nouns ending in round Taة, do not have similar plurals particularly if they are not verbal nouns.

Plurals as mentioned in this lesson are known as sound plurals for masculine and feminine genders respectively.

Exercises

1. Translate the following into Arabic:

The class was full. All the students were present in the class. They were sitting and reading their lesson. The teacher also was present. He was standing infront of the black board. He was writing difficult words on the black board.

Shamim, why were you not present yesterday?

Sir, I was sick.

Hassan, Shanker & Joseph, You were also absent. Yes sir, we were also sick.

Miss Kanta, you were also absent?

Yes sir, I was busy at home. My mother was sick.

Shiela, Leela & Zainab, were you present yesterday?

No sir, we were absent. Asha, Usha & Bi were present in the class.

Translate the following into English:

ذَهَبْنَا مَرَّةً فِى نُزْهَةٍ إِلَى شَاطِئِ بَحْرٍ. كَانَ الشَّاطِئُ جَمِيلًا وَ مُزْدَحِمًا بِالنَّاسِ. كَانَ النَّاسُ جَالِسِينَ وَ وَاقِفِينَ فِى جَمَاعَاتٍ. رَأَيْتُ بِنْتًا صَغِيرَةً. كَانَتْ جَالِسَةً فِى ظِلِّ شَجَرَةٍ. كَانَتْ بَاكِيَةً. مَنْ أَنْتِ؟ لِمَاذَا أَنْتِ تَبْكِينَ؟ سَأَلْتُهَا.

فَقَالَتِ الْبِنْتُ: أَنَا نِهَادُ. كُنْتُ لَاعِبَةً هُنَا مَعَ أَخِى سَمِيرٍ فَتَشَاجَرَ مَعِى وَ ذَهَبَ. لَمْ يَأْخُذَنِى مَعَهُ. فَأَخَذْتُهَا مَعِى. وَ ذَهَبْتُ مِنْ أُسْرَةٍ إِلَى أُسْرَةٍ حَتَّى رَأَتْهَا أُمُّهَا فَسَأَلَتْهَا: أَيْنَ كُنْتِ غَائِبَةً؟ وَفِى

نَفْسِ الْوَقْتِ ظَهَرَ الأَخُ وَ سَأَلَتْهُ اُمُّهُ: وَاَيْنَ كُنْتَ لاَعِباً؟

فَقَالَ الْوَلَدُ: كُنْتُ لاَعِباً مَعَ نِهَاد هُنَاك تَحْتَ الشَّجَرَةِ. فَقَالَتْ نِهَادُ: اَنْتَ ضَرَبْتَنِى وَ تَرَكْتَنِى. فَقَدِمَ الأَبُ وَقَالَ: اَيْنَ كُنْتُمْ كُلُّكُم؟ كُنْتُ بَاحِثًا عَنْكُمْ. فَتَرَكْتُهُمْ يَتَحَدَّثُونَ وَ ذَهَبْتُ اَتَجَوَّلُ مِن دُونِ هَدَفٍ.

3. Make sentences of all numbers and genders from the following nouns in simple past tense.

رَاجِعٌ . نَائِمٌ . سَاهِرٌ . كَاتِبٌ . قَادِمٌ.

Glossary   الكلمات العسيرة

Full; complete	مُكْتَمِلٌ/كَامِلٌ (Adj. SM)
Present; available	حَاضِرٌ (Adj. SM)
Calss; classroom	فُصُولٌ (P) فَصْلٌ (SM)
Reading; reader	قُرَّاءٌ (P) قَارِئ (Adj. SM)
Infront of	اَمَامَ (functions like a preposition)
Blackboard	سَبُّورَاتٌ (P) سَبُّورَةٌ (SF)
Yesterday	اَمْسِ* (indeclinable)
Sick	مَرْضَى (P) مَرِيضٌ (SM)
Absent	غَائِبُونَ (Adj. SM) غَائِبٌ (P)
Once	مَرَّةً (Adv. of time)
Beach; bank (of river)	شَوَاطِئُ(P) شَاطِئٌ (SM)
Room	غُرَفٌ (P) غُرْفَةٌ (SF)
Reading	قِراءَةٌ (NF)
Reading Room	غُرْفَةُ القِراءَةِ
Busy	مَشْغُولُونَ (Adj. SM) مَشْغُولٌ (P)

---

* Indeclinable word in Arabic retains its given vowel point at the terminal letter and it does not change in any circumstances. It is known as مَبْنِى in Arabic.

Mother	أُمٌّ (SF) أُمَّهَاتٌ (P)
Mother	وَالِدَةٌ (SF) وَالِداتٌ (P)
Picnic	نُزْهَةٌ (SF) نُزْهَاتٌ (P)
Sea	بَحْرٌ (SM) بِحَارٌ (P)
Shade	ظِلٌّ (SM) ظِلَالٌ (P)
Tree	شَجَرَةٌ (NUF)
To Cry, to weep	بَكَى / يَبْكِى / بُكَاءً
Crying, In the act of crying	بَاكٍ (بَاكٍ) (Adj. SM) بُكَاةٌ (P)
Crying, in the act of crying	بَاكِيَةٌ (Adj. SF) بَاكِيَاتٌ(P)
Family	أُسْرَةٌ (SF) أُسَرٌ (P)
To, unto	حَتَّى (Prep.)
At the same time	فى نَفْس الوقتِ
To appear, to give audience	ظَهَرَ / يَظْهَرُ / ظُهُورًا
To play	لَعِبَ / يَلْعَبُ / لَعِبًا
To roam around	تَجَوَّلَ / يَتَجَوَّلُ / تَجَوُّلًا
Player	لَاعِبٌ (SM) لاعِبُونَ (P)
Under	تَحْتَ (Prep.)
To beat, to hit	ضَرَبَ / يَضْرِبُ / ضَرْباً
To leave	تَرَكَ / يَتْرُكُ / تَرْكًا
Father	أَبٌ (SM) آباءٌ (P)
Father	وَالِدٌ (SM) وَالِدُونَ (P)
Goal, aim	هَدَفٌ (SM) أهدافٌ (P)
Without	مِنْ دُون
Aimlessly	مِنْ دُونِ هَدَفٍ

LESSON —16

الدرس—١٦

Negative Verb: Past And Present Imperfect
الفعل المنفى: الماضى والمضارع

One day Hamid went	فِىْ يَوم ذَهَبَ حَامِدٌ
to Shanker's house.	إِلَى بَيْتِ شَنْكَر.
Shanker received him with warmth	اِسْتَقْبَلَهُ شَنْكَرُ بِحَرَارَةٍ
and said:	وَ قَالَ:
Welcome! my friend.	مَرْحَباً! يَا صَدِيقِى.
Hamid: Thank you my brother.	حَامِدٌ: شُكْرًا لَكَ يَا أَخِى.
Shanker: How are you?	شَنْكَرٌ: كَيْفَ حَالُكَ؟
Hamid: God be praised. I am fine.	حَامِدٌ: اَلْحَمْدُ لِلّٰهِ، أَنَا بِخَيْرٍ.
And how are you?	وَ كَيْفَ أَنْتَ؟
Fine! Praises be to God.	بِخَيْرٍ! اَلْحَمْدُ لِلّٰه.
Shanker: I do not see you	شَنْكَر: لَا أَرَاكَ
in the college now-a-days.	فِى الْكُلِّيَّةِ فِى هَذِهِ الأَيَّام.
Hamid: Yes, I am very busy	حَامِد: نَعَمْ، أَنَا مَشْغُولٌ جِدًّا
these days.	فِى هَذِهِ الأَيَّام.
We have guests from London.	لَدَيْنَا ضُيُوفٌ مِنْ لُنْدُن.
That is why I did not go	لِذَلِك لَمْ أَذْهَبْ
to the college last week.	إِلَى الْكُلِّيَّةِ فِى الأُسْبُوع الْمَاضِى.
I shall not go to the college	لَاأَذْهَبُ إِلَى الْكُلِّيَّة
next week also.	فِى الأُسْبُوع الْقَادِم أَيْضًا.
I have come to inform you.	قَدِمْتُ لإِخْبَارِك.
And this is the leave application.	وَ هَذَا طَلَبُ الإِجَازَةِ.
Please give it to the professor.	أَعْطِه مِنْ فَضْلِك لِلأُسْتَاذ.

Shanker: fine! any other service?   شَنْكَر : طَيِّبٌ! اَىَّ خِدْمَةٍ اُخْرَىٰ؟

Hamid: Thanks a lot.   حَامِدٌ : شُكْرًا جَزِيْلاً.

Shanker: Mention not.   شَنْكَر : اَلْعَفْوِ.

The tea came and Hamid   اَتَىٰ الشَّاىٰ وَ شَرِبَ حَامِدٌ
and Shanker drank tea.   وَ شَنْكَر الشَّاىٰ.

Shanker: O! Hamid, did you go   شَنْكَر : يَا حَامِد، هَلْ ذَهَبْتَ
to London?   اِلَىٰ لُنْدُن:

Hamid: No, I did not go.   حَامِدٌ : لَا، مَا ذَهَبْتُ.

Shanker: Will you go   شَنْكَر : هَلْ تَذْهَبُ
with your guests?   مَعَ ضُيُوْفِكَ؟

Hamid: No, I will not go with them.   حَامِدٌ : لَا، لَا اَذْهَبُ مَعَهُم.

I will go to London next month   اَذْهَبُ اِلَى لُنْدُنَ فِىْ الشَّهْرِ الْقَادِمِ
only after the examinations.   فَقَطْ بَعْدَ الإِمْتِحَانَاتِ.

And after some time   وَبَعْدَ وَقْتٍ قَلِيْل
Hamid returned to his house.   رَجَعَ حَامِدٌ اِلَىٰ بَيْتِهِ.

Grammar:

Like anyother language, in Arabic also there are two kinds of statements:

    a) Positive statement   البيان المثبت

    b) Negative statement   البيان المنفى

a) The positive statement is the one which tells us about the happening of some act.

Example:

    The boy drank water   شَرِبَ الْوَلَدُ الْمَاءَ

    The boy drinks water   يَشْرَبُ الْوَلَدُ الْمَاءَ

b)   Negative statement is the one that negates the happening of some act.

Example:

    The boy did not drink water   مَا شَرِبَ الْوَلَدُ الْمَاءَ

    The boy does not drink water   لَا يَشْرَبُ الْوَلَدُ الْمَاءَ

To render the positive statement of the past tense into the negative statement we can employ two methods:

i) We can use the negative particle مَا before the past tense verb of the positive sense.

Example:

He drank	شَرِبَ
He did not drink	مَاشَرِبَ
He opened	فَتَحَ
He did not open	مَا فَتَحَ
He ate	أَكَلَ
He did not eat	مَا أَكَلَ
He went	ذَهَبَ
He did not go	مَاذَهَبَ
He came	قَدِمَ
He did not come	مَاقَدِمَ

ii) The other way to obtain the past negative is by using the particle لَمْ. However it is used before the present imperfect verb of the positive sense.

Example:

He drinks	يَشْرَبُ
He did not drink	لَمْ يَشْرَبْ

As it would be evident from the example above the negative particle لَمْ is used before the present imperfect verb of poistive sense. However, the meaning changes into the negative past. This negative particle لَمْ which is introduced before the present imperfect of the positive sense to bring about the past negative meaning, functions by causing 'sokoon' to the terminal letter of the present imperfect verb and additionally causing all the terminal 'noons' i.e. ن to drop except the 'noon' of II & III persons plurals of the feminine gender. In the following is given the full conjugation of يَشْرَبُ preceded by the negative particle لَمْ as explained above:

He did not drink	لَمْ يَشْرَبْ
They (PM) did not drink	لَمْ يَشْرَبُوا

She did not drink	لَمْ تَشْرَبْ
They (PF) did not drink	لَمْ يَشْرَبْنَ
You (SM) did not drink	لَمْ تَشْرَبْ
You (PM) did not drink	لَمْ تَشْرَبُوا
You (SF) did not drink	لَمْ تَشْرَبِى
You (PF) did not drink	لَمْ تَشْرَبْنَ
I (SMF) did not drink	لَمْ أَشْرَبْ
We (PMF) did not drink	لَمْ نَشْرَبْ

Similarly, the present imperfect verbs of the positive sense can be changed into the negative by just placing the negative particle لَا before it.

Example:

He drinks	يَشْرَبُ
He does not drink	لَا يَشْرَبُ
He opens	يَفْتَحُ
He does not open	لَا يَفْتَحُ
He eats	يَأْكُلُ
He does not eat	لَا يَأْكُلُ
He goes	يَذْهَبُ
He does not go	لَايَذْهَبُ
He comes	يَقْدَمُ
He does not come	لَا يَقْدَمُ

This combination of لَا and the present imperfect verb negates the statement in the present context as would be amply clear from the list of verbs above. It may also give the negative meaning in present continuous and future provided there is reason for it, For example:

| The student will not go
to the school tomorrow. | لَا يَذْهَبُ الطَّالِبُ
إِلَى الْمَدْرَسَةِ غَدًا |

Here the adverb of time غدا i.e. tomorrow in the sentence causes the act of the verb يذهب to extend to embrace futurity.

However, when لَنْ is introduced before the present imperfect verb of the positive sense the meaning changes into the future negative only. For example:

The boy will not/never drink water   لَنْ يَشْرَبَ الْوَلَدُ الْمَاءَ

In this case the last letter of the present imperfect takes the *fatḥa* and all the 'noon' letters are dropped except the 'noons' of the II & III persons plurals of the feminine gender. Below is produced the full conjugation of لَنْ يَّشْرَبَ for future guidance.

He will not drink	لَنْ يَشْرَبَ
They (PM) will not drink	لَنْ يَشْرَبُوا
She will not drink	لَنْ تَشْرَبَ
They (PF) will not drink	لَنْ يَشْرَبْنَ
You (SM) will not drink	لَنْ تَشْرَبَ
You (PM) will not drink	لَنْ تَشْرَبُوا
You (SF) will not drink	لَنْ تَشْرَبِى
You (PF) will not drink	لَنْ تَشْرَبْنَ
I (SMF) will not drink	لَنْ اَشْرَبَ
We (PMF) will not drink	لَنْ نَشْرَبَ

Note that (1) Maa i.e. مَا and Laa i.e. لَا are negative paricles which are placed before Maaḍi i.e. مَاضِى and muḍaari'a i.e. مضارع as shown in this lesson above. However, deviations in use are acceptable, specially in the spoken Arabic. Even though in the past negative Maa i.e. ما introduces the negative meaning in a sentence however, if this negative meaning is repeated then Laa i.e. لا is used for any number of times, e.g.

مَا أَكَلْتُ وَ لَا شَرِبْتُ

I did not eat and I did not drink i.e.

I did not eat & drink

or.

I did not eat nor did I drink.

and

مَا حَفِظْتُ وَ لَا قَرَأْتُ وَ لَا كَتَبْتُ

I did not memorize nor did I read or write. etc.

(2) Silencing vowel mark which is a small circle (°) above a letter in a word preceded by a vowelled letter is used to indicate a syllable. This circle is called sokoon i.e. سكون. For example: Sokoon above Raa in غُرْفَة indicates that غُرْ i.e. غ & ر together make one syllable, Fa with Fathah above makes another syllable and Ṭaa marboota makes the third syllable. Where sokoon is caused to be placed above the terminal letter of a word, it is known as Jazm i.e. جزم and the noun or verb is called Majzoom i.e. such a verb or noun is supposed to be in the apocopate and jussive mood respectively.

(3) When Lan i.e. لَنْ precedes the Mudaari'a verb, it causes Fathah to the last letter of the verb or causes all 'noons' to drop as explained in this lesson above. In this case the verb is considered to be in the subjunctive mood.

Exercises:

1. Translate the following into Arabic:

He is my friend Samir. He lives in Calcutta. This is his wife Sarita. She also lives in Calcutta with her husband and children. And these are Amir, Ritesh and Babu. They study in a college in Delhi.

Why have you come to Delhi, Mr. Samir? I have come to see my sons. And you, Mrs. Sarita Samir, why have you come? I have also come to see my children in the college.

Have your children come here to receive you? Yes, here they are. Hello! Children, how are you? Fine, sir. Thank you. Where will you all go now? Now we will go to our uncle. He lives here in Delhi. This is his daughter Shiela.

Hello, Miss Shiela, how are you? Fine! Thank you. Miss. Shiela, do you also study in the college? Yes, I study in a college in Delhi. Who are these girls? They are Sunaina, Priya and Zainab. They are my friends.

Hello! do you also go to the college? Yes, we go to the college with shiela.

O.K. I will go now. I will come tomorrow.

2. Translate the following into English:

رَجَعَ وَلَدٌ مِنْ مَدْرَسَتِهِ مُبَكِّرًا فِى يَوْمٍ فَقَالَتْ لَهُ أُمُّهُ: أَلَمْ تَذْهَبْ إِلَى مَدْرَسَتِكَ الْيَوْمَ يَا وَلَدِى؟ فَأَجَابَ الْوَلَدُ: ذَهَبْتُ وَ لَكِنِ اُسْتَاذِىَ لَمْ يَقْدَمْ. فَقَالَتِ الأُمُّ: وَهَلْ رَجَعَ كُلُّ الطُّلَّابِ؟ فَرَدَّ الْوَلَدُ: لَا، لَمْ يَرْجِعُوا. أَنَا وَحْدِى رَجَعْتُ. وَلِمَاذَا رَجَعْتَ إِلَى الْمَنْزِلِ؟ سَأَلَتْهُ أُمُّهُ. فَقَالَ الْوَلَدُ: ذَهَبَ الطُّلَّابُ إِلَى حَدِيقَةِ الْحَيَوَانَاتِ وَ أَنَا لَمْ أَذْهَبْ. وَبِالْمُنَاسَبَةِ، مَتَى تَذْهَبِينَ إِلَى السُّوقِ لِشِرَاءِ الْحَاجِيَاتِ؟ أُرِيدُ قَلَمًا. لَقَدِ انْكَسَرَ قَلَمِىْ. فَقَالَتِ الأُمُّ: نَذْهَبُ سَوِيًّا فِى الْمَسَاءِ. فَأَجَابَ الْوَلَدُ: لَا نَذْهَبُ هَذَا الْمَسَاءَ لأَنَّ أَصْدِقَائِى مِنَ الْمَدْرَسَةِ يَقْدَمُونَ إِلَيَّ. نَحْنُ نَذْهَبُ لِمُشَاهَدَةِ فِلْمٍ. فَقَالَتِ الأُمُّ: تَذْهَبُونَ لِلْفِلْمِ وَ لَا تَذْهَبُونَ لِزِيَارَةِ الأُسْتَاذِ الْمَرِيضِ، هَذَا غَيْرُ مَعْقُولٍ يَا وَلَدِى. فَخَجِلَ الْوَلَدُ وَقَالَ: اَحْسَنْتِ يَا أُمِّى. نَبَّهْتِنِى. لَنْ أَذْهَبَ لِلْفِلْمِ هَذَا الْمَسَاءَ. اَذْهَبُ لِزِيَارَةِ اُسْتَاذِى الْمَرِيضِ.

3. Write a paragraph in Arabic using verbs in jussive and subjunctive moods.

4. Choose some verbs to write their conjugations in jussive & subjunctive moods.

Glossary　　　　　　　　　　　　اَلْكَلِمَاتُ الْعَسِيرَةُ

To receive	اِسْتَقْبَلَ / يَسْتَقْبِلُ / اِسْتِقْبَالًا
With warmth; warmly	بِحَرَارَةٍ
To say	قَالَ / يَقُوْلُ / قَوْلًا
Saying (gerund)	قَائِلًا
O'	يَا
(vocative compulsorily used in Arabic but rarely translated in English)	
One day	فِى يَوْمٍ
Thank you	شُكْرًا لَكَ
To see	رَأَى / يَرَى / رُؤْيَةً
Busy	مَشْغُولٌ (SM) مَشْغُولُونَ (P)

Very; very much	جِدًّا (Adv. of manner)
We have	لَدَيْنَا
Guest	ضَيْفٌ(SM) ضُيُوفٌ(P)
To inform you	لِإِخْبَارِك

Infinitive meaning in Arabic is obtained by introducing ل meaning 'for' before the infinitive form (i.e. gerundal form) of the concerned verb. For example:

(1) He informed (Past imperfect) أَخْبَرَ

(2) He informs (Present imperfect) يُخْبِرُ

(3) To inform (Infinitive form) إِخْبَارٌ

The form mentioned at serial no. 3 is known as the infinitive form (gerundal form) and generally it is preceded by ل to render the meaning in the English infinitive.

Group	جَمَاعَةٌ (SF) جَمَاعَاتٌ (P)
People	إِنْسَانٌ (SM) أُنَاسٌ (P)
Shade	ظِلٌّ (SM) ظِلَالٌ (P)
Tree	شَجَرَةٌ (SF) شَجَرَاتٌ (P)
Weeping; crying	* بَاكِى (VN/ SM) بُكَاةٌ
To ask	سَأَلَ/ يَسْأَلُ/ سُؤَالاً
Playing; player	لَاعِبٌ (VN/ SM) لَاعِبُونَ
To quarrel	تَشَاجَرَ/ يَتَشَاجَرُ/ تَشَاجُرًا
Family	أُسْرَةٌ (SF) أُسَرٌ (P)
At the same time	فِى نَفْسِ الْوَقْتِ
To appear	ظَهَرَ/ يَظْهَرُ/ ظُهُورًا

---

* Verbal nouns i.e. nouns derived from verbs/ adjectives terminating in Yaa ى preceded by Kasrah are made into plural on the pattern of فُعَاةٌ as in the case of بَاكِى & بُكَاةٌ and سَاعِى & سُعَاةٌ (postman).

To beat	ضَرَبَ / يَضْرِبُ / ضَرْبًا
To leave	تَرَكَ / يَتْرُكُ / تَرْكًا
Searching (for) ; Looking (for) (VN/SM)	بَاحِثٌ (عَنْ)
To talk	تَحَدَّثَ / يَتَحَدَّثُ / تَحَدُّثًا
To roam about	تَجَوَّلَ / يَتَجَوَّلُ / تَجَوُّلاً
Without	مِنْ دُونِ
Aim	هَدَفٌ (SM) أَهْدَافٌ (P)
That is why	لِذَلِكَ
Application	طَلَبٌ (SM) طَلَبَاتٌ (P)
Leave	إِجَازَةٌ (SF) إِجَازَاتٌ (P)
To give	أَعْطَى / يُعْطِى / إِعْطَاءً
Please	مِنْ فَضْلِكَ
With	مَعَ (Prep.)
Only	فَقَطْ
Examination	اِمْتِحَانٌ (SM) اِمْتِحَانَاتٌ (P)
To return	رَجَعَ / يَرْجِعُ / رُجُوعًا
Calcutta	كَلْكُتَا
Wife	زَوْجَةٌ (SF) زَوْجَاتٌ (P)
Why	لِمَاذَا
To see	لِرُؤْيَةِ (infinitive)
Son	اِبْنٌ (SM) أَبْنَاءٌ (P)
I have come	قَدْ + قَدِمْتُ
Child	طِفْلٌ (SM) أَطْفَالٌ (P)
To receive	لِاسْتِقْبَالِ (infinitive)
Here they are	هَا هُمْ هَؤُلَاءِ
Hello	آلُو
Uncle	عَمٌّ (SM) عُمُومٌ (P) أَعْمَامٌ (P)
To live	سَكَنَ / يَسْكُنُ / سُكُونًا

Delhi	دِلْهِی
Daughter	بِنْتٌ (SF) بَنَاتٌ (P)
Who	مَنْ
O.K.	طَيِّبٌ
O.K.	حَسَنًا
Early	مُبَكِّرًا
To answer	أَجَابَ / يُجِيْبُ / اِجَابَةً
To say	قَالَ / يَقُولُ / قَوْلًا
Alone	وَحْدًا (وَحْدَهُ)
House	مَنْزِلٌ (SM) مَنَازِلُ (P)
To ask	سَأَلَ / يَسْأَلُ / سُؤَالًا
Zoo	حَدِيْقَةُ الْحَيَوَانَاتِ
Incidentally	بِالْمُنَاسَبَةِ
When	مَتَى
Market	سُوْقٌ (SF) أَسْوَاقٌ (P)
To buy	لِشِرَاءٍ(infinitive)
Needs (necessities)	حَاجِيَاتٌ
To want	أَرَادَ / يُرِيْدُ / إِرَادَةً
To break	اِنْكَسَرَ / يَنْكَسِرُ / اِنْكِسَارًا (Reflexive meaning)
Together	سَوِيًّا
All	كُلٌّ *
Evening	مَسَاءٌ

---

* كُلٌّ is a noun and it declines like any other noun. It is placed in construct position with another noun. It means 'every' before a singular common noun. For example:

كُلُّ وَلَدٍ Every boy/ Each boy

When it is placed before a plural defined noun it means 'all'. For example:

كُلُّ الأَوْلَادِ All the boys

Because	لِأَنَّ
To me	إِلَيَّ
To see/ watch (infinitive)	لِمُشَاهَدَةٍ
Film	فِلْم (SM) أَفْلَامٌ (P)
To be ashamed/ embarassed	خَجِلَ / يَخْجَلُ / خَجَلاً
To visit	لِزِيَارَةٍ (infinitive)
Sick	مَرِيْضٌ (SM) مَرْضَى (P)
Unbecoming; unreasonable	غَيْرُ مَعْقُوْلٌ
To do well	أَحْسَنَ / يُحْسِنُ / اِحْسَانًا
To remind, warn	نَبَّهَ / يُنَبِّهُ / تَنْبِيْهاً
To come	أَتَى / يَأْتِي / إِتْيَانًا

Derived Forms Of Verbs
الافعال المزيد فيها

One sunday in the noon I was sitting	ذَاتَ يَوْمِ أَحَدٍ فِى الظُّهْرِ كُنْتُ اَجْلِسُ
in my study-room	فِى غُرْفَةِ دِرَاسَتِى
reading a magazine	اَقْرَأُ مَجَلَّةً
when suddenly	إذْ
my youngest son entered.	دَخَلَ ابْنِى الأَصْغَرُ.
He stood beside me for a while,	فَوَقَفَ بِجَانِبِى قَلِيْلاً
then he proceeded towards my table	ثُمَّ تَقَدَّمَ اِلَى طَاوِلَتِى
and climbed up the chair placed	وَطَلَعَ الْكُرْسِىَّ الْمَوْضُوعَ
beside it.	بِجَانِبِهَا.
He started playing with the books	اَخَذَ يَلْعَبُ بِالْكُتُبِ
and the stationery placed on it.	وَاَدَوَاتِ الْكِتَابَةِ الْمَوْضُوعَةِ عَلَيْهَا.
He took my pen and a sheet of paper	اَخَذَ قَلَمِى وَوَرَقَةً
and started drawing lines	وَاَخَذَ يَرْسُمُ خُطُوطًا
on the paper as if he were writing.	عَلَى الْوَرَقَةِ، كَأَنَّهُ يَكْتُبُ.
I left the chair and walked	تَرَكْتُ الْكُرْسِىَّ وَ مَشَيْتُ
towards him.	نَحْوَهُ.
I went close to him but I found that he had	اِقْتَرَبْتُ مِنْهُ وَلَكِنَّنِى وَجَدْتُ اَنَّهُ
broken its nib.	كَانَ قَدْ كَسَّرَ رِيْشَهُ.
I put him down from the chair	فَأَنْزَلْتُهُ مِنَ الْكُرْسِىِّ
against his will.	عَلَى رَغْمِ اَنْفِهِ.
And I started restoring everything	وَاَخَذْتُ اُرْجِعُ كُلَّ شَىْ
to its place oɪ the table.	اِلَى مَكَانِهِ عَلَى الطَّاوِلَةِ.

When I was busy arranging	عِنْدَمَا كُنْتُ مَشْغُولًا أُرَتِّبُ
the table, he turned to the magazine	الطَّاوِلَةَ تَوَجَّهَ إِلَى الْمَجَلَّةِ
and (he) started turning its pages.	وَأَخَذَ يَتَصَفَّحُهَا .
When I was free from the table	وَلَمَّا فَرَغْتُ مِنَ الطَّاوِلَةِ
and paid attention to him,	وَالْتَفَتُّ إِلَيْهِ
I found that he had torn it.	وَجَدْتُ أَنَّهُ كَانَ مَزَّقَهَا .
I went to him	ذَهَبْتُ إِلَيْهِ
and held him by his hand	وَ مَسَكْتُهُ بِيَدِهِ
and turned him out of my room.	وَأَخْرَجْتُهُ مِنْ غُرْفَتِي .
He started weeping	فَأَخَذَ يَبْكِي
and went to his mother in the kitchen.	وَ ذَهَبَ إِلَى أُمِّهِ فِي الْمَطْبَخِ .
His mother started fondling him	أَخَذَتْ أُمُّهُ تُدَاعِبُهُ
and gave him milk in a cup to drink.	وَ أَعْطَتْهُ اللَّبَنَ فِي كُوبٍ لِلشُّرْبِ .
He became quiet and came to me	فَسَكَتَ وَجَاءَ إِلَيَّ
with the cup of milk.	بِكُوبِ اللَّبَنِ .
He sat on the floor	جَلَسَ عَلَى الْأَرْضِ
and drank the milk.	وَشَرِبَ اللَّبَنَ .
Then he tried to put the cup on	ثُمَّ حَاوَلَ أَنْ يَضَعَ الْكُوبَ عَلَى
the table.	الطَّاوِلَةِ .
The cup fell down and broke.	فَسَقَطَ الْكُوبُ وَانْكَسَرَ .
After that he came to me.	بَعْدَ ذَلِكَ قَدِمَ إِلَيَّ .
I pretended that I was angry	فَتَظَاهَرْتُ أَنَّنِي كُنْتُ غَاضِبًا
with him.	مِنْهُ .
He started talking to me about this	فَأَخَذَ يَتَحَدَّثُ عَنْ هَذَا
and that in his innocent voice inviting	وَ ذَاكَ بِصَوْتِهِ الْبَرِئِ يَسْتَلْفِتُ
my attention towards him.	اِنْتِبَاهِي إِلَيْهِ .
I laughed and began to tickle him till	فَضَحِكْتُ وَ أَخَذْتُ أُدَغْدِغُهُ حَتَّى
his cheeks turned red.	احْمَرَّتْ وَجْنَتَاهُ .

I let him off and he left the room.	فَتَرَكْتُهُ وَ خَرَجَ مِنَ الْغُرْفَةِ
After some time he returned with his toy.	وَبَعْدَ قَلِيلٍ رَجَعَ بِأُلْعُوبَتِهِ.
Then he pulled a chair and put it	ثُمَّ جَرَّ كُرْسِيًّا وَوَضَعَهُ
infront of me and we sat face to face	أَمَامِى وَجَلَسْنَا نَتَقَابَلُ
playing together (with each other).	وَ نَتَلَاعَبُ.

Grammar:

In terms of number of original letters that constitute an Arabic verb, there are three varieties of Arabic verbs. They are as follows:

(i) ثُلَاثِى , triliteral i.e. composed of three root letters. These triliteral verbs constitute the majority of the Arabic verbs.

(ii) رُبَاعِى , quadriliteral i.e. composed of four root-letters. We sparingly encounter these quadriliteral verbs. However they do exist and form the next majority or rather the major minority in the Arabic Verbs.

(iii) خُمَاسِى , quintuple i.e. composed of five root-letters. These verbs are the rarest to come across with. They are the counted few and are cited only as examples in the books of grammar. These verbs, composed of three or four or five original or root-letters are known in Arabic as الافعال المجردة i.e. verbs of the first stem.

When some other letters are added to these original verbs to extract fresh forms from the verbs, such extracted forms of the verbs are known in Arabic as الافعال المزيد فيها i.e. the derived forms of the verbs.

It has been explained in the foregoing lines that the triliteral verbs form the biggest majority of the Arabic verbs, so much so that we can easily dispense with the quadriliteral and quintuple verbs if we make a little effort. It is therefore, I shall tell you only about the triliteral verbs of the first stem and their derived forms.

In simple triliteral verbs (i.e. those consisting of three different consonant letters) the first and the third letters (III person singular masculine form) always, invariably carreis the fathah. The second letter may, however carry either *fathah* or *kasrah* or *dammah*. For example:

ذَهَبَ	He went
سَمِعَ	He heard
كَبُرَ	He was big

Another variety of triliteral verbs is that which consists of one or two weak letters beside one or two consonant letters. This weak letter or letters may either occur in the beginning or middle or the end. For example:

عَدَا	He ran
مَشَى	He went
قَالَ	He said

The foregoing variety of verbs is popularly known as irregualr triliteral verbs. It is slightly problematic to conjugate them. (For conjugation patterns of these verbs, see appendix.

The third variety of triliteral verbs is that which consists of two identical letters i.e. the second & the third letters are one and the same. It is therefore these two letters are written as one and said twice with the help of shaddah. On the face value, such verbs appear to be biliteral i.e. composed of two root- letters. However, in reality and for all practical purposes they are fully triliteral verbs. For example:

مَدَّ (مَدَدَ)	He stretched
فَرَّ (فَرَرَ)	He ran away

These triliteral verbs of the first stem are categorised under form (i). Now, let us take up the derived forms of the triliteral verbs. For our convenience we can divide them into three categories: A, B and C.

(A) Verbs having only one additional letter in excess of the three originals. This may be wrought:

(ii) By doubling the second root-letter e.g. رَجَّعَ to restore; to return s. th. (from رَجَعَ to return i.e. to come back or to go back).

In terms of meaning, it changes an intransitive or reflexive verb into transitive. Its normal infinitive verbal form is on the pattern of تَفْعِيْل as we find تَرْجِيْع in the case of رَجَّعَ .

(iii) By adding one Alif after the first root-letter e.g. دَاعَبَ to fondle (from دَعَبَ to joke).

In terms of meaning, it normally expresses the application of the act of the root form to another person. This form is always transitive. Its infinitive verb is always drawn on the pattern of مُفَاعَلَة as we find in the case of مُدَاعَبَة from دَاعَبَ

(iv) By adding one Alif before the first root-letter. e.g. أَنْزَلَ to take (s.o.) down (from نَزَلَ to get down).

This additional Alif changes the meaning of the intransitive verb into transitive and that of the transitive into double transitive. This form of verb is popularly known as causative. Its infinitive verb is drawn on the pattern of إِفْعَال as we find إِنْزَال from أَنْزَلَ.

(B) Verbs having two additional letters in excess of the three originals. This may be wrought:

(v) By placing ت before the first root-letter and doubling the second root-letter. e.g. تَقَدَّمَ to move ahead (from قَدِمَ to come).

In terms of meaning, this from is normally the reflexive of form (ii). For example قَدَّمَ means to move some one or some thing ahead and تَقَدَّمَ means to move ahead oneself.

Its infinitive verb is drawn on the pattern of تَفَعُّل , as we find تَقَدُّم in the case of تَقَدَّمَ.

(vi) By adding ت before the first root-letter and interfixing Alif after the first root letter. e.g. تَلَاعَبَ to play together (from لَعِبَ to play).

It is normally the reflexive of form (iii). For example لَاعَبَ means play with and تَلَاعَبَ means to play together. Also that لَاعَبَ pattern takes subject and the object. e.g. لَاعَبَ الْوَلَدُ بِنْتًا : The boy played with a girl , whereas تَلَاعَبَ takes only the subject, e.g.تَلَاعَبَ الْوَلَدُ وَالْبِنْتُ : the boy and the girl played together.

Its infinitive verb is drawn on the pattern تَفَاعُل, as we find تَلَاعُب from تَلَاعَبَ.

(vii) By adding ١ & ن before the three root-letters. e.g. اِنْكَسَرَ to be broken (from كَسَرَ to break).

It changes a transitive verb into a reflexive verb. It may also be treated as passive for all practical purposes. Its infinitive verb form is drawn on the pattern of اِنْفِعَال as we find اِنْكَسَار from اِنْكَسَرَ.

(viii) By adding ١ before the first and ت after the first root-letter.e.g. اِلْتَفَتَ to pay attention (from لَفَتَ to drawn attention).

It is difficult to relate it with any particular shade of meaning i.e. reflexive or intransitive or passive etc. however, in a large number of cases, this verb pattern changes the transitive verb into reflexive. Its infinitive verb is drawn on the pattern of اِفْتِعَال as in the case of اِلْتِفَات from اِلْتَفَتَ.

(ix) By adding ١ before the first root-letter and doubling the last root-letter.e.g. اِعْوَجَّ to be crooked (from عَوِجَ to be bent).

This verb pattern is reserved for describing colours or physical defects. Its infinitive verb is drawn on the pattern of اِفْعِلَال as in the case of اِعْوِجَاج from اِعْوَجَّ.

(C) Verbs having three additional letters in excess of the three root-letters. This is wrought:

(x) By adding ١ ، س & ت respectively before the three root-letters of the verb. e.g. إِسْتَلْفَتَ to request some one's attention (from لَفَتَ, to draw attention).

This verb pattern is employed to express desire or request and such other relative meanings. Its infinitive is drawn on the pattern of إِسْتِفْعَال, as in the case of إِسْتِلْفَات from إِسْتَلْفَتَ.

Apart from these verb patterns from (i) to (x) , there are five more patterns. However, they are sparingly used.

I have given alongside each verb pattern the shade of meaning for which it is ordinarily employed. However, it also should be made amply clear that it is not essential that a particular verb pattern from all verbs shall always have the same shade of meaning. It might have a different shade of meaning as well.

Theoretically speaking, we can derive all the verb patterns from a single verb consisting of three root-letters. However practically it does not obtain in the case of all the verbs. Some root-verbs might have only three verb-patterns in practical use. Some others might have four, five or six, while some others might have more than this. However, no verb can necessarily provide all the forms.

The conjugation of all the derived verbs is the same as that of the triliteral original verbs. In other words same prefixes, interfixes and suffixes are used in the conjugation of the derived verbs. Please see appendix for sample conjugations.

Exercises:

1. (a) Translate into Arabic:

 (1) Did you receive your brother's letter?

 (2) I want to employ one maid-servant for the house chores.

 (3) I don't expect any good from him now.

 (4) He threw a stone at the sleeping dog.

 (5) Has the postman delivered your parcel to you?

 (6) I know that you helped me a lot in that difficult time.

 (7) We sat together and spoke about our past days.

 (8) We shall meet here tomorrow again.

 (9) The bottle fell down and was broken.

 (10) Has he gone to his college?

 (b) I had great desire to visit Varanasi. This city of Varanasi is famous for its sarees, temples and the river Ganges. But every time I prepared to go there, some thing or other prevented me from it. No solid opportunity came my way to go there. One day I was very happy. Finally, a very solid opportunity was there. Banaras Hindu University

had invited me to conduct viva voce examination for two Ph. D
students in Arabic. On receiving this invitation I rushed to the railway
booking office to reserve my ticket. I always prefer train journey to air
journey. The booking office was crowded with people. People were
standing in long queues. I also stood in one queue. Soon I realised that
the queues were moving fast. In a few minutes time I found myself
facing the counter clerk. He received me with courtesy and smiled to
me gently. I handed over to him my reservation form with requisite
information. He passed a look at my form. After that his fingers began
to tap the keys of the computer. Fortunately reservation for my date
was available. He gently asked me money for the ticket. I took out my
purse from my pocket and gave him the money. He received the
money and handed over my ticket to me. I smiled to him in
thanks-giving and he smiled to me in return.

(2) Translate into English:

(a)

(1) أَرْكَبْتُهُ فِى سَيَّارَتِى وَ ذَهَبْتُ بِهِ إِلَى الْمُسْتَشْفَى.

(2) إِسْتَقْبَلَنِى مُضِيفِى عَلَى بَابِ مَنْزِلِه.

(3) قَدَّمَ لِىَ الغَارِسُون فِنْجَانَ شَاى سَاخِنٍ.

(4) كانَ يَمْشِى عَلَى الْمَاءِ فَانْزَلَقَ.

(5) هَلْ سَتُسَافِرُ إِلَى لُنْدُنْ فِى الشَّهْرِ القَادِمِ.

(6) لَا أَتَذَكَّرُ إِسْمَ مُدَرِّسِى.

(7) تَصْفَرُّ العَيْنانِ فِى مَرَضِ الْيَرْقَانِ.

(8) يَجِبُ اَنْ نَحْتَرِمَ أَسَاتِذَنَا.

(9) جَلَسْنَا نَتَبَادَلُ الحَدِيْث عَنْ ذِكْرَيَاتِ الماضِى.

(10) سَمِعْتُ صَوْتاً مُزْعِجاً وَاسْتَيْقَظْتُ مِنَ النَّوْمِ.

(b) بَعْدَ إِكْمَالِ دِرَاسَاتِى فِى الْجَامِعَةِ ضَيَّعْتُ كَثِيرًا مِنْ وَقْتِى الغَالِى فِى الْبَحْثِ عَنْ وَظِيفَةٍ
حُكُومِيَّةٍ. تَقَدَّمْتُ بِطَلَبَاتٍ إِلَى الوِزَرَاتِ والسِّفَارَاتِ وَالمَكَاتِبِ الْحُكُومِيَّةِ و غَيْرِ
الْحُكُومِيَّةِ وَ لَكِنْ لِلْأَسَفِ اَلْجَوَابُ كانَ 'لَا'.

ذَاتَ يَوْمٍ فِى الصَّبَاحِ كُنْتُ جَالِسًا فِى فِنَاءِ بَيْتِى أَتَصَفَّحُ الْجَرِيدَةَ إِذْ سَمِعْتُ طَرْقَةً عَلَى الْبَابِ. فَتَحْتُ الْبَابَ وَرَأَيْتُ صَدِيقِى. كَانَ زَمِيلِى فِى الدِّرَاسَةِ فِى الْجَامِعَةِ. فَأَدْخَلْتُهُ الْمَنْزِلَ وَرَافَقْتُهُ إِلَى غُرْفَةِ الإِسْتِقْبَالِ وَجَلَسْنَا نَتَقَابَلُ. عِنْدَمَا كُنَّا مَشْغُولِيْنَ فِى الْحَدِيثِ عَنِ الأَيَّامِ الْغَابِرَةِ جَاءَ ثُ أُخْتِى مَعَ الشَّاى و الْبَسْكُوِيت. سَأَلْتُ صَدِيقِى عَنْ عَمَلِهِ فَقَالَ: لِى مَصْنَعٌ صَغِيرٌ لِلألاَعِيبِ اللُّدْنِيَّةِ (الْبَلاَسْتِيكِيَّةِ). شَرَعْتُ الْعَمَلَ فِيهِ بِنَفْسِى أَوَّلاً، ثُمَّ رُوَيْدًا رُوَيْدًا إِسْتَخْدَمْتُ بَعْضَ الْعَامِلِينَ. وَالآنَ هُنَاك عِشْرُونَ شَخْصًا يَعْمَلُونَ فِى هَذَا الْمَصْنَعِ. وَأَنَاالْحَمْدُ لله سَعِيْدٌ. فَاقْتَرَبْتُ منه بِإِهْتِمَامٍ و سَأَلْتُهُ أَسْئِلَةً. فَبَادَلَنِى الإِهتِمَامَ بِالإِهْتِمَامِ وَ وَعَدَنِى بِكُلِّ الْمُسَاعدَةِ. فَعَزَمْتُ أَيْضًا عَلَى بَدْءِ عَمَلٍ مِثْلَهُ حَتَّى لَا يَضِيعَ الْمَزِيْدُ مِنْ وَقْتِى.

(3) Separate all the derived verbs from the foregoing passage and use them in sentences of your own in their different forms i.e. singular & plural forms etc.

Glossary	الكلمات العسيرة
To receive (s. th.)	إِسْتَلَمَ / يَسْتَلِمُ / إِسْتِيلاَمًا
To employ	إِسْتَخْدَمَ / يَسْتَخْدِمُ / إِسْتِخْدَامًا
Maid-servant	خَادِمَةٌ (SF) خَادِمَاتٌ (P)
House chores	أَعْمَالٌ مَنْزِلِيَّةٌ
To expect	تَوَقَّعَ / يَتَوَقَّعُ / تَوَقُّعًا
Good	خَيْرٌ (Adj. SM)
To throw	أَلْقَى / يُلْقِى / إِلْقَاءً
Stone	حَجَرٌ (SM) أَحْجَارٌ (P)
Sleeping	نَائِمٌ (Adj. SM)
Postman	سَاعِى الْبَرِيدِ
To deliver	سَلَّمَ / يُسَلِّمُ / تَسْلِيْمًا
Parcel	طَرْدٌ (SM) طُرُوْدٌ (P)
To help	سَاعَدَ / يُسَاعِدُ / مُسَاعَدَةً
A lot	كَثِير (Adj.)

Difficult	صَعْبٌ (Adj. SM)
To sit together	تَجَالَسَ / يَتَجَالَسُ / تَجَالُسًا
To speak (together)	تَحَادَثَ يَتَحَادَثُ / تَحَادُثاً
Day	يَوْمٌ (SM) اَيَّامٌ (P)
Past	مَاضِى (Adj. SM)
To meet; to assemble	اِجْتَمَعَ / يَجْتَمِعُ / اِجْتِمَاعًا
Once again	مَرَّةً اُخْرىٰ (Adv. of time)
Bottle	زُجَاجَةٌ (SF) زُجَاجَاتٌ (P)
To fall down	سَقَطَ / يَسْقُطُ / سُقُوْطاً
To be broken	اِنْكَسَرَ / يَنْكَسِرُ / اِنْكَسَارًا
College	كُلِّيَّةٌ (SF) كُلِّيَّاتٌ (P)
To make s. o. ride; to give a lift	اَرْكَبَ / يُرْكِبُ / اِرْكَاباً
To go	ذَهَبَ / يَذْهَبُ / ذَهَاباً
To take (s. o., s. th.) to	ذَهَبَ / يَذْهَبُ / ذَهَابًا (ب)
Hospital	مُسْتَشْفَى(SM) مُسْتَشْفَيَاتٌ (P)
To receive (s.o.)	اِسْتَقْبَلَ / يَسْتَقْبِلُ / اِسْتِقْبَالاً
House	مَنْزِلٌ (SM) مَنَازِلُ(P)
To offer	قَدَّمَ / يُقَدِّمُ / تَقْدِيْماً
Garcon, service boy	غَارْسُون
Waiter	نَادِلٌ (SM) نُدُلٌ (P)
Cup	فِنْجَانٌ (SM) فِنَاجِيْنُ(P)
Hot	سَاخِنٌ (Adj. SM)
To walk	مَشَى / يَمْشِى / مَشْيًا
To slip	اِنْزَلَقَ / يَنْزَلِقُ / اِنْزِلَاقًا
To travel	سَافَرَ / يُسَافِرُ / مُسَافَرَةً
London	لُنْدُن
Month	شَهْرٌ (SM) شُهُورٌ(P)

Next, coming	قَادِمٌ (VN/SM)
To turn yellow, to turn pale	اِصْفَرَّ / يَصْفَرُّ / اِصْفِرَارًا
Eye	عَيْنٌ (SF) عُيُونٌ (P)
Disease	مَرَضٌ (SM) أَمْرَاضٌ (P)
Jaundice	اَلْيَرْقَانُ
To be necessary	وَجَبَ / يَجِبُ / وَاجِبًا
To respect	اِحْتَرَمَ / يَحْتَرِمُ / اِحْتِرَامًا
Teacher; professor	أُسْتَاذٌ (SM) أَسَاتِذَةٌ (P)
To recall	تَذَكَّرَ / يَتَذَكَّرُ / تَذَكُّرًا
Memory	ذِكْرَى (SF) ذِكْرَيَاتٌ (P)
In the memory of	فِي ذِكْرَى
Sound; voice	صَوْتٌ (SM) أَصْوَاتٌ (P)

LESSON —18

الدرس—١٨

Numbers   الصيغة العددية

This is a class.	هَذَا فَصْلٌ.
The teacher is present.	اَلْأُسْتَاذُ مَوْجُودٌ.
He is sitting on the chair.	هُوَ جَالِسٌ عَلَى الْكُرْسِيِّ.
His book is open.	كِتَابُهُ مَفْتُوحٌ.
The (boy & girl) students	اَلطُّلَّابُ وَ الطَّالِبَاتُ
are sitting on the chairs.	جَالِسُونَ عَلَى الْكَرَاسِيِّ.
Their books are open.	كُتُبُهُمْ مَفْتُوحَةٌ.
The teacher said:	قَالَ الْأُسْتَاذُ:
We read a lesson yesterday and today	قَرَأْنَا دَرْسًا أَمْسِ وَالْيَوْمَ
we will read two lessons.	سَنَقْرَأُ دَرْسَيْنِ.
These two lessons talk	هَذَانِ الدَّرْسَانِ يَتَحَدَّثَانِ
about a lazy boy.	عَنْ وَلَدٍ كَسْلَانَ.
He did not work as he should have.	إِنَّهُ لَمْ يَعْمَلْ كَمَا يَجِبُ.
Therefore, he failed in life.	لِذَا فَشِلَ فِى الْحَيَاةِ.
He did not achieve	وَلَمْ يَحْصُلْ
anything worth mentioning.	عَلَى شَيْءٍ يُذْكَرُ.
When the teacher was busy in	عِنْدَمَا كَانَ الْأُسْتَاذُ مُنْهَمِكًا فِى
presenting the gist of this lesson,	تَقْدِيمِ خُلَاصَةِ هَذَا الدَّرْسِ،
Hamid & Shanker came	جَاءَ حَامِدٌ وَ شَنْكَرُ
and they entered the calss.	وَ دَخَلَا الْفَصْلَ.
The teacher closed his book	أَغْلَقَ الْأُسْتَاذُ كِتَابَهُ
and he paid attention (turned) to Hamid and	وَ تَوَجَّهَ إِلَى حَامِد
Shanker, and asked them:	وَشَنْكَر وَ سَأَلَهُمَا:

Where were you and why are you late	اَيْنَ كُنْتُمَا وَ لِمَاذَا تَأَخَّرْتُمَا
for the lesson?	عَنِ الدَّرْسِ؟
Hamid and Shanker replied.	فَاجَابَ حَامِدٌ وَ شَنْكَرَ:
We were sitting in the library	كُنَّا جَالِسَيْنَ فِى الْمَكْتَبَةِ
and we did not hear the bell.	وَ لَمْ نَسْمَعِ الْجَرَسَ.
About the same time	فِى نَفْسِ الْوَقْتِ
Asha & Usha came.	قَدِمَتْ آشَا وَ أُوْشَا.
The teacher asked them:	سَأَلَهُمَا الْأُسْتَاذُ:
O' Asha & Usha! Where were you?	أَيْنَ كُنْتُمَا يَا آشَا وَ أُوْشَا .
Why are you late for the lesson?	لِمَاذَا تَأَخَّرْتُمَا عَنِ الدَّرْسِ؟
They (both) said: sir, we left	فَقَالَتَا: يَا سَيِّدِى، خَرَجْنَا
house on time but we missed	مِنَ الْمَنْزِلِ فِى الْوَقْتِ وَلَكِنْ فَاتَنَا
the bus that is why we are late.	الْبَاصُ وَلِذَلِكَ تَأَخَّرْنَا.
We are very sorry.	نَحْنُ مُتَأَسِّفَتَان جِدًّا.
When the teacher was busy talking	بَيْنَمَا كَانَ الْأُسْتَاذُ مَشْغُولًا فِى الْحَدِيْثِ
he heard some sound in the class.	سَمِعَ صَوْتًا فِى الْفَصْلِ.
The (boy & girl) students were busy	كَانَ الطُّلَّابُ وَالطَّالِبَاتُ مَشْغُولِيْنَ
in talking among themselves.	فِى الْحَدِيْثِ بَعْضُهُمْ مَعَ الْبَعْضِ.
The teacher saw two girls talking.	رَأَى الْأُسْتَاذُ بِنْتَيْنِ تَتَحَدَّثَان.
The teacher scolded them and he said:	فَنَهَرَهُمَا الْأُسْتَاذُ وَ قَالَ:
Why are you talking, O' Maria & Leela.	لِمَاذَا تَتَحَدَّثَان يَا مَارِيَا وَلَيْلَا.
The (two) girls became silent.	فَسَكَتَتِ الْبِنْتَان.
Jameel & Joseph were	كَانَ جَمِيْلٌ وَ جُوزِيْف
busy with something.	مَشْغُولَيْنِ بِشَىٍّ.
The teacher asked them:	فَسَأَلَهُمَا الْأُسْتَاذُ:
What are you (both) doing	مَاذَا تَعْمَلَان
O' Jameel and Joseph?	يَا جَمِيْلُ وَ جُوزِيْف.

They (both) did not say anything	فَلَمْ يَقُولَا شَيْئاً
and they (both) sat without movement.	وَجَلَسَا بِدُوْنِ تَحَرُّكٍ.
The teacher said:	قَالَ الْأُسْتَاذُ:
It is very necessary for you (all) to come	مِنَ الضَّرُوْرِيِّ لَكُمُ الْقُدُومُ
to the class on time.	إِلَى الْفَصْلِ فِى الْوَقْتِ.
This will help you in future,	هَذَا يُفِيْدُكُمْ مُسْتَقْبَلاً،
God willing.	إِنْ شَاءَ اللّهُ.
After that, the teacher took the book and	بَعْدَ ذَلِكَ أَخَذَ الْأُسْتَاذُ الْكِتَابَ
read the lesson	وَ قَرَأَ الدَّرْسَ
and explained the meanings	وَشَرَحَ الْمَعَانِى
for the (boy & girl) students.	لِلطُّلَّابِ والطَّالِبَاتِ.

Grammar:

There are three numbers in Arabic. They are:

i) Singular number	١) صيغة المفرد
ii) Dual number	٢) صيغة التثنية
iii) Plural number	٣) صيغة الجمع

i) Singular number of a noun is that word which indicates one person, unit or item etc., as against two or more.

Example:

One boy	وَلَدٌ
One girl	بِنْتٌ
One dog	كَلْبٌ
One car	سَيَّارَةٌ
One city	مَدِيْنَةٌ
One officer	مُوَظَّفٌ

ii) Dual number is a characteristic of the Arabic language. As would be evident from the name, it indicates duality of a noun. It is very simple to make it from the original singular noun. We have to suffix to any noun of singular number اِن. The last letter of the singular noun will now be given a *Fatḥah* and the ن of this dual will have a *kasrah*.

Example:

Two boys	وَلَدٌ + اَن = وَلَدَاْنِ
Two girls	بِنتَانِ
Two dogs	كَلْبَانِ
Two cars	سَيَّارَتَانِ
Two cities	مَدِيْنَتَانِ
Two officers	مُوَظَّفَانِ

The dual number of the noun so obtained is supposed to be in the nominative case. For example we would say:

Two boys came	قَدِمَ وَلَدَانِ

It should be very clear from the sentence that وَلَدَانِ is the subject of the verb قَدِمَ. In the accusative and the genitive cases this اِن of the nominative case is replaced by ى ن. The letter preceding the ىretains its *fatḥah*. The ن of duality also continues to retain its *kasrah*.

Example:

Two boys	وَلَدَيْنِ
Two girls	بِنتَيْنِ
Two dogs	كَلْبَيْنِ
Two cars	سَيَّارَتَيْنِ
Two cities	مَدِيْنَتَيْنِ
Two officers	مُوَظَّفَيْنَ

Now to express the meaning:

I saw two boys

We would say:

رَأَيْتُ وَلَدَيْنِ

Similarly if we want to say-

I went to two boys   ذَهَبْتُ إِلَى وَلَدَيْنِ

iii) The plural number of a noun is that word which indicates in Arabic more than two persons or things etc.

Example:

Boys	اَوْلَادٌ
Girls	بَنَاتٌ
Dogs	كِلَابٌ
Cars	سَيَّارَاتٌ
Cities	مُدُنٌ
Officers	مُوَظَّفُوْنَ

Kinds of plural:

There are two kinds of plural in Arabic. They are:

i) Broken plural   ٢) اَلْجَمْعُ الْمُكَسَّرُ

ii) Sound Plural   ٢) اَلْجَمْعُ السَّالِمُ

i) Broken Plural   الجمع المكسر

Broken plural is formed from the singular noun by breaking the order of the letters composing a singular noun and by adding one or two or more letters. In some nouns one or two or more letters might have to be removed and the original vowel points replaced by some other vowel points. In brief we can say that wherever obtains replacement or displacement of letters or vowelpoints the plural so made is called broken plural.

Examples:

Boys	اَوْلَادٌ
Books	كُتُبٌ

Careful observation of the word اَوْلَادٌ will tell you that this plural has been made from the singular noun وَلَدٌ . one 'Alif ا' has been added before the original 'Waw و ' letter and another 'Alif ١ ' is inserted after the original 'laam ل' letter. Thus in this way by disturbing the order of the original letters and introducing additional letters we have made a broken plural of وَلَدٌ.

In the case of كُتُبٌ we have removed the original 'alif ١' of the singular noun كِتَابٌ which means one book. Original vowel points of كِتَابٌ have also been disturbed.

There are set patterns of broken plurals. However, they are so many. Similaly there are exceptions to the rules. It is therefore, suggested that the students should refer to teacher or dictionary to acquire plurals of those singular nouns from which we can not make sound plurals.

ii) Sound Plural اَلْجَمْعُ السَّالِمُ:

Unlike the broken plural, there is no deletion of letters in this kind of plurals. We don't have to prefix or interfix any letter or letters to the original form of the singular noun. We can make this kind of plural from certain fixed forms of singular nouns by suffixing to it certain letters. Sound plural is further divided into two forms as follows:

1) Sound plural for Masculine	اَلْجَمْعُ السَّالِمُ لِلْمُذَكَّرِ
2) Sound plural for Feminine	اَلْجَمْعُ السَّالِمُ لِلْمُؤَنَّثِ

1) Sound plural for Masculine:

Sound plural is generally made from the Active participle and the passive participle i.e. اسم الفاعل and اسم المفعول.

Sound plural masculine in the nominative case is obtained by suffixing to the singular noun waw و and ن noon. In this kind of plural waw و is always preceded by a *dammah* and the ن noon necessarily carries *fathah*. For example:

Murderers came.	قَدِمَ قَاتِلُونَ	قَاتِلٌ + وُنَ = قَاتِلُوْنَ
Muslims came.	قَدِمَ مُسْلِمُونَ	مُسْلِمٌ + وُنَ = مُسْلِمُونَ
Tailors came.	قَدِمَ خَيَّاطُونَ	خَيَّاطٌ + وُنَ = خَيَّاطُونَ

However, in the accusative and genitive cases we have to suffix ى Yaa and
ن noon. In this case the ى Yaa has to be necessarily preceded by *kasrah* and
the noon ن retains its *Fathah*. For example:

I saw murderers.	رَأَيْتُ قَاتِلِيْنَ	قَاتِلْ+يْنَ= قَاتِلِيْنَ
I saw muslims.	رَأَيْتُ مُسْلِمِيْنَ	مُسْلِمْ+يْنَ= مُسْلِمِيْنَ
I saw tailors.	رَأَيْتُ خَيَّاطِيْنَ	خَيَّاطْ+يْنَ= خَيَّاطِيْنَ

2) Sound plural for feminine:

It is generally wrought from nouns which terminate in Taa Marboota i.e.
round Taa ة, e.g.

notebook	كُرَّاسَةٌ
table	طَاوِلَةٌ

Procedure is as follows:

To obtain plural from such nouns we remove the round Taa i.e. ة and
instead we suffix elongative alif and normal stretched Taa ت.

Example:

Muslim woman	(SF)	مُسْلِمَةٌ
Muslim women	(PF)	مُسْلِمَاتٌ
Lady worker	(SF)	عَامِلَةٌ
Lady workers	(PF)	عَامِلَاتٌ

In the nominative case the letter before alif shall bear Fathah and the ت
carries *dammah* — double *dammah* if the noun is not defined with Al ال
and single if the noun is defined with Al or by way of Idaafat i.e.
ascription:

(Some) Muslim women came	قَدِمَتْ مُسْلِمَاتٌ
(Some) Lady workers entered	دَخَلَتْ عَامِلَاتٌ
The Muslim women came	قَدِمَتِ الْمُسْلِمَاتُ
The Indian Muslim women came	قَدِمَتْ مُسْلِمَاتُ الْهِنْدِ
The lady workers of the factory entered	دَخَلَتْ عَامِلَاتُ الْمَصْنَعِ

In the accusative & genitive cases the stretched Taa ت will accept *kasrah*—double or single as per conditions explained above.

Example:

I saw (some) Muslim women	رَأَيْتُ مُسْلِمَاتٍ
I saw the Muslim women	رَأَيْتُ الْمُسْلِمَاتِ
I ate with (some) Muslim women.	أَكَلْتُ مَعَ مُسْلِمَاتٍ

Notes:

1. Names of objects which do not have broken plurals, take sound feminine plural.

2. Verbal nouns generally take sound plurals.

There are three kinds of verbal noun in Arabic:

i) Verbal noun of infinitive meaning. This will be referred to as infinitive henceforth. This verbal noun generally takes sound feminine plural.

ii) Verbal noun extracted from the verb to mean the doer of some action. It is called in Arabic اسم الفاعل. Rules regarding the making of اسم الفاعل i.e. the English active participle are explained in lesson no. 19. Henceforth this verbal noun will be referred to as active participle.

iii) Verbal noun extracted from the verb to mean the receiver of the action. It is called in Arabic اسم المفعول i.e. the English passive participle. Rules regarding the making of it are explained in lesson no. 19. Hencefroth this verbal noun will be referred to as passive participle.

It should be remembered here that active participle i.e. اسم الفاعل is different from the subject i.e. فاعل.

Similarly the passive participle i.e. اسم المفعول is different from the object of the verb i.e. مفعول.

Exercises:

1)   Separate the sound plurals and the broken plurals from the
      following and use them in all the three cases (i.e. nominative,
      accusative and genitive cases) in sentences of your own:

(الف

١) اِجْتَمَعَ الطُّلَّابُ فِى النَّادِى.   ٢) مَا كَانَتِ الطَّالِبَاتُ مَوْجُودَاتٍ فِى الْفَصْلِ.

٣) لَا أُشَاهِدُ أَفْلَامًا كَثِيرَةً.   ٤) كَانَتِ السُّجُونُ مَمْلُوءَةً بِالْمُجْرِمِينَ.

٥) اَلْكِلَابُ نَائِمَةٌ تَحْتَ الشَّجَرَةِ.   ٦) كَانَتِ السَّيَّارَاتُ وَاقِفَةً فِى السَّاحَةِ.

٧) قَدِمَ الْمُدَرِّسُونَ مُبَكِّرًا إِلَى الْمَدْرَسَةِ.   ٨) مَا قَرَأْتُ شَيْئًا مِنْ هَذِهِ الْكُتُبِ.

٩) لَا نَفْتَحُ الْمَكْتَبَاتِ وَالْكُلِّيَّاتِ وَ الْجَامِعَاتِ وَالْمَكَاتِبَ فِى يَوْمِ عِيدِ الْاِسْتِقْلَالِ.

١٠) ذَهَبَتْ طَبِيبَاتٌ مَاهِرَاتٌ إِلَى الْإِمَارَاتِ الْعَرَبِيَّةِ الْمُتَّحِدَةِ.

(ب

هَذِهِ مَدْرَسَةٌ. هَذِهِ الْمَدْرَسَةُ جَيِّدَةٌ. هِىَ تُدَرِّسُ اللُّغَةَ الْإِنْجِلِيزِيَّةَ وَعُلُومَ الْإِجْتِمَاعِ. هُنَاكَ
عَدَدٌ لَابَأْسَ بِهِ مِنَ الْمُدَرِّسَاتِ فِى هَذِهِ الْكُلِّيَّةِ. اِنَّنِى اخْتَرْتُ هَذِهِ الْكُلِّيَّةَ مِنْ بَيْنِ جَمِيعِ
الْكُلِّيَّاتِ فِى نُيُودِلْهِى لِأَنَّهَا تُعْتَبَرُ أَحْسَنَ الْكُلِّيَّاتِ وَ السَّبَبُ فِى ذَلِكَ يَرْجِعُ إِلَى الْمُسْتَوَى
التَّعْلِيمِى فِى هَذِهِ الْكُلِّيَّةِ فِى جَمِيعِ الْمَوَادِّ. يُوجَدُ فِى هَذِهِ الْكُلِّيَّةِ مُدَرِّسُونَ أَيْضًا. هَؤُلَاءِ
الْمُدَرِّسُونَ وَ الْمُدَرِّسَاتُ تَخَرَّجُوا فِى جَامِعَاتٍ أَجْنَبِيَّةٍ وَ حَيْثُ أَنَّ الْكُلِّيَّةَ تَدْفَعُ مُرَتَّبَاتٍ
جَيِّدَةً لِلْمُدَرِّسِينَ وَ الْمُدَرِّسَاتِ فَلِذَلِكَ هُمْ كُلُّهُمْ يُخْلِصُونَ لِعَمَلِهِمْ. تَتَكَوَّنُ هَيْئَةُ
الْمُدِيرِينَ لِهَذِهِ الْكُلِّيَّةِ مِنْ كِبَارِ الْأَكَادِيمِيِّينَ مِنَ الْهُنُودِ وَالْأَجَانِبِ.

(ج

هَذَا الصَّبَاحَ مَتَى وَصَلْتُ مَكْتَبِى وَجَدْتُ اَنَّ الْبَابَ كَانَ مُغْلَقًا. كَانَ فَرَّاشَا الْمَكْتَبِ وَاقِفَيْنِ
أَمَامَ الْبَابِ. فَأَخْبَرَانِى اَنَّ الْمِفْتَاحَ لِلْبَابِ الْأَمَامِىِّ كَانَ ضَاعَ. وَقَالَا لِى اَنْ أَدْخُلَ مِنَ الْبَابِ
الْخَلْفِى. مَتَى دَخَلْتُ الْمَكْتَبَ رَأَيْتُ الْمُوَظَّفِينَ الْآخَرِينَ مَوْجُودِينَ، لَمْ أَرَ فَقَطْ كَاتِبَتَيْنِ.
كُنْتُ اَيْضًا مُتَأَخِّرًا. ذَهَبْتُ إِلَى طَاوِلَتِى وَ رَأَيْتُ كَوْمَةً مِنَ الْمِلَفَّاتِ. جَلَسْتُ عَلَى كُرْسِىٍّ
وَبَدَأْتُ اَتَصَرَّفُ مَعَ الْمِلَفَّاتِ.

Translate into Arabic:

(A) One pleasant after noon in winter I was going to the market with my daughter. When we reached the market we saw a crowd of people and a good number of police personnel. Though most of the shops were open, however, some uneasiness prevailed in the atmosphere. I asked one shopkeeper about the reason of the police presence in the market. He told me that one jewellery shop had been broken into the previous night. The thieves had taken away every thing from the shop. My daughter asked me: Are there only men thieves? I told her: there are women criminals also. There are women-thieves, lady pickpockets and lady murderers. They are not many. These women-criminals work in collaboration with men-criminals. My daughter asked: Who catches these women-criminals? Are their policewomen? I told her: Yes, there are policewomen also. We have lady officers in all our offices.

B)   The police man is a government employee. He wears an official uniform. He always has a stick in his hand. He moves from one place to another. He catches thieves, gamblers, drunkards and all bad people. Bad people are afraid of him.

3:   Translate into English the passages of question number one.

Glossary   الكلمات العسيرة

To assemble, to meet	إجْتَمَعَ/يَجْتَمِعُ/ إجْتِمَاعًا
Club	نَادِى (SM) نَوَادِى (P)
To see, to watch	شَاهَدَ/ يُشَاهِدُ/مُشَاهَدَةً
Film	فِلْمٌ (SM) أفْلَامٌ (P)
Gaol, jail	سِجْنٌ (SM) سُجُونٌ (P)
Full, filled up	مَمْلُوءٌ (Adj. SM)
Criminal	مُجْرِمٌ (SM) مُجْرِمُونَ (P)
Occasion of festivity	عِيدٌ (SM) أعْيَادٌ (P)

To become free, To become independent	إِسْتَقَلَّ / يَسْتَقِلُّ / إِسْتِقْلَالاً
Ladydoctor	طَبِيبَةٌ (SF) طَبِيبَيَاتٌ (P)
Expert, dexterous	مَاهِرٌ (Adj. SM)
United Arab Emirates	الإِمَارَاتُ العَرَبِيَّةُ الْمُتَّحِدَةُ
Dog	كَلْبٌ (SM) كِلَابٌ(P)
Open space, parking lot	سَاحَةٌ(SF)سَاحَاتٌ (P)
Sociology, social science	عُلُومُ الْإِجْتِمَاعِ
There	هُنَاكَ (Adv. of place)
Number	عَدَدٌ (SM) أَعْدَادٌ (P)
Considerable, not negligible, quite a few	لَا بَأْسَ بِ
To choose, to select	إِخْتَارَ / يَخْتَارُ / إِخْتِيَاراً
To consider	إِعْتَبَرَ / يَعْتَبِرُ / إِعْتِبَارًا
Reason	سَبَبٌ (SM) أَسْبَابٌ (P)
To go back, to return	رَجَعَ / يَرْجِعُ / رُجُوعًا
Standard, level	مُسْتَوَى (SM) مُسْتَوَيَاتٌ (P)
Standard of education	المُسْتَوَى التَّعْلِيمِى
Material; course (of study)	مَادَّةٌ (SF) مَوَادُّ (P)
To find	وَجَدَ / يَجِدُ / وُجُودًا
To be found	وُجِدَ / يُوجَدُ / وُجُودًا
To graduate	تَخَرَّجَ / يَتَخَرَّجُ / تَخَرُّجًا (فى)
Foreign, foreigner	أَجْنَبِىٌّ (Adj. SM)أَجَانِبُ (P)
To be sincere, to devote	أَخْلَصَ / يُخْلِصُ / إِخْلَاصًا
To consist of	تَكَوَّنَ / يَتَكَوَّنُ / تَكَوُّنًا
Body, board	هَيْئَةٌ (SF) هَيْئَاتٌ(P)
Director	مُدِيرٌ (SM) مُدِيرُونَ (P)
Academician, academic	أَكَادِيمِىٌّ(SM)
Closed	مُغْلَقٌ (PP/SM)

To inform	أَخْبَرَ / يُخْبِرُ / إِخْبَارًا
Key	مِفْتَاحٌ (SM) مَفَاتِيْحُ(P)
Back, behind	خَلْفَ(Adv. of place)
Only	فَقَطْ
Pile	كَومَةٌ (SF) كَومَاتٌ (P)
File	مِلَفٌّ(SM) مِلَفَّاتٌ(P)
To begin	بَدَأَ/ يَبْدَأُ/ بَدْءَ
To dispose of	تَصَرَّفَ / يَتَصَرَّفُ/ تَصَرُّفًا
Pleasant	لَطِيفٌ (Adj. SM)
Good	جَمِيْلٌ (Adj. SM)
Afternoon	عَصْرٌ (SM) عُصُورٌ(P)
Market	سُوقٌ (SM/F) أَسْوَاقٌ (P)
When	عِنْدَمَا (Adv. of time)
People	إِنْسَانٌ(SM) أُنَاسٌ /نَاسٌ(P)
Good number, large number	عَدَدٌ كَبِيرٌ
Crowd	زِحَامٌ(SM) زَحْمَةٌ (SF)
Police personnel	رِجَالٌ مِنَ الشُّرْطَةِ
Though, despite	بِالرَّغْمِ مِنْ / عَلَى الرَّغْمِ مِنْ
Uneasiness	إِضْطِرَابٌ(SM)
To prevail	سَادَ/ يَسُودُ/ سِيَادَةً
To be broken into	سُرِقَ / يُسْرَقُ/ سَرِقَةً
Jewellery	مُجَوْهَرٌ(SM) مُجَوْهَرَاتٌ (P)
Night	لَيْلَةٌ(SF) لَيَالِى (P)
Previous night, last night	لَيْلَةَ أَمْسِ
Thief	لِصٌّ(SM) لُصُوصٌ(P)
Criminal (man)	مُجْرِمٌ (SM) مُجْرِمُونَ(P)
Criminal (lady/ woman)	مُجْرِمَةٌ (SF) مُجْرِمَاتٌ (P)
Pickpocket	نَشَّالٌ (SM) نَشَّالُونَ (P)

Murderer	قَاتِلٌ (SM) قَتَلَةٌ/ قَاتِلُونَ (P)
In collaboration with	بِالتَّعَاوُنِ مَعَ
To catch	مَسَكَ/ يَمْسُكُ/ مَسْكًا
To arrest, to catch	أَلْقَى/ يُلْقِى الْقَبْضَ على
Policeman	شُرْطِيٌّ(SM) شُرْطِيُّونَ (P)
Policewoman	شُرْطِيَّةٌ/ شُرْطِيَّاتٌ (P)
Officer/ captain	ضَابِطٌ(SM) ضُبَّاطٌ
Dress, uniform	زِيٌّ (SM) ازْيَاءٌ (P)
Official dress/ uniform	زِيٌّ رَسْمِيٌّ
Stick	عَصَا(SF) عِصِيٌّ (P)
Gambler	مُقَامِرٌ(SM) مُقَامِرُونَ
Drunkard	سَكْرَانُ (SM) سُكَارَىْ (P)
Afraid, fearful	خَائِفٌ (Adj. SM) خَائِفُونَ (P)
To hear, to listen	سَمِعَ/ يَسْمَعُ/ سَمْعًا
Sorry, regretful	مُتَأَسِّفٌ (Adj. SM) مُتَأَسِّفُونَ (P)
To become silent	سَكَتَ/ يَسْكُتُ/ سُكُوتًا

| Verbal Nouns: | الاسماء الفعلية: |

Active Participle And Passive Participle
اسم الفاعل و اسم المفعول

I am a research scholar in the centre of	اَنَا طَالِبٌ بَاحِثٌ فِى مَرْكَزِ
Arabic and African Studies	الدِّرَاسَاتِ الْعَرَبِيَّةِ وَالإفْرِيْقِيَّةِ
in the school of languages	فِى كُلِّيَةِ اللُّغَاتِ
in Jawaharlal Nehru University.	بِجَامِعَةِ جَوَاهَرْ لَال نِهْرُو.
This University is famous all over the	هَذِهِ الْجَامِعَةُ مَشْهُورَةٌ فِى كُلِّ
world for its high academic standard.	الْعَالَمِ لِلْمُسْتَوَى الْعِلْمِى الْعَالِى.
During last winter break	خِلَالَ عُطْلَةِ الشِّتَاءِ الْمَاضِيَّةِ
I went to Hyderabad	ذَهَبْتُ إِلَى حَيْدَر آبَاذ
on an educational tour.	فِى رِحْلَةٍ دِرَاسِيَّةٍ.
I went to Usmania University and	ذَهَبْتُ إِلَى الْجَامِعَةِ الْعُثْمَانِيَّةِ وَ قَابَلْتُ
I met (men) teachers and (lady) teachers of	الْمُدَرِّسِيْنَ وَالْمُدَرِّسَاتِ
the Arabic language.	لِنُغَةِ الْعَرَبِيَّةِ.
I also met (boy) students	وَقَابَلْتُ اَيْضًا اَلدَّارِسِيْنَ وَالدَّارِسَاتِ.
and (girl) students.	
I had work in the University library.	كَانَ لِىَ الْعَمَلُ فِى مَكْتَبَةِ الْجَامِعَةِ.
Therefore, I took a letter from	لِذَا أَخَذْتُ مَكْتُوبًا مِنْ
the head of the Arabic department	رَئِيْسِ الْقِسْمِ الْعَرَبِى
for the Librarian.	إِلَى اَمِيْنِ الْمَكْتَبَةِ.
I visited the library on the same day	زُرْتُ * الْمَكْتَبَةَ فِى نَفْسِ الْيَوم
in the afternoon and I saw in the library	بَعْدَ الظُّهْرِ وَ رَأَيْتُ بِالْمَكْتَبَةِ

---

* For conjugation Pattern see Appendix.

a large number of (men) workers

and (lady) workers.

عَدَدًا كَبِيراً مِنَ الْعَامِلِيْنَ وَالْعَامِلَاتِ.

I went to the room of the Librarian.

ذَهَبْتُ إِلَى غُرْفَةِ أَمِيْنِ الْمَكْتَبَةِ.

The Librarian sent me

بَعَثَنِى الأَمِيْنُ

to his assistant.

إِلَى مُسَاعِدِهِ.

The assistant librarian helped me in my
work and similarly other employees of the
Library helped me.

سَاعَدَنِى الأَمِيْنُ الْمُسَاعِدُ فِى عَمَلِى وَ
كَذَلِكَ سَاعَدَنِى الْمُسْتَخْدَمُوْنَ
الآخَرُوْنَ فِى الْمَكْتَبَةِ.

I spent two days in work

أَنْفَقْتُ يَوْمَيْنِ فِى الْعَمَلِ

in the Library and on the third day

بِالْمَكْتَبَةِ وَ فِى الْيَومِ الثَّالِثِ

I went to the Central Institute

ذَهَبْتُ إِلَى الْمَعْهَدِ الْمَرْكَزِى

of English and Foreign Languages,

لِلُّغَةِ الانْجِلِيزِيَّةِ وَ اللُّغَاتِ الأَجْنَبِيَّةِ،

and I met all the (men) teachers and (lady)
teachers

وَقَابَلْتُ جَمِيْعَ الْمُدَرِّسِيْنَ
وَ الْمُدَرِّسَاتِ

in the department of Arabic.

بِالْقِسْمِ الْعَرَبِى.

A new teacher helped me

سَاعَدَنِى مُدَرِّسٌ جَدِيْدٌ

a lot in my work.

فِى عَمَلِى كَثِيْراً.

This new teacher accompanied me

رَافَقَنِى هَذَا الْمُدَرِّسُ الْجَدِيْدُ

to the historical places.

إِلَى الأَمَاكِنِ التَّارِيْخِيَّةِ.

I returned to Delhi on the fourth day.

عُدْتُ إِلَى دِلْهِى فِى الْيَومِ الرَّابِعِ.

Grammar:

Verbal nouns or the active and the passive participles of the Arabic
language are drawn from the verbs on certain set patterns as per details
given below:

i) Active Participle اسم الفاعل

Active participle is a noun (adjectival) which is formed on the pattern of
فاعل from the triliteral verbs i.e. the original three-letterd verbs, like:

ذَهَبَ   كَتَبَ

In this case we interfix one 'alif ١ ' after the first original letter and
compulsorily give a kasrah to the second original letter of the concerned
three-lettered verb.

Example:

Verb	(He wrote)	كَتَبَ : كَـتَـبَ
Active participle	(Writer)	كَـ+ اُ+ تـبٌ =كَاتِبٌ
Verb	(He went)	ذَهَبَ: ذَ هَـبَ
Active participle	(Goer)	ذَ+ ا +هِـبٌ = ذَاهِبٌ

In the case of verbs which have more than three letters, we have to prefix to
them one مـ with dammah (except where it is alif ١) and the penultimate
letter is given kasrah.

Example:

Verb	(He travelled)	سَافَرَ: سَـا فَـرَ
Active participle (Traveller)		مـ+ سـا فـر = مُسَافِرٌ
Verb	(He begged)	تَسَوَّلَ : تَـسَـوَّ لَ
Active participle (Begger)		مُـ + تَـسَـوّ لٌ = مُتَسَوِّلٌ

And where the first letter happens to be' alif ١ ' the alif ١ is dropped and
the process explained above is applied.

Example:

Verb	(He used)	إسْتَخْدَمَ: اِسْـتَـخْـدَ مَ
Active participle	(User)	مُـ+ سـتَـخْـدِمٌ= مُسْتَخْدِمٌ
Verb	(He gave to drink)	أشْرَبَ: أَشْـرَبَ
Active participle	(Giver to drink)	مُـ + شْـرِبٌ = مُشْرِبٌ

ii. Passive participle

Passive participle is also a noun (adjectival). It is formed from the three-lettered verbs by adding one م with *fathah* before the first original letter and by placing a 'waw و' after the second original letter. Additionally the first original letter will be given a Sokoon and the second letter a *ḍammah*.

Example:

Verb	(He wrote)	كَتَبَ : كَ تَ بَ
Passive participle	(Written)	مَ + كْ تُ + وْ بّ = مَكْتُوبّ

In the case of verb having more than three letters, one م with *ḍammah* is placed before the verbs (except those which have alif ١ as the first letter) and the penultimate letter is given a *fathah*.

Example:

Verb	(He addressed)	خَاطَبَ : خَ ا طَ بَ
Passive participle		مُ + خَ ا طَ بّ = مُخَاطَبّ
Addressee/ Addressed)		

And where the first letter is alif ١ , the alif is dropped before adding the 'meem م' . The penultimate letter shall have *fathah*.

Example:

Verb	(He employed/ He used)	اِسْتَخْدَمَ : ا سْ تَ خْ دَ مَ
Passive participle		مُ + سْ تَ خْ دَ مَ = مُسْتَخْدَمّ
(Employee/ Used)		

It should be remembered that the passive participles can not be made from the verbs which have reflexive meanings.

Example:

To be broken	اِنْكَسَرَ
To change (by itself)	تَغَيَّرَ

All the active and the passive participles i.e. أسماء الفاعل و المفعول made in the way and manner explained above are masculine in gender. They may be changed into feminine gender merely by suffixing the round 'Ta ة' to them.

Example:

A man clerk	كَاتِبٌ
A woman clerk	كَاتِبَ + ة = كَاتِبَةٌ
A man traveller	مُسَافِرٌ
A woman traveller	مُسَافِرَ + ة = مُسَافِرَةٌ

It may also be remembered as a general rule that all the active and the passive participles have sound plurals as explained in lesson no. 18.

Beside what has been said about the active participle and its making from the triliteral verbs and the verbs having more than three letters, there is another form of the active participle with rather quite intensive meaning. The pattern of this intensive active participle is the فَعَّالٌ pattern. It is made only from the triliteral verbs by doubling the second original letter of the verb and placing one 'alif ا', after this redoubled letter. This elongative 'alif ا' is preceded by *fathah*.

Example:

To cook	طَبَخَ / يَطْبُخُ / طَبْخًا
A cook	طَبَّاخٌ
To cultivate (land)	فَلَحَ يَفْلَحُ فَلْحًا
A cultivator (of land), A farmer	فَلَّاحٌ

It may be remembered here that this intensive active participle is mostly employed for the professionals.

Nouns of this pattern also decline like anyother active participle.

Exercises:

1. Make active and passive participles from the following verbs and suitably use them in sentences of your own in all the three numbers and cases:

He drank	شَرِبَ	He killed	قَتَلَ
He heard	سَمِعَ	He beat	ضَرَبَ
He helped	سَاعَدَ	He sought help	اِسْتَنْجَدَ
He offered	قَدَّمَ	He elected	اِنْتَخَبَ
He helped	نَصَرَ	He overpowered	غَلَبَ
He accepted Islam	أَسْلَمَ	He sent	أَرْسَلَ

2. Translate into Arabic:

(A) In Delhi in the mornings and in the evenings you will find the buses very crowded. They are mostly crowded with the office goers and the school going children. And particularly in the morning when the timings of the office goers and the school going children coincide. Unfortunately the bus drivers in Delhi are very careless. It is therefore , you will always find the commuters complaining about the unco-operative behaviour of the drivers in general. I believe the commuters are in the right. The conductors are also unco-operative and often use harsh language. I hope the local authorities will take steps to improve the quality of service in the near future.

(B) We find that recently there is a lot of openness in the world societies. Now not only European societies but also the Asian and African societies have allowed a lot of freedom to ladies. As a result we find lady-workers working shoulder-to-shoulder with men-workers in all walks of life. They are teachers. They are telephone operators. They are ministers, engineers, journalists, computer engineers and scientists. It is impossible to see any work place without lady workers holding all kinds of positions.

3. Translate into English:

(A) اَوَدُّ اَنْ اَتَحَدَّثَ اِلَيْكُمْ هُنَا عَنْ مَصْنَعِ زُجَاجٍ يَقَعُ قُرْبَ دِلْهِى. يَعْمَلُ فِى هَذَا الْمَصْنَعِ عَدَدٌ كَبِيرٌ مِنَ الْعَامِلِينَ وَالْعَامِلَاتِ. مِنْهُمُ الْمُهَنْدِسُونَ وَ الْمُهَنْدِسَاتُ وَالْكَاتِبُونَ وَالْكَاتِبَاتُ وَالْفَرَّاشُوْنَ وَالْفَرَّاشَاتُ. هَؤُلَاءِ كُلُّهُم مُسْتَخْدَمُونَ مِنْ صَاحِبِ الْمَصْنَعِ لِلْعَمَلِ فِى مَصْنَعِهِ. هَؤُلَاءِ الْمُوَظَّفُونَ وَالْمُوَظَّفَاتُ يَعْمَلُونَ سَوِيًّا لِصَالِحِ الْمَصْنَعِ وَ صَاحِبِ الْمَصْنَعِ. هَذَا الْمَصْنَعُ يَشْتَغِلُ لَيْلَ نَهَارَ وَالْمُسْتَخْدَمُونَ يَعْمَلُونَ فِيهِ فِى نَوْبَاتٍ نَهَارِيَّةٍ وَلَيْلِيَّةٍ. كُلُّهُمْ رَاضُونَ بَعْضُهُمْ عَنْ بَعْضٍ.

(B) تَجِدُ فِى دِلْهِى كَثِيرًا مِنَ الآثَارِ التَّارِيْخِيَّةِ. مِنْهَا (مَنَارَةُ قُطْبْ) وَالْقَلْعَةُ الْحَمْرَاءُ وَ الْقَلْعَةُ الْقَدِيمَةُ وَالْمَسْجِدُ الْجَامِعُ وَ مَقْبَرَةُ صَفْدَرْ جَنْك. هَذِهِ الآثَارُ الْقَدِيمَةُ مَشْهُورَةٌ جِدًّا فِى كُلِّ الْعَالَمِ. يَقْدَمُ السَّائِحُونَ وَالسَّائِحَاتُ مِنْ كُلِّ اَنْحَاءِ الْعَالَمِ لِرُؤْيَةِ هَذِهِ الآثَارِ التَّارِيْخِيَّةِالْقَدِيمَةِ لَقَدْ فَتَحَتْ حُكُومَةُ الْهِنْدِ الْمَرْكَزِيَّةُ مَكَاتِبَ السِّيَاحَةِ فِى الْهِنْدِ وَخَارِجَهَا لِتَطْوِيرِ السِّيَاحَةِ. يَعْمَلُ بِهَذِهِ الْمَكَاتِبِ عَدَدٌ كَبِيرٌ مِنَ الْمُسْتَخْدَمِينَ وَ الْمُسْتَخْدَمَاتِ.

بِجَانِبِ هَذِهِ الآثَارِ يُوجَدُ هُنَاك أَمَاكِنُ الإهْتِمَامِ الْأُخْرَى مِنْ أَمْثَالِ الْمَتْحَفِ الْقَوْمِىِّ وَمَكْتَبِ الْأَرَاشِيفِ الْقَوْمِى وَمَرَاكِزِ الثَّقَافَةِ وَالبَحْثِ العِلْمِى. دِلْهِى مَدِينَةٌ كَبِيرَةٌ وَ مَعْرُوفَةٌ فِى كُلِّ الْعَالَمِ.

4. Separate all the active and passive participles from the foregoing passages and use them in sentences of your own.

Glossary:	الكلمات العسيرة
Morning	صُبْحْ (SM) أَصْبَاحْ (P)
And	وَ (Conjunctive)
Evening	مَسَاءْ (MS) أَمْسِيَاتْ (P)
To find	وَجَدَ/يَجِدُ/ وُجُودًا
Bus	أُوتُوبِيْس (SM) أُوتُوبِيْسَاتْ (P)
Crowded	مُزْدَحِمٌ(AP/SM)

Mostly	(Adv. of manner) فِى أَكْثَرِ الأَحْيَانِ / كَثِيرًا مَا
Goer	ذَاهِبٌ (AP/SM)
Office goer/going to office	ذَاهِبٌ الَى الْمَكْتَبِ
Particularly	(Adv. of manner) خَاصَّةً
To coincide	تَوافق / يَتَوَافقُ / تَوَافُقًا
Timing	مَوعِدٌ (SM) مَوَاعِدُ (P)
Unfortunately	لِسُوْءِ الْحظِّ
Careless	مُهمِلٌ (AP/SM)
Always	(Adv. of time) دَائِمًا
Commuter, passenger	رَاكِبٌ (AP/SM) رُكَّابٌ (P)
To complain (About)	شَكا / يَشْكُو / شِكَايَةً (عَن)
Behaviour	سُلُوكٌ (SM)
In general, generally	بِشَكْلٍ عَامٍ
To believe	إِعْتَقدَ / يَعْتقِدُ / إعتِقَادًا
Correct, right, in the right	مُصِيبٌ (AP/SM) مُصِيبُونَ (P)
Uncooperative	غَيْرُ مُتَعَاوِنٍ
Conductor	مُحَصِّلٌ (AP/SM)
Hard words/harsh language	كَلِمَاتٌ خَشِنَة
To hope	أَمَلَ / يَأْمُلُ / أَمَلاً
Local	مَحَلِّى (Adj. SM)
Authorities	سُلْطَةٌ (SF) سُلْطَاتٌ (P)
To take (A measure, step)	إتَّخَذَ / يَتِّخِذُ / إتِّخَاذًا (إجراءً)
Measure/ step	إجْرَاءٌ (SM) إجْرَاءَاتٌ (P)
To improve	حَسَّنَ / يُحَسِّنُ / تَحْسِينًا
Quality; type	نَوْعِيَّةٌ (SF)
Quality of service; type of service	نَوْعِيَّةُ الْخِدمَة

In the near future	فِى الْقَرِيبِ الْعَاجِلِ
Recently	أَخِيْرًا (Adv. of time)
Openness	إِنْفِتَاحٌ (SM)
Society	مُجْتَمَعٌ (SM) مُجْتَمَعَاتٌ (P)
Europe	أُوْرُوْبًّا
European	أُوْرُوْبِّى
Asia	آسِيَا
Asian	آسْيَوِى
Africa	إِفْرِيْقِيَا
African	إِفْرِيقِى
To allow	سَمَحَ / يَسْمَحُ / سَمَاحًا
Freedom	حُرِّيَّةٌ (SF)
Woman	إِمْرَأَةٌ (SF) نِسَاءٌ (Pl.-irregular)
Shoulder- to-shoulder	جَنْبًا لِجَنْبٍ
Field/ scope	مَجَالٌ (SM) مَجَالَاتٌ (P)
Telephone operator	عَاهِلُ التِّلِفُون
Minister	وَزِيْرٌ (SM) وُزَرَاءُ (P)
Engineer	مُهَنْدِسٌ (SM) مُهَنْدِسُوْنَ (P)
Scientist	عَالِمٌ (SM) عُلَمَاءُ (P)
Computer	كُومْبِيُوتَر (SM) كُومْبِيُوتَرَاتٌ (P)
Holding, holder	مَاسِكُ (AP/SM) مَاسِكُونَ (P)
To wish, desire, want	وَدَّ / يَوَدُّ / وِدَادًا
To talk	تَحَدَّثَ / يَتَحَدَّثُ / تَحَدُّثًا
Plant, industrial unit, factory	مَصْنَعٌ (SM) مَصَانِعُ (P)
Glass	زُجَاجٌ (SM)
To be situated	وَقَعَ / يَقَعُ / وُقُوعًا

Near, close	قُرْبَ (Adv. of place)
In the interest of the factory	فِى صَالِحِ الْمَصْنَعِ
To work	إِشْتَغَلَ / يَشْتَغِلُ / إِشْتِغَالاً
Day in & day out	لَيْلَ نَهَارَ
Shift	نَوْبَةٌ (SF) نَوْبَاتٌ(P)
Day time	نَهَارٌ (SM) أَنْهُرٌ (P)
Night	لَيْلٌ (SM) لَيَالِى
Day	نَهَارِىٌّ (Adj. SM)
Night, nocturnal	لَيْلِىٌّ (Adj. SM)
Pleased, happy	رَاضِى (Adj. SM) رَاضُونَ (P)
Relic, monument	أَثَرٌ (SM) آثَارٌ (P)
Historical	تَارِيخِىٌّ (Adj. SM)
Qutb Minar	مَنَارَةُ قُطْبٍ
Red fort	اَلْقَلْعَةُ الْحَمْرَاءُ
Old fort	اَلْقَلْعَةُ الْقَدِيمَةُ
Tomb, mausoleum	مَقْبَرَةٌ (SF) مَقَابِرُ (P)
To come	قَدِمَ / يَقْدَمُ / قُدُومًا
Tourist	سَائِحٌ (SM) سَائِحُونَ(P)
Corner	نَحْوٌ (SM) أَنْحَاءٌ {P}
Centre	مَرْكَزٌ (SM) مَرَاكِزُ (P)
Central	مَرْكَزِىٌّ (Adj. SM)
Government	حُكُومَةٌ (SF) حُكُومَاتٌ (P)
Outside/ out	خَارِجَ (Adv. of place)
To develop	طَوَّرَ / يُطَوِّرُ / تَطْوِيْرًا
In addition to, beside	بِجَانِبِ
Place	مَكَانٌ (SM) أَمَاكِنُ (P)

Places of interest	اَمَاكِنُ الإِهْتِمَامِ
Like	مِثلٌ (SM) أَمْثَالٌ
Museum	مَتحَفٌ (SM) مَتَاحِفُ (P)
National	قَوْمِيٌّ (Adj. SM)
Archives	مَكْتَبُ الاَرَاشِيْفِ
Cultural centres	مَرَاكِزُ الثَّقَافَةِ
Research	بَحْثٌ (SM) بُحُوْثٌ (P)
Scientific research	اَلْبَحْثُ الْعِلْمِىُّ
Known, famous	مَعْرُوفٌ (Adj. SM)

Dual Of The Verbs And Pronouns
المثنى للفعل و الضمائر

I was sitting in my room	كُنْتُ جَالِسًا فِىْ غُرْفَتِى
in the University preparing lessons	فِى الْجَامِعَةِ أُعِدُّ دُرُوْسًا
for the next day. Suddenly	لِلْيَوْمِ التَّالِى. اِذْ
Mohammed and Ram came to me	جَاءَ نِى مُحَمَّدٌ وَرَام
and (they both) said to me:	وَقَالَا لِى:
Sir, we need your help.	سَيِّدِىْ، نَحْنُ مُحْتَاجَانِ مُسَاعَدَتَك
We two and Asha and Kiran	نَحْنُ الإثْنَيْنِ وَ آشَا وَكِيْرَان
would like to go to attend	نَوَدُّ الذَّهَابَ لِحُضُورِ
the marriage of our friend Ahmad.	زَوَاجِ صَدِيْقِنَا اَحْمَد.
We request your permission.	نَرجُوا اِذْنَ سِيَادَتِك.
I said: O. K., but you (both) should write	قُلْتُ: طَيِّبٌ، وَلَكِنْ يَجِبُ
a leave application mentioning	اَنْ تَكْتُبَا طَلَبَ اِجَازَةٍ مَعَ ذِكْرِ
the days of absence.	اَيَّامِ الْغَيَاب.
As regards Asha and kiran, they should	أَمَّا آشَا وَ كِيْرَانَ فَيَلْزَمُ
come to me to give	اَنْ تَاتِيَانِى حَتَّى تُقَدِّمَا
the leave application.	طَلَبَ الإجَازَة.
Ram and Mohammed felt happy	فَرَضِىَ مُحَمَّد وَ رَام
and left my room.	وَخَرَجَا مِنْ غُرْفَتِى.
After some time Asha and Kiran came	بَعْدَ قَلِيْلٍ قَدِمَتْ آشَا وَكِيْرَان
and (they both) submitted	وَ قَدَّمَتَا
the leave application.	طَلَبَ الإجَازَة.
I asked them (both):	فَسَأَلْتُهُمَا:

When will you (both) return	مَتَى سَتَعُودَانِ
from the marriage.	مِنَ الزَّوَاجِ.
They (both) said: after two days,	فَقَالَتَا: بَعْدَ يَوْمَيْنِ
God willing.	إِنْ شَاءَ اللّٰهُ.
I said: please convey my congratulations	فَقُلْتُ: اَرْجُوا اَنْ تُبَلِّغَا تَهَانِيَ
to Ahmad & his bride.	لِأَحْمَد وَ عَرُوْسَتِه.
They (both) said: sure sir.	فَقَالَتَا: وَهُوَ كَذَلِكَ يَا سَيِّدِى.
Kiran said: Ahmad & his wife	قَالَتْ كِيْرَان: أَحْمَد وَ عَرُوْسَتُهُ
have sent their greetings for you.	بَلَّغَا سَلَامَهُمَا لِسِيَادَتِكَ.
They are (two) good people.	هُمَا إِنْسَانَانِ طَيِّبَانِ.
I said: O.K., God willing, we will meet	فَقُلْتُ: طَيِّبٌ إِنْ شَاءَ اللّٰهُ نَلْتَقِى
after two days.	بَعْدَ يَوْمَيْنِ.

Grammar:

(a) Dual of the verbs:

It has been explained in lessons nos. 13 & 14 that the verb in Arabic has to agree with its subject in gender when it precedes it. It has to agree with the subject in number also when it occurs after the subject.

i) To obtain the dual form of the past third person masculine verb one 'alif ١' has to be suffixed to the past third person masculine verb of singular number. For example:

١. ذَهَبَ

1. He went

They (MD) went ذَهَبَ + ١ = ذَهَبَا

٢. كَتَبَ

2. He wrote

They (MD) wrote كَتَبَ + ١ = كَتَبَا

ii) In the third person feminine also one '١ alif' has to be suffixed to the singular form of the feminine verb. In this case the silent Taa ت will be given a *fathah*.

Example:

1. She went   ذَهَبَتْ . ١

   They (FD) went   ذَهَبَتَا = ا + ذَهَبَتْ

2. She wrote   كَتَبَتْ . ٢

   They (FD) Wrote   كَتَبَتَا = ا + كَتَبَتْ

iii) In the case of second person of both the genders 'ما' has to be sufixed to the respective verb of singular number and the ' Taa ت' in both these cases is given a *dammah*. Examples:

1. You (SM)went   ذَهَبْتَ

   You (MD) went   ذَهَبْتُمَا = مَا + ذَهَبْتُ

2. You (SF) went   ذَهَبْتِ

   You (FD) went   ذَهَبْتُمَا= مَا + ذَهَبْتُ

iv) In the case of the present tense verb ان is suffixed to the singular verbs of both the genders except the feminine singular verb of the second person where the ى ن is first elided and then the ان is added. However, in all these cases the letter preceding 'alif' is given *fathah* and the 'noon ن' carries *Kasrah*.

Example:

He goes   يَذْهَبُ

   They (MD) go   يَذْهَبَانِ = انَ + يَذْهَبُ

She goes   تَذْهَبُ

   They (FD) go   تَذْهَبَانِ = انَ + تَذْهَبُ

You (SM) go   تَذْهَبُ

   You (MD) go   تَذْهَبَانِ =ان + تَذْهَبُ

You (SF) go   تَذْهَبِينَ

   You (FD) go   تَذْهَبَانِ =ان+ تَذْهَبُ

b) Of the nouns

ب) لِلاسماء

Dual of the noun and its cases have been explained in full details in lesson no: 18.

c) Of the personal (pro) nouns.

ج) للضَّمائر

Details regarding personal (pro) nouns have been given in lesson no. 9 and 10. In case of their dual forms they happen to be fixed words. They are:

They two girls or boys هُمَا

You two girls or boys اَنْتُمَا

In case of the possessive pronouns also the forms are fixed as given below:

Their (MFD) هُمَا

Your (MFD) كُمَا

These two pronouns of the dual number are used in both the accusative and the genitive cases.

d) Of the demonstrative pronouns

د) أسماء الأشارة

The following words are used to indicate the dual of the demonstrative pronouns:

These (MD)	هَذَان
These (FD)	هَاتَان
Those (MD)	ذَانِك
Those (FD)	تَانِك

The demonstrative pronouns are indeclinable except their dual forms. The forms metioned above are said to be in the nominative case. In the accusative and the genitive cases the following forms are used:

These (MD)	هَذَيْن
These (FD)	هَاتَيْن
Those (MD)	ذَيْنِك
Those (FD)	تَيْنِك

Exercises:

1. Conjugate the following verbs in the past and the present tenses and then use them in sentences of your own:

To sit	جَلَسَ / يَجْلِسُ / جُلُوْسًا
To stand	وَقَفَ / يَقِفُ / وُقُوفاً
To ride	رَكِبَ / يَرْكَبُ / رُكُوبًا
To alight; to get down	نَزَلَ / يَنزِلُ / نُزُوْلاً
To enter	دَخَلَ / يَدْخُلُ / دُخُولاً

2. Rewrite complete tables of personal, possessive and demonstrative (pro) nouns and use them in sentences of your own keeping in mind the three cases.

3. Translate into Arabic:

Ramu is a young boy . My son Abid is also about the same age. They are friends. They study in the same school. They go to school every morning together. They play together and do their homework together. They are always together. One day the teacher asked them: why do you sit so close and behave so alike? Are you twins? Another boy got up and said: No sir, they are not twins. They are two good friends. And these two are their favourite seats. They like to sit on these seats.

4. Translate into English:

كَانَ الْوَقْتُ صَبَاحاً مُبَكِّرًا. خَرَجْتُ لِلتَّنَزُّهِ وَفْقًا لِعَادَتِى بَيْنَهَا عَبْرَ سَنَوَاتٍ مُتَتَالِيَةٍ. وَلَدَىْ وُصُوْلِى مُنْعَطَفَ الطَّرِيقِ وَجَدْتُ مُوْهَان وَ جَمِيْل فِىْ انْتِظَارِئْ. هَذَانِ الرَّجُلَانِ مِنْ اَصْدِقَائِى آخُذُهُمَا مَعِى مِنْ هَذَا الْمُنْعَطَفِ. هُمَا يَعْمَلَانِ اَيْضاً مَعِىَ فِى مَكْتَبِى. فَمَشَيْنَا نَحْوَ الْحَدِيْقَةِ. وَلَدَىْ دُخُولِنَا بَابَ الْحَدِيْقَةِ رَأَيْنَا بِنْتَيْنِ تَمْشِيَانِ عَلَى الْعُشْبِ الْأَخْضَرِ النَّاعِمِ. مَا كُنْتُ رَأَيْتُ هَاتَيْنِ الْبِنْتَيْنِ قَبْلَ الْيَوْمِ. فَسَأَلْتُ مُوْهَان وَ جَمِيْل: هَلْ رَأَيْتُمَا هَاتَيْنِ الْبِنْتَيْنِ قَبْلَ الْيَوْمِ. فَقَالَا: لَا، مَارَأَيْنَاهُمَا قَبْلَ الْيَوْمِ. فَذَهَبْتُ إِلَيْهِمَا وَ سَأَلْتُ: مَنْ اَنْتُمَا؟ فَقَالَتَا: نَحْنُ مِنَ الْحَىِّ الْمُجَاوِرِ لَكَ يَا عَمُّ. فَسَأَلْتُهُمَا: هَلْ اَنْتُمَا تَأْتِيَانِ إِلَى هَذِهِ الْحَدِيْقَةِ كُلَّ صَبَاحٍ. فَقَالَتَا: لَا.

Glossary:	الكلمات العسيرة
Young; small	صَغِيرٌ (Adj SM) صِغَارٌ (P)
Son, boy	اِبْنٌ (SM) أَبْنَاءٌ (P)
About	عَنْ (Preposition)
Same/ the same	نَفْسٌ
School	مَدْرَسَةٌ (SF) مَدَارِسُ (P)
Together	مَعًا
To do	* قَامَ / يَقُومُ / قِيَامًا بِـ
Home work	اَلْوَاجِبُ الْمَدْرَسِى
Always	دَائِمًا
One day/ on one day	ذَاتَ يَوْمٍ / فِىْ يَوْمٍ
To ask	سَأَلَ / يَسْأَلُ / سُؤَالاً
Why	لِمَاذَا
Close/ close by	عَلَى مَقْرُبَةٍ مِّنْ
So/ so much; to this extent	إِلَى هَذَا الْحَدِّ
To behave	تَصَرَّفَ / يَتَصَرَّفُ / تَصَرُّفًا
Alike; similar	بِصُوْرَةٍ مُتَشَابِهَةٍ
Twin	تَوْأَم (SM) تَوَائِمُ (P)
Another	آخَرُ
To get up	نَهَضَ / يَنْهَضُ / نُهُوْضًا
Good	طَيِّبٌ (Adj SM) طَيِّبُونَ (P)
Favourite	مُفَضَّلٌ (Adj SM)
Seat	مَقْعَدٌ (SM) مَقَاعِدُ (P)
To love	أَحَبَّ / يُحِبُّ / مَحَبَّةً

---

* For conjugation pattern, please see appendix.

No, not	لَيْسَ *
To walk	تَنَزَّهَ / يَتَنَزَّهُ / تَنَزُّهًا
According to	وَفْقاً لِ
Habit	عَادَةٌ (SF) عَادَاتٌ (P)
To Build up	بَنَى / يَبْنِى / بِنَاءً **
Accross	عَبْرَ
Year	سَنَةٌ (SF) سَنَوَاتٌ / سِنِيْنَ (P)
Continuous	مُتَتَالِيَةٌ
On; at the time of	لَدَى
To reach	وَصَلَ / يَصِلُ / وُصُولاً **
Turn (Of the road)	مُنْعَطَفٌ (SM) مُنْعَطَفَاتٌ (P)
Road	طَرِيقٌ (SMF) طُرُقٌ (P)
To find	وَجَدَ / يَجِدُ / وُجُودًا **
To wait	إِنْتَظَرَ / يَنْتَظِرُ / اِنْتِظَاراً
Waiting for me	فِى اِنْتِظَارِى
To walk; to go	مَشَى / يَمْشِى / مَشْيًا **
Towards, to	نَحْوَ
To enter	دَخَلَ / يَدْخُلُ / دُخُولاً

---

* This verb does not have the present indefinite form. It gives the
intensified meaning of 'لَا' . It functions like 'Kaana كَانَ' to govern the
subject i.e. مُبْتَداً and خَبَر the predicate i.e. it gives ḍammah to the subject
and causes *fatḥah* to the predicate. The conjugation of لَيْسَ is given
hereunder for ready reference & future use:

لَسْنَ	لَيْسَتَا	لَيْسَتْ	لَيْسُوا	لَيْسَا	لَيْسَ
لَسْتُنَّ	لَسْتُمَا	لَسْتِ	لَسْتُمْ	لَسْتُمَا	لَسْتَ
		لَسْنَا	لَسْتُ		

** For conjugation pattern, please see appendix

to see	رَأَى ⁄ يَرَى ⁄ رُؤْيَةً **
Grass	عُشْبٌ (SM) أَعْشَابٌ (P)
Soft	نَاعِمٌ (Adj. SM)
Before	قَبْلَ(used as prepositon)
Area; colony	حَيٌّ (SM) أَحْيَاءٌ (P)
Neighbouring	مُجَاوِرٌ (VNSM)
To come	أَتَى ⁄ يَأْتِى ⁄ إِتْيَانًا **

** For conjugation pattern see appendix.

LESSON – 21

الدرس – ٢١

Possessed & Possessor Or The Construct Phrase

الملكية والمالك او المركب الاضافى

This is a boy.	هَذَا وَلَدٌ.
He is a teacher's son.	هُوَ ابْنُ مُدَرِّسٍ.
The teacher's son is a disciplined boy.	ابْنُ الْمُدَرِّسِ وَلَدٌ مُؤَدَّبٌ.
This is his school.	هَذِهِ مَدْرَسَتُهُ.
His school is quite far from his house.	مَدْرَسَتُهُ بَعِيدَةٌ جِدًّا مِنْ بَيْتِهِ.
He rides his bi-cycle	هُوَ يَرْكَبُ دَرَّاجَتَهُ
from his house to his school.	مِنْ بَيْتِهِ إِلَى مَدْرَسَتِهِ.
These are his friends.	هَؤُلَاءِ أَصْدِقَاؤُهُ.
His friends like him.	أَصْدِقَاؤُهُ يُحِبُّونَهُ.
And he likes his friends.	وَهُوَ يُحِبُّ أَصْدِقَائَهُ.
This is their class.	هَذَا فَصْلُهُمْ.
And this is their teacher.	وَهَذَا مُدَرِّسُهُمْ.
The students are sitting.	اَلطُّلَّابُ جَالِسُونَ.
And their teacher is standing	وَ أُسْتَاذُهُمْ وَاقِفٌ
infront of the blackboard.	أَمَامَ السَّبُّورَةِ.
He is writing difficult words	هُوَ يَكْتُبُ الْكَلِمَاتِ الصَّعْبَةَ
on the blackboard.	عَلَى السَّبُّورَةِ.
His students are writing	طُلَّابُهُ يَكْتُبُونَ
these words in their copybooks	هَذِهِ الْكَلِمَاتِ فِى كُرَّاسَاتِهِم
with their meanings.	مَعَ مَعَانِيهَا.

Grammar:

The genitive case of the Arabic language is popularly known as possessed & possessor. It is called الاضافة in Arabic.

This kind of phrase indicates that some thing or some quality belongs to some one or some thing. This very relation of belonging is expressed by placing any two (nouns) in construct position or by using in English 'of' or the apostrophe 's' . However, in Arabic there does not exist any such word. This meaning is obtained by the placement of nouns in certain order with the adjustment of the vowelpoints. This is known as construct phrase or المركب الاضافى. As has been explained in the foregoing the relation of belonging between two objects in Arabic is created by placing two or more nouns in certain order. This kind of placement of nouns causes *kasrah* to the terminal letter of the possessor which noun precisely is known to be in the genitive case. *

The following things are to be borne in mind while making these kinds of construct phrases or sentences:

i) The object possessed is placed before the possessor.
ii) The possessor is placed immediately after the possessed.
iii) The object possessed does not admit nunnation i.e. the double vowel points.
iv) The possessed object in such possessive phrases and sentences does not take the definite article.

Example:

A teacher's son came.   قَدِمَ اِبْنُ مُدَرِّسٍ.
I saw a teacher's son.   رَأَيْتُ إِبْنَ مُدَرِّسٍ.
I went with a teacher's son.   ذَهَبْتُ مَعَ إِبْنِ مُدَرِّسٍ.

---

* Nouns carrying *kasrah* for whatever grammatical reasons are known or categorised to be in the genitive case.

In the three sentences above the possessed object is إبن . It is therefore placed before مُدَرِّسٌ which is the possessor here. Now it would be seen that إبن has only one dammah in sentence no. 1, where it serves as subject of the verb قَدِمَ. In sentence no. 2: إبن has *fathah*. Here it is serving as object of the verb رَأَيْتُ. In sentence no. 3: إبن has *kasrah* because it is preceded by a preposition. Hence we find that the possessed objects carry vowelpoints according to their placement after the verb and the preposition. However, مُدَرِّسٌ the possessor invariably has *kasrah*. It has double *kasrah* because it is not defined with the definite article الـ. When the possessor is defined it admits only one *kasrah*. For example:

The teacher's son came	قَدِمَ ابْنُ الْمُدَرِّسِ.
I saw the teacher's son.	رَأَيْتُ ابْنَ الْمُدَرِّسِ.
I went with the teacher's son.	ذَهَبْتُ مَعَ ابْنِ الْمُدَرِّسِ.

In case of the dual and the sound plural masculine the 'noon ن' drops out when it is placed in construct position with another noun. For example إبْنَان is a dual noun meaning two sons. It will be put in construct position with the noun مُدَرِّسٌ in the following manner:

The two sons of the teacher came.	قَدِمَ ابْنَا الْمُدَرِّسِ.
I saw the two sons of the teacher.	رَأَيْتُ ابْنَى الْمُدَرِّسِ.
I went with the two sons of the teacher.	ذَهَبْتُ مَعَ ابْنَى الْمُدَرِّسِ.

مُدَرِّسُونَ is a sound plural of the singular مُدَرِّسٌ. When this مُدَرِّسُونَ is placed in construct postion with another noun كُلِّيَّةٌ it will decline in the following manner:

The teachers of the college came.	قَدِمَ مُدَرِّسُو الْكُلِّيَّةِ.
I saw the teachers of the college .	رَأَيْتُ مُدَرِّسِى الْكُلِّيَّةِ.
I went with the teachers of the college.	ذَهَبْتُ مَعَ مُدَرِّسِى الْكُلِّيَّةِ.

This kind of placement of two nouns beside causing the meaning of belonging can also show that something is part of something . For example.

A cup of water/ a water cup	كُوبُ مَاءٍ
A window of glass/ a glass window	شُبَّاكُ زُجَاجٍ

Exercises:

1. Put the following pairs of nouns in construct position to show belonging and use them in sentences of your own:

مَكْتَبَةٌ: جَامِعَةٌ/بَابٌ: بَيْتٌ/عَمِيْدٌ: كُلِّيَّةٌ/كُرَّاسَةٌ: بِنْتٌ/عَرُوْسَةٌ: طِفْلٌ

طَالِبٌ: مَدْرَسَةٌ/قَلَمٌ: مُدَرِّسٌ/سَيَّارَةٌ: سَفِيْرٌ/مَائِدَةٌ: طَعَامٌ

2. Repeat exercise no: 1. with the duals & the plurals of the nouns.

3. Translate into Arabic:

This is my friend Hamid. He works in an office in Delhi. Hamid's office is in Krishi Bhavan. He goes to the office in the morning and comes back in the evening. Hamid likes to work hard. Hamid also likes to spend time with his office colleagues. He sits with the office colleagues in the lunch break. On sundays and holidays he likes to visit office colleagues and friends. This is Hamid's house. It has two rooms only. Hamid's wife keeps the two rooms of the house very clean. They are a small family of four including their two sons who are big enough.

4. Translate into English:

أَدْرُسُ فِيْ جَامِعَةِ جَوَاهَرْ لَال نِهْرُو. أَدْرُسُ فِيْ كُلِّيَّةِ اللُّغَاتِ. اَنَا اَدْرُسُ اللُّغَةَ الْعَرَبِيَّةَ. كُلِّيَّةُ اللُّغَاتِ وَاحِدَةٌ مِنْ كُلِّيَّاتٍ عَدِيْدَةٍ فِيْ جَامِعَةِ نِهْرُو. وَ فِيْ كُلِّ كُلِّيَّةٍ مَرَاكِزُ مُخْتَلِفَةٌ. اِسْمُ مَرْكَزِى هُوَ مَرْكَزُ الدِّرَاسَاتِ الْعَرَبِيَّةِ وَالْأَفْرِيْقِيَّةِ. هَذَا مَكْتَبُ الْجَامِعَةِ. مُوَظَّفُو مَكْتَبِ الْجَامِعَةِ أُنَاسٌ طَيِّبُونَ. اَنَا بِصِفَتِى دَارِسًا أُقَابِلُ مُوَظَّفِى الْجَامِعَةِ مِنْ وَقْتٍ اِلَى وَقْتٍ طِوَالَ السَّنَةِ. وَكَذَلِكَ هُنَاك مُنَاسَبَاتٌ اَجْتَمِعُ فِيْهَا مَعَ مُوَظَّفِى الْجَامِعَةِ. هَذِهِ مَكْتَبَتُنَا. مَكْتَبَةُ جَامِعَةِ نِهْرُو غَنِيَّةٌ جِدًّا مِنْ حَيْثُ الْكُتُبُ فِى الْعُلُوْمِ وَ الآدَابِ وَاللُّغَاتِ وَ كُلِّ فُرُوْعِ الْمَعْرِفَةِ. جَامِعَةُ جَوَاهَرْ لَال نِهْرُو جَامْعَةٌ دَاخِلِيَّةٌ. لَهَا مَدِيْنَةٌ سَكَنِيَّةٌ كَبِيْرَةٌ. لِهَذِهِ الْمَدِيْنَةِ السَّكَنِيَّةِ بَابَان رَئِيْسَان. تَرَى بَابَى الْجَامِعَةِ مَفْتُوحَيْنِ لَيْلًا وَنَهَارًا. يَجْلِسُ عَلَى بَابَى الْجَامِعَةِ رِجَالُ الأَمْنِ بِالتَّنَاوُبِ.

Glossary:　　　　　　　　　　　　　الكلمات العسيرة

Some; a few	عَدِيْدَةٌ (Adj. SF)
Centre	مَرْكَزٌ (SM) مَرَاكِزُ (P)
Different; various	مُخْتَلِفٌ (Adj. SM)
Humanbeing, man	إِنْسَانٌ (SM) أُنَاسٌ (P)
Good	طَيِّبٌ (Adj. SM) طَيِّبُوْنَ (P)
Capacity	صِفَةٌ (SF)
In my capacity as a student	بِصِفَتِي دَارِسًا
Student	دَارِسٌ (SM) دَارِسُوْنَ (P)
To meet	قَابَلَ / يُقَابِلُ / مُقَابَلَةً
Whole, all...long	طِوَالَ
All the year round	طِوَالَ السَّنَةِ
Dean	عَمِيْدٌ (SM) عُمَدَاءُ (P)
Doll	عَرُوْسَةٌ (SF) عَرَائِسُ (P)
Ambassador	سَفِيْرٌ (SM) سُفَرَاءُ (P)
Table (dining)	مَائِدَةٌ (SF) مَوَائِدُ ،مَائِدَاتٌ(P)
Food	طَعَامٌ (SM) أَطْعِمَةٌ (P)
To work	عَمِلَ / يَعْمَلُ / عَمَلاً
To like: to love	أَحَبَّ / يُحِبُّ / مَحَبَّةً
To work hard	اِجْتَهَدَ / يَجْتَهِدُ / اِجْتِهَادًا
To spend	أَنْفَقَ / يُنْفِقُ / اِنْفَاقاً
Colleague	زَمِيْلٌ (SM) زُمَلَاءُ(P)
Lunch	غَدَاءٌ (SM)
Break, interval, period	فَتْرَةٌ (SF) فَتَرَاتٌ (P)
Holiday	عُطْلَةٌ (SF) عُطْلَاتٌ (P)
To visit	زَارَ / يَزُوْرُ / زِيَارَةً

To keep	اَبْقَى / يُبْقِى / اِبْقَاءٌ
Family	اُسْرَةٌ (SF) اُسْرَاتٌ (P)
Small	صَغِيرٌ (Adj. SM) صِغَارٌ (P)
Of four	مِنْ اَرْبَعَةِ
Including	بِانْضِمَامِ
Big	كَبِيرٌ (Adj. SM) كِبَارٌ (P)
Enough, adequate	بِشَكْلٍ كَافٍ

LESSON — 22

الدرس—٢٢

Adjective & the Noun Qualified

الصفة والموصوف

In fact I am a teacher.	<div dir="rtl">فِى الوَاقِعِ اَنَا مُدَرِّسٌ .</div>
I work in a secondary school.	<div dir="rtl">اَعْمَلُ فِى مَدْرَسَةٍ ثَانَوِيَّةٍ.</div>
The covered area of this school is very big.	<div dir="rtl">اَلْمِسَاحَةُ الْمُغَطَّاةُ لِهَذِهِ الْمَدْرَسَةِ كَبِيرَةٌ جِدًّا.</div>
Besides, it has a big playground.	<div dir="rtl">عِلَاوَةً عَنْ ذَلِكَ لَهَا مَيْدَانٌ كَبِيرٌ .</div>
We have combined education in this school.	<div dir="rtl">لَنَا التَّعْلِيمُ الْمُخْتَلِطُ فِى هَذِهِ الْمَدْرَسَةِ.</div>
There are about two thousand boys and girls in this school.	<div dir="rtl">هُنَاك حَوَالَى اَلْفَى وَلَدٍ وَ بِنْتٍ فِى هَذِهِ الْمَدْرَسَةِ.</div>
We have small girls and small boys in our school.	<div dir="rtl">لَنَا بَنَاتٌ صَغِيرَاتٌ وَ اَوْلَادٌ صِغَارٌ فِى مَدْرَسَتِنَا.</div>
We also have big girls and big boys in this school.	<div dir="rtl">لَنَا اَيْضًا بَنَاتٌ كَبِيرَاتٌ وَ اَوْلَادٌ كِبَارٌ فِى هَذِهِ الْمَدْرَسَةِ.</div>
We have two hundred teachers.	<div dir="rtl">لَنَا مِئَتَا مُدَرِّسٍ .</div>
I have a big class.	<div dir="rtl">لِى فَصْلٌ كَبِيرٌ .</div>
Other teachers also have big classes.	<div dir="rtl">لِلْمُدَرِّسِينَ الآخَرِينَ اَيْضًا فُصُولٌ كَبِيرَةٌ</div>
We have only two small classes.	<div dir="rtl">لَنَا فَقَطْ فَصْلَان صَغِيرَان.</div>
Our principal has recently bought a new car.	<div dir="rtl">عَمِيدُنَا اِشْتَرَى اَخِيراً سَيَّارَةً جَدِيدَةً.</div>
Other teachers also have cars.	<div dir="rtl">لِلْمُدَرِّسِينَ الآخَرِينَ اَيْضًا سَيَّارَاتٌ.</div>
Those are old cars.	<div dir="rtl">تِلْك سَيَّارَاتٌ قَدِيمَةٌ</div>

This is the office of the principal. هَذَا مَكْتَبُ الْعَمِيدِ.

You will always see two sturdy peons سَوْفَ تَرَوْنَ دَائِمًا فَرَّاشَيْنِ قَوِيَّيْنِ

sitting at his door. جَالِسَيْنِ عَلَى بَابِهِ.

These two sturdy peons هَذَانِ الْفَرَّاشَانِ الْقَوِيَّانِ

always go with our dear principal دَائِمًا يَذْهَبَانِ مَعَ عَمِيدِنَا الْعَزِيْزِ

wherever he goes. حَيْثُمَا يَذْهَبُ.

These two peons have their quarters هَذَانِ الْفَرَّاشَانِ مَنْزِلَاهُمَا

in the school campus. فِيْ مَدِيْنَةِ الْمَدْرَسَةِ.

Beside poultry birds بِجَانِبِ الطُّيُورِ الدَّاجِنَةِ

they also keep beautiful اِنَّهُمْ اَيْضًا يَقْتَنُونَ كِلَابًا جَمِيْلَةً

and tiny dogs. I also have taken وَ صَغِيْرَةً. اَنَا اَيْضًا قَدْ اَخَذْتُ

one tiny dog from them. كَلْبًا صَغِيْرًا مِنْهُمَا.

I love my tiny dog very much. اُحِبُّ كَلْبِى الصَّغِيْرَ جِدًّا.

Do you also love dogs? هَلْ اَنْتَ اَيْضًا تُحِبُّ الْكِلَابَ؟

Grammar:

Adjective in Arabic is known as صفة and the noun qualified by the adjective is called مَوْصُوف. They are also known as نعت and مَنْعُوت respectively.

In Arabic the:

    i) Adjective follows the noun it qualifies.

    ii) Adjective completely agrees with its noun in:

    a) case

    b) definiteness and indefiniteness.

    c) number

    d) gender

Example:

    A big boy came قَدِمَ وَلَدٌ كَبِيْرٌ

The foregoing sentence is composed of three parts:

(He) came	قَدِمَ	intransitive verb
A boy	وَلَدٌ	a common noun
big	كَبِيرٌ	adjective

In this setence وَلَدٌ is a masculine noun of singular number. It is cosidered to be a common noun because it is not defined with the definite article اَلْ. It is in the nominative case being the subject of the intransitive verb قَدِمَ. Hence , the adjective كَبِيرٌ agrees with the noun in all aspects as mentioned above under (a) (b) (c) (d).

Similarly in the cases of the dual and plural nouns the adjective will fully agree with the noun it qualifies. For Example we would say:

Two boys came	قَدِمَ وَلَدَان
Two big boys came	قَدِمَ وَلَدَان كَبِيرَان
Boys came	قَدِمَ اَوْلَادٌ
Big boys came	قَدِمَ اَوْلَادٌ كِبَارٌ

And where the noun is defined with the definite article ال the adjective also will have to be defined with اَلْ. For example:

| The big boy came | قَدِمَ الْوَلَدُ الْكَبِيرُ |

If the noun qualified is in the accusative or genitive cases the adjective also will follow. For example:

| I saw a big boy | رَأَيْتُ وَلَداً كَبِيراً |

' Boy' in this sentence is the object of the transitive verb رَأَيْتُ and therefore, it is in the accusative case. The adjective here shall have to be placed in the accusative case.

And if we say:

| I went to a big boy | ذَهَبْتُ اِلِى وَلَدِ كَبِيرٍ |

We would find that the noun ولد is preceded by a preposition which functions in Arabic to cause *kasrah* to the terminal letter of the noun it precedes. It is therefore, the adjective also will have *kasrah*.

Similarly, if the noun is of the feminine gender the adjevctive also has to be feminine. All the Arabic adjectives of the masculine gender including the verbal nouns of the active and the passive voices which give adjectival meaning can be changed into the feminine gender by suffixing to them the round 'Taaة '. For example the adjective كَبِيْرٌ of the masculine gender will become كَبِيْرَةٌ after the round Taa ة is suffixed to it. This كَبِيْرَةٌ will decline to agree with the noun in case, number and all other aspects as explained above.

The plural of such feminine adjectives and adjectival nouns will be sound plural as explained in lesson no. 18. They will decline also as explained in the said lesson.

It should be remembered here that plurals of objects indicating non-humanbeings are treated on par with singular feminine for all purposes as explained in lesson no. 8. For example we would say:

The new books are expensive.   اَلْكُتُبُ الْجَدِيْدَةُ ثَمِيْنَةٌ

It may be noted here that 'books اَلْكُتُبُ' is a nonhuman plural. It is therefore, the feminine singular adjective 'اَلْجَدِيْدَةُ new' is used.

Exercises:

1. Translate into Arabic:

This huge building is an office complex. They are mostly governmental offices. This huge and tall building has nine floors including the ground floor. The ground floor mainly consists of public canteens and a big co-operative store run by the government employees themselves. Besides, there are covered parking places for the official cars. For the visiting cars there is a big open space to park them. The ground floor and the surrounding area is very unsafe and unclean. There are bad people who roam about in this area. They are mostly tricksters and pickpockets. Besides, you can always see tens of dirty dogs loitering about . At other floors there are offices of different ministries. There is mixed working force in all these offices. There are big officials and small officilas in these offices. There are men-officials and women-officials.

2. Given below are the masculine adjectives of singular number. Use them in sentences of your own. Also use suitably their dual and plural forms in sentences of your own.

سَرِيعٌ، رَخِيصٌ، صَعْبٌ، سَهْلٌ، قَبِيْحٌ، جَمِيْلٌ، قَصِيرٌ، طَوِيْلٌ، قَدِيْمٌ، جَدِيْدٌ.

3. Render the adjectives in exercise no. 2 into those of the feminine gender for all numbers and suitably use them in sentences of your own.

4. Translate into English:

الف: هَذِهِ جَامِعَةُ جَوَاهِرْ لَآلِ نِهْرُو. هَذِهِ جَامِعَةٌ كَبِيرَةٌ. يَدْرُسُ فِىْ هَذِهِ الْجَامِعَةِ الْكَبِيْرَةِ الطُّلَّابُ الْكِبَارُ مَعَ الطَّالِبَاتِ الْكَبِيْرَاتِ. هٰؤُلَاءِ الطُّلَّابُ الْكِبَارُ وَالطَّالِبَاتُ الْكَبِيْرَاتُ يُتَابِعُوْنَ دِرَاسَاتِهِمْ فِى الْعُلُوْمِ الْعَصْرِيَّةِ وَاللُّغَاتِ الْحَدِيْثَةِ. تُقَدِّمُ الْجَامِعَةُ كُوْرِسَاتٍ مُنْتَظِمَةٍ كَامِلَةِ الدَّوَامِ فِى النَّهَارِ وَكُورِسَاتٍ وَجِيْزَةِ نِصْفِ الدَّوَامِ فِى الْمَسَاءِ. اَنَا طَالِبٌ فِىْ قِسْمِ اللُّغَةِ الْعَرَبِيَّةِ الْحَدِيْثَةِ. لَنَا فَصْلٌ صَغِيْرٌ وَ غُرْفَةٌ كَبِيْرَةٌ. لِلْغُرْفَةِ الْكَبِيْرَةِ بَابَانِ وَاسِعَانِ وَ شُبَّاكَانِ ضَيِّقَانِ. كَرَاسِيُّ الْغُرْفَةِ جَدِيْدَةٌ وَ مُرِيْحَةٌ. سَوْفَ تَرَى هَذَيْنِ الْبَابَيْنِ الْوَاسِعَيْنِ مَفْتُوحَيْنِ دَائِمًا خِلَالَ سَاعَاتِ دَوَامِ الْجَامِعَةِ. يَدْخُلُ طُلَّابُ هَذِهِ الْغُرْفَةِ مِنْ هَذَيْنِ الْبَابَيْنِ الْوَاسِعَيْنِ وَيَخْرُجُونَ مِنْهُمَا.

ب: قَالَتِ الْمُدَرِّسَةُ: نَحْنُ الْآنَ فِىْ اَوَائِلِ الشِّتَاءِ. هَذِهِ الْأَيَّامُ لَيْسَتْ حَارَّةً وَلَابَارِدَةً. هِىَ اَيَّامٌ لَطِيْفَةٌ جِدًّا. لِمَاذَا لَانَذْهَبُ فِى نُزْهَةٍ. نَذْهَبُ مَثَلاً إِلَى حَدِيْقَةِ الْحَيَوَانَاتِ لِنَرَى اَنْوَاعًا مُخْتَلِفَةً مِّنَ الْحَيَوَانَاتِ وَالطُّيُورِ. تَتَوَاجَدُ فِىْ حَدِيْقَةِ الْحَيَوَانَاتِ حَيَوَانَاتٌ مُفْتَرِسَةٌ. وَكَذَلِكَ نَجِدُ فِى الْحَدِيْقَةِ حَيَوَانَاتٍ نَادِرَةً وَ طُيُورًا غَرِيْبَةً. فَصَفَّقَ جَمِيْعُ الطُّلَّابِ الْحَاضِرِيْنَ وَ الطَّالِبَاتِ الْحَاضِرَاتِ.

فَقَالَتِ الْمُدَرِّسَةُ: نَذْهَبُ إِنْ شَاءَ اللهُ، إِلَى حَدِيْقَةِ الْحَيَوَانَاتِ فِى يَوْمِ السَّبْتِ الْقَادِمِ. نَجْتَمِعُ فِى فِنَاءِ الْمَدْرَسَةِ فِى السَّبْتِ الْقَادِمِ فِى السَّاعَةِ الثَّامِنَةِ وَ مِنْ هُنَاكَ نَذْهَبُ إِلَى حَدِيْقَةِ الْحَيَوَانَاتِ. وَافَقَ الْجَمِيْعُ عَلَى ذَلِكَ. بَعْدَ ذَلِكَ أَخَذَتِ الْمُدَرِّسَةُ تُدَرِّسُنَا دَرْسًا جَدِيْداً.

Glossary:	الكلمات العسيرة
Reality	وَاقِعٌ
Teacher	مُدَرِّسٌ(SM) مُدَرِّسُونَ (P)
To work	عَمِلَ / يَعْمَلُ / عَمَلاً
Secondary	ثَانَوِيٌّ (Adj. SM)
Area; terrain, sector	مِسَاحَةٌ (SF) مِسَاحَاتٌ(P)
Covered	مُغَطَّى (VNSM)
Apart from	عِلَاوَةً عَنْ
Ground; square	مَيْدَانٌ (SM) مَيَادِينُ (P)
Mixed, combined	مُخْتَلِطٌ
Around	حَوَالَى
One thousand	أَلْفٌ
Small, young	صَغِيرٌ (Adj. SM) صِغَارٌ (P)
Small, young	صَغِيرَةٌ (Adj. SF) صَغِيرَاتٌ (P)
One hundred	مِائَةٌ / مِئَةٌ
Calss	فَصْلٌ (SM) فصول (P)
Principal	عَمِيدٌ(SM) عُمَدَاءُ (P)
To buy	اِشْتَرَى / يَشْتَرِى / اِشْتِرَاءً
New	جَدِيدٌ (Adj. SM) جُدُدٌ (P)
Old	قَدِيمٌ (Adj. SM) قُدَامَى (P)
To see	رَأَى / يَرَى / رُؤْيَةً
Peon; attendant	فَرَّاشٌ (SM) فَرَّاشُونَ (P)
Strong	قَوِيٌّ (Adj. SM) اقوياء (P)
Always	دَائِمًا
With	مَعَ (Preposition)

Dear; beloved	عَزِيزٌ (Adj. SM) أَعِزَّاءُ (P)
Wherever	حَيْثُمَا
House	مَنْزِلٌ (SM) مَنَازِلُ (P)
Ground	أَرْضِيٌّ (Adj. SF)
Ground floor	اَلدَّوْرُ الْأَرْضِيُّ
Bird	طَائِرٌ (SM) طُيُورٌ (P)
Poultry, domesticated (animals/ birds)	دَاجِنٌ (دَاجِنَةٌ)
Beside; in addition to	بِجَانِب
To keep; to acquire	اِقْتَنَى / يَقْتَنِي / اِقْتِنَاءً
To take	أَخَذَ / يَأْخُذُ / أَخْذًا
Expensive; costly	ثَمِينٌ (Adj. SM)
Fast	سَرِيعٌ (Adj. SM) سِرَاعٌ (P)
Cheap	رَخِيصٌ (Adj. SM) رِخَاصٌ (P)
Difficult	صَعْبٌ (Adj. SM) صِعَابٌ (P)
Easy	سَهْلٌ (Adj.SM)
Ugly	قَبِيحٌ (Adj. SM) قِبَاحٌ (P)
Beautiful, handsome	جَمِيلٌ (Adj. SM)
Short	قَصِيرٌ (Adj. SM) قِصَارٌ (P)
Tall	طَوِيلٌ (Adj. SM) طِوَالٌ (P)
To study	دَرَسَ / يَدْرُسُ / دِرَاسَةً
To pursue	تَابَعَ / يُتَابِعُ / مُتَابَعَةً
Studies	دِرَاسَةٌ (SF) دِرَاسَاتٌ (P)
Science	عِلْمٌ (SM) عُلُومٌ (P)
Modern	حَدِيثٌ (Adj. SM)
Course (of study)	كُورس (SM) كُورسَاتٌ (P)

Regular	مُنْتَظِمٌ
Full time	كَامِلُ الدَّوَامِ
Brief; short	(Adj. SM) وَجِيْزٌ
Part-time	نِصْفُ الدَّوَامِ
Narrow	(Adj. SM) ضَيِّقٌ
Wide; broad	(Adj.SM) وَاسِعٌ
Comfortable	(Adj. SM) مُرِيْحٌ

LESSON — 23

الدرس — ٢٣

Imperative Verb And Negative Verb

فعل الامر و فعل النهى

That day was very hot in midsummer.	كَانَ ذَلِكَ الْيَوْمُ حَارًّا جِدًّا فِى أَوَاسِطِ الصَّيْفِ.
We were present in the class (room) waiting for the teacher.	كُنَّا مَوْجُودِينَ فِى الْفَصْلِ فِى اِنْتِظَارِ الْأُسْتَاذِ.
The teacher was late today.	كَانَ الْأُسْتَاذُ مُتَأَخِّرًا الْيَوْمَ.
The teacher came	جَاءَ الْأُسْتَاذُ
and he entered the class (room).	وَ دَخَلَ الْفَصْلَ.
We greeted him.	سَلَّمْنَا عَلَيْهِ.
The teacher returned the greetings	رَدَّ الْأُسْتَاذُ السَّلَامَ
and he said:	وَقَالَ:
Today is very hot, then he said to me:	اَلْيَوْمَ حَارٌّ جِدًّا ثُمَّ قَالَ لِى:
Ram Kumar, put on the light	يَا رَام كُومَار، اَشْعِلِ النُّورَ
and turn on the fan & open	وَافْتَحِ الْمِرْوَحَةَ
the window.	وَالشُّبَّاك.
After that the teacher said:	بَعْدَ ذَلِكَ قَالَ الْأُسْتَاذُ:
Open your book O Adil.	اِفْتَحْ كِتَابَكَ يَا عَادِلُ.
Boys, open your books.	اِفْتَحُوا كُتُبَكُمْ يَا أَوْلَادُ.
The teacher began to teach	أَخَذَ الْأُسْتَاذُ يُدَرِّسُ
and he wrote the difficult words	وَكَتَبَ الْكَلِمَاتِ الصَّعْبَةَ
on the blackboard.	عَلَى السَّبُّورَةِ.

The students began to write	أَخَذَ الطُّلَّابُ يَكْتُبُونَ
the meanings in their notebooks.	الْمَعَانِيَ فِى كُرَّاسَاتِهِم.
The teacher asked Asha:	سَأَلَ الْأُسْتَاذُ آشَا:
Where is your note book, Asha?	أَيْنَ كُرَّاسَتُكِ يَا آشَا؟
Open your notebook and write	إِفْتَحِى كُرَّاسَتَكِ وَاكْتُبِى
these words with their meanings	هَذِهِ الْكَلِمَاتِ مَعَ مَعَانِيْهَا
and do not talk with others.	وَلَاتَتَحَدَّثِى مَعَ الآخَرِيْنَ.
Why do you write on	لِمَاذَا تَكْتُبُ عَلَى
the book , Adil?	الْكِتَابِ يَا عَادِلُ؟
Don't write on the book, Adil.	لَا تَكْتُبْ عَلَى الْكِتَابِ يَا عَادِلُ.
Don't write on the book, boys.	لَا تَكْتُبُوا عَلَى الْكِتَابِ يَا أَوْلَادُ.
Don't write on the book, Miss.	لَا تَكْتُبِى عَلَى الْكِتَابِ يَا آنِسَةُ.
Don't write on the book, girls.	لَا تَكْتُبْنَ عَلَى الْكِتَابِ يَا بَنَاتُ.
During the lesson the teacher cast	خِلَالَ الدَّرْسِ أَلْقَى الْأُسْتَاذُ
a look at the class and asked	نَظْرَةً عَلَى الْفَصْلِ وَسَأَلَ
about Hamid: Where is Hamid?	عَنْ حَامِد، أَيْنَ حَامِد؟
Munir said: Sir, Hamid is unwell.	قَالَ مُنِير: سَيِّدِى ، حَامِدٌ مَرِيْضٌ.
The teacher said: Let Hamid take rest	قَالَ الْأُسْتَاذُ: فَلِيَسْتَرِحْ حَامِدٌ
for two or three days.	لِبَومَيْنِ أَوْثَلَاثَةِ أَيَّام.
After his recovery from illness	بَعْدَ إِفَاقَتِهِ مِنَ الْمَرَضِ
I will repeat this lesson for him.	أُعِيْدُ لَهُ هَذَا الدَّرْسَ.
Let us continue the lesson now.	فَلْنُوَاصِلْ الدَّرْسَ الآنَ.
During the lesson	خِلَالَ الدَّرْسِ
the school principal came	قَدِمَ عَمِيْدُ الْمَدْرَسَةِ
and he entered the room.	وَ دَخَلَ الْغُرْفَةَ.

The teacher rose for him	فَقَامَ لَهُ الْأُسْتَاذُ
and he said: Sir, please come.	وَقَالَ: تَفَضَّلْ يَا سَيِّدِئ.
The principal spoke to the teacher	تَحَدَّثَ الْعَمِيدُ إِلَى الْمُدَرِّسِ
for a while and returned.	قَلِيلًا وَعَادَ.
The bell rang and the lesson ended.	دَقَّ الْجَرَسُ وَانْتَهَى الدَّرْسُ.

Grammar:

The imperative verb i.e. فعل الأمر and the negative verb i.e. فعل النهى are formed from those forms of the present imperfect verb i.e. الفعل المضارع which indicate second person i.e. صيغة الحاضر. In the case of the triliteral verbs i.e. verbs which have three original letters, we have to drop the symbol of مضارع which will necessarily be ت in all cases. After removing the symbol of مضارع we look at the first original letter. In most of the cases it will have a sokoon and we can not read any word in Arabic which begins with a silent letter. Therefore, we prefix to it one alif with Hamza ء. If the second original letter has *fathah* or *kasrah* then this alif ا is given *kasrah*. If the second original letter has dammah then the 'Alif ا' so prefixed is given darnmah. The last letter of the verb is given Sokoon ْ. For example:

To go ذَهَبَ يَذْهَبُ تَذْهَبُ
إِذْهَبْ

In this case the ت of تَذْهَبُ is dropped. Now we find that the letter ذ bears sokoon. Therefore, we prefix to it alif with Hamza ء and because the second original letter has *fathah*, therefore, we give *kasrah* to this alif. The last letter which is ب in this case, is given sokoon. Now we read this form of the verb as:

Idh hab   إِذْهَبْ

In the case of the singular feminine, the dual masculine and the dual feminine and the plural masculine forms of the verb, the letter noon ن is dropped. The last letter alif ا Yaaى and و waw are considered to be carrying sokoon as elongative vowels, therefore, we don't add any letter at the end of these forms of the verb except the plural maculine form of the verb. We suffix to it one 'Alif ١' which is Known as protective 'Alif ١'*.

For example:

singular feminine	تَذْهَبِيْنَ	إِذْهَبِي
dual masculine	تَذْهَبَان	إِذْهَبَا
dual feminine	تَذْهَبَانَ	إِذْهَبَا
Plural masculine	تَذْهَبُوْنَ	إِذْهَبُوا

In the case of the plural feminine the letter noon ن is retained with its original *fathah*. For example:

تَذْهَبْنَ   إِذْهَبْنَ

In the case of verbs which have more than three letters- whether original or additional-after removing the symbol of مضارع, if we find that the next letter has a vowel, then in that case we only give sokoon to the last letter of the verb and follow the procedure as explained above for obtaining other forms i.e. dual and plural etc, of the verb.

Example:

سَافَرَ يُسَافِرُ تُسَافِرُ to travel

After removing the symbol of مضارع we have سَافِرُ form of the verb. In this case س is having a *fathah*, Therefore, we only give sokoon to the last letter

---

*   In the plural masculine form of the imperative we suffix one Alif to the original letters of the verb. This Alif is called "protective Alif" which disappears when the verb is followed by any linkable personal pronoun.

Example:
Beat him (you all men)   إِضْرِبُوه

However, this alif has to make physical apperance in written Arabic if the verb is followed by any other noun, pronoun or proper-noun.

Beat the boy (you all men)	إِضْرِبُوا الْوَلَدَ
Beat this boy (you all men)	إِضْرِبُوا هَذَا الْوَلَدَ
Beat Hamid (you all men)	إِضْرِبُوا حَامِدًا

which is Raa in this case and in this way, we obtain the following form:

سَافِرْ

For other forms of the verb we follow the procedure as explained above:

singular masculine	سَافِرْ	تُسَافِرُ
dual masculine	سَافِرَا	تُسَافِرَانِ
plural masculine	سَافِرُوْا	تُسَافِرُونَ
singular feminine	سَافِرِيْ	تُسَافِرِيْنَ
dual feminine	سَافِرَا	تُسَافِرَانِ
plural feminine	سَافِرْنَ	تُسَافِرْنَ

If we find that after removing the symbol of مضارع , the next letter has sokoon, then in that case we prefix to such a verb one Alif/ Hamza with *kasrah* and give sokoon to the last letter. For example:

اِسْتَقْبَلَ يَسْتَقْبِلُ to receive (s.o.) تَسْتَقْبِلُ

اِسْتَقْبِلْ

If the verb is causative on the pattern of أَفْعَلَ/يُفْعِلُ then in that case after removing the symbol of مضارع we prefix to it Alif/ Hamza with *fathah* and give sokoon to the last letter . For example:

أَجْلَسَ يُجْلِسُ to seat تُجْلِسُ

أَجْلِسْ

In the case of verbs which end with two identical letters and written as one with the help of shadda, we, after dropping the symbol of the present imperfect, either separate them and write them as two separate entities and prefix to them one Alif with appropriate vowel point or read them with a *fathah* at the terminal letter while at the same time retaining the existing vowel point on the letter after dropping symbol of the present indicative. For example:

to stretch	تَمُدُّ	مَدَّ يَمُدُّ
singular masculine	أُمْدُدْ	مُدَّ

dual masculine	اُمْدُدَا	مُدَّا
plural masculine	اُمْدُدُوا	مُدُّوا
singular feminine	اُمْدُدِى	مُدِّى
dual feminine	اُمْدُدَا	مُدَّا
plural feminine	اُمْدُدْنَ	اُمْدُدْنَ

In the case of triliteral verbs which have ا، و or ى as the medial letter preceded by an even vowel, we would drop this letter in the singular masculine and plural feminine imperative verbs while retaining it in the other four forms for obvious reasons.

Examples:

		تَقُولُ	to say	يَقُولُ	قَالَ
قُلْنَ	قُوْلَا	قُولِىْ	قُولُوا	قُولَا	قُلْ
		تَنَامُ	to sleep	يَنَامُ	نَامَ
نَمْنَ	نَامَا	نَامِى	نَامُوا	نَامَا	نَمْ

Arabic imperative verb may also be used in the meaning of request e.g. إِجْلِسْ which means "sit down", may also mean in the given circumstances "Please sit down". However, the phrase. مِنْ فَضْلِكَ meaning 'Please" is normally appended to the imperative, e.g. إِجْلِسْ، مِنْ فَضْلِكَ is the standard and widely followed form of rendering the dictative meaning of the imperative into the polite meaning of request.

The negative form of the verb is obtained by using the negative particle لَا before the present imperfect verb without disturbing the order of the letters of the verb. Only the last letter of the verb is given sokoon. Other forms of the verb i.e. dual and plural etc, are obtained by applying the same procedure as in the case of the imperative verb. That is to say, we drop all the 'noons ن' and retain only the noon ن of the plural feminine with its original *fathah*. We also suffix the protective alif ا , to the plural masculine form of the verb subject to rules as explained in the imperative. For example:

singualr masculine	لَا تَذْهَبْ	تَذْهَبُ
dual masculine	لَاتَذْهَبَا	تَذْهَبَانِ
plural masculine	لَاتَذْهَبُوا	تَذْهَبُونَ
singular feminine	لَا تَذْهَبِى	تَذْهَبِينَ
dual feminine	لَاتَذْهَبَا	تَذْهَبَانِ
plural feminine	لَاتَذْهَبْنَ	تَذْهَبْنَ

تَفَضَّلْ is the most apt equivalent of "please" which might be used at any occasion without using the required word. For example, opening the door you can invite your visitor inside the house by merely saying تَفَضَّلْ without saying أُدْخُلْ which alone means "enter". Or pointing to a chair you can simply say تَفَضَّلْ and in the context it would mean ''please sit down''. ,

تَفَضَّلْ is aslo thoroughly conjugated on the تَفَعَّلْ pattern.

Imperative for the third & the first persons

For obvious reasons, the third and the first person nouns can not be ordered or dictated to do anything. However, suggestions may be made to them as they may be made to the second person nouns.

This meaning in English is conveyed by the verbs "let, should, must or ought to". Beside other ways of conveying the same meaning in Arabic, we use one ل with *kasrah*. This ل is known in the grammar terminology of the Arabic language as the ل of imperative i.e. لام الامر. This "laam" causes a sokoon to the terminal letter of the present indicative and causes removal of all the ن letters except those of the third and second persons of plural feminine. The meaning of a verb bedecked with this "laam" is interpreted with 'should' or 'let' or any other word with a similar meaning.

If this "laam" is preceded by و and ف "And" and "Then", then this " laam" is given a "sokoon".

And he should go	وَلْيَذْهَبْ
Then he should go	فَلْيَذْهَبْ

Exercises:

1) Make the imperatives and the negatives from the following verbs and use them in sentences of your own:

To drink	شَرِبَ/ يَشْرَبُ/شُرْبًا
To kill	قَتَلَ / يَقْتُلُ/قَتْلًا
To break	كَسَرَ / يَكْسِرُ/كَسْراً
To come forward, to apply	تَقَدَّمَ / يَتَقَدَّمُ/تَقَدُّماً
To be happy	سَعِدَ/ يَسْعَدُ/ سَعَادَةً
To hear; to listen	سَمِعَ/ يَسْمَعُ/ سَمْعًا
To seat	أَجْلَسَ / يُجْلِسُ/ إِجْلَاسًا
To inform	أَخْبَرَ/ يُخْبِرُ/ إِخْبَارًا
To break (into pieces)	كَسَّرَ/ يُكَسِّرُ/ تَكْسِيرًا
To tear	مَزَّقَ/ يُمَزِّقُ/ تَمْزِيقاً
To drive	سَاقَ/ يَسُوقُ/ سَوْقًا
To lead	قَادَ/ يَقُودُ/ قِيَادَةً

2) Translate into Arabic:

(A) 1. Open (PM) your books and read lesson no. 21.

2. Eat (SF) your breakfast and go to your school. You must reach there before eight O' clock.

3. Read (DM) Your lesson aloud and learn it by heart.

4. Please don't shout (PF) at me like this.

5. Don't break (SM) the glass; it is very expensive.

6. Don't enter (PM) his room without his permission.

7. Knock (SF) the door before you enter.

8. Don't drive (SM) the car without licence.

9. Please don't stand (PM) in the passage.

10. Write (SM) a letter immediately after reaching there.

(B) It was a very nice day in the early monsoon season. My children asked me to go to the Zoo. I agreed to this proposal. We started making preparation. My younger daughter took some of her toys. I told her: Don't take your toys. You will have no time to play with them. I told my son: Don't forget drinking water. I told my wife: Please take one or two umbrellas also. When we reached the Zoo I gave money to my children and told them: Go together. Stand in the queue and buy four tickets. Inside the Zoo when we were offering groundnuts to the monkeys, one watchman approached us. He said: Please don't offer anything to the animals. It is not allowed. We moved on from cage to cage and saw many animals and birds. In the evening when we returned home, we were very tired.

3. Translate into English:

بَعْدَ غِيَابٍ يَوْمَيْنِ أَوْ ثَلاَثَةِ أَيَّامٍ ذَهَبْتُ إِلَى الْمَدْرَسَةِ لِحُضُورِ فَصْلِي. رَآنِي الْأُسْتَاذُ وَاسْتَوْقَفَنِي فَوَقَفْتُ. سَأَلَنِي الْأُسْتَاذُ: أَيْنَ كُنْتَ؟ فَقُلْتُ لَهُ: سَيِّدِي، كُنْتُ مَرِيضاً. قَالَ الْأُسْتَاذُ: إِذْهَبْ الآنَ إِلَى نَاظِرِ الْمَدْرَسَةِ وَقَدِّمْ لَهُ طَلَبَ الإِجَازَةِ.

عِنْدَمَا وَصَلْتُ غُرْفَةَ النَّاظِرِ كُنْتُ خَائِفًا. وَلَكِنَّ النَّاظِرَ اسْتَقْبَلَنِي بِبَشَاشَةٍ وَحَرَارَةٍ. فَشَرَحْتُ لَهُ مَطْلُوبِي فَقَالَ لِيَ النَّاظِرُ: اُكْتُبْ لِي طَلَبًا وَجِيْزًا وَوَقِّعْ عَلَيْهِ. وَسَيُوَقِّعُ عَلَيْهِ أَيْضًا وَالِدُكَ. غَدَا تَقَدَّمْ إِلَيَّ بِالطَّلَبِ. بَعْدَ ذَلِكَ عُدْتُ إِلَى فَصْلِي. فَقَالَ الْأُسْتَاذُ: اِجْلِسْ وَ اسْمَعْ إِلَى الدَّرْسِ بِانْتِبَاهٍ وَلاَتُزْعِجْ زُمَلاَئَكَ. فِى نَفْسِ الْوَقْتِ أَخَذَ الطُّلاَّبُ يَتَحَدَّثُونَ فِيمَا بَيْنَهُم فَقَالَ الْأُسْتَاذُ: يَا أَوْلاَدُ، لاَتَتَحَدَّثُوا وَاقْرَءُوا دَرْسَكُمْ جَيِّدًا.

4) Separate the imperative and the negative forms of the verbs from the exercise no. 3 above and use them in sentences of your own.

Glossary:

الكلمات العسيرة:

Before — قَبْلَ

8'O clock — اَلسَّاعَةُ الثَّامِنَةُ

Aloud — بِصَوْتٍ عَالِي / بِصَوْتٍ عَالٍ

To learn by heart	اِسْتَظْهَرَ / يَسْتَظْهِرُ / اِسْتِظْهَارًا
To shout	صَرَخَ / يَصْرُخُ / صُرَاخًا
(He shouted) at me	(صَرَخَ) فِيَّ
Like this	هَكَذَا
To enter	دَخَلَ / يَدْخُلُ / دُخُولاً
Without	بِدُوْنِ ، بِغَيْرِ
Permission/ permit	إِذْنٌ (SM) أُذُونٌ (P)
To break	كَسَرَ / يَكْسِرُ / كَسْرًا
Glass	زُجَاجٌ (SM) زُجَاجَاتٌ (P)
Expensive	ثَمِيْنٌ (Adj. SM)
To knock	طَرَقَ / يَطْرُقُ / طَرْقًا
To drive	سَاقَ / يَسُوقُ / سَوْقًا
Licence	رُخْصَةٌ (SF) رُخَصٌ (P)
To stand	وَقَفَ / يَقِفُ / وُقُوفًا
Passage, way	مَمَرٌّ (SM) مَمَرَّاتٌ (P)
Letter	خِطَابٌ (SM) خِطَابَاتٌ (P)
Immediately after	فَوْرَ
Immediately	فَوْرًا
To search (for)	بَحَثَ / يَبْحَثُ عَنْ (بَحْثًا عَنْ)
To contact (s.o.)	اِتَّصَلَ / يَتَّصِلُ بـ / اِتِّصَالاً
To ask; to request	سَأَلَ / يَسْأَلُ / سُؤَالاً
To beware	اِحْتَرَسَ / يَحْتَرِسُ / اِحْتِرَاسًا
Lesson	دَرْسٌ (SM) دُرُوسٌ (P)
House	بَيْتٌ (SM) بُيُوتٌ (P)
Thief	سَارِقٌ (SM) سَارِقُونَ (P)
Thief	لِصٌّ (SM) لُصُوصٌ (P)
Train	قِطَارٌ (SM) قِطَارَاتٌ (P)
Season	فَصْلٌ (SM) فُصُولٌ (P)

Summer season	صَيْفٌ / فَصْلُ الْصَيْفِ
Because, that is why	لِذَلِك
Journey	سَفَرٌ (SM) أَسْفَارٌ (P)
Comfortable	مُرِيْحٌ (VNSM)
Wine	خَمْرٌ (SMF) خُمُورٌ (P)
To collect; to assemble	جَمَّعَ / يُجَمِّعُ / تَجْمِيعاً
To receive (s.o)	اِسْتَقْبَلَ / يَسْتَقْبِلُ / اِسْتِقْبَالاً
To allow entry	اَدْخَلَ / يُدْخِلُ اِدْخَالاً
Respect	اِحْتِرامٌ

Adjective Of The Comparative And The Superlative Degrees
اسم التفضيل

The city of Delhi is a big city.	مَدِيْنَةُ دِلْهِيْ مَدِيْنَةٌ كَبِيْرَةٌ .
It is divided into Old Delhi	هِيَ مُنْقَسِمَةٌ فِى مَدِيْنَةِ دِلْهِى الْقَدِيْمَةِ
and New Delhi.	وَ دِلْهِى الْجَدِيْدَةِ.
New Delhi is bigger	دِلْهِىْ الْجَدِيْدَةُ اَكْبَرُ
than Old Delhi.	مِنْ دِلْهِى الْقَدِيْمَةِ.
Old Delhi is more congested	دِلْهِى الْقَدِيْمَةُ اَكْثَرُ اِزْدِحَامًا
than New Delhi.	مِنْ دِلْهِىْ الْجَدِيْدَةِ.
In New Delhi the houses are big	فِىْ دِلْهِى الْجَدِيْدَةِ اَلْبُيُوتُ كَبِيْرَةٌ
and the roads are wide.	وَالشَّوَارِعُ وَاسِعَةٌ.
In Old Delhi the houses are small	فِى دِلْهِى الْقَدِيْمَةِ اَلْبُيُوتُ صَغِيْرَةٌ
and the roads are narrow.	وَالشَّوارِعُ ضَيِّقَةٌ.
In New Delhi you will find	فِى دِلْهِى الْجَدِيْدَةِ تَجِدُ
the most important offices	اَهَمَّ الْمَكَاتِبِ
of the government of India.	لِلْحُكُومَةِ الْهِنْدِيَّةِ.
In Delhi you will find the	فِىْ دِلْهِى سَوْفَ تَجِدُ
historical buildings including	الْمَبَانِى التَّارِيْخِيَّةَ بِانْضِمَام
Qutub Minar.	قُطْبْ مِيْنَار.
It is the tallest minaret in India.	هِيَ اَطْوَلُ مَنَارَةٍ فِى الْهِنْدِ.
It is not the oldest building in India.	هِيَ لَيْسَتْ اَقْدَمَ الْمَبَانِىْ فِى الْهِنْدِ.
Beside these monuments	بِجَانِبِ هذِه الآثَارِ
there are found	يُوجَدُ هُنَاك

other places of importance	أَمَاكِنُ الإِهْتِمَامِ الأُخْرَى
like the National Museum	مِن أَمْثَالِ الْمَتْحَفِ الْقَومِى
and the National Archives,	وَمَكْتَبِ الأَرَاشِيفِ الْقَومِى
and the cultural centres	وَمَرَاكِزِ الثَّقَافَةِ
and the scientific research .	وَالْبَحْثِ الْعِلْمِى.
Delhi is a big city	دِلْهِى مَدِينَةٌ كَبِيرَةٌ
and it is known all over the world.	وَهِىَ مَعْرُوفَةٌ فِى كُلِّ الْعَالَمِ.

Grammar:

Indeed the comparative and the superlative dgrees are different forms of simple stative adjective.

In Arabic all such adjectives and adjectival/verbal nouns which are based on triliteral verbs can easily be changed into adjectives of comparative degree by prefixing one alif with fathah to the original or the root letters of the verbs.

In this case the first original letter will have Sokoon, the second letter will have fathah and the third *dammah*.

For example we take the adjective قَصِيرٌ. It means short (in stature or length). This adjective is originally derived from قصر. Now to obtain the comparative degree we have to apply the formula explained above:

$$أَ + قْصَرُ = أَقْصَرُ$$

This form of the adjective will mean: shorter. In English the comparative is followed by 'than', which meaning in Arabic is obtained by using مِنْ.

Thus if we want to say that:

This boy is short......we would say in Arabic هَذَا الْوَلَدُ قَصِيرٌ and if we want to say 'This boy is shorter', we would say in Arabic: هَذَا الْوَلَدُ أَقْصَرُ

However, if we want to say that:

This boy is shorter than that boy, then we would say in Arabic:

هَذَا الْوَلَدُ أَقْصَرُ مِنْ ذَلِكَ الْوَلَدِ.

It may be remembered that the majority of such derived adjectives consists of four letters. In the following are given a few examples of simple adjectives and adjectival nouns being changed into adjectives of comparative degree. Let us take for example:

قَصِيرٌ (من قصر) أَقْصَرُ short Shorter

عَاقِلٌ (من عقل) أَعْقَلُ wise Wiser

جَمِيْلٌ (من جمل) أَجْمَلُ beautiful more beautiful

And if we want to express the superlative degree of the adjective we use only the adjectival noun of comparative degree immediately followed by the plural of the noun bedecked with the definite article ال. In this case also the last letter of the plural noun will have a *kasrah*. Let us suppose that we want to say that: He is the shortest man or He is the 'Shortest' of the men. In Arabic we would express this meaning as under:

هُوَ أَقْصَرُ الرِّجَالِ

There is another way of expressing superlative degree. We can use the comparative degree of the adjective immediately followed by the concerned noun in singular number and in this case the singular noun will not admit the definite article and the terminal letter will take double *kasrah*. Example:

هُوَ أَقْصَرُ رَجُلٍ He is the shortest man

It should also be clarified that this اقصر من in the case of comparative and only أَقْصَرُ in the case of superlative degree respectively are treated as fixed patterns or forms which are used with all nouns irrespective of their number and gender as would become amply evident if you carefully peruse the following sentences:

This man is short.	هَذَا الرَّجُلُ قَصِيرٌ.
This man is shorter than that man.	هَذَا الرَّجُلُ أَقْصَرُ مِنْ ذَلِكَ الرَّجُلِ.
This is the shortest man.	هَذَا أَقْصَرُ الرِّجَالِ.
This boy is tall.	هَذَا الْوَلَدُ طَوِيْلٌ.
This boy is taller than that boy.	هَذَا الْوَلَدُ أَطْوَلُ مِنْ ذَلِكَ الْوَلَدِ.

This is the tallest boy.	هَذَا أَطْوَلُ الأَوْلادِ.
This train is fast.	هَذَا الْقِطَارُ سَرِيعٌ.
This train is faster than that train.	هَذَا الْقِطَارُ أَسْرَعُ مِنْ ذَلِكَ الْقِطَارِ.
This is the fastest train.	هَذَا أَسْرَعُ الْقِطَارَاتِ.
This pen is cheap.	هَذَا الْقَلَمُ رَخِيصٌ.
This pen is cheaper than that pen.	هَذَا الْقَلَمُ أَرْخَصُ مِنْ ذَلِكَ الْقَلَمِ.
This is the cheapest pen.	هَذَا أَرْخَصُ الأَقْلامِ.
This house is beautiful.	هَذَا الْبَيْتُ جَمِيلٌ.
This house is more beautiful than that house.	هَذَا الْبَيْتُ أَجْمَلُ مِنْ ذَلِكَ الْبَيْتِ.
This is the most beautiful house.	هَذَا أَجْمَلُ الْبُيُوتِ.
This girl is tall.	هَذِهِ الْبِنْتُ طَوِيلَةٌ.
This girl is taller than that girl.	هَذِهِ الْبِنْتُ أَطْوَلُ مِنْ تِلْكَ الْبِنْتِ.
This is the tallest girl.	هَذِهِ أَطْوَلُ الْبَنَاتِ.
This girl is taller than that boy.	هَذِهِ الْبِنْتُ أَطْوَلُ مِنْ ذَلِكَ الْوَلَدِ.
This boy is taller than those two boys.	هَذَا الْوَلَدُ أَطْوَلُ مِنْ ذَيْنِكَ الْوَلَدَيْنِ.

In the case of such adjectival nouns which are drawn from the verbs other than the triliteral verbs and in the case of such triliteral verbs where it is not possible to express the adjectival meaning of the comparative degree through the pattern explained above, we use a supporting word (either أَكْثَرُ or أَشَدُّ) of the said pattern followed by the infinitive forms of the verb in the accusative case. For example, if we want to say that: This boy is hardworking, we would say in Arabic:

هَذَا الْوَلَدُ مُجْتَهِدٌ

However, if we want to say that: this boy is more hardworking than that boy, we would say:

هَذَا الْوَلَدُ اَكْثَرُ اِجْتِهَادًا مِنْ ذَلِكَ الْوَلَدِ.

You should carefully note the expression " اَكْثَرُ اِجْتِهَادًا " in the sentence above.

In the case of the superlative meaning this اَكْثَرُ will be immediately followed only by the plural of the concerned noun bedecked with the definite article and this noun will be in the genitive case i.e. its terminal letter will have **kasrah** and then the infinitive form of the verb will come in the accusative case. Suppose here we want to say that: He is the most hardworking boy, we would say in Arabic:

هُوَ اَكْثَرُ الاَوْلَادِ اِجْتِهَاداً

This pattern of comparative degree i.e. اَفْعَلُ is diptote i.e. in the nominative case it takes dammah and in the accusative and genetive cases it takes only fathah unless otherwise it is in the construct phrase where it admits **kasrah** also.

To understand it better, carefully note the following sentences:

قَدِمَ اِلَيَّ وَلَدٌ اَقْصَرُ مِنْ اِبْنِك

(There) came to me a boy shorter than your son.

In the sentence above وَلَدٌ is the subject of the verb قَدِمَ and thus it takes dammah and اَقْصَرُ is the adjective in the comparative degree for qualifying the nominative noun وَلَدٌ and agrees with it beside other things, in case also and it is precisely because of this reason that اقصر is also in the nominative case. Now let us see the following sentence:

رَاَيْتُ وَلَدًا اَقْصَرَ مِنْ اِبْنِك   I saw a boy shorter than your son.

In this sentence the noun وَلَد is the object of the verb رأى and it is therefore in the accusative case marked by fathah and the adjective of the comparative degree qualifying the وَلَدًا agrees with it, beside other things, in case also.

Now there remains with us only the genitive case. Let us see this sentence:

ذَهَبْتُ اِلَى وَلَدٍ اَقْصَرَ   I went to a shorter boy.

Note that the noun وَلَدٍ is in the genitive case as it is preceded by the preposition الى and the adjective of comparative degree اَقْصَرُ should also have

been in the genitive case i.e. it should have borne a *kasrah* at its terminal
letter. However, it is not so because this pattern of اَقْصَرُ is diptote. Hence,
although in the sentence above, it is qualifying a noun of the genitive case,
yet it can admit only fatḥah.

However, if this pattern of comparative adjectival meaning is placed in
construct phrase then it can admit *kasrah* also. For example:

I went to the shortest boy   ذَهَبْتُ إِلَى اَقْصَرِ وَلَدٍ
in the calss.   فِى الْفَصْلِ

I went to the shortest of the boys in   ذَهَبْتُ إِلَى اَقْصَرِ الْاَوْلَادِ
the class.   فِى الْفَصْلِ

In the foregoing two sentences اقصر is in construct phrase with ولد and
الاولاد and it is preceded by preposition الى , therefore, it carries *kasrah*.

Other changing patterns of اَفْعَلُ viz. فُعْلَى for feminine singular or اَفْعَلَانِ
or فُعْلَيَانِ for masculine & feminine dual & فُعْلٌ for plural are very
sparingly used as stative adjectives. For example, we can say هِىَ الْبِنْتُ
الصُّغْرَى She is the youngest daughter. In sum, we can not and we should
not say: هِىَ صُغْرَى مِنْ تِلْكَ الْبِنْتِ . افعل pattern is good enough for expressing
comparative & superlative adjectival meaning as explained above.

Exercises:

(1) Translate into Arabic:

(A)   (1) He is poorer than his brother.

(2) Is your sister bigger than my brothers and sisters.

(3) He is the tallest boy in our class.

(4) I saw a man fatter than your peon.

(5) The girls are more intelligent than the boys.

(6) My brother is more hardworking than you are.

(7) My book is cheaper than your book.

(8) Is your garden more beautiful than my garden.

(9) Do you think that this worker is more honest than those
       workers.

(10) This teacher is more sincere than the students.

(B)

This is our school building. It is an old building. It is older than the mosque beside it. It has many rooms. Some rooms are big and some rooms are small. Calss rooms are bigger than the teachers' rooms. The hall in this school is the biggest of all rooms. This is my classroom. It is a big room. There are thirty boys and girls in my class. Girls are more hardworking than boys.

2) Translate into English:

هَذِهِ حَدِيقَةٌ كَبِيرَةٌ. هِيَ اَكْبَرُ الْحَدَائِقِ فِى كُلِّ الْمَدِينَةِ. فِيهَا اَشْجَارٌ طَوِيلَةٌ وَ اَشْجَارٌ قَصِيرَةٌ. فِيهَا اَشْجَارُ الْأُوْكَالِبْتُوس اَيْضاً. هِيَ اَطْوَلُ مِنْ اَشْجَارِ التِّيْنِ وَلَكِنَّهَا اَهْزَلُ مِنْ اَشْجَارِ التِّيْنِ. لَقَدْ عَشَّشَتِ الطُّيُورُ فِىْ هَذِهِ الْاَشْجَارِ. تُفَضِّلَ الطُّيُورُ الْاَشْجَارَ الطَّوِيلَةَ. فَهِىَ قَلَّمَا تُعَشِّشُ فِى الْاَشْجَارِ ذَاتِ الثِّمَارِ. تَرَى فِىْ هَذِهِ الْحَدِيقَةِ طُيُورًا كَثِيرَةً. بَعْضُهَا صَغِيرَةٌ وَبَعْضُهَا كَبِيرَةٌ. بَعْضُهَا جَمِيْلَةٌ وَبَعْضُهَا عَادِيَةٌ. اَلْحِدَأَةُ اَكْبَرُ مِنَ الْغُرَابِ. اَلْبَبْغَاءُ اَجْمَلُ مِنَ الْغُرَابِ. اَلْعَنْدَلِيْبُ اَصْغَرُ مِنَ الْاِثْنَيْنِ. هُنَاك حَيَوَانَاتٌ كَبِيرَةٌ وَصَغِيْرَةٌ فِىْ هَذِهِ الدُّنْيَا.

(3) Make adjectives of the comparative & the superlative degrees from the following & use them in sentences / paragraphs of your own.

عَالِمٌ/ عَاقِلٌ/ ثَقِيْلٌ/ خَفِيْفٌ/ رَخِيْصٌ/ غَالِى/ غَالِى/ قَصِيْرٌ/ طَوِيْلٌ/ رَحِيْمٌ

(4) Where and how do you make adjectives of comparative & superlative degrees by using words اَشَدُّ / اَكْثَرُ / اَكْبَرُ and اَصْغَرُ. Write a paragraph by using such adjectives.

Glossary:

الكلمات العسيرة

Divided	(Adj. SM) مُنْقَسِمٌ
Bigger	(Adj. com.) اَكْبَرُ
More	(Adj. com.) اَكْثَرُ
Crowd	إِزْدِحَامٌ
Street, road	شَوَارِعُ (SM) شَارِعٌ (P)
Wide, broad	(Adj. SM) وَاسِعٌ

Narrow	ضَيِّق (Adj. SM)
More important	أَهَمُّ
To find	وَجَدَ، يَجِدُ، وُجُودًا
You will find	سَوْفَ تَجِدُ
Building	مَبْنًى (SM) مَبَانِى (P)
Including	بِإِنْضِمَام
Taller, longer	أَطْوَلُ (Adj. com.)
Old	قَدِيمٌ (Adj. SM)
Older	أَقْدَمُ (Adj. com.)
Monument	أَثَرٌ (SM) آثَارٌ (P)
Historical	تَارِيخِىّ (Adj. SM)
Place	مَكَانٌ (SM) أَمَاكِنُ (P)
Places of interest	أَمَاكِنُ الإِهْتِمَام
Museum	مَتْحَفٌ (SM) مَتَاحِفُ (P)
National	قَوْمِىٌّ (Adj. SM)
Archives	أَرْشِيفٌ (SM) أَرَاشِيفُ (P)
Known, well known, famous	مَعْرُوفٌ (Adj. SM)
Poor	فَقِيرٌ (Adj. SM) فُقَرَاءُ (P)
Poorer	أَفْقَرُ (Adj. com.)
Intelligent	ذَكِىٌّ (Adj. SM) أَذْكِيَاءُ (P)
More intelligent	أَذْكَى (Adj. com.)
Hardworking	مُجْتَهِدٌ (Adj. SM) مُجْتَهِدُونَ (P)
More hardworking	أَكْثَرُ إِجْتِهَادًا (Adj. com.)
Cheap	رَخِيصٌ (Adj. SM)
Cheaper	أَرْخَصُ (Adj. com.)
Beautiful	جَمِيلٌ (Adj. SM)
More beautiful	أَجْمَلُ
To think	إِفْتَكَرَ، يَفْتَكِرُ، إِفْتِكَارًا

Honest	أَمِيْنٌ (Adj. SM) أُمَنَاءُ (P)
More honest	أَكْثَرُ أَمَانَةً
Worker	عَامِلٌ (SM) عُمَّالٌ (P)
Sincere	مُخْلِصٌ (Adj. SM) مُخْلِصُونَ (P)
More sincere	أَكْثَرُ إِخْلَاصًا (Adj. com.)
Mosque	مَسْجِدٌ (SM) مَسَاجِدُ (P)
Garden	حَدِيْقَةٌ (SF) حَدَائِقُ (p)
Fig	تِيْنٌ (CNM)
Thin	هَزِيْلٌ (Adj. SM) هَزْلَى (P)
Thinner	أَهْزَلُ (Adj. com.)
To nestle	عَشَّشَ / يُعَشِّشُ / تَعْشِيْشًا
To prefer	فَضَّلَ / يُفَضِّلُ / تَفْضِيْلًا
Hardly	قَلَّمَا(Adv. manner)
Fruit	ثَمَرٌ (SM) ثِمَارٌ (P)
Birds	طَائِرٌ (SM) طُيُورٌ (P)
Ordinary	عَادِيٌّ (Adj. SM)
Kite (bird)	حِدَأَةٌ (SF) حِدَآتٌ (P)
Crow	غُرَابٌ (SM) غِرْبَانٌ (P)
Nightangle	عَنْدَلِيْبٌ (SM) عَنَادِلُ (P)
Animal	حَيَوَانٌ (SM) حَيَوَانَاتٌ (P)
Heavy	ثَقِيْلٌ (Adj. SM)
Light	خَفِيْفٌ (Adj. SM)
High, lofty	عَالِى(Adj. SM)(عَالٍ)
Dear, expensive	غَالِى (Adj. SM)(غَالٍ)
Kind	رَحِيْمٌ (Adj. SM)
Hard, tough	شَدِيْدٌ (Adj. SM)
Harder, tougher	أَشَدُّ (Adj. com)

Adjectives Of Colours & Physical Defects
الالوان والعيوب البدنية

John works in a private office	يَعْمَلُ جَون فِى مَكْتَبٍ خَاصٍّ
in New Delhi.	بِنِيُو دِلْهِى.
John goes to his office in his car.	يَذْهَبُ جَون اِلَى مَكْتَبِهِ فِىْ سَيَّارَتِه.
The colour of his car is red.	لَوْنُ سَيَّارَتِهِ اَحْمَرُ.
John bought it one year ago or so.	اِشْتَرَاهَا جَون قَبْلَ عَامٍ اَوْ كَذَا.
This is Sheela.	هَذِهِ شِيْلَا.
She is John's wife.	هِىَ زَوْجَةُ جَون.
She works in the Home Ministry.	هِىَ تَعْمَلُ فِى وِزَرَاةِ الدَّاخِلِيَّةِ.
This is her personal car.	هَذِهِ سَيَّارَتُهَا الْخَاصَّةُ.
It is black.	هِىَ سَوْدَاءُ.
Sheela bought it one year ago or so.	اِشْتَرَتْهَا شِيْلَا قَبْلَ عَامٍ اَوْ كَذَا.
The red & black cars	اِنَّ السَّيَّارَاتِ الْحَمْرَاءَ وَالسَّوْدَاءَ
are many in our city.	كَثِيْرَةٌ جِدًّا فِىْ مَدِيْنَتِنَا.
However, men & women,	اَمَّا الرِّجَالُ وَالنِّسَاءُ
we are brown and black.	فَنَحْنُ سُمْرٌ وَسُوْدٌ.
This is Faheem.	هَذَا فَهِيْمٌ.
He too works in the Home Ministry.	هُوَ اَيْضًا يَعْمَلُ فِى وِزَارَةِ الدَّاخِلِيَّةِ.
The Goverment has reserved some jobs	خَصَّصَتِ الْحُكُومَةُ عَدَدًا مِنَ الْوَظَائِفِ
for the blind & the lame.	لِلْعُمْى وَالْعُرْجِ.
This man is black.	١ هَذَا الرَّجُلُ اَسْوَدُ.
These two men are black.	٢ هَذَانِ الرَّجُلَانِ اَسْوَدَانِ.

These men are black.	3 هٰؤُلَاءِ الرِّجَالُ سُودٌ.
This girl is black.	4 هٰذِهِ الْبِنْتُ سَوْدَاءُ
These two girls are black.	5 هَاتَانِ الْبِنْتَانِ سَوْدَاوَانِ.
These girls are black.	6 هٰؤُلَاءِ الْبَنَاتُ سُودٌ.
This dog is black.	7 هٰذَا الْكَلْبُ اَسْوَدُ.
These two dogs are black.	8 هٰذَانِ الْكَلْبَانِ اَسْوَدَانِ.
These dogs are black.	9 هٰذِهِ الْأَكْلَابِ سَوْدَاءُ.
This bitch is black.	10 هٰذِهِ الْكَلْبَةُ سَوْدَاءُ.
These two bitches are black.	11 هَاتَانِ الْكَلْبَتَانِ سَوْدَاوَانِ.
These bitches are black.	12 هٰذِهِ الْكَلْبَاتُ سَوْدَاءُ.
This car is black.	13 هٰذِهِ السَّيَّارَةُ سَوْدَاءُ.
These two cars are black.	14 هَاتَانِ السَّيَّارَتَانِ سَوْدَاوَانِ.
These cars are black.	15 هٰذِهِ السَّيَّارَاتُ سَوْدَاءُ.
What colour is the car.	16 مَالَوْنُ السَّيَّارَةِ؟
The car is black.	17 اَلسَّيَّارَةُ سَوْدَاءُ.
The colour of the car is black.	18 لَوْنُ السَّيَّارَةِ اَسْوَدُ.

Grammar

The adjectives of colour and physical defect have a set pattern in the Arabic language.

It is drawn on اَفْعَلُ pattern for a masculine object of singular number and on the فَعْلَاءُ pattern for a singular feminine object.

In the case of dual number ان is suffixed to the singular number of both the genders, however, in the case of the feminine, the terminal Hamza ء is changed into و.

In the case of plural noun the فُعْلٌ pattern is used. However, its use is confined to the plurals of such nouns only which indicate humanbeings. See sentences numbers 3 & 6.

For plurals of such nouns which indicate non-humanbeings the singular feminine form is used irrespective of the gender of the noun qualified by the adjective of colour and physical defect. See sentences numbers 9, 12 & 15 above.

Adjective of colour and physical defect comes after the noun it qualifies like any other ordinary adjective in Arabic.

It completely agrees with its noun as explained in lesson No:22. The adjective of colour and physical defect is diptote and admits one dammah in the nominative case and one fathah in the accusative and genitive cases.

Example:

A black boy came.	قَدِمَ وَلَدٌ اَسْوَدُ.
I saw a black boy.	رَأَيْتُ وَلَدًا اَسْوَدَ.
I went to a black boy.	ذَهَبْتُ إِلَى وَلَدٍ اَسْوَدَ.

In the case of comparative meaning, the word اَشَدُّ/اَكْثَرُ is used followed by the noun of colour and the infinitve form of the verb of physical defect in the accusative case. Suppose that we want to say: This man is blacker (more black) than that man, we would say in Arabic:

هَذَا الرَّجُلُ اَكْثَرُ / اَشَدُّ سَوَادًا مِنْ ذَلِكَ الرَّجُلِ

Adjectival noun of dual number denoting colour and physical defect is declinable as per rules regarding the dual noun.

Example:

قَدِمَ رَجُلَانِ اَسْوَدَانِ.

رَأَيْتُ رَجُلَيْنِ اَسْوَدَيْنِ.

ذَهَبْتُ إِلَى رَجُلَيْنِ اَسْوَدَيْنِ.

Where the meaning of the superlative degree is required the word اَشَدُّ / اَكْثَرُ is immediately followed by the plural of the concerned noun bedecked with the definite article Al الـ which in turn is followed by the noun of clour in the accusative case.

Example: He is the blackest man هُوَ اَكْثَرُ الرِّجَالِ سَوَادًا

The word for colour is لَوْنٌ, Its plural is اَلْوَانٌ i. e. colours.

When we want to ask about the colour of some person or some other thing, we use the interrogative pronoun مَا meaning what, followed by the word لون and then the concerned noun is placed in the genitive case bedecked with the definite article Al الـ or else it should be placed in construct position with a pronoun or a proper noun or a defined noun.

Example:

What colour is the shirt?	مَا لَوْنُ الْقَمِيْصِ؟
Or	
What is the colour of the shirt?	
What colour is your shirt?	مَالَوْنُ قَمِيْصِك
What colour is the car?	مَا لَوْنُ السَّيَّارَةِ؟

In reply if we want to say that:

The shirt is black, we would say in Arabic:

اَلْقَمِيْصُ اَسْوَدُ

Here, because the shirt i.e. القميص is a masculine gender noun of singular number, therefore, we use اسود the adjective of colour on the اَفْعَلُ pattern which is used for singular masculine. However, if we want to reply the second question i.e. ما لون السيارة؟

We would say:

اَلسَّيَّارَةُ سَوْدَاءُ

Here, in this case the car i.e. اَلسَّيَّارَةُ is a feminine gender noun of singular number, therefore, we say سَوْدَاءُ on the فَعْلَاءُ pattern which pattern is used for singular feminine. As has been made amply clear in lesson number 22, that the adjective agrees with its noun in number, gender, definiteness, indefiniteness and cases, except that the plural of the non-personal noun whether masculine or feminine, is treated as singular of the feminine gender. For example, if we want to say that: The cars are black, we would say:

اَلسَّيَّارَاتُ سَوْدَاءُ

or if we want to say: The shirts are black, we would say:

اَلْقُمْصَانُ سَوْدَاءُ

We can also say as follows:

The cars' colour is black, or   لَوْنُ السَّيَّارَاتِ اَسْوَدُ

The shirts' colour is black.   لَوْنُ الْقُمْصَانِ اَسْوَدُ

It may be added here that in this case in fact, اسود qualifies the word لون
which may be written before اسود. However, because context dictates that,
therefore, it is not written.

The plural of اَفْعَلُ and فَعْلَاءُ is drawn on the pattern of فُعْلٌ and this pattern
indicating plural is used only for personal nouns i.e. humanbeings.

Example:

The man is red (SM)   اَلرَّجُلُ اَحْمَرُ

The woman is red (SF)   اَلْمَرْأَةُ حَمْرَاءُ

The men are red (PM)   اَلرِّجَالُ حُمْرٌ

The women are red (PF)   اَلنِّسَاءُ حُمْر

The adjectives of physical defects are used similarly i.e. they also have to be
in complete agreement with their nouns they qualify.

Example:

A lame boy came.   قَدِمَ وَلَدٌ اَعْرَجُ

I saw a lame boy.   رَأَيْتُ وَلَدًا اَعْرَجَ

I went with a lame boy.   ذَهَبْتُ مَعَ وَلَدٍ اَعْرَجَ

Note: It may be mentioned here that the adjectives of the colour and the
physical defect of the singular number are treated as diptote as shown in
examples above while the duals and plurals are triptote. However, if the
singular adjective of colour or physical defect is bedecked with the definite
article 'al ال' then it is treated as triptote. In fact all diptote nouns in Arabic
are treated as triptotes if they carry al ال or if they are in construct position.
For example we would say:

I went with the lame boy   ذَهَبْتُ مَعَ الْوَلَدِ الْاَعْرَجِ

Some colours

بعض الالوان

	جمع	مفرد مؤنث	مفرد مذكر
White	بِيْضٌ	بَيْضَاءُ	اَبْيَضُ
Red	حُمْرٌ	حَمْرَاءُ	اَحْمَرُ
Blue	زُرْقٌ	زَرْقَاءُ	اَزْرَق
Brown/ Tan	سُمْرٌ	سَمْرَاءُ	اَسْمَرُ
Green	خُضْرٌ	خَضْرَاءُ	اَخْضَرُ
Yellow	صُفْرٌ	صَفْرَاءُ	اَصْفَرُ

Some physical defects:

بعض العيوب البدنية

One eyed	عُوْرٌ	عَوْرَاءُ	اَعْوَرُ
Blind	عُمْىٌ	عَمْيَاءُ	اَعْمَى
Lame	عُرْجٌ	عَرْجَاءُ	اَعْرَجُ
Dumb	بُكْمٌ	بَكْمَاءُ	اَبْكَمُ
Deaf	صُمٌّ	صَمَّاءُ	اَصَمُّ

Exercises:

1. Translate into Arabic:

A: 1)   Is he blind?

2)   Are they lame?

3)   I saw a red car.

4)   Did you meet the two deaf boys?

5)   He met the Red Indians.

6)   These two black girls are from Sudan.

7)   What colour are your dogs?

8)   My dogs are black.

9)   I want to see a dumb boy.

10) These trees are tall and they have green leaves and yellow flowers.

(B)   One day, in the early morning I went out for a walk. I came out of my house and saw a black dog. This black dog is in fact an unpaid watchman of this locality. There is a big group of dogs and bitches. There is a black bitch in this group. It has two black puppies and seven brown puppies. There are many other bitches in this group. Two bitches are black and five are brown. In this group there is a lame dog and a blind bitch. Two other dogs are blind and two more bitches are lame.

These lame and blind dogs and bitches do not move much from their place. The other healthy dogs and bitches take care of them. They help them with food. These are animals. Humanbeings are not this good. They have reasons and reasons to trouble and harm other people. I know an old and blind man. His people have abondoned him. Now he lives with other blind and lame people on the street. This black girl has a very sad story. She was lured away from her house by a handsome and brown boy. He exploited her and abondoned her. Now she lives on the street with all kinds of people. They are black. They are white. They are brown. Let us hope our society will do something to prevent the sufferings of the people. I was walking with so many things on my mind. I did not know the passage of the time. I had completed my round and now I was standing at my door. I had come back home.

2. Separate the adjectives of colours and physical defects from question no. 2 and 3 and use them in your own sentences.

3. Translate into English:

الف: ١. اِشْتَرَيْتُ سَيَّارَةً سَوْدَاءَ.

٢. قَدِمَتْ إِلَيَّ إِمْرَأَتَانِ عَمْيَاوَانِ.

٣. مَالَوْنُ قَمِيصِكَ؟

٤. قَدَّمَتِ الْحُكُوْمَةُ مُسَاعَدَاتٍ مَالِيَّةً لِلنِّسَاءِ الْعُمْيِ.

٥. زُرْتُ مِنْطَقَةً خَضْرَاءَ جِدًّا فِى وِلَايَةٍ كِيْرَالَا بِالْهِنْدِ.

٦. اَلسُّودُ وَالْبِيْضُ سَوَاءٌ.

٧. اَلْجَامُوْسَةُ سَوْدَاءُ وَالْبَقَرَةُ بَيْضَاءُ.

٨. زُرْتُ وَلَدَيْنِ اَعْرَجَيْنِ فِى الْمُسْتَشْفَىٰ.

٩. عَالَجَ الدُّكْتُورُ بِنْتًا عَرْجَاءَ بِنَجَاحٍ.

١٠. هَلْ تَعْرِفُ اَنَّهُ اَصَمُّ وَاَبْكَمُ؟

ب: مَرَّةً رَأَيْتُ مَنْظَرًا مُدْهِشًا لِلْغَايَةِ. كُنْتُ أَذْهَبُ فِى سَيَّارَتِى السَّوْدَاءِ إِلَى كُلِّيَّتِى. كَانَ الشَّارِعُ الرَّئِيْسُ مُزْدَحِمًا لِلْغَايَةِ بِالسَّيَّارَاتِ. رَأَيْتُ وَلَداً اَعْمَى مَعَ وَلَدٍ اَعْرَجَ. بَدَا أَنَّهُمَا صَدِيْقَانِ وَ يَسْكُنَانِ وَيَعْمَلَانِ سَوِيًّا. جَلَسَ الْوَلَدُ الْأَعْرَجُ عَلَى مَنْكِبَى الْوَلَدِ الْأَعْمَىٰ. وَاَرْشَدَ الْوَلَدُ الْأَعْرَجُ الْوَلَدَ الْأَعْمَىٰ حَتَّى عَبَرَا الطَّرِيْقَ بِسَلَامَةٍ. تَعَجَّبْتُ كَثِيْرًا مِنْ هَذِهِ الصَّدَاقَةِ الْعَمَلِيَّةِ بَيْنَ الْأَعْمَىٰ وَ الْأَعْرَجِ. بَدَأْتُ اُفَكِّرُ فِى مَوْضُوعِ التَّعَاوُنِ بَيْنَ الْجَمِيْعِ عَلَى نِطَاقٍ اَوْسَعَ لِتَحْقِيْقِ الرَّخَاءِ وَ الرَّفَاهِيَّةِ فِى هَذِهِ الدُّنْيَا.

Glossary	الكلمات العسيرة
Colour	لَوْنٌ (SM) اَلْوَانٌ (P)
Defect	عَيْبٌ (SM) عُيُوبٌ (P)
Red	أَحْمَرُ (SM) حَمْرَاءِ (SF) حُمْرٌ (P)
To buy	إِشْتَرَى / يَشْتَرِى / إِشْتِرَاءً
Year	عَامٌّ (SM) اَعْوَامٌ (P)
Husband, spouse,	زَوج (SM) ازوَاجٌ (P)
Wife	زَوجَةٌ (SF) زَوجَاتٌ (P)
To work	عَمِلَ / يَعْمَلُ / عَمَلاً
Ministry	وِزَارَةٌ (SF) وِزَارَاتٌ (P)
Home ministry	وِزَارَةُ الدَّاخِلِيَّةِ
Black	اسوَدُ (SM) سَوداءُ (SF) سُودٌ (P)
Tan, wheatish, brown	أَسمَرُ (SM) سَمْرَاءُ (SF) سُمْرٌ (P)

To allocate , to set apart	خَصَّصَ / يُخَصِّصُ / تَخْصِيصًا
Number	عَدَدٌ (SM) أَعْدَادٌ (P)
Blind	أَعْمَى (SM) عَمْيَاءُ (SF) عُمْىٌ (P)
Shirt	قَمِيْصٌ (SM) قُمْصَانٌ (P)
To offer, to present	قَدَّمَ / يُقَدِّمُ / تَقْدِيْمًا
Help, relief	مُسَاعَدَةٌ (SF) مُسَاعَدَاتٌ (P)
Financial, monetary	مَالِيٌّ (Adj. SM)
To visit	زَارَ / يَزُورُ / زِيَارَةً
Green	أَخْضَرُ (SM) خَضْرَاءُ (SF) خُضْرٌ (P)
White	أَبْيَضُ (SM) بَيْضَاءُ (SF) بِيْضٌ (P)
Buffalo	جَامُوسٌ (SM) جَامُوسَةٌ (SF) جَوَامِيْسُ (P)
Cow	بَقَرٌ (SM) بَقَرَةٌ (SF)
Lame	أَعْرَجُ (SM) عَرْجَاءُ (SF) عُرْجٌ (P)
Hospital	مُسْتَشْفَى (SM) مُسْتَشْفَيَاتٌ (P)
To treat; to handle	عَالَجَ / يُعَالِجُ / مُعَالَجَةً
Success	نَجَاحٌ (SM) نَجَاحَاتٌ (P)
Deaf	أَصَمُّ (SM) صَمَّاءُ (SF) صُمٌّ (P)
Dumb	أَبْكَمُ (SM) بَكْمَاءُ (SF) بُكْمٌ (P)
Strange, awe striking	مُدْهِشٌ (Adj. SM)
To live	سَكَنَ / يَسْكُنُ / سُكُونًا
Together	سَوِيًّا
Shoulder	مَنْكِبٌ (SF) مَنَاكِبُ (P) *
To guide	أَرْشَدَ / يُرْشِدُ / إِرْشَادًا

---

* Generally body parts in pairs are treated as feminine gender nouns.

To cross	عَبَرَ / يَعْبُرُ / عُبُورًا
Safety	سَلَامَةٌ (SF) سَلَامَاتٌ (P)
To wonder	تَعَجَّبَ / يَتَعَجَّبُ / تَعَجُّبًا
Practical	عَمَلِيٌّ (Adj. SM)
To begin	بَدَأَ / يَبْدَأُ / بَدْءَ
To think	فَكَّرَ / يُفَكِّرُ / تَفْكِيرًا
Topic, subject	مَوضُوعٌ (SM) مَوضُوعَاتٌ (P)
Cooperation	تَعَاوُنٌ (SM)
Wide, broad	وَسِيعٌ (Adj. SM)
Wider, broader	أوسَعُ (Adj. com)
Scale, level	نِطَاقٌ (SM) نِطَاقَاتٌ (P)
Prosperity	رَخَاءُ (SM)
Prosperity	رَفَاهِيَّةٌ (SF)
To achieve, to realise	حَقَّقَ / يُحَقِّقُ / تَحْقِيقًا

LESSON – 26

الدرس –٢٦

The Number & The Noun Qualified
By The Number

العدد والمعدود

Cardinal Number

العدد الاصلى

This is a private school for teaching the foreign languages.	هَذِهِ مَدْرَسَةٌ خَاصَّةٌ لِتَعْلِيمِ اللُّغَاتِ الْأَجْنَبِيَّةِ.
For this school i.e. this school has a grand building.	لِهَذِهِ الْمَدْرَسَةِ مَبْنًى فَخْمٌ.
In it i.e. it has three floors.	فِيهِ ثَلَاثَةُ أَدْوَارٍ.
This school organises private lessons in all the major languages of the world including German, French, Chinese, Japanese, Arabic, English and Russian.	تُنَظِّمُ هَذِهِ الْمَدْرَسَةُ الدُّرُوسَ الْخُصُوصِيَّةَ فِى جَمِيعِ لُغَاتِ الْعَالَمِ الرَّئِيسِيَّةِ، مِنْهَا اَللُّغَةُ الْأَلْمَانِيَّةُ وَاللُّغَةُ الْفَرَنْسِيَّةُ وَاللُّغَةُ الصِّينِيَّةُ وَاللُّغَةُ الْيَابَانِيَّةُ وَاللُّغَةُ الْعَرَبِيَّةُ وَاللُّغَةُ الانجِلِيزِيَّةُ وَاللُّغَةُ الرُّوسِيَّةُ.
These are seven languages.	هِىَ سَبْعُ لُغَاتٍ.
I study the Arabic language.	اَدْرُسُ اللُّغَةَ الْعَرَبِيَّةَ.
There are fifteen girl students and fifteen boy students in my class.	هُنَاك خَمْسَ عَشَرَةَ طَالِبَةً وَخَمْسَةَ عَشَرَ طَالِباً فِى فَصْلِى.
They are thirty boy & girl students in my class.	هُمْ ثَلَاثُونَ طَالِبًا وَطَالِبَةً فِى فَصْلِى.

There work in this school	هُنَاكَ يَعْمَلُ فِىْ هَذِهِ الْمَدْرَسَةِ
twenty five male teachers	خَمْسَةٌ وَّ عِشْرُونَ مُدَرِّسًا
and twenty five female teachers.	وَ خَمْسٌ وَّ عِشْرُونَ مُدَرِّسَةً.
The number of boy & girl students	يَبْلُغُ عَدَدُ الدَّارِسِيْنَ وَ الدَّارِسَاتِ
in this school	فِى هَذِهِ الْمَدْرَسَةِ
is estimated at one hundred	(يَبْلُغُ) مِئَةَ
(boy) students and one hundred thirty	طَالِبٍ وَمِئَةً وَّ ثَلَاثِيْنَ
(girl) students.	طَالِبَةً.

Numerals:

		For feminine Nouns	For Masculine Nouns	Arabic Numerals
1	One	وَاحِدَةٌ	وَاحِدٌ	١
2	Two	إِثْنَتَان	إِثْنَان	٢
3	Three	ثَلَاثٌ	ثَلَاثَةٌ	٣
4	Four	أَرْبَعٌ	أَرْبَعَةٌ	٤
5	Five	خَمْسٌ	خَمْسَةٌ	٥
6	Six	سِتٌّ	سِتَّةٌ	٦
7	Seven	سَبْعٌ	سَبْعَةٌ	٧
8	Eight	ثَمَان (ثَمَانِى)	ثَمَانِيَةٌ	٨
9	Nine	تِسْعٌ	تِسْعَةٌ	٩
10	Ten	عَشَرٌ	عَشَرَةٌ	١٠
11	Eleven	إِحْدىٰ عشرة	أَحَدَعَشَرَ	١١
12	Twelve	إِثْنَتَا عَشَرَةَ	إِثْنَا عَشَرَ	١٢
13	Thirteen	ثَلَاثَ عَشَرَةَ	ثَلَاثَةَ عَشَرَ	١٣
14	Fourteen	أَرْبَعَ عَشَرَةَ	أَرْبَعَةَ عَشَرَ	١٤
15	Fifteen	خَمْسَ عَشَرَةَ	خَمْسَةَ عَشَرَ	١٥

16	Sixteen	سِتَّ عَشَرَةَ	سِتَّةَ عَشَرَ	١٦
17	Seventeen	سَبْعَ عَشَرَةَ	سَبْعَةَ عَشَرَ	١٧
18	Eighteen	ثَمَانِى عَشَرَةَ	ثَمَانِيَةَ عَشَرَ	١٨
19	Nineteen	تِسْعَ عَشَرَةَ	تِسْعَةَ عَشَرَ	١٩
20	Twenty	عِشْرُوْنَ	عِشْرُونَ	٢٠
30	Thirty	ثَلَاثُونَ	ثَلَاثُونَ	٣٠
40	Forty	أَرْبَعُونَ	أَرْبَعُونَ	٤٠
50	Fifty	خَمْسُونَ	خَمْسُونَ	٥٠
60	Sixty	سِتُّونَ	سِتُّونَ	٦٠
70	Seventy	سَبْعُونَ	سَبْعُونَ	٧٠
80	Eighty	ثَمَانُونَ	ثَمَانُونَ	٨٠
90	Ninety	تِسْعُونَ	تِسْعُونَ	٩٠
100	Hundred	مِائَةٌ/مِئَةٌ	مِائَةٌ/مِئَةٌ	١٠٠

Group One

Three boys came to my house.
قَدِمَ ثَلَاثَةُ أَوْلَادٍ إِلَى بَيْتِى.

Three girls came to my house.
قَدِمَتْ ثَلَاثُ بَنَاتٍ إِلَى بَيْتِى.

I saw three boys in the playground.
رَأَيْتُ ثَلَاثَةَ أَوْلَادٍ فِى الْمَلْعَبِ.

I saw three girls in the playground.
رَأَيْتُ ثَلَاثَ بَنَاتٍ فِى الْمَلْعَبِ.

I sat with three boys in the restaurant.
جَلَسْتُ مَعَ ثَلَاثَةِ أَوْلَادٍ فِى الْمَطْعَمِ.

I sat with three girls in the restaurant.
جَلَسْتُ مَعَ ثَلَاثِ بَنَاتٍ فِى الْمَطْعَمِ.

Group Two

Thirteen boys came to my house.
قَدِمَ ثَلَاثَةَ عَشَرَ وَلَدًا إِلَى بَيْتِى.

Thirteen girls came to my house.
قَدِمَتْ ثَلَاثَ عَشَرَةَ بِنْتًا إِلَى بَيْتِى.

I saw thirteen boys in the playground.
رَأَيْتُ ثَلَاثَةَ عَشَرَ وَلَداً فِى الْمَلْعَبِ.

I saw thirteen girls in the playground.
رَأَيْتُ ثَلَاثَ عَشَرَةَ بِنْتًا فِى الْمَلْعَبِ.

I sat with thirteen boys	جَلَسْتُ مَعَ ثَلَاثَةَ عَشَرَ وَلَداً
in the restaurant.	فِى الْمَطْعَمِ.
I sat with thirteen girls	جَلَسْتُ مَعَ ثَلَاثَ عَشَرَةَ بِنْتاً
in the restaurant.	فِى الْمَطْعَمِ.

Group Three

One hundred boys came to my house.	قَدِمَ مِئَةُ وَلَدٍ إِلَى بَيْتِى.
One hundred girls came to my house.	قَدِمَتْ مِئَةُ بِنْتٍ إِلَى بَيْتِى.
I saw one hundred boys	رَأَيْتُ مِئَةَ وَلَدٍ
in the playground.	فِى الْمَلْعَبِ.
I saw one hundred girls	رَأَيْتُ مِئَةَ بِنْتٍ
in the playground.	فِى الْمَلْعَبِ.
I sat with one hundred boys	جَلَسْتُ مَعَ مِئَةِ وَلَدٍ
in the canteen.	فِى الْمَطْعَمِ.
I sat with one hundred girls in the restaurant	جَلَسْتُ مَعَ مِئَةِ بِنْتٍ فِى الْمَطْعَمِ.

Grammar:

The usage of Arabic numerals is slightly typical. It is therefore essential to read this lesson very carefully and note the important points.

We have known that all nouns which have Taa Marboota ة as their teminal letter, are feminine in gender. These Arabic numerals too are (adjectival) nouns and the same rule applies to them also. For example ثَلَاث (three) is a masculine gender noun because it does not end with Taa Marboota ة and if we suffix to it the Taa Marbuta ة and say ثَلَاثَةٌ it would be treated as a feminine gender noun because of the presence of the Taa marboota.

To learn the usage of these numerals quickly and correctly, following points have to be borne in mind:

The numbers given above are cardinal numbers i.e. العدد الاصلى.

The cardinal number in Arabic always precedes the noun it qualifies.

The numbers one and two i.e. وَاحِدٌ & اِثْنَانِ in the case of masculine nouns and وَاحِدَةٌ & اِثْنَتَان in the case of feminine nouns are normally not used to indicate the singularity and duality of the noun as the same is denoted by the nouns themselves. For example كِتَابٌ or كِتَابًا or كِتَابٍ in their respective cases shall mean only one book and likewise the dual form of the nouns shall enable us to dispense with the number indicating two. For example كِتَابَان & كِتَابَيْنِ shall mean only two books in their respective cases. And where these numbers are used, they shall be used only after the nouns they qualify as their adjectives and render their meaning into emphatic. For example كِتَابٌ وَاحِدٌ and كِتَابَانِ اِثْنَانِ shall mean "only one book" or "only two books" respectively.

For the convenience of the readers usage of Arabic numerals has been explained under three groups as follows:

Group One

The factual usage of the Arabic numerals begins from three onwards.

From three to ten if the noun qualified by the number is masculine, in that case:

1) The number shall be feminine i.e. the number with Taa marboota ة will be used.

2) The noun qualified shall be plural.

3) The noun qualified shall not admit the definite article.

4) The noun qualified shall be in the genitive case i.e. its terminal letter shall bear *kasrah*.

For Example:

Three boys came to my house.   قَدِمَ ثَلَاثَةُ أَوْلَادٍ إِلَى بَيْتِي.

I saw three boys in the playground   رَأَيْتُ ثَلَاثَةَ أَوْلَادٍ فِى الْمَلْعَبِ.

I sat with three boys in the restaurant.   جَلَسْتُ مَعَ ثَلَاثَةِ أَوْلَادٍ فِى المطْعَمِ.

Where the noun qualified by the number is feminine, in that case:

the number shall be masculine in gender i.e. the number shall be without Taa marboota ة, and other instructions shall remain the same as in the case of the masculine nouns as explained above.

For Example:

Three girls came to my house.	قَدِمَتْ ثَلَاثُ بَنَاتٍ إِلَى بَيْتِى.
I saw three girls in the playground.	رَأَيْتُ ثَلَاثَ بَنَاتٍ فِى المَلْعَبِ.
I sat with three girls in the restaurant.	جَلَسْتُ مَعَ ثَلَاثِ بَنَاتٍ فِى المَطْعَمِ.

Group Two

From eleven to ninetynine the noun qualified by the number shall be singular in the accusative case and the number shall be as per details below:

The "tens" from twenty onwards are common for both the genders i.e. twenty & thirty etc. will be used for the nouns of both the genders and also they will decline according to the case. In the nominative case these will end with وُنَ. For example if we want to say that: twenty boys/girls came to my house, we would say in Arabic:

قَدِمَ عِشْرُونَ طَالِباً إِلَى بَيْتِى.

قَدِمَتْ عِشْرُونَ طَالِبَةً إِلَى بَيْتِى.

In the accusative and genitive cases the number shall take ين termination.

Example:

I saw twenty boys.	رَأَيْتُ عِشْرِينَ وَلَداً.
I saw twenty girls.	رَأَيْتُ عِشْرِينَ بِنْتاً.
I sat with twenty boys.	جَلَسْتُ مَعَ عِشْرِينَ وَلَداً.
I sat with twenty girls.	جَلَسْتُ مَعَ عِشْرِينَ بِنْتاً.

In the case of eleven & twelve both the components of the compound number shall have to agree with their noun in gender. For example:

(A)

i)	Eleven boys came to my house.	قَدِمَ أَحَدَ عَشَرَ وَلَداً إِلَى بَيْتِى.
ii)	Twelve boys came to my house.	قَدِمَ اثْنَا عَشَرَ وَلَداً إِلَى بَيْتِى.

(B)

i)	Eleven girls came to my house.	قَدِمَتْ إِحْدَى عَشَرَةَ بِنْتاً إِلَى بَيْتِى.

ii) Twelve girls came to my house.   قَدِمَتْ اِثْنَتَا عَشَرَةَ بِنْتًا اِلَى بَيْتِى.

In the case of twelve, the first component i.e. the unit only of this compound number in both the genders shall decline in the accusative and genitive cases. For example:

I saw twelve boys.   رَأَيْتُ اِثْنَى عَشَرَ وَلَداً.

I saw twelve girls.   رَأَيْتُ اِثْنَتَى عَشَرَةَ بِنْتاً.

I sat with twelve boys.   جَلَسْتُ مَعَ اِثْنَى عَشَرَ وَلَدًا.

I sat with twelve girls.   جَلَسْتُ مَعَ اِثْنَتَى عَشَرَةَ بِنْتاً.

Eleven & thirteen onwards unto nineteen both the components of the compound number are indeclinable i.e. both the components shall carry fathah irrespective of the case of the noun they qualify in terms of nominative, accusative and genitive cases. For example, we would say:

Thirteen boys came.   قَدِمَ ثَلَاثَةَ عَشَرَ وَلَداً

I saw thirteen boys.   رَأَيْتُ ثَلَاثَةَ عَشَرَ وَلَداً

I sat with thirteen boys.   جَلَسْتُ مَعَ ثَلَاثَةَ عَشَرَ وَلَداً.

In the case of twentyone & twentytwo & other similar numbers the "ten" component of the compound number shall be commonly used for nouns of both the genders and the "unit" component shall agree in gender with the noun they qualify and both the components of the number shall be declinable according to the case.

Example:

21 boys came.   قَدِمَ وَاحِدٌ وَّعِشْرُونَ وَلَداً.

I saw 21 boys.   رَأَيْتُ وَاحِداً وَّ عِشْرِينَ وَلَداً.

I sat with 21 boys.   جَلَسْتُ مَعَ وَاحِدٍ وَّ عِشْرِينَ وَلَدًا.

In the case of twenty three and other numbers till ninetynine (barring 31, 32 and similar numbers) the first component of the compound number shall be feminine in the case of a masculine noun and in the case of a feminine noun the same shall be in the masculine gender. Both the components shall decline according to the case.

Example:

23 boys came.	قَدِمَ ثَلاثَةٌ وَّ عِشْرُونَ وَلَداً.
I saw 23 boys.	رَأَيْتُ ثَلاثَةً وَّعِشْرِينَ وَلَداً.
I sat with 23 boys.	جَلَسْتُ مَعَ ثَلاثَةٍ وَّ عِشْرِينَ وَلَدَا.
23 girls came.	قَدِمَتْ ثَلاثٌ وَّ عِشْرُونَ بِنْتاً.
I saw 23 girls.	رَأَيْتُ ثَلاثًا وَّ عِشْرِينَ بِنْتاً.
I sat with 23 girls.	جَلَسْتُ مَعَ ثَلاثٍ وَّ عِشْرِينَ بِنْتاً.

Group Three

In the case of hundred the noun qualified shall always be singular and in the genitive case. The number shall be declinable according to the case.

Example:

One hundred boys came.	قَدِمَ مِائَةُ وَلَدٍ.
I saw one hundred boys.	رَأَيْتُ مِائَةَ وَلَدٍ.
I sat with one hundred boys.	جَلَسْتُ مَعَ مِائَةِ وَلَدٍ.
One hundred girls came.	قَدِمَتْ مِائَةُ بِنْتٍ.
I saw one hundred girls.	رَأَيْتُ مِائَةَ بِنْتٍ.
I sat with one hundred girls.	جَلَسْتُ مَعَ مِائَةِ بِنْتٍ.

Figures of numbers in Arabic are written and read from left to right in declining order. For example: 120 i.e. one hundred twenty, would be rendered in Arabic similarly, i.e. one hundred will precede twenty and we would say مِائَةٌ وَ عِشْرُونَ.

The biggest number (in figures) is written at the extreme left followed by smaller numbers in order as in English except that from eleven unto ninetynine the unit shall precede the ten. For example in English we say twenty three but in Arabic we would say three and twenty (ثَلاثَةٌ وَ عِشْرُونَ).

All components of the compound numbers in Arabic are linked with the conjunctive particle وَ except that in the case of eleven unto nineteen no conjunctive is used.

All numbers in Arabic are declinable according to their case except that in the case of eleven and thirteen unto nineteen the number shall never decline.

From three to ten the noun shall be plural and in the genitive case.

From eleven to ninetynine the noun shall be singular & in the accusative case.

From hundred onwards the noun shall be singular and in the genitive case.

In a bigger number the position i.e.اعراب of the nouns shall be determined in accordance with the smallest unit of the number. Suppose we want to say: one thousand one hundred boys. We would say this in Arabic as follows:

أَلْفٌ وَّمِائَةُ وَلَدٍ

It is because the smallest unit in this big number is hundred which takes singular noun in the genitive case as explained undergroup 3 above. However, if we want to say:

One thousand one hundred fifty boys, then we would say this in Arabic as follows:

أَلْفٌ وَمِائَةٌ وَخَمْسُونَ وَلَداً

In this case the smallest unit is fifty which takes a singular noun in the accusative case as explained under group2 above. If we want to say:

One thousand one hundred three boys, we would say in Arabic:

أَلْفٌ وَ مِائَةٌ وَّثَلَاثَةُ أَوْلَادٍ

The smallest unit here is three in which case the noun shall be plural and in the genitive case as explained under group 1 above.

Exercises:

1) Translate into Arabic:

(A)

    1) I have a new book.

    2) I hav read these two magazines.

3) There were five boy-students in the class.
4) I bought eight note-books.
5) I have studied in four colleges.
6) There are fifteen boys and fifteen girls in my class.
7) Who has taken eighteen spoons from my cupboard.
8) There are one thousand fifty students in my school.
9) I bought this pen for twentyfive rupees.
10) Two thousand is a big number.

(B) Yesterday I went to the market. I bought one pen and two books. I also bought two notebooks. I paid Rs. 50/- for pen and Rs. 150 for the two books. The notebooks were of course cheap. I paid only Rs. 6/- for them both. On my way back home, I saw an accident. Two buses had collided. Three girls died on the spot while fifteen men and eleven women received serious injuries. About three hundred persons had assembled there. In the meantime the police came and dispersed the crowd.

Translate into English:

فِى الأُسْبُوعِ سَبْعَةُ أَيَّامٍ وَهِىَ:

يَوْمُ الثُّلَاثَاءِ. 　　يَوْمُ الإِثْنَيْنِ. 　　يَوْمُ الأَحَدِ. 　　يَوْمُ السَّبْتِ.

يَوْمُ الْجُمْعَةِ. 　　يَوْمُ الْخَمِيْسِ. 　　يَوْمُ الأَرْبِعَاءِ.

فِى السَّنَةِ اِثْنَا عَشَرَ شَهْرًا وَهِىَ:

تَمُّوْز	‐	يُولْيُو	٧.	كَانُون الثَّانِى	‐	يَنَايِر	١.
آب	‐	أُغُسْطُس	٨.	شُبَاط	‐	فِبْرَايِر	٢.
أَيْلُول	‐	سِبْتِمْبر	٩.	آذَار	‐	مَارِس	٣.
تِشْرِينَ الأَوَّل	‐	أُكْتُوبر	١٠.	نِيْسَان	‐	إبْرِيْل	٤.
تِشْرِيْنَ الثَّانِى	‐	نُوفِمْبِر	١١.	أَيَّار	‐	مَايُو	٥.
كَانُون الأَوَّل	‐	دِيْسِمْبِر	١٢.	حَزِيْران	‐	يُونْيُو	٦.

عِنْدَمَا كُنْتُ جَالِسًا فِي غُرْفَتِي قَدِمَ إِلَيَّ طَالِبَانِ وَ قَدَّمَا لِيْ طَلَبًا لِلْمَعُونَةِ الْمَالِيَّةِ مِنَ الْجَامِعَةِ. قُلْتُ لَهُمْ: هَنَاكَ لَجْنَةٌ تَتَكَوَّنُ مِنْ ثَمَانِيَةِ أَعْضَاءَ لِاعْتِبَارِ مِثْلِ هَذِهِ الطَّلَبَاتِ وَعِنْدَنَا حَوَالَى خَمْسِيْنَ طَلَبًا. سَتَجْتَمِعُ هَذِهِ اللَّجْنَةُ قَرِيْبًا لِاتِّخَاذِ الْقَرَارِ. مِنَ الضَّرُورِيِّ أَنْ تَعْرِفُوا اَنَّ الْمَبْلَغَ الْمُتَوَافِرَ لَدَيْنَا لِهَذَا الْغَرَضِ هُوَ فَقَطْ أَرْبَعَةُ آلَافِ رُوْبِيَةٍ. وَإِذَا قَسَّمْنَا هَذَا الْمَبْلَغَ بَيْنَ جَمِيعِ الْمُتَقَدِّمِيْنَ فَسَيَحْصُلُ كُلُّ مُتَقَدِّمٍ عَلَى ثَمَانِيْنَ رُوْبِيَةً فَقَطْ.

Glossary:	الكلمات العسيرة
I have	لِيْ / عِنْدِى
Magazine	مَجَلَّةٌ (SF)/ مَجَلَّاتٌ (P)
To buy	اِشْتَرَى / يَشْتَرِى / اِشْتِرَاءُ
To study	دَرَسَ / يَدْرَسُ / دَرْساً
Who	مَنْ / اَلَّذِى / اَلَّتِى
To take	أَخَذَ / يَأْخُذُ / أَخْذًا
Spoon	مِلْعَقَةٌ (SF) مَلَاعِقُ (P)
Cupboard, vault	خَزِيْنَةٌ (SF)/خَزَائِنُ (P)
Cupboard	دُوْلَابٌ (SM)/دَوَالِيْبُ (P)
Number	عَدَدٌ(SM) أَعْدَادٌ(P)
Day	يَوْمٌ (SM)/ أَيَّامٌ (P)
Saturday	(يَوْمُ) السَّبْتِ
Sunday	(يَوْمُ) الأَحَد
Monday	(يَوْمُ) الإِثْنَيْنِ
Tuesday	(يَوْمُ) الثُّلاثَاء
Wedneseday	(يَوْمُ) الأَرْبِعَاء
Thursday	(يَوْمُ) الخَمِيس
Friday	(يَوْمُ) الجُمُعَة

Help	مَعُونَةٌ (SF) مَعُونَاتٌ (P)
To consist (of)	تَكَوَّنَ / يَتَكَوَّنُ / تَكُوُّنًا
To be available	تَوَافَرَ / يَتَوَافَرُ / تَوَافُرًا
To divide	قَسَّمَ / يُقَسِّمُ / تَقْسِيْمًا
Applicant	مُتَقَدِّمٌ (SM) مُتَقَدِّمُونَ (P)
Committee	لَجْنَةٌ (SF) لِجَانٌ (P)
To consider	إِعْتَبَرَ / يَعْتَبِرُ / إِعْتِبَاراً

The Number & The Noun Qualified
By The Number
العدد والمعدود

Ordinal Numbers		العدد الوصفى
	Masculine	**Feminine**
First	الاول	اَلْأُوْلَى
Second	اَلثَّانِى	اَلثَّانِيَةُ
Third	الثَّالِثُ	الثَّالِثَةُ
Fourth	الرَّابِعُ	الرَّابِعَةُ
Fifth	اَلْخَامِسُ	اَلْخَامِسَةُ
Sixth	اَلسَّادِسُ	اَلسَّادِسَةُ
Seventh	اَلسَّابِعُ	اَلسَّابِعَةُ
Eighth	اَلثَّامِنُ	اَلثَّامِنَةُ
Ninth	اَلتَّاسِعُ	اَلتَّاسِعَةُ
Tenth	اَلْعَاشِرُ	اَلْعَاشِرَةُ
Eleventh	اَلْحَادِىَ عشَرَ	اَلْحَادِيَةَ عَشَرَةَ
Twelfth	اَلثَّانِى عَشَرَ	اَلثَّانِيَةَ عَشَرَةَ
Thirteenth	اَلثَّالِثَ عَشَرَ	اَلثَّالِثَةَ عَشَرَةَ
Fourteenth	الرَّابِعَ عَشَرَ	اَلرَّابِعَةَ عَشَرَةَ
Fifteenth	اَلْخَامِسَ عَشَرَ	اَلْخَامِسَةَ عَشَرَ
Sixteenth	اَلسَّادِسَ عَشَرَ	اَلسَّادِسَةَ عَشَرَةَ
Seventeenth	اَلسَّابِعَ عَشَرَ	اَلسَّابِعَةَ عَشَرَةَ

Eighteenth	اَلثَّامِنَ عَشَرَ	اَلثَّامِنَةَ عَشَرَةَ
Nineteenth	اَلتَّاسِعَ عَشَرَ	اَلتَّاسِعَةَ عَشَرَةَ
Twentieth	اَلْعِشْرُونَ	اَلْعِشْرُونَ
Twenty-first	اَلْحَادِى وَالْعِشْرُونَ	اَلْحَادِيَةُ وَالْعِشْرُونَ
Twenty-second	اَلثَّانِى وَالْعِشْرُونَ	اَلثَّانِيَةُ وَالْعِشْرُونَ
Twenty-third	اَلثَّالِثُ وَالْعِشْرُونَ	اَلثَّالِثَةُ وَالْعِشْرُونَ

Thirtieth	اَلثَّلَاثُونَ
Fourtieth	اَلْاَرْبَعُونَ
Fiftieth	اَلْخَمْسُونَ
Sixtieth	اَلسِّتُّونَ
Seventieth	السَّبْعُونَ
Eightieth	اَلثَّمَانُونَ
Ninetieth	اَلتِّسْعُونَ
Hundredth	اَلْمِئَةُ

Ordinal numbers are those which indicate the position of a person, place or thing. This meaning of the number is expressed by "First, second and third" etc. in the English language. Similarly, we have ordinal numbers in Arabic. In Arabic all the ordinal numbers are derived from the cardinal numbers except the "first". The word to indicate this is الاَوَّل.

While discussing cardinal numbers, it was emphasized that from three to ten the gender of the number shall be opposite to the gender of the noun. And in the case of 13 & 14, 23 & 24 and similar compound numbers the first component of the number shall be opposite to the gender of the noun.

However, in the case of ordinal numbers this does not obtain. Here gender of the number shall have to be in agreement with the gender of the noun as per details given below : From one to ten the masculine noun will take masculine number i.e. without Taa marboota ة and it shall be used like an adjective after the noun it qualifies.

This is the third part of the book.   هَذَا الْجُزْءُ الثَّالِثُ لِلْكِتَابِ.

I bought the third part of the book.   اِشْتَرَيْتُ الْجُزْءَ الثَّالِثَ لِلْكِتَابِ.

I read this idiom   قَرَأْتُ هَذَا التَّعْبِيْرَ

in the third part of the book.   فِى الْجُزْءِ الثَّالِثِ لِلْكِتَابِ.

Where the ordinal number is used in a meaning similar to that of the superlative, it is used before the plural of the noun defined either by the definite article or that plural noun should be in construct phrase.

Example:

The third son of his father came.   قَدِمَ ثَالِثُ أَوْلَادِ اَبِيْهِ.

I saw the third son of his father.   رَأَيْتُ ثَالِثَ أَوْلَادِ اَبِيْهِ.

I sat with the third son of his father.   جَلَسْتُ مَعَ ثَالِثِ أَوْلَادِ اَبِيْهِ.

The third daughter of her father came.   قَدِمَتْ ثَالِثَةُ بَنَاتِ أَبِيْهَا.

From eleventh to nineteenth, although both the components of the compound number shall agree in gender with the noun they qualify, however, both these components shall be in the accusative case irrespective of the position they hold in the sentence.

Example:

The thirteenth boy came.   قَدِمَ الْوَلَدُ الثَّالِثَ عَشَرَ.

I saw the thirteenth boy.   رَأَيْتُ الْوَلَدَ الثَّالِثَ عَشَرَ.

I went with the thirteenth boy.   ذَهَبْتُ مَعَ الْوَلَدِ الثَّالِثَ عَشَرَ.

The thirteenth girl came.   قَدِمَتِ الْبِنْتُ الثَّالِثَةَ عَشَرَةَ.

I saw the thirteenth girl.   رَأَيْتُ الْبِنْتَ الثَّالِثَةَ عَشَرَةَ.

I went with the thirteenth girl.   ذَهَبْتُ اِلَى الْبِنْتِ الثَّالِثَةَ عَشَرَةَ.

From twentieth onwards-whatever the number the number agrees with the noun in gender and they are thoroughly declinable according to the case:

Example:

The twentyfifth boy came	قَدِمَ الْوَلَدُ الْخَامِسُ وَالْعِشْرُوْنَ.
I saw the twentyfifth girl	رَأَيْتُ الْبِنْتَ الْخَامِسَةَ وَالْعِشْرِيْنَ.
I sat with the ninetyninth girl	جَلَسْتُ مَعَ الْبِنْتِ التَّاسِعَةِ وَالتِّسْعِيْنَ
The hundredth boy came.	قَدِمَ الْوَلَدُ الْمِئَةُ
The one thousand and hundredth girl came.	قَدِمَتِ الْبِنْتُ الْمِئَةُ وَالْأَلْفُ.

It is important to note that all the components of the ordinal number take the definite article.

It may be mentioned here that both the cardinal numbers and the ordinal numbers generally have sound plurals on the pattern of sound plural feminine.

Example:

Three	ثَلَاثَةٌ/ثَلَاثٌ : ثَلَاثَاتٌ
Fours	اَرْبَعَةٌ/اَرْبَعٌ : اَرْبَعَاتٌ
Fives	خَمْسَةٌ/خَمْسٌ : خَمْسَاتٌ
Twenties	عِشْرُونَ : عِشْرُونَاتٌ
Fifties	خَمْسُونَ : خَمْسُونَاتٌ

These plurals decline as per rules explained in respect of sound plural.

Fractions are expressed as follows:

half	½	نِصْفٌ
one third	1/3	ثُلُثٌ
one fourth	¼	رُبْعٌ
one fifth	1/5	خُمْسٌ
one sixth	1/6	سُدْسٌ
one seventh	1/7	سُبْعٌ
one eighth	1/8	ثُمْنٌ

one ninth	1/9	تُسْعٌ
one tenth	1/10	عُشْرٌ

Suppose we want to say 1/6, 2/6 & 3/6 we would say in Arabic:

1/6	سُدْسٌ
2/6	سُدْسَانِ
3/6	ثَلاثَةُ اَسْدَاسٍ

These fractions are common for nouns of both the genders and they are declinable.

Suppose we want to say 55 upon 250, we would say in Arabic:

خَمْسَةٌ وَّ خَمْسُونَ على مِئَتَينِ وَ خَمْسِينَ

If we have decimated figure, then we would say:

خَمْسَةٌ وَعِشْرُونَ وَثَمَانِيَةُ اجزاءٍ مِنْ عشَرَةٍ   25.8

These figures are generally separated with ر in Arabic, as follows: 25ر 8. Every increasing figure after decimal shall be subtracted from the next figure. Example:

خَمْسَةٌ و عِشْرُونَ وثَمَانِيَةٌ وَّ ثَمَانُونَ جُزءً مِنْ مِئَةٍ   25.88

Exercises:

(1) Translate into Arabic:

(A) 1)   He left India for Japan on 31st of May last.

    2)   She is my first daughter

    3)   The first item on the agenda is confirmation of the minutes of the last meeting.

    4)   He is the twentysixth president of our co-operative society.

    5)   Divide this amount into three equal parts and give one-third to the servant and the remaining two-thirds to the shopkeeper.

6) He has completed his hundredth year on eleventh January last but he still looks quite healthy.

7) I shall receive my hundred- twenty first salary next month.

8) Sir, I want to marry your second daughter.

9) He spends one-fourth of his salary on smoking; another one-fourth on drinking; the third one-fourth on gambling and the remaining one-fourth on eating. This is the reason that he is so weak and looks pale.

10) I have taken this idea for my story from the fourteenth story of the book you had given me.

(B)

Now we have entered the twentyfirst Century. Though we have made a lot of progress in all the fields of human life & information, but peace is still far away. With the advent of nuclear weaponry the threat of the third war is hanging over our heads. This thought is hair raising because if it happens, God forbid, then the destruction will be much more than what it was during the first & the second world wars. It is feared that the entire world would be ruined.

(2) Translate into English:

فِى الشَّهْرِ الْقَادِمِ فِى الْيَوْمِ الثَّالِثَ عَشَرَ سَوْفَ نَحْتَفِلُ بِعِيْدِ زَوَاجِنَا الْخَامِسِ وَالْعِشْرِيْنَ. إِنَّا أَخَذْنَا هَذِهِ الْفِكْرَةَ مِنْ جَارِنَا سَمِيْرٍ الَّذِى احْتَفَلَ بِعِيْدِ زَوَاجِهِ الرَّابِعِ وَالثَّلَاثِيْنَ فِى الْعِشْرِيْنَ مِنَ الشَّهْرِ الْمَاضِى. سَمِيْرٌ يَسْكُنُ فِى الْبَيْتِ الْمُلَاصِقِ لِبَيْتِنَا مُنْذُ مَا يَقِلُّ عَنْ ثَلَاثَةِ أَعْوَامٍ. هُوَ كَبِيْرُ السِّنِّ وَ لَكِنَّهُ إِنْسَانٌ نَشِيْطٌ وَ يَوَدُّ الإِحْتِفَالَاتِ. وَنَصَحَنِى أَنْ لَا أَدَعَ فُرْصَةً تُفْلِتُ وَ أَنْ أُقِيْمَ حَفَلَاتٍ لِأَقْرَبِ الأَقْرِبَاءِ وَ الأَصْدِقَاءِ لِأَنَّ الْحَفَلَاتِ تُكَوِّنُ مُنَاسَبَاتٍ لِتَجْدِيْدِ وَ تَوْثِيْقِ عُرَى الْقَرَابَاتِ وَالصَّدَاقَاتِ. فَأَخَذْتُ هَذِهِ النَّصِيْحَةَ مِنْهُ بِجِدِّيَّةٍ وَهَذِهِ أَوَّلُ حَفْلَةٍ أَقَمْتُهَا فِى بَيْتِى. أَتَطَلَّعُ إِلَى إِقَامَةِ مَزِيْدٍ مِنَ الْحَفَلَاتِ فِى الأَيَّامِ الْقَادِمَةِ، إِنْ شَاءَ اللهُ. وَمَا رَأْيُكَ فِى هَذِهِ الْفِكْرَةِ؟

Glossary: الكلمات العسيرة

To leave	غَادَرَ / يُغَادِرُ / مُغَادَرَةً
Japan	اَلْيَابَان
Item	بَنْدٌ (SM) بُنُودٌ (P)
Agenda	جَدْوَلٌ (SM) جَدَاوِلُ (P)
To confirm	أَكَّدَ / يُؤَكِّدُ / تَأْكِيْداً
Minutes (of a meeting)	مَحْضَرٌ (SM) مَحَاضِرُ (P)
Meeting	إِجْتِمَاعٌ (SM) إِجْتِمَاعَاتٌ (P)
President	رَئِيْسٌ (SM) رُؤَسَاءُ (P)
Society	مُجْتَمَعٌ (SM) مُجْتَمَعَاتٌ (P)
Co-operative	تَعَاوُنِيٌّ (Adj. SM)
To divide	قَسَّمَ / يُقَسِّمُ / تَقْسِيْمًا
Amount	مَبْلَغٌ (SM) مَبَالِغُ (P)
To give	أَعْطَى / يُعْطِى / إِعْطَاءً
Part	جِزْءٌ (SM) اجزاءٌ (P)
Equal	مُسَاوِى (Adj. SM)
Servant	خَادِمٌ (SM) خَدَمٌ (P)
Shopkeeper	صَاحِبُ الْمَحَلِّ، أَصْحَابُ الْمَحَلَّاتِ
Master; owner	صَاحِبٌ (SM) أَصْحَابٌ (P)، مَالِكٌ / مُلَّاكٌ
Shop	دُكَّانٌ (SM) دَكَاكِيْنُ (P)، مَحَلٌّ (SM) مَحَلَّاتٌ (P)
To look; to appear	ظَهَرَ / يَظْهَرُ / ظُهُورًا
To receive	إِسْتَلَمَ / يَسْتَلِمُ / إِسْتِلَامًا
Salary	مُرَتَّبٌ (SM) مُرَتَّبَاتٌ (P)
To want	أَحَبَّ / يُحِبُّ / مَحَبَّةً
To marry	تَزَوَّجَ / يَتَزَوَّجُ / تَزَوُّجًا
To spend	أَنْفَقَ / يُنْفِقُ / إِنْفَاقًا
To smoke	دَخَّنَ / يُدَخِّنُ / تَدْخِيْنًا

Another; other	آخَرُ (SM) آخَرُونَ(P)، أُخْرَىٰ (SF) أُخْرَيَاتٌ (P)
To drink	شَرِبَ / يَشْرَبُ / شُرْباً
To gamble	قَامَرَ / يُقَامِرُ / مُقَامَرَةً
To eat	أَكَلَ / يَأْكُلُ / أَكْلاً
Reason	سَبَبٌ(SM)/ أَسْبَابٌ(P)
That	أَنْ
That he is	أَنَّهُ / إِنَّهُ
Weak	ضَعِيفٌ (Adj. SM) ضُعَفَاءُ(P)
Idea	فِكْرَةٌ (SF) فِكَرٌ(P)
Story	قِصَّةٌ (SF) قِصَصٌ(P)
To publish: To announce	أَعْلَنَ / يُعْلِنُ / إِعْلاَنًا
Result	نَتِيجَةٌ (SF) نَتَائِجُ(P)
A.D, Christian era	لِلْمِيلَادِ
To consist (of)	اِشْتَمَلَ / يَشْتَمِلُ / اِشْتِمَالاً (عَلَى) *
Page	صَفْحَةٌ (SF) صَفْحَاتٌ(P)
To teach	دَرَّسَ / يُدَرِّسُ / تَدْرِيساً
Class-room	فَصْلٌ (SM) فُصُولٌ(P)
Office	مَكْتَبٌ(SM) مَكَاتِبُ(P)
Administrative	إِدَارِيٌّ (Adj. SM)
To remain	بَقِيَ / يَبْقَى / بَقَاءٌ
House	بَيْتٌ (SM) بُيُوتٌ(P)
Teacher	مُدَرِّسٌ (SM) مُدَرِّسُونَ(P)
To dirty; to make dirty	وَسَّخَ/يُوَسِّخُ/ تَوْسِيخًا

---

* Like in English, Arabic has verbs which take direct objects, e.g. أَكَلَ الْمَوْزَ i.e.
'he ate banana' and it also has verbs which take indirect objects i.e. there
would be a preposition between the verb and the object e.g.

This class consists of fifty students. هَذَا الْفَصْلُ يَشْتَمِلُ عَلَى خَمْسِينَ طَالِبًا.

To get up, to stand up	وَقَفَ / يَقِفُ / وُقُوفاً
To deliver (lecture)	اَلْقَى / يُلْقِى / اِلْقَاءَ
Lecture	مُحَاضَرَةٌ (SF) مُحَاضَرَاتٌ(P)
About	حَوْلَ / عَن
Necessity	ضَرُوْرَةٌ (SF) ضَرُوْرَاتٌ(P)
To bring near	قَرَّبَ / يُقَرِّبُ / تَقْرِيْباً
Different	مُخْتَلِفٌ(Adj SM)**
Component	مُكَوِّنٌ (SM) مُكَوِّنَاتٌ(P)
People	إِنسانٌ (SM) أُنَاسٌ (P)
Milk	لَبَنٌ (SM) اَلْبَانٌ(P)
To mint (money, coins)	سَكَّ / يَسُكُّ / سَكَّا
Remaining	بَاقِى(Adj SM)

** Before a plural noun of either gender, it is always مُخْتَلَفٌ and where it follows a noun it is read as مُخْتَلِفٌ and agrees with the noun in gender.

LESSON — 28

الدرس — ٢٨

Particles That Cause Fatḥah To The Present Imperfect And Particles That Cause Fatḥah To The Nouns, Pronouns

نَوَاصِبُ الْفِعْلِ الْمُضَارِعِ وَ نَوَاصِبُ الأَسْمَاءِ

One evening,	مَسَاءَ يَوْمٍ،
Mr. Ramamurti returned	عَادَ السَّيِّدُ رَامَا مُورْتِى
from his office early.	مِنْ مَكْتَبِهِ مُبَكِّراً.
He was very tired.	كَانَ مُتْعَبًا جِدًّا.
His wife saw him and went to him	رَأَتْهُ زَوْجَتُهُ، وَذَهَبَتْ اِلَيْهِ
in order to know the reason.	لِكَىْ تَعْرِف السَّبَبَ.
And she asked him: How are you?	وَاِنَّهَا سَأَلَتْهُ: كَيْفَ أَنْتَ؟
What happend to you?	مَاذَا حَصَلَ لَكَ؟
He said: It seems that	فَقَالَ: يَبْدُو اَنَّهُ
fever has struck me (I caught fever)	قَدْ اَصَابَتْنِى الْحُمَّى.
I remained feverish	بَقِيتُ مَحْمُومًا
all the day long.	طُوْلَ النَّهَارِ.
She said: Did you go to the doctor	فَقَالَتْ: هَلْ ذَهَبْتَ اِلَى الدُّكْتُورِ
to take medicine?	لِتَأْخُذَ الدَّوَاءَ.
He said: No, I do not want to go to	قَالَ: لَا، لَا اُرِيدُ اَنْ اَذْهَبَ اِلَى
the doctor because the fever	الدُّكْتُورِ لِأَنَّ الْحُمَّى
has gone down now.	قَدْ تَخَفَّفَتْ الآنَ.
It is enough that you prepare half cup of	يَكْفِى أَنْ تُعِدِّى نِصْفَ كُوْب مِنْ
boiled water with a little ginger	الْمَاءِ الْمَغْلِىّ مَعَ قَلِيلٍ مِنَ الزَّنْجَبِيْلِ
and some sugar and black pepper,	وَقَلِيلٍ مِّنَ السُّكَّرِ وَالْفِلْفِلِ الأَسْوَدِ
so that I (can) drink it.	لِكَى اَشْرَبَهُ.

And after one hour, God so willing,	وَبَعْدَ سَاعَةٍ، اِنْ شَاءَ اللَّهُ،
everything will be (as desired)	سَيَكُونُ كُلُّ شَىْءٍ
all right.	(عَلَى مَايُرَام) حَسَناً.
The wife touched his forehead	لَمَسَتِ الزَّوْجَةُ جَبِينَهُ
and said that the fever	وَقَالَتْ اِنَّ الْحُمَّى
had not yet gone down and this	لَمَّا يَتَخَفَّفْ وَ اِنَّ هَذَا
indigenous medicine	الدَّوَاءَ الْبَلَدِى
will not benefit you.	لَنْ يُفِيدَكَ.
Let us go to the doctor.	فَلْنَذْهَبْ اِلَى الدُّكْتُورِ.
He might give you some medicine	اِنَّهُ قَدْ يُعْطِيكَ دَوَاءً
that will cure you quickly.	يَشْفِيكَ بِسُرْعَةٍ.
Perhaps the doctor gives you an injection	لَعَلَّ الدُّكْتُورَ يُعْطِيكَ اِبْرَةً
which will cure you immediately.	قَدْ تَشْفِيكَ فَوْرًا.
He said: I wish I were able	قَالَ: لَيْتَنِى كُنْتُ قَادِرًا
to walk, but I am feeling	عَلَى الْمَشْيِ. لَكِنَّى اَشْعُرُ
extremely weak as if the strength	بِضُعْفٍ شَدِيدٍ كَأَنَّ الْقُوَّةَ
has been extracted from my body.	قَدِ اسْتُخْرِجَتْ مِنْ بَدَنِى.
She said: Then I contact the doctor	قَالَتْ: اِذَنْ اَتَّصِلَ بِالدُّكْتُورِ
on telephone in order to call him	عَلَى التِّلِفُونِ لِكَىْ اَطْلُبَهُ
to our home.	اِلَى بَيْتِنَا.
Mr. Ramamurti kept quiet as though he	سَكَتَ السَّيِّدُ رَامَا مُورْتِى كَأَنَّهُ
agreed with her.	يَتَّفِقُ مَعَهَا.

Grammar

There are particles which cause fatḥah to the terminal letter of the present imperfect verb. These particles are as follows:

That	اَنْ
Never	لَنْ

So that, in order that   كَيْ

Then, in the case   إذَنْ

Anyone of these four particles above and a few more like حتّى cause fatḥah to the terminal letter of the present imperfect that it precedes and the verb is considered to be in the subjunctive mood and in places where the fatḥah can not be given, they cause all the "noons" i.e. the letter ن to drop except in the case of III & II person plural feminine.

لن defines the meaning of the present imperfect verb to the future negative. For example لا يَذهَبُ may mean depending on the context:

(1) He does not go.

(2) He is not going.

(3) He will not go.

However, لَن يَّذهَبَ shall mean: He will not go or the emphatic: He will never go.

أن، كَى، إذن generally define the meaning of the present imperfect to 'causative'. For example: كَى أذهَبَ will mean: So that I go and so on. Particle إذن literally would mean: 'in that case' and it is used before an imperfect verb to answer or complement an intention. For example if you say: سَوفَ أزُورُك غَداً i.e. I will visit you tomorrow then the addressee would say: إذَنْ تَشْرَبَ الشَّايَ مَعَنَا : in that case (or then) you will drink tea with us.

The particle أن, besides being followed by a verb in the subjunctive mood, is usually preceded by a verb expressing desire. For example: أريد أنْ أذهَبَ

In this case the meaning is rendered into infinitive. Hence, the sentence above would mean: I want to go.

It may also be preceded by a verb indicating probability or a similar meaning in which case the meaning in English would be expressed by 'might or may'. For example: يُحْتَمَلُ أنْ أزُوْرَك غداً I might visit you tomorrow.

Following is the sample conjugation with one of the foregoing particles that cause fatḥah to the present imperfect:

S.M	III	person	He will never go	لَنْ يَذْهَبَ
D.M.	III	person		لَنْ يَذْهَبَا

P.M.	III	person	لَنْ يَذْهَبُوا
S.F.	III	person	لَنْ تَذْهَبَ
D.F.	III	person	لَنْ تَذْهَبَا
P.F.	III	person	لَنْ يَذْهَبْنَ
S.M.	II	person	لَنْ تَذْهَبَ
D.M.	II	person	لَنْ تَذْهَبَا
P.M.	II	person	لَنْ تَذْهَبُوا
S.F.	II	person	لَنْ تَذْهَبِى
D.F.	II	person	لَنْ تَذْهَبَا
P.F.	II	person	لَنْ تَذْهَبْنَ
S.M. &	F I	person	لَنْ أَذْهَبَ
PM &	F I	Person.	لَنْ نَذْهَبَ

إِنَّ، أَنَّ، كَأَنَّ، لَيتَ، لكِنَّ & لَعلَّ are particles which cause fatḥah to the terminal letter of a noun and in case of pronouns, only the 'inseparable' pronouns are used. أَنَّ & إِنَّ are used in the meaning of 'that' to connect two parts of a sentence. For example:

He said that he wants to visit me.   قَالَ إِنَّهُ يُرِيدُ زِيَارَتِى.

I heard that he has expired.   سَمِعْتُ أَنَّهُ تُوُفِّىَ.

إِنَّ is used after قَالَ and its different forms while أَنَّ is used after all other verbs.

كَأَنَّ means 'as if' 'as though' For example:

The teacher scolded me   وبَّخَنى المُدرِّسُ

as if I had committed the mistake.   كَأَنِّى أَخْطَأتُ.

There is one causative 'ل' with kasrah under it, however, it causes **fatḥah** to the present imperfect. For example:

He is coming to take you with him.   هُوَ قَادِمٌ لِيَأْخُذَكِ معَه

This causative 'ل' is used as above and occasionally it is prefixed to كى to say لِكى . For example:

لَيت means: 'would that, I wish'. For example:

I wish the boy had passed the examination   لَيتَ الوَلَدَ نجَحَ فى الإمْتِحان

لكِنَّ means: 'but, however'. For example:

The teacher beat the boy but   ضرَبَ المُدرِّسُ الوَلَدَ لكِنَّ

the princip١al did not interfere.   العَمِيْدَ لَمْ يَتَدَخَّلْ

لَعَلَّ means: 'perhaps'. For example:

Perhaps the teacher is present
لَعَلَّ الْأُسْتَاذَ مَوْجُودٌ

in the room.
فِى الْغُرْفَةِ

Point should also be noted that occasionally لكِنَّ is used as لكِنْ i.e. with sokoon on its terminal ن and in this case لكِنْ is generally followed by a verb, e.g. لكِنْ لَا أُرِيْدُ أَنْ آكُلَ i.e. but I don't want to eat.

Exercises

1) Translate into Arabic:

Once upon a time there lived an ascetic at the top of a mountain. He had taken an oath that he would not move from his place in order to beg for food. He said that he would eat only the fruits. He also promised himself that if he does not find food he will drink only water and express his gratitude to God. This place was infact very beautiful and had plenty of fruits and a spring of water. This place appeared as though it were a piece of heaven. But perhaps God had decided to put this ascetic to test. Soon the trees started withering till all of them dried up in two or three months' time. The ascetic got up one morning and found that the spring of water also had dried up. The ascetic looked upto the sky as though he was complaining but did not come down for food or water. He spent the day without water and food but in the evening he felt the pinch of hunger and thirst. He left his hut in the evening and climbed down the mountain in search of food.

Translate into English:

ذَهَبَ وَلَدٌ رَاعٍ إِلَى مَرْجٍ فِى الْجِبَالِ خَارِجَ الْقَرْيَةِ لِيَرْعَى غَنَمَهُ فَأَرَادَ أَنْ يَمْزَحَ مَعَ أَهْلِ الْقَرْيَةِ. فَصَاحَ بِأَعْلَى صَوْتِهِ: الذِّئْبُ...الذِّئْبُ... جَاءَ أَهْلُ الْقَرْيَةِ مَعَ الْعِصِيِّ وَ الْمَنَاجِلِ كَىْ يُسَاعِدُوهُ و يُخْرِجُوهُ مِنَ الْمَأْزِقِ. وَلكِنَّهُمْ انْدَهَشُوا عِنْدَمَا رَأَوْا الْوَلَدَ الرَّاعِيَ جَالِساً مُتَّكِئاً صَخْرَةً صَغِيرَةً وَ هُوَ يَضْحَكُ. غَضِبَ أَهْلُ الْقَرْيَةِ مِنَ الْوَلَدِ وَ نَهَرُوهُ وَعَادُوْا إِلَى الْقَرْيَةِ. فَمَضَتْ أَيَّامٌ وَجَاءَ ذِئْبٌ مَرَّةً حَقّاً إِلَى الْمَرْعَى وَ أَخَذَ الْوَلَدُ يَصِيْحُ لِلنَّجْدَةِ و لكِنْ لِلْأَسَفِ لَمْ يَاتِ اَحَدٌ مِنَ الْقَرْيَةِ لِنَجْدَتِهِ وَ فَتَكَ الذِّئْبُ بِعَدَدٍ مِنَ الْغَنَمِ. فَقَالَ الْوَلَدُ فِىْ قَلْبِهِ: لَيْتَنِى لَمْ أَمْزَحْ مَعَ النَّاسِ فِى الْمَرَّةِ السَّابِقَةِ.

Glossary   الكلمات العسيرة

Once upon a time	فِيْ زَمَنٍ مِنَ الأَزْمَانِ
Ascetic	نَاسِك (SM) نُسَّاك (P)
Top, peak	قِمَّة (SF) قِمَم (P)
Mountain	جَبَلٌ (SM) جِبَالٌ (P)
To take an oath, to swear	أَقْسَمَ / يُقْسِمُ / إِقْسَامًا
To move	تَحَرَّكَ / يَتَحَرَّكُ / تَحَرُّكًا
In order to, so that	لِكَيْ
To beg	شَحَذَ / يَشْحَذُ / شَحْذًا
To eat	أَكَلَ / يَأْكُلُ / أَكْلاً
To promise	وَعَدَ / يَعِدُ / وَعْدًا
To express	أَعْرَبَ / يُعْرِبُ / إِعْرَابًا (عن)
Gratitude, thanks	شُكْرٌ
Infact	فِى الْحَقِيقَةِ
Plenty	كَثِيرٌ
Spring (of water)	عَيْنٌ (SF) عُيُونٌ (الماء)
To appear	بَدَا / يَبْدُو / بِدَايَةً
Hut	كُوخٌ (SM) أَكْوَاخٌ (P)
To climb down	نَزَلَ / يَنْزِلُ / نُزُولاً
In search of	بَحْثًاعَنْ
Shepherd	رَاعٍ (رَاعِى) (SM) رُعَاةٌ (P)
Meadow	مَرْجٌ (SM) مُرُوجٌ (P)
Village	قَرْيَةٌ (SF) قُرًى (P)
To tend, to graze	رَعَى / يَرْعَى / رِعَايَةً
To intend, to want	أَرَادَ / يُرِيْدُ / إِرَادَةً
To joke	مَزَحَ / يَمْزَحُ / مَزْحًا
To shout	صَاحَ / يَصِيْحُ / صِيَاحًا
Wolf	ذِئْبٌ (SM) ذِئَابٌ (P)
Baton, stick	عَصًا (SF) عِصِىٌّ (P)

Sickle	مِنْجَلٌ (SM) مَنَاجِلُ (P)
So that, in order to	كَيْ / لِكَى
To help	سَاعَدَ / يُسَاعِدُ / مُسَاعَدَةً
To save, to extricate	أَخْرَجَ / يُخْرِجُ / إِخْرَاجًا
Difficult situation	مَأْزِقٌ (SM) مَآزِقُ (P)
To be surprised	إِنْدَهَشَ / يَنْدَهِشُ / اِنْدِهَاشًا
To recline (on)	اِتَّكَأَ / يَتَّكِئُ / اِتِّكَاءً (عَلَى)
Rock	صَخْرٌ (SM) (صَخْرَةٌ) صُخُورٌ (P)
To laugh	ضَحِكَ / يَضْحَكُ / ضَحْكًا
To become angry	غَضِبَ / يَغْضَبُ / غَضَبًا
To chide	نَهَرَ / يَنْهَرُ / نَهْرًا
To return	عَادَ / يَعُودُ / عَوْدَةً
To pass	مَضَى / يَمْضِى / مُضِيًّا
In fact, in reality, really	حَقًّا
Help	نَجْدَةٌ
For help	لِلنَّجْدَةِ
Sorrow, grief	أَسَفٌ
Unfortunately	لِلْأَسَفِ
To come	أَتَى / يَأْتِى / إِتْيَانًا
Nobody came	لَمْ يَأْتِ أَحَدٌ
To slay, to kill	فَتَكَ / يَفْتِكُ / فَتْكًا
I wish, how I wish	لَيْتَنِى

LESSON — 29

الدرس — ٢٩

Exceptives ادوات الاستثناء

Hamid is our classmate.	حَامِدٌ زَمِيْلُنَا فِى الْفَصْلِ.
He is intelligent and hardworking.	هُوَ ذَكِىٌّ وَ مُجْتَهِدٌ
Also he is a big sportsman.	كَمَا وَهُوَ رِيَاضِىٌّ كَبِيْرٌ.
We see him either in the class-room	نَرَاهُ اِمَّا فِى الْفَصْلِ
or in the library or in the playground.	أَمْ فِىْ الْمَكْتَبَةِ أَمْ فِى مَيْدَانِ اللَّعِبِ.
We find him busy all the day long.	نَرَاهُ مَشْغُولاً طُولَ النَّهَارِ.
In the last final examination	فِى الْإِمْتِحَانِ النِّهَائِى الْأَخِيْرِ
Hamid passed with distinction.	نَجَحَ حَامِدٌ بِدَرَجَةِ الْإِمْتِيَازِ.
At this occasion he held	وَبِهَذِهِ الْمُنَاسَبَةِ أَقَامَ
a big tea-party in his house,	حَفْلَةَ شَاى كَبِيْرَةً فِى بَيْتِهِ،
and invited all his classmates.	وَ دَعَا اِلَيْهَا جَمِيْعَ زُمَلَائِهِ.
I reached his house five minutes before the scheduled time.	وَصَلْتُ اِلَى مَنْزِلِهِ قَبْلَ الْمَوْعِدِ بِخَمْسِ دَقَائِقَ.
Nobody had come by that time except Nabeel and he is his fast friend.	مَا كَانَ جَاءَ حَتَّى ذَلِكَ الْوَقْتِ إلَّا نَبِيْلٌ وَ هُوَ صَدِيْقُهُ الْحَمِيْمُ.
At he scheduled time the invitees started reaching	وَفِى الْوَقْتِ الْمَحَدَّدِ اَخَذَ الْمَعْزُومُونَ يَصِلُونَ
in groups and singly.	فِى جَمَاعَاتٍ وَ فُرَادَى.
In half an hour time all the students had come except one (student).	وَ فِى نِصْفِ سَاعَةٍ وَصَلَ جَمِيْعُ الطُّلَّابِ اِلّا طَالِباً.

All (the students) sat in	جَلَسَ الْجَمِيْعُ فِى
the drawing room and started talking on	غُرْفَةِ الْاِسْتِقْبَالِ وَأَخَذُوا يَتَحَدَّثُوْنَ فِى
different topics.	مَوْضُوعَاتٍ شَتَّى
including studies & examinations.	بِمَا فِيْهَا الدِّرَاسَاتُ وَالْاِمْتِحَانَاتُ.
Then slowly the convesation shifted to	ثُمَّ رُوَيْداً رُوَيْداً اِنْتَقَلَ الْحَدِيْثُ اِلَى
Hamid's grand (distinguished) success.	نَجَاحِ حَامِدٍ الْمُمْتَازِ.
Some of us decided	فَصَمَّمَ بَعْضُنَا
to have with him heart-to-heart talk	عَلَى مُفَاتَحَتِهِ
regarding the secret	حَوْلَ سِرٍّ
of his distinguished success.	نَجَاحِهِ الْمُمْتَازِ.
At this very moment Hamid appeared	فِىْ نَفْسِ الْوَقْتِ ظَهَرَ
to us and invited us to	لَنَا حَامِدٌ وَ دَعَانَا اِلَى
the house garden where	حَدِيْقَةِ الْمَنْزِلِ حَيْثُ
he had arranged the party.	كَانَ نَظَّمَ الْحَفْلَةَ.
We got up and moved towards	فَقُمْنَا وَتَحَرَّكْنَا نَحْوَ
the garden where we found	الْحَدِيْقَةِ حَيْثُ وَجَدْنَا
every thing ready.	كُلَّ شَئٍ جَاهِزاً.
I proceeded towards Hamid	فَتَقَدَّمْتُ نَحْوَ حَامِدٍ
till I got close to him.	حَتَّى اِقْتَرَبْتُ مِنْهُ.
We (both) stood facing all (others) and I	فَوَقَفْنَا نَتَقَابَلُ الْجَمِيْعَ
said: Dear friends!	وَقُلْتُ: أَصْدِقَائِى الْأَعِزَّاءُ!
In fact it is a very happy occasion	إِنَّ هَذِهِ الْمُنَاسَبَةَ سَارَّةٌ جِدّاً
not because it is a tea-party	وَذَلِك لَيْسَ لِأَنَّهَا حَفْلَةُ شَاي
but because it is an occasion to celebrate the	وَلَكِنْ لِأَنَّهَا مُنَاسَبَةٌ نَحْتَفِلُ فِيْهَا
success of our dear friend.	بِنَجَاحِ صَدِيْقِنَا الْعَزِيْزِ.

In fact there is a lesson in his success	إِنَّ فِى نَجَاحِهِ دَرْساً
for all of us, the students.	لِجَمِيعِنَا نَحْنُ الطُّلَّابَ.
Now, when we congratulate	وَالآنَ، إِذْ نَحْنُ نُهَنِّىءُ
our friend on his success and wish	صَدِيقَنَا عَلَى نَجَاحِهِ وَ نَتَمَنَّى
all good for him in the future,	لَهُ كُلَّ خَيْرٍ فِى الْمُسْتَقْبَلِ،
we also request him to tell us	نَلْتَمِسُ إِلَيْهِ أَنْ يَقُولَ لَنَا
in a few words the secret	فِى كَلِمَاتٍ سِرَّ
of his all round success in life	نَجَاحِهِ الشَّامِلِ فِى الْحَيَاةِ
so that we take guidance from it.	حَتَّى نَسْتَرْشِدَمِنْهُ.
All the people welcomed this idea	فَرَحَّبَ الْجَمِيعُ بِهَذِهِ الْفِكْرِةِ
and supported it .	وَأَيَّدُوهَا.
Hamid said: My dear friends, I	قَالَ حَامِدٌ: أَصْدِقَائِى الأَعِزَّاءُ، إِنَّنِى
seize this opportunity to thank you	لَأَغْتَنِمُ هَذِهِ الْفُرْصَةَ لَأَشْكُرَكُمْ جَمِيعاً
all for attending my party.	لِحُضُورِ حَفْلَتِى.
I would also say that I don't have anything	وَأَقُولُ إِنَّهُ لَا يُوْجَدُ عِنْدِى
that you don't have except that I set my	شَىْءٌ لَايُوْجَدُ عِنْدَكُم سِوَى
time-table.	أَنَّنِى رَتَّبْتُ بَرْنَامَجِى.
There is time for every thing	لِكُلِّ شَىْءٍ وَقْتٌ
in my time table.	فِى بَرْنَامَجِى.
Dear friends, there is nothing on the surface	أَصْدِقَائِى الأَعِزَّاءُ، لَا شَىْءَ عَلَى
of this earth which could enable a	وَجْهِ الأَرْضِ يُمَكِّن
human-being to acquire success except	إِنْسَاناً مِنْ إِحْرَازِ
regularity, punctuality	النَّجَاحِ إِلَّا الإِنْتِظَامُ وَالْمُوَاظَبَةُ
and sincere efforts to realise his goals	وَالْجُهُودُ الْمُخْلِصَةُ لِتَحْقِيقِ أَهْدَافِهِ
in life.	فِى الْحَيَاةِ.
I think it is sufficient to say	أَكْتَفِى بِهَذَا
and invite you all to take tea.	وَادْعُوكُمْ جَمِيعًا لِتَنَاوُلِ الشَّاي.

Grammar:

Before explaining the "Exceptives", and their specific and peculiar usage in the Arabic language, it is necessary to point out that exception so made can only be of person/s from a group of persons and of articles from a group of similar articles and of animate or inanimate objects from a gorup of similar animate or inanimate objects. That is to say , we cannot except a monkey from a group of human-beings and/or otherwise (except where the usage is rhetoric). So also we cannot except an inanimate object like table from a group of animals and/or otherwise.

As should be amply clear from the foregoing details the exceptive is a word which singles out object/s from a group of similar objects. For this purpose, in English we use the word "except" or "save". In Arabic we use quite a few words for the purpose. Of these إلّا is the most frequently used. It is used as per details given below:

1. The noun excepted is placed after إلّا.

2. The noun excepted is placed in the accusative case i.e. its terminal letter is given fatḥah.

Example:

1. The students have come except one student.　قَدِمَ الطُّلَّابُ إلَّا طَالِبًا.

2. I saw the students except one student.　رَأَيْتُ الطُّلَّابَ إلا طَالِبًا.

You can see for yourself that in the two sentences above, the nouns excepted are placed in the accusative case. If you keenly observe sentence no (1) above, you will find that the excepted noun is supposedly in the nominative case as this would simply mean that:

The students came　قَدِمَ الطُّلَّابُ

and one student did not come.　وَلَمْ يَقْدَمْ طَالِبٌ وَاحِدٌ

and in sentence no (2) above, the excepted noun is in the accusative case as it would mean that:

I saw the students and I did not see one student　رَأَيْتُ الطُّلَّابَ وَلَمْ أَرَطَالِباً

However, in both the cases the excepted noun is طَالِبٌ and it should be in the accusative case as per rules explained in the foregoing lines in this regard.

Another factor worth noting is that the first parts of the two sentences preceding the exceptive إلّا are in the positive sense. In this case the excepted noun shall be always in the accusative case.

However, where the sentences are negative, the noun/s after the exceptive may be in the accusative case. For example:

1) The students did not come except

one student.

أ. مَاقَدِمَ الطُّلَّابُ
إلاطَالِباً

2) I did not see the students

except one student.

ب. مَا رَأَيْتُ الطُّلَّابَ
إلَّا طَالباً.

3) I did not sit with the students

except one student.

ج. مَا جَلَسْتُ مَعَ الطُّلَّابِ
إلَّا طَالباً.

It may also be noted here that in such cases the case terminal of the excepted noun may be in accordance to the sense of the meaning. For example the sentence (A) above would mean that 'only one student came' and hence rules permit to say:

مَاقَدِمَ الطُّلَّابُ إلَّا طالبٌ (يعنى قَدِمَ طالبٌ فَقَط)

Similarly, sentence 'B' would mean that 'I saw only one student', and hence 'student' is object of the verb رَأَيْتُ and therefore we would say:

مَارَأَيْتُ الطُّلَّابَ إلَّا طَالِبًا (يَعنى رأَيْتُ طَالِبًا فقط)

In the case of the third sentence i.e. sentence 'C', it would mean that 'I sat with only one student' and hence, rules permit to say:

مَاجَلَسْتُ مَعَ الطُّلَّابِ إلَّا طَالِبٍ (يَعنى جلسْتُ مَعَ طالبٍ فَقَط).

In brief we can say that the 'exceptive' إلّا:

(i) Causes fatḥah to the terminal letter of the noun that follows it provided that the clause preceding it is in the positive sense.

(ii) May cause Fathah to the terminal letter of the noun that follows it even where the clause preceding it is in the negative sense.

iii) May cause the applicable case terminal if the sentence were rendered in positve sense.

Apart from the exceptive إِلَّا there are a few more words which are less frequently used as the exceptives. they are:عدا ، خلا

These exceptives normally cause *kasrah* to the terminal letters of the nouns. For example:

The students came except one student.	قَدِمَ الطُّلَّابُ عَدَا طَالِبٍ.
The students came except one student.	قَدِمَ الطُّلَّابُ خَلَا طَالِبٍ.

However, where the exceptives عدا and خلا are preceded by the word ما they admit only the accusative case to the excepted noun.

The students came except one student.	قَدِمَ الطُّلَّابُ مَاعَدَا طَالِبًا.
The students came except one student.	قَدِمَ الطُّلَّابُ مَا خَلَا طالباً.

In addition to the exceptives mentioned above, there are some more words used as exceptives or in a way very similar to them.

I have also dealt in this lesson with لا of General Negation i.e. لا نفى الجنس. This لا of General Negation is followed by a Common Noun of singular number in the accusative case with only one *Fathah*. For example we say:

There is no body (not a soul) in the house.	لَا رَجُلَ فِى الدَّارِ
There is no doubt in it	لَا رَيْبَ فِيْهِ

Exercises:

1. Translate into English:

كَانَ الوَقْتُ صَبَاحَا——حوالى السَّاعَةِ الْعَاشِرَةِ. كُنْتُ أَجْلِسُ فِى غُرْفَةِ الدِّرَاسَةِ إِذْ دَقَّ جَرَسُ الْبَابِ. فَأَوْمَأْتُ لِلْخَادِمِ لِيَذْهَبَ إِلَى الْبَابِ وَيَفْتَحَ الْبَابَ. عَادَ الْخَادِمُ وَبَلَّغَنِى عَنْ قُدُومِ الطُّلَّابِ. فَطَلَبْتُ مِنْهُ أَنْ يُجْلِسَهم فِى غُرْفَةِ الإِسْتِقْبَالِ. وَتَوَجَّهْتُ أَيْضًا إِلَى غُرْفَةِ الإِسْتِقْبَالِ. وَبَعْدى دَخَلَ الطُّلَّابُ الغُرْفَةَ. كَانَ قَدِمَ كُلُّ الطُّلَّابِ إِلَّا طَالِبَيْنِ——حَمِيْدًا وحَامِدًا. سَأَلْتُ الْمَوْجُودِينَ عَنْ حَمِيْدٍ وحَامِدٍ فَرَدَّ عَلَىَّ طَالِبٌ: وَقَعَ حَمِيْدٌ مِنَ الأُوتُوبِيْس وَأَخَذْنَاهُ إِلَى المُسْتَشْفَى. عُدْنَا جَمِيْعًا بَعْدَ إِدْخَالِهِ المُسْتَشْفَى مَاعَدا حَامِدًا. هُوَ الآنَ مَعَ حَمِيْدٍ فِى المُسْتَشْفَى. سَأَلْتُهُم: هَل بَلَّغْتُم مُدِيْرَ

الْجَامِعَةِ. قَالُوا: ذَهَبْنَا إِلَى سَكَنِهِ وَلَكِنْ لَا أَحَدَ يُوجَدُ فِي بَيْتِهِ سِوَى حَارِسَيْنِ وَكَلْبٍ. فَوَدِدْنَا أَنْ نُبَلِّغَ سِيَادَتَكَ. سَمِعْتُ كَلَامَهُم وَ بَدَاتُ أَحَاوِلُ الْإِتِّصَالَ على التلفون بالأشخاص الْمَعْنِيِّينَ فِى الادَارِةِ و لكن لسوء الحظ لَم أَتَوَفَّقْ أَنْ أَجِدَ الْمُدِيرَ ولَا نَائِبَ الْمُدِيرِ وَلَا الْمُسَجِّلَ إِلَّا مُرَاقِبَ الدَّاخِلِيَّةِ. فَطَلَبْتُ مِنْهُ أَنْ يَّذْهَبَ إِلَى الْمُسْتَشْفَى لِلْعِنَايَةِ بِحَمِيْدٍ. طَمْأَنْتُ الطَّلَبَةَ وَطَلَبْتُ مِنْهُمُ الْعَوْدَةَ إِلَى دَاخِلِيَّتِهِم.

2. Translate into Arabic:

Yesterday I took the students of my class to the city's zoological garden. It is the biggist zoological garden in our country. It has a large number of animals and birds. I requested to see the director of the zoo. The director received me with a courtesy smile in his office. I told him we needed a guide to conduct us systematically in the zoo. He told me he had no guides. However, he called one senior employee and instructed him to accompany us and to show us through the zoo. We started our tour inside the zoo from cage to cage in the wild animals corner. All cages had ferocious animals like lions, tigers, leopards, wild cats etc. except one huge cage. It was empty. Out of curiosity I asked why that cage was empty. Our companion told us that the cage was meant for a pair of white tigers. The tigress begot three cubs two months ago. For some unknown reason two of the three cubs died. The pair became suspicious of everyone approaching the cage. They did not allow anyone to go close the cage except an old employee. One day this old employee entered the cage. In affection he lifted the cub but the pair were angry and attacked the old man who died inside the cage itself. The pair were furious. With great difficulty we removed the tiger family to seclusion and took away the dead body of the old man. Later the pair stopped eating anything as if they were in mourning for the old man they had killed. The mother did not have any milk to feed the cub. In a few days time they all died one by one.

3: Make sentences/ running paragraph using all/some of the exceptives given below:

سوى/ ماسوى، خلا/ ماخلا، عدا/ماعدا، إلا، غير

4: Use لا of general negation in your sentences/paragraph.

Glossary

الكلمات العسيرة

Intelligent (adj)	ذَكِيٌّ (Adj SM) اَذْكِيَاءُ(P)
Sportsman	رِيَاضِيٌّ (Adj SM) رِيَاضِيُّونَ (P)
Either.....or	إمَّا....أَمْ
Decision	قَرَارٌ(SM) قَرَارَاتٌ(P)
Occasion	مُنَاسَبَةٌ (SF) مُنَاسَبَاتٌ (P)
To hold (party)	اَقَامَ/ يُقِيْمُ (حَفْلَةً) إِقَامَةً
Party, function	حَفْلَةٌ(SF) حَفَلَاتٌ (P)
To invite	دَعَا/ يَدْعُو / دَعْوَةً
To reach; to arrive (at)	وَصَلَ/ يَصِلُ/ وُصُولًا
Residence; house	بَيْتٌ(SM) بُيُوتٌ(P)
Before; ahead of	قَبْلَ(Adv. of time used as preposition)
Minute	دَقِيْقَةٌ (SF) دَقَائِقُ (P)
To come	قَدِمَ/ يَقْدَمُ / قُدُومًا
Close friend, bosom friend	صَدِيْقٌ حَمِيْمٌ/ أَصَدِقَاءُ حَمِيْمُونَ
Specified, scheduled	مُحَدَّدٌ (Adj SM)
Invitee	مَعْزُومٌ (SM) مَعْزُوْمُونَ(P)
Group	مَجْمُوعَةٌ (SF) مَجْمُوعَاتٌ (P)
Individual	فَرْدٌ (SM) أَفْرَادٌ (P)
In groups & singly	جَمَاعَاتٍ وَ فُرَادَىٰ(Adverb of manner)
To receive, to welcome	اِسْتَقْبَلَ / يَسْتَقْبِلُ / اِسْتِقْبَالًا
Drawing-room	غُرْفَةُ الإسْتِقْبَال
To exchange	بَادَلَ/ يُبَادِلُ / مُبَادَلَةً
Conversation, talk (P)	حَدِيْثٌ (SM) أَحَادِيْثُ، جِوَارٌ (SM) حِوَارَاتٌ
Topic, subject	مَوضُوعٌ (SM) مَوضُوعَاتٌ(P)
Different	مُخْتَلِفٌ(Adj SM)

Studies	دِرَاسَةٌ (SF) دِرَاسَاتٌ (P)
Then Slowly slowly	فَرُوَيْداً رُوَيداً(Adv. of manner)
To shift, to drift (conversation)	اِنْتَقَلَ / يَنْتَقِلُ / اِنْتِقَالاً
Success	نَجَاحٌ (SM) نَجَاحَاتٌ (P)
Great, grand	عَظِيمٌ (Adj SM)
To be determined (upon)	مُصَمِّمٌ (عَلَى) (Adj SM)
Some, a few	عَدَدٌ (SM) أَعْدَادٌ (P)
To have heart -to-heart talk	فَاتَحَ / يُفَاتِحُ / مُفَاتَحَةً
Secret	سِرٌّ (SM) اَسْرَارٌ (P)
To appear	ظَهَرَ / يَظْهَرُ / ظُهُورًا
To organize, to arrange	نَظَّمَ / يُنَظِّمُ / تَنْظِيماً
To stand up; to get up	قَامَ / يَقُومُ / قِيَاماً
To move	تَحَرَّكَ / يَتَحَرَّكُ / تَحَرُّكًا
Where	أَيْنَ
To find	وَجَدَ / يَجِدُ / وُجُوداً
Ready	مُسْتَعِدٌّ، جَاهِزٌ (Adj SM)
To proceed to, to head towards	تَوَجَّهَ / يَتَوَجَّهُ / تَوَجُّهًا(إِلَى)
Towards	نَحْوَ (Adv. of place)
Dear	عَزِيزٌ (Adj SM) اَعِزَّاءُ
To celebrate	اِحْتَفَلَ / يَحْتَفِلُ / اِحْتِفَالاً(ب)
To congratulate	هَنَّأَ / يُهَنِّئُ / تَهْنِئَةً
To wish	وَدَّ / يَوَدُّ / وُدًا
Future	مُسْتَقْبَل
To request	رَجَا / يَرْجُو / رَجَاءً
Word	كَلِمَةٌ (SF)كَلِمَاتٌ (P)
Comprehensive	شَامِلٌ (Adj. SM)

Advice	نَصِيحَةٌ (SF) نَصَائِحُ (P)
To give lesson, to take (class)	أَدَارَ/ يُدِيرُ/ إِدَارَةً (دَرْساً)
To become	أَصْبَحَ/ يُصْبِحُ/ إِصْبَاحاً
To welcome	رَحَّبَ/ يُرَحِّبُ/ تَرْحِيْباً(ب)
To second; to support	أَيَّدَ/ يُؤَيِّدُ/ تَأْيِيْداً
To grab; to seize (opportunity)	اِغْتَنَمَ/ يَغْتَنِمُ/ اِغْتِنَاماً
Opportunity	فُرصَةٌ (SF) فُرَصٌ (P)
To thank	شَكَرَ/ يَشْكُرُ/ شُكْراً
To attend; to be present	حَضَرَ/ يَحْضُرُ/ حُضُوراً
To be found	وُجِدَ/ يُوْجَدُ/ وُجُودًا
Except	إلاّ/ غَيْر
Programme	بَرْنَامَجٌ (SM) بَرَامِجُ (P)
To allocate	خصّصَ يُخصّصُ/ تَخْصِيْصاً
To enable	مَكَّنَ/ يُمَكِّنُ/ تَمْكِيْناً
Regularity	إنْتِظَامٌ
Punctuality	مُوَاظَبَةٌ
Effort	مُحَاوَلَةٌ (SF) مُحَاوَلَاتٌ (P)
Sincere	مُخْلِصٌ (Adj SM)
To realise; to achieve (goal)	حَقَّقَ /يُحَقِّقُ/ تَحْقِيْقاً
Goal	هَدَفٌ (SM) أَهْدَافٌ (P)
To be sufficient	كَفَى/ يَكْفِي/ كِفَايَةً
Inception	بِدَايَةٌ (SF) بِدَايَاتٌ (P)
To clean	نَظَّفَ/ يُنَظِّفُ/ تَنْظِيْفًا
To decorate	زَيَّنَ/ يُزَيِّنُ/ تَزْيِيْناً
Calss	فَصْلٌ (SM) فُصُولٌ (P)
Private; characteristic	خُصُوصِيَةٌ (SF) خُصُوصِيَّاتٌ (P)

Teacher	مُدَرِّسٌ(SM) مُدَرِّسُونَ (P)
Sick	مَرِيضٌ (SM) مَرْضَى (P)
Dress; uniform	زِيٌّ (SM) أَزْيَاءٌ (P)
School (pertaining to)	مَدْرَسِيّ (Adj. SM)
To send back, to return	أَعَادَ/ يُعِيْدُ/ إِعَادَةً، رَجَّعَ/ يُرَجِّعُ/ تَرْجِيعاً
Peon	فَرَّاشٌ(SM) فَرَّاشُوْنَ (P)
Staff	عَامِلٌ (SM)عُمَّالٌ (P)
Finally	نِهَائِياً
To ask; to request	طَلَبَ/ يَطْلُبُ/ طَلَباً
Of, about	حَوْلَ/ عَنْ
General knowledge; General information	مَعْلُومَاتٌ عَامَّةٌ
To answer	أَجَابَ/ يُجِيْبُ/ إِجَابَةً
Question	سُؤَالٌ (SM) أَسْئِلَةٌ (P)
Happy	مَسْرُورٌ (SM) مَسْرُورُونَ، سَعِيْدٌ (SM) سُعَدَاءُ (P)
(Grass) pasturage	عُشْبٌ
Performance	أَدَاءٌ (SM) أَدَاءَاتٌ (P)
Strange; wonderful	عَجِيْبٌ، غَرِيْبٌ (Adj. SM)
If	إِذَا، إِنْ
To need; to want	إِحْتَاجَ/ يَحْتَاجُ/ إِحْتِيَاجاً
Hurry	عَجَلَةٌ/ سُرْعَةٌ
In need of	مُحْتَاجٌ إِلَى
Sociology	عُلُومُ الإِجْتِمَاعِ
Well-known	مَعْرُوْفٌ
To search (for), to look for	بَحَثَ/ يَبْحَثُ (عن)
Catalogue	فِهْرِسٌ (SM) فَهَارِسُ(P)
Classified	مبوَّب

To copy; to note down	اِسْتَنْسَخَ / يَسْتَنْسِخُ / اِسْتِنْسَاخاً
Department; section	قِسْمٌ (SM) أَقْسَامٌ (P)
As per, according to	طِبْقاً لِـ / وَفْقاً لِـ
Written	مَكْتُوبٌ
Recorded; written	مُسَجَّلٌ / مَكْتُوبٌ
To waste	أَضَاعَ / يُضِيعُ / إِضَاعَةً
Exercise; training	تَدْرِيبٌ (SM) تَدْرِيبَاتٌ (P)
To accompany	رَافَقَ / يُرَافِقُ / مُرَافَقَةً
To make tired	أَتْعَبَ / يُتْعِبُ / اِتْعَاباً
Empty handed	صِفْرُ الْيَدَيْنِ
To determine (upon)	صَمَّمَ / يُصَمِّمُ (عَلَى)
To ring	رَنَّ / يَرِنُّ / رَنَّةً
Bell	جَرَسٌ (SM) أَجْرَاسٌ (P)
Study/ Study room	غُرْفَةُ الدِّرَاسَةِ
To tap, to rap, to knock, to ring	دَقَّ / يَدُقُّ / دَقًّا
The bell rang	دَقَّ الْجَرَسُ
To gesture, to beckon	أَوْمَأَ / يُومِئُ / إِيمَاءَةً
To inform	بَلَّغَ / يُبَلِّغُ / تَبْلِيغًا
Drawing room	غُرْفَةُ الإسْتِقْبَالِ
To answer, to reply	رَدَّ / يَرُدُّ / رَدًّا
To be lucky	تَوَفَّقَ / يَتَوَفَّقُ / تَوَفُّقًا
To fall, to be situated	وَقَعَ / يَقَعُ / وُقُوعًا
Vice chancellor	مُدِيرُ الْجَامِعةِ
Concerned people	اَلشَّخْصُ الْمَعْنِيُّ / الأَشْخَاصُ الْمَعْنِيُّونَ
Warden of the hostel	مُرَاقِبُ الدَّاخِلِيَّةِ
To reassure	طَمْأَنَ / يُطَمْئِنُ
Zoological garden	حَدِيقَةُ الْحَيَوَانَاتِ

Courtesy smile	إِبْتِسَامَةُ الْمُجَامَلَة
Guide	دَلِيلٌ / دَلِيلُونَ
To guide, to conduct	أَرْشَدَ / يُرْشِدُ / إِرْشَادًا
Systematically	بِشَكْلٍ تَرْتِيبِى
Senior employee	مُوَظَّفٌ كَبِيرٌ
To instruct, to give instructions	أَعْطَى / يُعْطِى تَعْلِيمَاتٍ
Out of curiosity	عَلَى سَبِيلِ الْفُضُول
Companion	مُرَافِقٌ (SM) مُرَافِقُونَ (P)
Cub	شِبْلٌ (SM) أَشْبَالٌ (P)
To be suspicious, to suspect	تَشَكَّكَ / يَتَشَكَّكُ / تَشَكُّكًا
To approach	إِقْتَرَبَ / يَقْتَرِبُ / إِقْتِرَابًا (مِنْ)
In affection	إِظْهَارًا لِلْحُبِّ
To lift	رَفَعَ / يَرْفَعُ / رَفْعًا
Pair, spouse	زَوْجٌ / أَزْوَاجٌ
To be angry	غَضِبَ / يَغْضَبُ / غَضَبًا
Furious, angry	غَاضِبٌ
With great difficulty	بِصُعُوبَةٍ كَبِيرَةٍ
To remove, to drive away	أَبْعَدَ / يُبْعِدُ / إِبْعَادًا
To take out	أَخْرَجَ / يُخْرِجُ / إِخْرَاجًا
To stop	تَوَقَّفَ / يَتَوَقَّفُ (عن)
To mourn	نَدَبَ / يَنْدُبُ / نَدْبًا
In (the state of) mourning	فِى حَالَةِ نَدْب
To feed, to suck (at mother's breast)	رَضِعَ / يَرْضَعُ / رَضْعًا
To nurse, to suckle	أَرْضَعَ / يُرْضِعُ / إِرْضَاعًا
In a few days time	فِى أَيَّام
One by one, one after the other	وَاحِداً بَعْدَ وَاحِدٍ

Verb For Mixed Plurals And Adverbs
الفعل للجموع المختلطة والظروف

The boy students and the girl students	الطلابُ والطَّالِباتُ
were waiting for the teacher.	كانوا يَنْتَظِرُونَ لِلْمُدَرِّسِ.
The bell rang. The teacher opened	رَنَّ الْجَرسُ. فَتَحَ الأستاذُ
the door gently and entered	أَلْبَابَ بِهدُوءٍ ودخَلَ
the room gracefully.	الغرفةَ بوَقَارٍ.
The (boy and girl) students got up	قَامَ الطلَّابُ وَالطَّالِبَاتُ
as a mark of respect for him.	اِحْتِرَامًا لَه.
Then they sat on the chairs	بَعْدَ ذَلِك جَلَسُوا عَلَى الْكَرَاسِى
calmly and put	صَامِتِيْنَ وَ وَضَعُوا
their satchels infront of them.	حَقَائِبَهُمْ أَمَامَهُم.
After that each student tookout	بَعدَ ذَلِك أَخْرَجَ كُلُّ طَالِبٍ
his book from his satchel silently	كِتَابَهُ مِنْ حَقِيْبَتِه سَاكِتًا
and opened it on the lesson of the day	وفَتَحَه عَلَى دَرْسِ الْيَوْمِ
carefully.	بِاحْتِرَاسٍ.
The teacher took a book and a piece	أَخَذَ الْمُدَرِّسُ كتاباً و قطعَةً
of chalk. He walked to the	من الطَّباشِيرِ وَمَشَى نَحْوَ
blackboard slowly.	السَّبُّورةِ بِبُطءٍ.
He started writing on the blackboard	بَدَأَ يَكْتُبُ عَلى السَّبُّورة
difficult words with their meanings.	الْكلِمَاتِ الصَّعْبَةَ مَعَ مَعَانِيها.
Then he explained the lesson	بَعْدَ ذلك شَرَحَ الدرسَ
in simple words.	بِكلِمَاتٍ سَهْلةٍ.

The teacher closed the book	أَغْلَقَ الْأُسْتَاذُ الْكِتَابَ
and returned it to its owner.	وَ رَجَّعَهُ إِلَى صَاحِبِهِ.
Then he cast a look at the class	ثُمَّ أَلْقَى نَظْرَةً عَلَى الْفَصْلِ
and asked them about the homework.	وَ سَأَلَهُم عَنِ الْوَاجِبِ الْمَدْرَسِى.
All the boy students	قَدَّمَ جَمِيعُ الطُّلَّابِ
and the girl students	وَالطَّالِبَاتِ
gave their notebooks to the teacher.	كُرَّاسَاتِهِم لِلْأُسْتَاذِ.
The teacher took the notebooks	أَخَذَ الْأُسْتَاذُ الْكُرَّاسَاتِ
and said with a smile:	وَقَالَ بِابْتِسَامَةٍ:
My children, you are	أَوْلَادِى، أَنْتُمْ
hardworking students.	طُلَّابٌ مُجْتَهِدُونَ .
Next time you all shall write	فِى الْمَرَّةِ الْقَادِمَةِ سَوفَ تَكْتُبُونَ
an essay on historical monuments	مَقَالاً فِى الْآثَارِ الْقَدِيْمَةِ
in Delhi.	فِى دِلْهِى.
Then he left for another class.	بَعْدَه خَرَجَ لِفَصْلٍ آخَرَ.

Grammar:

As explained earlier, the verbs in Arabic have to agree with their subjects in number and gender.

This you have seen in examples separately set for masculine and feminine gender nouns. But what shall obtain in case of a mixed plural subject?

In this case the masculine element of a mixed plural subject dominates. In other words the verb in such cases will be of masculine gender. For example you want to say that: Shankar, Asha and Usha went to see a film.

This would be expressed in Arabic as follows:

ذَهَبَ شَنْكَر وَآشَا وَأُوْشَا لِمُشَاهَدَةِ فِيْلَم

You can see that the verb used for this mixed plural subject is that we normally use with a masculine subject.

Where the verb for such mixed plural subject has to be used after the subject, in that case not only that it will be masculine but it will also have to agree with the subject in number.

For example:

شنكر و آشا و أوشا ذَهَبُوا لِمُشَاهَدَةٍ فِيْلَم.

Preposition in Arabic is called حرف الجر i.e. Ḥarf al-Jarr. This particle or preposition causes **kasrah** to the terminal letter of the noun it precedes. Such a noun is called مجرور i.e. in the genitive case. This point has also been discussed earlier in detail.

The English adverb of place or adverb of manner etc. can be expressed in Arabic with a preposition preceding the noun.

For example:

The teacher opened the door calmly.   فَتَحَ الاُسْتَاذُ الْبَابَ بِهُدُوءٍ.

Adverbs in Arabic are generally expressed with the noun in the accusative case. For example:

The students stood respectfully for him   قَامَ الطُّلَّابُ اخْتِرَامًا لَّه .

I will visit you in the evening.   اَزُورُك مساءً.

He came almost running   جاءَ مُهَرْوِلًا.

He entered the room smilingly.   دَخَلَ الْغُرْفَةَ مُبْتَسِمًا

Let me further explain to clarify that adverbial meaning for indicating manner is expressed mostly by placing the noun—verbal or infinitive form of the verb—in the accusative case. Verbal noun in this case may be singular or dual or plural according to the contextual requirement. However, this infinitive form of the verb shall always be singular.

Let us see the following examples:

The boy entered the room smilingly.   (٢) دَخَلَ الْوَلَدُ الْغُرْفَةَ مُبْتَسِمًا.

The (two) boys entered the room smilingly.   (٣) دَخَلَ الْوَلَدان الغُرْفَةَ
مُبْتَسِمَيْنِ.

The boys entered the room smilingly.   (٣) دَخَلَ الأَوْلادُ الْغُرْفَةَ مُبْتَسِمِينَ.

In the preceding examples مُبْتَسِمٌ is a verbal noun (active participle) and hence, as explained in the foregoing, it is being used as adverb in the accusative case in singular, dual & plural.

Examples with infinitive form of the verb:

The boy got up respectfully (i.e. out of respect) for the teacher.	(١) قَامَ الوَلَدُ إحْتِرامًا للمُدرِّسِ
The (two) boys got up respectfully (i.e. out of respect) for the teacher.	(٢) قَامَ الوَلَدان إحْتِرامًا للمُدرِّسِ.
The boys got up respectfully (i.e. out of respect) for the teacher.	(٣) قَامَ الأوْلَادُ إحْتِرامًا للمُدرِّسِ.

It may also be borne in mind that there are certain adverbs which function exactly like the prepositions. For example:

Above	(Adv. of place)	فوقَ
Under	(Adv of place)	تَحْتَ
Behind	(Adv. of place)	وَراءَ
Infront of	(Adv. of place)	أمامَ

These adverbs as above and more like them cause Kasrah to the terminal letter of the noun they precede.

-Adverb of manner is known in Arabic as الحال.

-Adverb of time is known in Arabic as ظرف الزمان

-Adverb of place is known in Arabic as: ظرف المكان

Exercises:

Translate into Arabic:

One day I got up early in the morning. In fact it is not my habit to get up early. Normally I go to sleep very late in the night, say one O'clock or two O'clock when I have a lot of work, but in any case never before mid-night. I have been having this habit since I joined a college in Delhi and started my hostel life. During my hostel life I used to keep awake till very late preparing my lessons or doing my home assignment. This continued for complete five years during which period I completed my B.A. & M.A.

degrees. And now when I am no more a student, this old habit still persists
with me. I have always known that early sleeping and early rising is good
for health but my very sincere attempts at giving up this old habit have
failed.

2. Translate into English:

فى الأُسْبُوعِ الْمَاضِىْ اُقِيْمَتِ الْحَفْلَةُ الرِّيَاضِيَّةُ فِى كُلِّيَتِنَا. كَانَتْ كُلِّيَّتُنَا مَزْدَحِمَةً مُنْذُ وقتٍ مُبَكِّرٍ
فِى الصَّبَاحِ. قَدِمَ الطُّلَّابُ الْمُشْتَرِكُونَ فِى مُخْتَلَفِ الْفَعَالِيَّاتِ مُبَكِّرِيْنَ حَتَّى يَأْخُذُوا الاسْتِعْدَادَ
لِلْمُشَارَكَةِ حَسْبَ تَعْلِيْمَاتِ الْمُدَرِّسِ الرِّيَاضِى. قَدِمَ الْمُدَرِّسُ الرِّيَاضِى اَيْضاً مُبَكِّراً. كَانَ مِنَ
الْمُقَرَّرِ أَنْ تَبْدَأَ اَعْمَالُ الْحَفْلَةِ فِى السَّاعَةِ الْعَاشِرَةِ تَمَاماً. بَدَأَ الطُّلَّابُ وَالطَّالِبَاتُ وَالْمُدَرِّسُونَ
وَالْمُدَرِّسَاتُ يَصِلُونَ الْكُلِّيَّةَ حَوَالَى السَّاعَةِ التَّاسِعَةِ وَالنِّصْفِ. كَانَ الطُّلَّابُ وَالطَّالِبَاتُ لَابِسِيْنَ
اَحْسَنَ اَزْيَائِهِمْ وَ يَمْشُونَ هُنَا وَ هُنَاكَ وَيَتَمَازَحُونَ فِيْمَا بَيْنَهُم مُبْتَسِمِيْنَ وَمُبْتَهِجِيْنَ. وَصَلَ مُدِيْرُ
الْكُلِّيَّةِ فِى السَّاعَةِ الْعَاشِرَةِ إِلَّا الرُّبْعِ. ذَهَبَ المدرِّسُونَ وَالمُدَرِّسَاتُ مُهَرْوِلِينَ اِلَى بَوَّابةِ قَاعةِ
الْحَفْلَةِ وَاستَقْبَلُوهُ مُرَحِّبِيْنَ بِهِ وَ ملوِّحِيْنَ لهُ أغصَانَ الْوَرْدِ. دَخَلَ المديرُ قَاعَةَ الْحَفْلَةِ وَ قامَ
الحاضِرُونَ مِنَ الطُّلابِ وَالطَّالِباتِ وَالضُّيوفِ اِحْتِراماً لَه. جَلسَ المديرُ حَتَّى النِّهايَةِ وَبَعْدَهَا اَلْقَى
خِطَابًا وَجِيْزًا مُقَدِّرًا المجهوداتِ المَبْذُولَةَ مِنَ الاَسَاتِذةِ وَالطُّلابِ لإِنْجاحِ الْحَفْلَةِ.ثُمَّ وَزَّعَ
الجَوَائِزَعلَى النَّاجِحِيْنَ والنَّاجِحَاتِ فِى مُخْتَلَفِ الْفَعَالِيَّاتِ. ثُمَّ غَادَرَ الْجَمِيْعُ الكلِّيَّةَ مَسْرُورِيْنَ
قبلَ السَّاعةِ السابعةِ مساءً. إِنَّ الطلابَ والطالباتِ الذينَ يَسكُنُونَ فِى الدَّاخِليةِ فَهُم تَأَخَّروا قَلِيْلًا
مَعَ المُدَرِّسِ الرِّيَاضِى وَالْفَرَّاشِيْنَ لإِعَادَةِ الاَثَاثِ والاَشْيَاءِ الأُخْرىٰ داخلَ الكُلِّيةِ.

3) Pick out all adverbs from the lesson & the exercises & use them in
sentences of your own.

Vocabulary:

Habit	عَادَةٌ (SF) عَادَاتٌ (P)
Normally	عَادَةً (Adv)
Very	جِدًّا (Adv. of manner)
Late, Delay	تأخيرٌ (NM)
When	متى
I have	عِندى

In any case	عَلَى كُلِّ حالٍ
Ever, always (also often used for never)	أَبَدًا
Before	قَبْلَ
Mid-night	نِصف اللَّيْل
Since	مُنْذُ
To join	إلْتَحقَ/ يَلْتَحقُ/ إلْتِحَاقًا
Life	الحَيَاةُ
Hostel	داخِليةٌ
During	خِلالَ
To prepare	أَعَدَّ/ يُعِدُّ/ إعدادًا
Home assignment	الوَاجِبُ المَدْرَسيُّ
To continue	واصلَ/ يُواصِلُ/ مُواصَلَةً
To complete	أكمَلَ/ يُكْمِلُ/ إكمَالاً
B. A.	بكالُورْيُوس
M. A.	مَاجِسْتير
Degree	شَهَادَةٌ (SF) شَهاداتٌ(P)
To remain	بَقِيَ/ يَبْقَى/ بَقَاءً
Health	صِحَّةٌ
Useful, good	مُفيدٌ
Sincere	مُخْلِصٌ
Attempt, effort	مُحَاوَلَةٌ (SF) مُحاولاتٌ (P)
To give up	تَركَ/ يَتْرُكُ/ تَرْكًا
To fail (in exam)	رسبَ/ يَرسُبُ/ رُسُوباً
To fail (in doing s. th. or in exam)	فَشِلَ/ يَفْشَلُ/ فَشْلاً
Suddenly	فَجْأةً

LESSON — 31

الدرس — ٣١

Passive Voice verb	الفعل المجهول
Kana + Past Tense	كان + الماضى
Kana+ Present Tense	كان + المضارع

We lived in a village	كُنَّا نَعِيْشُ فِىْ قَرْيَةٍ
beside a jungle.	عَلَى كَثَبٍ مِنْ غَابَةٍ .
There lived in this jungle	عَاشَ فِى هَذِهِ الْغَابَةِ
beasts of prey.	حَيَوَانَاتٌ مُفْتَرِسَةٌ .
There was a lion also. The lion used	كَانَ هُنَاكَ أَسَدٌ اَيْضاً. كَانَ الاَسَدُ
to come to our village every night.	يَأْتِى اِلَى قَرْيَتِنَا كُلَّ لَيْلَةٍ.
The village-residents were afraid	كَانَ سُكَّانُ الْقَرْيَةِ خَائِفِيْنَ
of this lion because this lion	مِنْ هَذَا الْأَسَدِ لِأَنَّ هَذَا الْأَسَدَ
had killed a boy.	كَانَ قَتَلَ وَلَداً.
The village-residents called a hunter	طَلَبَ سُكَّانُ الْقَرْيَةِ صَيَّاداً
to kill it.	لِقَتْلِه.
The hunter sat in a dark place	جَلَسَ الصَّيَّادُ فِى مَكَانٍ مُظْلِمٍ
one night.	ذَاتَ لَيْلَةٍ.
The lion came as usual	قَدِمَ الأَسَدُ كَعَادَتِه
and the hunter fired a shot at the lion.	وَاَطْلَقَ الصَّيَّادُ طَلْقَةً عَلَى الأَسَدِ.
The lion was killed and the lion's dead	قُتِلَ الأَسَدُ وَ حُمِلَتْ
body was carried to the house	جُثَّةُ الاَسَدِ اِلَى بَيْتِ
of the village chief	رَئِيْسِ الْقَرْيَةِ
and a cash prize was presented (given)	وَ قُدِّمَتْ جَائِزَةٌ نَقْدِيَّةٌ
to the hunter.	لِلصَّيَّادِ.

Grammar:

We have seen that when كان is followed by a verbal noun in the accusative case as its predicate, it gives the meaning in past continuous. For example:

كان الولد جالساً

The boy was sitting.

When the verb كان is placed before a past tense verb, it changes the meaning into the past perfect. For example: ذَهَبَ means: he went; but if we say كان ذهبَ, then it would mean: he had gone. In this form of the verb the verb كان may immediately be followed by the second verb. However in Arabic it is preferable that كان should be followed by the subject and then the second verb should be placed. For example:

كَانَ الوَلَدُ قَتَلَ الأَسدَ

The boy had killed the lion

If the object is a linkable pronoun then the construction order shall change slightly, e.g.

كان ضربه الأُستاذ.

The teacher had beaten him.

In the sentence above the verb كَانَ is followed by the second verb ضَرَبَ followed by linkable pronoun which plays object and finally the overt subject.

If the verb كَانَ is placed before the present indicative verb, then in this case the meaning of the verb indicates habit or a continuous process in the past. For example the verب يَذهب means: he goes; but if we say: كَانَ يَذْهَبُ , it would mean; he used to go. Similarly يَسْكُنُ means "he lives" but كَانَ يَسْكُنُ would means "he lived" or "he used to live" which meaning indicates a continuous process of living in the past.

Passive Voice Verb: صيغة الفعل المجهول

Always a verb is either intransitive or transitive. An intransitive verb requires at least a subject and a transitive verb requires at least a subject and an object to make a complete meaningful sentence.

Passive voice can not be made from intransitive verbs. Passive voice cannot be made from reflexive verbs.

Passive voice is made from the transitive verbs.

Passive voice is sparingly used in Arabic. It is very simple to change a transitive verb into passive voice.

i) The first letter of a verb is given a *dammah*.

ii) The penultimate letter is given a *kasrah* in the case of the past tense verb and in the case of present imperfect verb the penultimate letter is given a *fathah*.

iii) The terminal letter retains original diacritical mark which is Fathah in the case of the past tense verb and dammah in the case or the present tense verb.

Example:

Past tense active voice		Past tense passive voice	
He killed	قَتَلَ	He was killed	قُتِلَ
He carried	حَمَلَ	He was carried	حُمِلَ
He presented	قَدَّمَ	He was presented	قُدِّمَ

(iv) In certain derived verbs i.e. forms of verbs derived from triliteral verbs not only that the first letter/ syllable is given a *dammah* but the second syllable is also given a *dammah*.

Example:

He received	إِسْتَقْبَلَ	He was received	أُسْتُقْبِلَ
He exceeded	تَجَاوَزَ	He was exceeded	تُجُووِزَ

Present tense active voice		Present tense passive voice	
He kills	يَقْتُلُ	He is killed	يُقْتَلُ
He carries	يَحمِلُ	He is carried	يُحْمَلُ
He exceeds	يَتَجَاوَزُ	He is exceeded	يُتَجَاوَزُ
He receives, he welcomes	يَسْتَقْبِلُ	He is received/ He is welcomed	يُسْتَقْبَلُ

All passive voice verbs in past and present are conjugated similarly as in the active voice. For sample conjugation please see appendix.

In the case of active voice verb, the verb takes object beside the subject. We have known that the subject takes ḍammah and the object takes *Fatḥah*. For example:

The boy killed the lion   قَتَلَ الْوَلَدُ الْأَسَدَ

In the sentence above the subject الولدُ takes ḍammah and الْأَسَدَ which is the object terminates with Fatḥah.

However, in the case of passive voice, the subject does not make physical appearance in the sentence. It is the object which figures in the sentence. In this case, the object is given ḍammah and it is known in Arabic Grammar terminology as agent of the subject (نائب الفاعل). It is worth pointing here that in English also only the object appears and the subject is not mentioned. It is only understood from the context. For example, we say in English:

The lion was killed.

It would be seen that in the sentence above the suject is nowhere mentioned. So also in Arabic we would say:

The lion was killed   قُتِلَ الْأَسَدُ

Here also we mention only the object and give it ḍammah. as explained earlier.

Theoretically speaking, we can render all the transitive verbs into the passive voice. However, all verbs are not used in passive voice. Specially for the humanbeings the Arabic passive verb is used sparingly and it is used only in such places where there is no escape from it.

Besides, there is another way of giving expression to the passive without taking recourse to the actual passive verb. We use for this purpose the verb تَمَّ followed by the infinitive form of the verb in the nominative case as shown hereunder:

A solution to the problem has been found.   تَمَّ إِيجَادُ حَلٍّ لِلْمُشْكِلَةِ.

The Conference will be held	سَيَتِمُّ عَقْدُ الْمُؤْتَمَرِ
in Geneva next month.	فِيْ جِنِيْف الشَّهْرَ الْقَادِمَ.

In this kind of sentences the infinitive form of the verb and the noun governed by it shall be placed in construct position i.e. مضاف/ مضاف اليه. The infinitive verb concurrently plays the role of subject and hence it would take ḍammah while the noun governed by it shall have *kasrah*.

In passive voice the expression "by" is very often used in English, e.g.

The glass was broken (by) a worker. The meaning of (by) in the Arabic passive voice is expressed by using (مِنْ). For example in Arabic we would say:

The glass was broken by a worker	كُسِرَ الزُّجاجُ مِن عَامِلٍ

Period of time or point of time مُدَّةُ الزَّمَنِ أَوْ نُقْطَةُ الزَّمَنِ

I have been working in this factory (for)	أَعمَلُ فِى هَذَا الْمَصْنَعِ
the past twenty years.	(مُنْذُ) عِشْرِيْنَ عَاماً الْمَاضِيَةِ.

In the sentence above (for) is used to indicate period of time which is expressed by using (مُنْذُ) in Arabic.

I have been working in this factory	أَعْمَلُ فِى هَذِهِ الْمَصْنَعِ
(since) 1990.	(مُنْذُ) أَلْفٍ وَتِسْعِمِائَةٍ وَ تِسْعِينَ.

In the foregoing sentence (since) is used to indicate point of time which is expressed by using (مُنْذُ) in Arabic.

In Arabic both (1) period of time and (2) point of time, are expressed by using (مُنْذُ). We can also use only (مِنْ) in both these cases, e.g.

(١) أَعْمَلُ فِى هَذَا الْمَصْنَعِ مِنْ عِشْرِيْنَ عَاماً

(٢) أَعْمَلُ فِى هَذَا الْمَصْنَعِ مِنْ عَامِ أَلْفٍ وَ تِسْعِمِائَةٍ وَتِسْعِيْنَ

Exercises:

1. Translate into Arabic:

(a) A dinner-party was held when the son of a big businessman passed in his B.A. examination. Many big people were invited to the party. The house of the businessman was decorated lavishly. The street was swept and washed. The carpets were spread and the chairs and the tables were arranged properly. The guests were received warmly and seated at proper places. They were offered the best kinds of food and drink.

(b)   (1)   I had seen this film last week also.

(2)   Had he gone to meet his relatives there?

(3)   I used to wish him every day.

(4)   She lived in this house two years ago.

(5)   The elephant had been killed with gun.

(6)   He will be punished for his misbehaviour.

(7)   They will be trained before they are sent abroad.

(8)   He is being punished for his negligence.

2) Rewrite the following sentences correctly after replacing the verbs of active voice with those of the passive voice:

1   أَخْرَجَ الْأُسْتَاذُ الْكِتَابَ وَ بَدَأَ التَّدْرِيسَ.

2   كَتَبَ حَامِدٌ إِلَيْنَا رِسَالَةَ الْأُسْبُوعَ الْمَاضِى.

3   إِسْتَقْبَلَ وَزِيرُ خَارِجِيَّةِ الْهِنْدِ رَئِيسَ الْوُزَرَاءِ الْبَاكِسْتَانِى.

4   قَتَلَ الصَّيَّادُ عَدَداً كَبِيراً مِنَ الْحَمَامِ.

5   اَنْفَقَتِ الْحُكُومَةُ أَمْوَالاً كَثِيرَةً عَلَى بِناءِ هَذِهِ الْعِمَارَةِ.

6   فَتَحَ الْفَرَّاشُ الْأَبْوَابَ وَالشَّبَابِيْكَ.

7   أَصْلَحَتِ الْوَرْشَةُ سَيَّارَتِى قَبْلَ يَوْمَيْنِ.

8   سَرَقَ اللُّصُوصُ أَمْوَالاً كَثِيرَةً مِنْ هَذَا الْبَنْكِ.

9   قَدَّمَ لِى صَدِيْقِى هَذَا الْقَامُوسَ.

10   كَسَرَ ابْنِى هَذِهِ الطَّاوِلَةَ قَبْلَ يَوْمَيْنِ أَوْ ثَلَاثَةِ أَيَّامٍ.

Translate into English:

خَرَجَ الطُّلَّابُ مِنْ مُخْتَلَفِ الْمَعَاهِدِ التَّعْلِيمِيَّةِ فِى تَظَاهُرَةٍ ضِدَّ تَوْصِيَاتِ لَجْنَةِ مَانْدَال حَوْلَ حَجْزِ الْوَظَائِفِ فِى الْمَكَاتِبِ الْحُكُومِيَّةِ لِلْمُتَخَلِّفِينَ وَ ذَهَبُوا إِلَى مَبْنَى الْبَرْلَمَانِ فِى مَوْكِبٍ ضَخْمٍ. إِجْتَمَعَ الطُّلَّابُ يُظْهِرُونَ عَدَمَ رِضَاهُمْ بِاللُّجُوءِ إِلَى أَعْمَالِ الْعُنْفِ. فَأُلْقِيَتِ الْحِجَارَةُ عَلَى

السَّيَّارَاتِ وَ مَبْنَى البَرلِمَان وَ كَذلِكَ اُحْرِقَتْ سَيَّارَةٌ حُكُومِيَّةٌ وَسَيَّارَاتٌ عُمُومِيَّةٌ. وَ بِالنَّتِيجَةِ اُجْبِرَتِ الشُّرْطَةُ على إِطْلَاقِ النَّارِ عَلَى المُحْتَشِدِينَ مِن الطُّلَابِ. قُتِلَ طالِبٌ بِالْمَوقِعِ وَ جُرِحَ عدَدٌ كَبِيرٌ مِنْهم. وَ كَذلِكَ اُلْقِىَ القَبْضُ عَلَى عَددٍ مِّنَ الْمُحْتَجِّيْنَ مِنَ الطُّلابِ.

4) Separate all the passive voice verbs from the foregoing paragraph and use them in sentences of your own.

Glossary:	الكلمات العسيرة:
Dinner	عَشَاءٌ
Party	حَفْلَةٌ (SF) حَفَلَاتٌ (P)
A dinner party	حَفْلَةُ عَشَاءٍ
To hold (a party)	أَقَامَ / يُقِيمُ / إِقَامَةً
He held (organised) a party.	أَقَامَ حَفْلَةً
When	مَتَى
To pass (examination)	إِجْتَازَ / يَجْتَازُ / إِجْتِيَازًا
Examination	إِمْتِحَانٌ (SM) إمتحانَاتٌ (P)
B. A.	بَكَالُورِيُوس
Many	عَدَدٌ (مِنْ)
To invite	دَعَا / يَدعُو / دَعْوَةً ، عَزَمَ / يَعْزُمُ / عُزُومَةً
To be invited	دُعِىَ / يُدْعَى / دَعْوَةً
To decorate	زَيَّنَ / يُزَيِّنُ / تَزْيِيناً
Lavishly	بِتَرَفٍ
To sweep	كَنَسَ / يَكْنِسُ / كَنْساً
To wash	غَسَلَ / يَغْسِلُ / غُسْلاً
Carpet	سَجَّادَةٌ (SF) سَجَاجِيْدُ (P)
To spread (bed/carpet)	نَشَرَ / يَنشُرُ / نَشْراً
To arrange	رَتَّبَ / يُرَتِّبُ / تَرتِيْباً
Properly	بِشَكْلٍ مُناسِبٍ
To receive (s. o.), to welcome	إِسْتَقْبَلَ / يَسْتَقْبِلُ / اِسْتِقْبَالاً

To receive (s. th.)	إِسْتَلَم / يَسْتَلِمُ / اِسْتِلاماً
Warmly	بِحَرَارَةٍ
Place	مَكَانٌ (SM) أَمْكِنَةٌ (P)
Proper	مُنَاسِبٌ (Adj. SM)
To offer, to give	قَدَّمَ / يُقَدِّمُ / تَقْدِيماً
Kind	رَحِيمٌ (Adj. SM)
Food	طَعَامٌ (SM) أَطْعِمَةٌ (P)
Drink	مَشْرُوبٌ (SM) مَشْرُوْبَاتٌ (P)
To see (film etc)	شاهد / يُشاهِدُ / مُشَاهَدَةً
Film; movie	فِلْمٌ (SM) أفلام (P)
To wish, to love	أَحَبَّ / يُحِبُّ / مَحَبَّةً
Gun	بُنْدُقِيَّةٌ (SF) بنادِقُ
To punish	عَاقَبَ / يُعَاقِبُ / مُعَاقَبَةً
Misbehaviour	سُوءُ السُّلُوكِ
To train	دَرَّبَ / يُدرِّبُ / تَدْرِيباً
Abroad	خَارِجَ الْبِلَادِ
Negligence	إهْمَالٌ
To neglect	أَهْمَلَ / يُهْمِلُ / إهْمَالاً
To appoint	عَيَّنَ / يُعَيِّنُ / تَعْيِيناً
Government	حُكُومَةٌ (SF) حُكُومَاتٌ (P)
Additional	إضَافِيٌّ (Adj. SM)
Guard, watchman	حَارِسٌ (SM) حُرَّاسٌ (P)
Sanctuary	حَرَمٌ
Mercilessly	بِقَسَاوَةٍ
To shift (s. th.)	نَقَلَ / يَنْقُلُ / نَقْلاً
To clean	نَظَّفَ / يُنَظِّفُ / تَنْظِيفاً
Director: manager	مُدِيرٌ (SM) مُدِيرُونَ (P)
Dining-table, table	مَائِدَةٌ (SF) مَوائِدُ (P)

To deliver, to handover	سَلَّمَ / يُسَلِّمُ / تَسْلِيماً
Postman	سَاعِى الْبَرِيدِ
Fruit seller	فَاكِهَانِى
Fruit	فَاكِهَةٌ (SF) فَوَاكِهُ (P)
To arrange in rows	صَفَّ / يَصُفُّ / صَفّاً
Tidily	بِأَنَاقَةٍ
Mirror	مِرْآةٌ / مَرَايَا
Tree	شَجَرَةٌ(SF) شَجَرَاتٌ (P)
To call, to send for	أَرْسَلَ / يُرْسِلُ (لِ) / إِرْسَالاً
Factory	مَصْنَعٌ (SM) / مَصَانِعُ
Position (job)	وَظِيفَةٌ (SF) / وَظَائِفُ
Vacant	شَاغِرٌ(Adv. SM)
Vacancy	شَاغِرَةٌ (SF) / شَوَاغِرُ (P)

Vocatives, Interrogatives, Weak Verbs
أَدَوَاتُ النِّدَاء، أَدواتُ الإِستِفهام، الافعال الناقصةِ

Hamid is a studious & serious student.	حَامِدٌ طَالِبٌ مُجْتَهِدٌ وَ جِدِّيٌّ .
All (boy & girl) students love him,	يُحِبُّهُ جَمِيعُ الطُّلَّابِ وَ الطَّالِبَاتِ
and the teachers also love him.	وَالأَسَاتِذَةُ أَيْضاً يُحِبُّونَه.
Once it happened that he absented (himself)	حَصَلَ مَرَّةً أَنَّهُ غَابَ
from the school for two days.	لِيَوْمَيْنِ عَنِ الْمَدْرَسَةِ.
His classmates wanted to go	وَدَّ زُمَلَاؤُهُ الذَّهَابَ
to him in order to know the reason	إِلَيهِ لِيَعْرِفُوا السَّبَبَ
for his absence.	لِغِيَابِهِ.
On the third day of his absence	فِى الْيَوم الثَّالِثِ لِغِيَابِهِ
they went to his house after the school.	ذَهَبُوا إِلَى بَيْتِهِ بَعْدَ الْمَدْرَسَةِ.
They found him at home. However, he	وَجَدُوهُ فِى الْبَيْتِ. وَلكِنَّهُ
appeared tired.	بَدَا مُتْعَباً .
Some of them asked him:	فَسَأَلَهُ بَعْضُهُمْ:
O' Hamid, what happened to you?	يَا حَامِدُ مَاذَا حَصَلَ بِكَ؟
You have not been attending the school for	لَا تَحْضُرُ الْمَدْرَسَةَ
three days.	مُنْذُ ثَلَاثَةِ أَيَّامٍ.
Hamid said: My friends,	قَالَ حَامِدٌ: أَصْدِقائي،
I was sick.	كُنْتُ مَرِيضًا.
I had gone with some of my relatives	كُنْتُ ذَهَبْتُ مَعَ بَعْضِ أَقْرِبَائِى
to the zoo three days ago.	الَى حَدِيقَةِ الْحَيوَانَاتِ قَبْلَ ثَلَاثَةِ أَيَّامٍ.
It (the weather) was very hot.	كَانَ الْجَوُّ حَارًّا.
The winds were like fire and violent.	كَانَتِ الرِّيَاحُ مِثْلَ النَّارِ وَ شَدِيدَةً.

And in this heat we roamed about	وَفِى هٰذِهِ الْحَرَارَةِ تَجَوَّلْنَا
in the zoo from one cage	فِى حَدِيقَةِ الْحَيَوَانَاتِ مِنْ قَفَصٍ
to another and we continued walking whole	إِلَى قفصٍ وَ اسْتَمْرَرْنَا فِى الْمَشْى
day long.	طُولَ النَّهَارِ.
We did not take rest at all.	لَم نَسْتَرِحْ أَبَدًا.
We became tired. Then in the evening	أَصْبَحنا مُتَعَبِينَ. ثُمَّ فِى الْمَسَاءِ
we returned to our house/ home.	رَجَعْنَا إِلَى بَيْتِنَا.
I felt that I was extermely tired.	شَعَرْتُ بِأَنَّنِى كُنْتُ مُتْعَباً جِدًّا.
I did not eat anything.	لَمْ آكُلْ شَيْئاً.
I went to my bed early in the night.	ذَهَبْتُ إِلَى سَرِيرِى مُبَكِّراً بِاللَّيْلِ.
I spent the whole night in fever.	أَنفَقْتُ طُولَ اللَّيْلِ فِى الْحُمَّى.
My people thought that I was tired	ظَنَّ أَهْلِى أَنَّنِى كُنْتُ مُتْعَبًا
and nothing (else).	وَ لَاشَئَ آخَرَ.
But when they found me feverish in	ولٰكِنْ عِندَمَا وَجَدُونِى مَحْمُوْماً فِى
the morning also, they became worried and	الصَّبَاحِ أَيْضاً، أَصْبَحُوْا مُتَفَكِّرِينَ
called a doctor.	وَ دَعَوا دُكْتُوْرًا.
The doctor examined me properly	فَحَصَنِى الدُّكْتُورُ جَيِّدًا
and said that I had a sun-stroke.	وَقَالَ إِنَّنِى مُصَابٌ بِضَرْبَةِ شمسٍ.
He gave me medicine and now	أَعْطَانِى الدَّوَاءَ وَالآنَ
by God's grace I have improved greatly.	الحمد لِلّهِ تَحَسَّنْتُ كَثِيرًا.
In a day or two I will be all right .	فِى يَوم أَوْ يَومَيْنْ سَوفَ أَشْفِى.
The tea came and all of them drank tea.	جَاءَ الشَّاى وَ كُلُّهُم شَرِبُوا الشَّاىَ.
Then they got up to leave wishing	ثُمَّ قَامُوْا لِلْخُرُوجِ مُتَمَنِّيْنَ
fast recovery for Hamid	الشِّفَاءَ السَّرِيعَ لِحَامِدٍ
and praying to God for his health.	وَدَاعِيْنَ اللّهَ لِصِحَّتِه.
Hamid thanked his friends	شَكَرَ حَامِدٌ أَصِدْقَاءَه
for their vistit	لِلزِّيَارَةِ
and bade them farewell saying:	وَوَدَّعَهُم قَائِلاً:

See you, brothers/ friends.   الَى اللّقَاء، إخْوَانِى.

We shall meet, God so willing after   نَلتَقِى، إنْ شَاءَ اللّهُ بَعْدَ

two days in the school itself.   يَومَينِ فى الْمَدْرَسَةِ نَفْسِهَا.

Grammar:

Vocative·

Vocative in Arabic is called حرف النداء which literally means "particle for inviting attention of some one." The word used for this purpose in Arabic is يا which is equivalent of O' of the English language.

We hardly use this O' when we call some one. So also in Arabic. However, at places and particularly in the written Arabic we use this يا more often. يا is used before a noun or a pronoun.

Noun after this vocative will not take ال and it will be in the nominative case i.e. its terminal letter shall have *dammah* (only one *dammah*) for example:

O' boy	يا ولدُ
O' children	يا اولادُ
O' Hamid	يا حامدُ

Where for reasons we can not give a clear *dammah* to the noun, it shall be supposed to be having *dammah*. For example:

O' Usha	يا اوشا
O' Mala	يا مَالا
O' you	يَا هذا

Where the noun is in construct position with another noun, in that case the noun so adressed shall be in the accusative case i.e. the terminal letter of the first noun shall have a *Fathah*. For example:

O' street boy	يَا ولَدَ الشَّارِعِ
O' school boys	يَا اولَادَالمدرسةِ

O' Abdullah   يَا عبدَاللّه

Another popular vocative is أَيُّهَا for masculine and أَيَّتُهَا for feminine meaning the same as above. In this case the noun shall have ال. For example:

O' boy   اتّها الوَلَدُ

O' boys   أَيُّهَا الأَولادُ

O' girl   أَيَّتُهَا الْبِنْتُ

At places يَا and أَيَّتُهَا /اَيُّهَا may be combinedly used as follows:

O' boy   يا اَيُّهَا الوَلَدُ

O' girls   ياأَيَّتُهاالبناتُ

In case of the vocative أَيُّهَا and يَا اَيُّهَا no noun or pronoun etc can be used in construct position. We have seen in earlier lessons that the Arabic language is very sensitive about the masculine and feminine genders. For example: if the subject is masculine, then the verb also has to be masculine etc. However, in the case of voctive the same (masculine) vocative can be used with all nouns irrespective of its gender and number.

Interrogatives:

Same is the case with interrogative pornouns. For example: مَا meaning "what", مَنmeaning "who", will be used with all nouns irrespective of their number and gender saving only that مَا is used with objects other than humanbeings and مَن strictly and only with objects meaning humanbeings. For example:

What is this?   مَا هَذا؟

This is a book.   هَذا كِتابٌ.

This is a lion   هَذا أَسَدٌ.

The same مَا هذا may be used for questioning about objects of feminine gender also unless otherwise we know for certainty that the object questioned about is a feminine gender noun where alone we shall use?مَا هذه.

Following examples shall amply clarify the usage of مَن"who".

Who is he?	مَن هُوَ؟
Who is she?	مَن هِيَ؟
Who are you? (S.M.)	مَنْ أَنْتَ؟
Who are you? (S.F.)	مَنْ أَنْتِ؟
Who are they? (P.M.)	مَنْ هُم؟

هَلْ is also an interrogative pronoun which , when placed alone, does not have any meaning; However, when it is palced before a nominal sentence of positive sense, it renders it into question. For example هووَلد means: he is a boy, but if we say?هَلْ هُوَ وَلَدٌ, it would mean: Is he a boy?

When this هل is placed before a verbal sentence, in this case it has to be translated as : did, do, will & shall etc. in apposition to the tense of the verb. For example:

Did you go to the school?	هَلْ ذَهَبْتَ إِلَى الْمَدْرَسَةِ؟
Do you go to the school?	هَلْ تَذْهَبُ إِلَى الْمَدْرَسَةِ؟
Will you go to the school?	هَل سَتَذهَبُ إِلَى الْمَدْرَسَةِ؟

It is important to note that هَلْ is used only with the sentences of positive meanings where the answer may be given by نَعم Yes or لَا No.

There is another particle or interrogative pronoun which is called همزة الاستفهام i.e. Hamza for interrogation. It is used with the nominal and verbal sentences with the same meaning as above. For example:

| Is he a boy? | أَهُوَ وَلَدٌ؟ |
| Did you go to the school? | أ ذَهَبْتَ إِلَى الْمَدْرَسَةِ؟ |

However, another quality of this أ is that it can be used with sentences of negative meanings also.

For example:

The boy is not sitting	لا يجلسُ الطالبُ.
Is not the boy sitting?	أَلَا يَجْلِسُ الطَّالِبُ؟
You did not go the school.	لَم تَذهبْ الَى الْمَدْرَسَةِ.

Did you not go to the school?	أَلَم تَذهَبْ إِلَى الْمَدْرَسَةِ؟
Do you not go to the school?	أَلا تَذهَبُ الَى الْمَدْرَسَةِ؟
(Don't you go to the school?)	

Another characteristic of أ is that it indicates choice. In other terms, where the answer can not be made in "yes" or "no" only أ is used for interrogation. In this case, أ is followed by أَمْ meaning "or". For example:

Did you eat apple or banana?	أَ أَكَلْتَ التُّفَّاحَ أَمِ الْموزَ؟

In this case, as it is clear , the answer can not be made by 'yes' or 'no'. We have to answer in a full sentence or at least we have to mention the object eaten by its name, saying I ate apple أَكلتُ التُّفَّاح

In brief, we can say that " أ " can be used in place of " هل " , but we can not use " هل " in place of أ .

Besides, there are many other interrogatives like لما ذا meaning "why", أين meaning "where", etc and all these have to be used in their abstract forms with nouns of all genders and numbers as explained above.

The defective verbs:

In Arabic, verbs which necessarily cause *dammah* to the subject i.e.Mubtada and *fathah* to the predicate i.e. Khabar are known as "defective verbs" i.e. الافعال الناقصة . They are also known as sisters of كانَ. They fuction in the same manner as كان , i.e. they allow *dammah* to its Mubtada and *fathah* to its Khabar.

The most popular & widely used defective verbs are as follows:

To be	كَانَ / يَكُونُ / كونًا
To become	صَارَ / يَصِيْرُ / صَيْرُورَةً
To be, to become (with special reference to morning time)	أَصْبَحَ / يُصْبِحُ / إِصْبَاحاً
To be, to become (with special reference to evening time)	أَمْسَى / يُمْسِي / إِمْسَاءً

To be, to become   أَضْحَى / يُضْحِى / إِضْحَاءَ
(with special reference to forenoon)

To be, to become   بَاتَ / يَبِيتُ / بَيَاتاً
(with special reference to forenoon)

These verbs have been very carefully used in this lesson to indicate their
appropriate and specialized meaning and usage. However, these verbs are
loosely used without reference to time factor. For example اصبح is used in
the meaning of " to become" without its being restricted to morning time
alone and similarly أمسى and other verbs.

Besides, there are some other verbs which grammatically fall under the
category of defective verbs.

Some of these verbs may be rendered into present indicative while some
others can be fully conjugated and a few have fixed forms.

There is a defective verb which can not be rendered into present imperfect.
This verb is لَيْسَ. It is employed to render a sentence of positive sense into
that of negative sense. However, it functions exactly like any other
defective verb. For example: الْوَلَدُ جَالِسٌ is a nominal sentence meaning: the
boy is sitting. And when we say: لَيْسَ الولَدُ جَالِساً it would mean: The boy is
not sitting. The predicate after ليس may also be in the genitive case
provided it is preceded by a preposition. For exampleلَيْسَ الوَلَدُ بِجَالِسٍ,
however meaning remains the same: 'The boy is not sitting'. Another
characteristic of this "past defective verb" is that it gives the meaning in the
present indicative.

All these verbs, like other ordinary verbs are preferably used before their
subjects where they agree with them only in gender. However, if they have
to be used after the subjects, they will have to agree with them in gender
and number also.

Exercises:

1. Translate into Arabic:

(a) My friend Uday was an intelligent and a hardworking student. He was
my classmate in M. Com. He used to remain busy all the time (with)

reading books on his subject and the related topics. As a result of his continuous and systematic reading, he became very proficient in his subject. Teachers were happy with him and so were the students. He passed his M. com. with distinction in each paper. and soon after that he got a big post in the government with huge salary. Now we do not meet but I still remember him. I don't know whether he remembers me or not.

(b) I am not a difficult person. This is perhaps the reason that people take me for a ride. I often think that I should change my habits, but now it is not possible. Who can change at my ripe age of 50 years. Yesterday I had gone to the electricity office to pay my bill. The queue was long and I was getting late for office. In the meantime some one called me from behind and said: Good man, do you recognise me? My name is Sashank. Don't you remember me? You once helped me. I was getting late for my interview and on my request you gave me a lift on your scooter to the place of my interview. I am now working in that office only because of you. I was very pappy to know that. I thought it was really not bad to be good. Somewhere, some time you do get recognition—your reward of being good.

2. Translate into English:

نَحْنُ أَصْلاً مِنْ قَرْيَةٍ فِى الوِلاَيَةِ الشِّمَالِيَّةِ. كَانَتْ جَدَّتى تَحكى لَنَا قِصَصاً عَنْ قَرْيَتِنَا. هِىَ قَارَنَتْ دَائِماً الحَيَاةَ المَدَنِيَّةَ والحياةَ الرِّيِفِيَّةَ. وَقَالَتْ إِنَّ النَّاسَ فِى المُدُنِ مُعْرِضُونَ ولاَ يُفَكِّرُونَ فى مَصَالِحِ الآخَرِينَ بَيْنَمَا إِنَّ القَرَوِيِّينَ بُسَطَاءُ و هُم دائِما مُسْتَعِدُّونَ لِمُسَاعَدَةِ الآخَرِينَ و قَالَتْ أَيْضاً إِنَّ الحَيَاةَ فِى القُرىٰ احسَنُ بكثيرٍ مِنَ الحَيَاةِ فِى المُدُنِ و بِخَاصَّةٍ فِى المُدُنِ الكُبرىٰ مِثْل دِلهى. رُوَيْداً رُوَيداً وُلِدَتْ لَدَىَّ رَغْبَةٌ شَدِيدَةٌ فِى الذَّهَابِ الى قريةٍ لِأَرَى بِعَيْنَىَّ الحَيَاةَ الرِّيِفِيَّةَ وأُدْرِكَ بالفَرْقِ بَيْنَ الحَيَاةِ المَدَنِيَّةِ و الحَيَاةِ الرِّيِفِيَّةِ. وَحَصَلَ أَن سَنَحَتْ لى فُرصَةٌ عِندَما كُنتُ فى الصفِّ العاشِرِ. قَرَّرَتِ المَدْرَسَةُ على الذَّهابِ إِلَى قَرِيَةٍ قُرْبَ دِلهى فى رِحْلَةٍ دِراسِيَّةٍ حتَّى نَتَعَرَّفَ علىَ كَيْفِيَّةِ المَعِيشَةِ الرِّيِفِيَّةِ وَأَنْ نُقَدِّمَ مَا أَمكَنَ لَنَا مِنَ المُسَاعَدَةِ لِأَهْلِ القَرْيَةِ فى تَحْسِينِ حالَتِهِم المَعِيشِيَّةِ.

جَاءَ يَوْمُ الرِّحْلَةِ و ذَهَبْنَا بِمَعِيَّةِ أُسْتَاذٍ إِلى قَرْيَةِ ماندى. هذه القرية قَرِيْبَةٌ مِنْ دِلهى. وَصَلْنَا هَذِهِ القَرْيَةَ فى سَاعَتَيْنِ تَقْرِيباً. عِندَما وَصَلْنَا هذه القَرْيَةَ رَأينَا أَنَّ كِبَارَالقَرْيَةِ كَانُوا مَوْجُودِيْنَ خَارِجَ

الْقَرْيَةِ لِاسْتِقْبَالِنَا. فَرَحَّبُوا بِنَا بِحَفَاوَةٍ وصِرْنَا مَسْرُورِينَ لِلْغَايَةِ. كُنَّا تَعْبَانِينَ. فَأَخَذَنَا كِبَارُ الْقَرْيَةِ إِلَى مَبْنَى الْهَيْئَةِ الرِّيْفِيَّةِ و قَدَّمُوا لَنَا الشَّايَ والفَطَائِرَ. بَعْدَ شُرْبِ الشَّاى اسْتَرَحْنَا قَلِيلًا و حَوَالَى السَّاعَةِ الرَّابِعَةِ مَسَاءً خَرَجْنَا بِمَعِيَّةِ دَلِيلٍ لِنُقَابِلَ النَّاس و نَتَعَرَّفَ عَلَى أَحْوَالِهِم. رَأَيْنَا أَنَّ الْجَوَّ فِى الْقَرْيَةِ كانَ نَقِيًّا و أَنَّ الْمَنَاظِرَ كَانَتْ جَذَّابَةً. فَمَشَيْنَا عَلى مَهْلِنَا نَتَفَرَّجُ عَلَى الْمَنَاظِرِ الشَّيِّقَةِ حَتَّى أَمْسَيْنَا عَائِدِينَ إِلَى مَبْنَى إِقَامَتِنَا بَعْدَ غُرُوْبِ الشَّمْسِ. كَانَ كِبَارُ الْقَرْيَةِ مَوْجُودِينَ فَقَدَّمُوا لَنَا الطَّعَامَ و بَعْدَ أَكْلِ الطَّعَامِ جَلسْنَا نَتَحَدَّثُ لِوَقْتٍ قَلِيلٍ. ثُمَّ عَادَ كِبَارُ الْقَرْيَةِ وَبِتْنَا لَيْلَةً مُرِيحَةً فِى جَوِّ الْقَرْيَةِ اللَّطِيْفِ. أَصْبَحْنَا مُبَكِّرِينَ و خَرَجْنَا نَمْشِى نَتَمَتَّعُ بِالْمَنَاظِرِ الطَّبِيعِيَّةِ الخَلَّابَةِ وعِنْدَمَا أَضْحَيْنَا تَعْبَانِيْنَ عُدْنَا إِلَى مقَرِّنَا. وأَكَلْنَا فُطُورَنَا. بَعْدَ ذلِك جَاءَ أَهْلُ القَرْيَةِ وجَلسْنَا نَتَحَدَّثُ إِلَى الْقَرَوِيِّنَ. عَرَفْنَا خِلَالَ حَدِيثِنَا مَعَهُمْ أَنَّ مُعْظَمَ القَرَوِيِّنَ أُمِّيُونَ. فَظَلِلْنَا نَتَحَدَّثُ فِى هَذا المَوْضُوعِ فِيْمَا بَيْنَنَا ونُعِدُّ بَرَامِجَ لِتَعْلِيمِ القَرَوِيِّنَ فِى الْعُطْلَةِ الصَّيْفِيَّةِ القَادِمَةِ. أَمْضَيْنَا يَومَيْنِ فِى القَرِيَةِ وعُدْنَا فِى الْيَومِ الثَّالِثِ مَعَ الأَمَلِ والوَعْدِ أَنَّنَا نَعُودُ إِلَيهِم مَرَّةً أُخرى فِى العُطْلَةِ الصَّيْفِيَّةِ القَادِمَةِ بِمَشْرُوعٍ إِزَالَةِ الأُمِّيَّةِ مِن تِلْكَ القَرْيَةِ.

3) Separate all the defective verbs from the foregoing passage and use them in sentences/ paragraph of your own.

Vocabulary:

Uday (proper noun)	أُودَاى
Intelligent	ذَكِىٌّ (Adj. SM) أذْكِياء(P)
M. Com.	ما جِسْتِير فِى عُلُومِ التِّجَارَة
All the time	كُلَّ ذلِك الوَقْتِ
Subject, topic	مَوضُوعٌ (SM) مَوضُوعَاتٌ (P)
As a result (of)	بِالنَّتِيجَةِ (لِ)
Continuous	مُسْتَمِرٌّ(Adj. SM)
Systematic	مُنَظَّمٌ (Adj. SM)
And so	وهَكَذا
To pass (examination)	إِجتازَ/ يَجْتازُ/ إِجتيازًا (الإمتِحان)
With distinction	بِامتِيازٍ

Each; every	كلٌّ
And soon after that	و بعدَ ذلك فوراً
To get	حصلَ / يحصُلُ / حُصُولاً (على)
Salary	مُرَتَّبٌ (SM) مُرَتَّباتٌ (P)
Post, job, position	وَظِيْفَةٌ (SM) وَظَائِفُ (P)
To remember	تذكّرَ / يتَذَكَّرُ / تذكُّراً، ذَكَرَ / يَذكُرُ / ذِكْراً
I still remember (him)	أذْكُرُه للآن
Either.......or	إمَّا، أم
To walk (slowly)	مَشَى / يَمْشِى / (ببطءٍ) مَشْيًا
Aimlessly	بِدُون هَدَفٍ
Road	شارِعٌ (SM) شَوَارِعُ (P)
Weather	جَوٌّ (SM) أجْوَاءٌ (P)
Reward	جَائِزَةٌ (SF) جَوَائِزُ (P)
To take for a ride, to cheat	خَدَعَ / يَخْدَعُ / خِدَاعًا
Ripe age	سِنٌّ نَاضِجَةٌ
Electricity office	مَكتَبُ الكَهرَبَاءِ
Queue	طَابُورٌ (SM) طَوَابِيْرُ (P)
To know, to recognise	عَرَفَ / يَعْرِفُ / عِرْفَانًا
Scooter	دَرَّاجَةٌ بُخَارِيَّةٌ
Interview, meeting	لِقَاءٌ (SM) لِقَاء اتٌ(P)
To transport, to give a lift	نَقَلَ / يَنْقُلُ / نَقْلًا
Pleasant	لطيفٌ (Adj. SM)
Slowly	بِبُطءٍ
To look (at)	نَظَرَ / يَنْظُرُ / نَظَرًا (إلَى)
Commodity, goods	سِلْعَةٌ (SF) سِلَعٌ (P)
To display	عَرَضَ / يَعْرِضُ / عرْضاً
Displayed	معروضٌ (Adj. SM)
Showroom; exhibition	مَعْرِضٌ (SM) مَعَارِضُ(P)

Voice; sound	صَوتٌ (SM) أَصْوَاتٌ(P)
Shop	مَحَلٌّ (SM) مَحَلَّاتٌ (P) دُكَّانٌ (SM) دَكَاكِيْنُ (P)
To call; to accost	نادى / يُنادى / مُنَاداةً
From behind	مِن وَراءِ
To turn (to)	تَحوَّلَ / يَتَحوَّلُ / تَحَوُّلًا (إلى)
Of mine, my	لِى
Dear (to me)	عَزِيزٌ (SM) أَعِزَّاءُ (P)
For, since	مُنذُ، مِنْ
Year	سَنَةٌ (SF) سِنُونٌ (P) سَنَةٌ (SF) سَنَوَاتٌ (P)
To rush: to walk hastily	هَرْوَلَ / يُهَرِولُ / هَرْوَلَةً
Arm	سَاعِدٌ (SF) سَواعِد (P)
To kiss	قَبَّلَ / يُقَبِّلُ / تَقْبِيلًا
Warmth	حَرارةٌ (NF)
Meaning	مَعْنى (SM) مَعَانِى (P)
Thing	شَىءٌ (SM) أَشْيَاءُ (P)
About many things	عَنْ كَثِيرٍ مِنَ الأَشْيَاءِ
To revive	أَحْيى / يُحْيى / إِحْيَاءً
Memory	ذاكِرةٌ (NF)
Hour, watch	سَاعَةٌ (SF) سَاعَاتٌ (P)
For hours together	لساعاتٍ فى وقتٍ واحِدٍ
To feel	شعرَ / يَشْعُرُ / شُعوراً
To pass (some place)	مَرَّ / يَمُرُّ / مُرُورًا (ب)
Passage (of time)	مُرُورُ الزَّمَنِ
Tiredness; weariness	تَعَبٌ (NM)
Neither ....nor	لَا ....ولَا
To close	اغلَقَ / يُغْلِقُ / إغْلاقاً

Time & Date
الزمن والتاريخ

One morning	صَباحَ يَومٍ
at 8 o'clock	فى السَّاعَةِ الثَّامِنَةِ
or 8.15	أوفى السَّاعَةِ الثَّامِنَةِ وَالرُّبعِ
I was standing in queue	كنتُ واقِفاً فى الطَّابُورِ
at a bus stop.	بِمَحَطَّةِ بَاصٍ.
It was the time when the (bus) stops are	هُوَ الوَقْتُ حَيْثُ تَكونُ الْمَحَطَّاتُ
crowded with those going	مُزْدَحِمَةً بالذَّاهِبينَ
to the offices and the schools.	الَى الْمَكاتِبِ وَالمَدارِسِ.
I was standing waiting for the bus	كنتُ واقِفاً فى انْتِظارِ الْبَاصِ
when suddenly I heard a person	إذْ سَمِعْتُ فَجْأَةً شَخْصًا
behind me grumbling.	وَرائى يتَذَمَّرُ.
I turned towards him and (I) saw	تحوَّلْتُ نَحوَهُ وَ رَأيتُ
a thin and middle aged person.	شَخْصًا هَزيلاً وكَهْلاً.
It was evident from his appearance	تَبَيَّنَ من مَظْهَرِهِ
that he was a clerk in some office.	أنَّهُ كان كاتِباً فى مَكْتَبٍ.
When he saw me turning towards him,	مَتَى رآنى أتَحوَّلُ نَحوَهُ،
he asked me befriendingly:	سَألَنى مُتودِّدًا:
What is the time, my (dear) brother?	السَّاعَةُ كَمْ يَا اَخِى؟
I looked at my watch and replied (to him):	ألقَيتُ نَظْرَةً على ساعَتى وأجَبْتُ (لَه)
It is half past eight (or 8.30).	هِى الثَّامِنَةُ والنِّصْفُ.
The stranger continued	استَمَرَّ الأجْنَبِيُّ
the conversation saying:	فى الْحَديثِ قَائِلاً:

It always happens like this. I leave	دائماً يَحْصُلُ هَكَذا. أَخْرُجُ
every day quite early for the office but I	كُلَّ يَوم مُبكّراً جِدًّا لِلمكتبِ، ولكنَّى
reach there late	أَصِلُه مُتَأَخِّراً
most of the time.	فى أكْثَرِ الأحْيَانِ.
We don't have any system	لَيسَ عِنْدَنَا نِظامٌ
and there is none to take to task	ولايُوجَدُ هناك شَخْصٌ يُحَاسِبُ
these government employees.	هؤُلاءِ الْمُوَظَّفِينَ الْحُكُومِيِّينَ.
We , the employees of private offices,	نَحْنُ الْمُوظَّفِينَ لِلْمَكَاتِبِ الخاصَّةِ
work like donkeys.	نَعْمَلُ مِثْلَ الحَمِيرِ.
But (despite that)	ولكن (بالرَّغْمِ مِنْ ذٰلك)
Our employer is never happy with us.	لا يُسَرُّ بِنَا صاحبُ عَمَلِنا.
The employees	إنَّ العَامِلِينَ
of Delhi Transport Corporation	بهَيْئةِ نَقْلِ دلهى
do not know the value of time.	لا يَعْرِفُونَ قِيمَةَ الوَقْتِ.
They are always late and cause	هُم دائمًا يتأخَّرُونَ و يُسَبِّبُونَ
delay to us.	لَنا التَّأخِيرَ.
Look my dear sir, I leave every day for my	شُفْ يا سَيِّدى، أخْرُجُ كُلَّ يَومٍ لِمَكْتَبِى
office at eight o'clock exactly so that I can	فى السَّاعةِ الثامنةِ بالضَّبْطِ حَتَّى أتَمَكَّنَ
reach my office on time.	مِنَ الوُصُولِ لِمَكْتَبِى فى الوَقْتِ.
Inspite of this I am late for office	بالرَّغْمِ من ذٰلك أتأخَّرُ عَن المَكْتَبِ
for a week or ten days	أُسْبُوعًا أو عَشَرَةَ أيَّامٍ
every month.	كُلَّ شَهْرٍ.
The boss scolds me	يُوبِّخُنى صاحِبُ العَمَلِ
and cuts my salary.	و يَقْتَطِعُ مُرَتَّبى.
He thinks I am lazy,	هُو يَفْتَكِرُ بأنَّى كسلان،
don't make hurry.	لا أُسرِعُ.
Last Friday, on 18th	الجُمُعَةَ السَّابِقَةَ فى الْيَوم الثَّامِن عَشَر

instant I was late	للشَّهرِ الجَارى تَأَخَّرْتُ
for half an hour and I reached office	بنِصْفِ سَاعَةٍ وَوصَلْتُ المَكْتَبَ
at half past ten.	فِى السَّاعَةِ العَاشِرَةِ والنصْفِ .
As soon as I reached there,	فَوْرَ وُصُولى هُنَاك
my employer called me to his room.	طَلَبَنى صَاحِبُ العَمَل لِغُرْفَتِه .
I went to his room with my heart	ذَهَبْتُ الَى غُرفَتِه و قَلْبى
beating (hard)	يَنبِضُ (بِشِدَّةٍ)
and my head bowed down.	و رَأسى ناكِسٌ .
The master cast at me an examining look	ألقىْ صاحبُ العَمَلِ عَلَىَّ نظرةً فاحصةً
and reminded me angrily	وذكّرنى بغَضَبٍ
that I was late	أنَّنى تَأَخَّرْتُ
on 6th, 9th, 10th,	فِى اليَومِ السادس والتَّاسع والعاشر و
13th, & 16th	الثالِث عشر والسادسَ عشر
instant.	للشهر الجارى .
After giving me a normal dose	وبَعْدَ أنْ أعطانى جُرعَةً عاديةً
of scolding and chiding, he gave me	مِن التَّوبِيخ والتعنِيف أعطانى
the final notice, saying:	الإشعارَ النهائى قائلاً :
If you are late after today,	إذَا تَأخَّرْتَ بعد اليوم
I shall remove you from your job.	فَسَوفَ أُبعدك عن العَمَل
And here the stranger stopped	و هنا تَوقَّفَ الأجنبِىُّ
and heaved a deep sigh as if he was	وأخَذَ نَفَسًا عميقاً كأنَّه
preparing to resume the conversation	يَستعِدُّ لإستِئْنَافِ الحديثِ
when suddenly there appeared a bus	إذ ظَهَرَ باصٌّ
at some distance.	على مَسافَةٍ .
He cancelled the conversation	إنّه ألْغَى الحَدِيثَ
and got ready for boarding	وَ استَعَدَّ لِلرُّكُوب
as if he was preparing	كأنَّه يَسْتعِدُّ
to attack his worst enemy.	لِمُهَاجَمَةِ ألَدّ اَعْدَائِه .

The bus came and stopped

وصلَ الباصُ و توقَّفَ

and the queue moved .

و تحرَّك الطابُورُ .

The people started getting in

بدأ النّاسُ يَرْكَبُونَ

one by one.

و احداً بَعْدَ واحِدٍ .

When I entered the conductor said:

وَعِندَمَا دَخَلْتُ قالَ المُحَصِّلُ :

It is complete.

تمامٌ.

I looked back and saw the stranger was

نَظَرتُ وَرائي وَرَأيتُ الاجنبيَّ

on the verge of weeping.

عَلَى وَشَكِ الْبُكاءِ .

I got down immediately and gave him

فنَزَلْتُ فوراً و أعطيتُه

my turn so that he could reach

نَوبَتى حتَّى يَتَمَكَّنَ منَ الوُصُولِ

his office on time, and is not removed

لمَكتَبِه فى الوقتِ ولا يُفصَلَ

from his job.

عن عملِه.

As far as I am concerned (or as regards me),

أمَّا أنا،

I am a government employee.

فأَنا مُوظَّفٌ حُكوميٌّ

There is none

لا يُوجَدُ هُناك شَخْصٌ

to scold me in the office.

فى الْمَكْتَبِ يُوَبِّخُني.

I am a confirmed employee

أنا عامِلٌ ثابتٌ

and nobody can remove me

و لا يَستطِيعُ احدٌ أن يَفْصِلَني

from my job.

عَن عَمَلِي.

I get my salary every month .

آخذُ راتِبي كلَّ شهرٍ.

What if I am late today intentionally

لا بَأْسَ إذا تَأَخَّرتُ اليَومَ عَمْدًا

for a good cause.

لِسَبَبٍ حَسَنٍ.

Grammar:

In Arabic, the word meaning hour or o'clock is سَاعَةٌ. It is preceded by the definite article Al اَلْ while it is used to tell or ask time.

The noun كم before or after الساعة means 'what', for example:

What is the time?

كَمِ السّاعَةُ؟ or السّاعَةُ كَمْ؟

Either of the two expressions given above may be used to ask time.

In standard Arabic, only the ordinal numbers are used for telling time except for 'one' where alone the cardinal number meaning one i.e. وَاحدة is used.

As is evident, the word السّاعة is a feminine gender noun because it ends with the Taa Marboota ة. It is therefore, the "full hour" is expressed in Arabic by an ordinal number of feminine gender. For example eight o'clock and nine o'clock will be expressed thus:

8 o'clock	السَّاعَةُ الثَّامِنَةُ
9 o'clock	الساعة التاسعةُ

For half in Arabic we say النِّصْفُ and for quarter the word used is اَلرُّبْعُ. These partitive nouns are used as they are without any change.

For example:

Half past nine or 9.30 (literally: nine & half)	السَّاعَةُ التَّاسِعَةُ وَالنِّصْفُ
Quarter past eighth or 8.15	السَّاعَةُ الثَّامِنَةُ والرُّبْعُ

The preposition 'at' with reference to time means 'فِى' in Arabic.

For example:

at 8 O'clock	فِىْ السَّاعَةِ الثَّامِنَةِ.

The preposition فى functions normally i.e. it gives *kasrah* to all the temporal nouns which are governed by it except eleven and where the Arabic compound numbers are treated as indeclinable.

The word for minute in Arabic is دَقِيقَةٌ. Its plural is دَقَائِقُ

ثَانِيَةٌ means second of which the plural is ثَوَانِى.

The meaning of 'past' as in the combinations: half past or five minutes past, is expressed by the conjunctive وَ. For example:

1) Five minutes past eight (O'clock)	اَلسَّاعَةُ الثَّامِنَةُ وَ خَمْسُ دَقَائِقَ
2) Half past eight or 8.30	السَّاعَةُ الثَّامِنَةُ والنِّصْفِ.

The meaning of 'to' as in the combinations: quarter to eight or five minutes to eight, is expressed by إلّا. For example:

at quarter to eight	فى السَّاعَةِ الثَّامِنَةِ الا الرُّبع
at five minutes to eight	فى الساعة الثامنة إلا خمس دقائق

It is important to note that minutes are expressed by cardinal numbers.

A. M., is expressed by the word صباحاً or فى الصباح. For example:

7.00 A.M. or 7.00 O'clock	السَّاعَةُ السَّابِعَةُ صَباحاً أَو
in the morning	فِىْ الصَّبَاحِ.

'P.M.' is exprssed by the word مَساءً or فِى الْمَساءِ. For example:

5.00 P. M. or 5.00 O'clock	السَّاعَةُ الخَامِسَةُ مَساءً أَو
in the evening.	فِى الْمَساءِ

In Arabic a day of twenty four hours is called يَوْم plural is أَيَّام.

Day-time is called نَهارٌ and the night لَيْلٌ or لَيْلَةً.

"Today" has the fixed form of اليَوْم .

"Week" means أُسْبُوعٌ, plural is أَسَابِيع . Following are the Arabic names of the days of the week.

Sunday	(يَوْمُ) الأَحد
Monday	(يَوْمُ) الاثنين
Tuesday	(يَوْمُ) الثلاثاء
Wednesday	(يَوْمُ) الاربعاء
Thursday	(يَوْمُ) الخميس
Friday	(يَوْمُ) الجُمْعَة
Saturday	(يَوْمُ) السَّبْتِ

"Month" in Arabic is شَهْرٌ with the plural أَشْهُرٌ or شُهُورٌ .

Following are the names of the months:

Arabic Names	Christian Names	
كانُون الثَّانى	January	يَنَايِر
شُباط	February	فِبْرَايِر
آذار	March	مَارِس

نِيسَان	April	إبرِيْل
أَيَّار	May	مَايُو
حَزِيرَان	June	يُونْيُو
تَمّوز	July	يُولْيُو
آب	August	اُغُسْطُس
أيلُول	September	سِبْتِمْبِر
تِشرينَ الأوّل	October	أَكْتُوبِر
تِشرين الثَّانى	November	نُوفِمْبِر
كانون الأوَّل	December	دِيْسِمِبر

"Year" in Arabic generally means سنةٌ with the plural سِنُونٌ or سَنَواتٌ . Another word is عَامٌ, plural أَعْوَامٌ.

For season in Arabic we use the word فَصْلٌ. Its plural is فُصُولٌ. There are four seasons in the year. They are as follows:

Summer	(season)	(فَصْلُ) الصَّيفِ
Winter	(season)	(فَصْلُ) الشِّتَاءِ
Spring	(season)	(فَصْلُ) الرَّبيعِ
Autumn	(season)	(فَصْلُ) الخَريفِ

Date in standard Arabic is expressed by using ordinal number. It is normally preceded by the word اَلْيَوم . For example:

I will visit	أزورُ
Your office	مَكْتَبَكُم
On 18th instant	فِى الْيَومِ الثَّامِن عَشَر للشَّهْرِ الْجَارى

We may drop the word اليوم i.e. day, however, we still use the ordinal number to express date. For example:

I will visit	أزور
Your office	مَكْتَبَكُم
On 18th	فِى الثَّامنَ عشَرَ
instant	للشَّهْرِ الْجَارى

There is another small grammar point which we have casully dealt with in the main body of this lesson. It is called إِخْتِصَاصٌ - ikhtisas. When a noun is used to qualify a pronoun of the I person, it is always placed in the accusative case. This qualifying noun also restricts the meaning & makes it emphatic in a way . It is conveyed as follows: نحنُ الهُنودَ We the Indians.

Note:

However, practically in the day-to-day life, in the spoken language, generally the cardinal numbers are used for indicating time & date etc. For example, we would say:

It is now 9:30	السَّاعَةُ الآنَ تسعة ونُصْ (نِصْف)
I'll meet you at 5.15 PM	أُقَابِلُك فِى السَّاعة خَمْسَة وَرُبْع مَسَاءً
It is 14 January to day	نَحنُ اليَومَ فِى اربَعَةَعشرَ ينايَرَ

Exercises:

(1) Translate into Arabic:

Gopal is a young boy. He is a student in Delhi Public School. His school opens at 9.00 A.M. Gopal has never been late for school. He gets up early in the morning at about six O'clock. After waking up, he goes to the bathroom and cleans his teeth and washes his face. At 6.30 he goes for short walk and returns home at 7.00 O'clock. Then he takes his bath and puts on clean clothes. And after that he throws a cursory glance at the newspaper. At 8.00 O'clock he takes his breakfast. At 8.15 sharp always he leaves his home for the bus-stop where he gets his school bus at 8.25 or 8.30.

And this bus normally takes twenty minutes to reach the school. In this way Gopal always reaches the school before 9.00 O'clock . Last Monday, 16th April, Gopal did not go to the school. Then the following two days i.e. on 17th and 18th April also he could not go to the school. His classmates got worried and on the evening of the 18th April after the school, they went to his house to see him. Gopal was better. He thanked them for visiting him and told them he would go to school from 23rd April.

2) Translate into English:

هَذَا جَارِى. إِسْمُهُ شَنْكَر. شَنْكَر تَاجِرٌ صَغِيرٌ. لَهُ دُكَّانُ بِقَالَةٍ فِى حَىِّ يُوسُفْ سَرَاى، إِنَّ شَنْكَر
اِنْسَانٌ مُهَذَّبٌ وَمُؤَدَّبٌ. وَ هُوَ مُتَدَيِّنٌ لِلْغَايَةِ. قَلَّمَا يَحِيد عَنْ بَرْنَامَجِهِ. يَقُومُ شَنْكَر
دَائِماً مِنْ نَوْمِهِ مُبَكِّراً فِى السَّاعَةِ السَّادِسَةِ وَ بَعْدَ الاِسْتِحْمَامِ يَخْرُجُ إِلَى مَعْبِدِ الْحَىِّ فِى السَّاعَةِ
السَّابِعَةِ. يَعُودُ شَنْكَر مِنَ الْمَعْبِدِ فِى السَّاعَةِ السَّابِعَةِ وَ النِّصْفِ. وَيَقْرَأَ الْجَرَائِدَ حَتَّى السَّاعَةِ
الثَّامِنَةِ.

يَأْكُلُ شَنْكَر فُطُورَهُ فِىْ السَّاعَةِ الثَّامِنَةِ وَ يَخْرُجُ لِدُكَّانِهِ فِى السَّاعَةِ الثَّامِنَةِ وَالنِّصْفِ. إِنَّ دُكَّانَهُ بَعِيْدٌ
مِنْ مَنْزِلِهِ. يَصِلُ شَنْكَر لِدُكَّانِهِ فِى السَّاعَةِ التَّاسِعَةِ تَقْرِيباً. يَعُودُ شَنْكَر اِلَىٰ الْمَنْزِلِ فِى السَّاعَةِ
الْسَابِعَةِ مَسَاءً كُلَّ يَوْمٍ.

يَفْتَحُ شَنْكَر دُكَّانَهُ فِىْ كُلِّ الشَّهْرِ اِلَّا يَوْمَيْنِ. فَهُوَ يُغْلِقُ دُكَّانَهُ فِى الْيَومِ الْخَامِسَ عَشَرَ وَالْيَوم
الثَّلَاثِيْنَ كُلَّ شَهْرٍ. وَيَذْهَبُ إِلَى السُّوقِ لِشِرَاءِ حَاجِيَاتِ الدُّكَّانِ وَالْمَنْزِلِ.

3. Write a paragraph on a situation using therein time, dates & days for as many times as possible.

4. Write a paragraph on the activities of the mosque in your neighbourhood.

5. Rewrite names of months & days and use them in sentences of your own.

Vocabulary: الكلمات العسيرة

To wake up	إِسْتَيْقَظَ ⁄ يَسْتَيْقِظُ ⁄ إِسْتِيْقَاظاً
Bathroom	حَمَّامٌ (SM) حَمَامَاتٌ (P)
To clean, to wash	غَسَلَ ⁄ يَغْسِلُ ⁄ غُسْلاً
Face	وَجْهٌ (SM) وُجُوهٌ (P)
To take bath	إِسْتَحَمَّ ⁄ يَسْتَحِمُّ ⁄ اِسْتِحْمَامًا
Clothe/ dress	ثَوْبٌ (SM) ثِيَابٌ (P) مَلْبَسٌ (SM) مَلَابِسُ (P)
To throw	أَلْقَىٰ ⁄ يُلْقِى ⁄ اِلْقَاءَ، طَرَحَ ⁄ يَطْرَحُ ⁄ طَرْحاً
Glance	نَظْرَةٌ (SF) نَظَرَاتٌ (P)
Cursory glance	نَظْرَةٌ عَابِرَةٌ
Newspaper	صَحِيْفَةٌ (SF) صُحُفٌ (P) جَرِيْدَةٌ (SF) جَرَائِدُ (P)

Sharp (time)	بِالضَّبْطِ/ مَضْبُوطٌ
Always	دَائِماً
Normally	عَادَةً
Break, intermission	فَتْرَةُ الإِسْتِرَاحَةِ
Programme	بَرْنَامَجٌ (SM) بَرَامِجُ (P)
Culture	ثَقَافَةٌ (SF) ثَقَافَاتٌ (P)
Cultural	ثَقَافِيٌّ (Adj. SM)
To continue	إِسْتَمَرَّ/ يَسْتَمِرُّ/ اِسْتِمْرَارًا
To distribute	وَزَّعَ/ يُوَزِّعُ/ تَوْزِيعاً
Prize; award	جَائِزَةٌ (SF) جَوَائِزُ (P)
Winner	فَائِزٌ (SM) فَائِزُونَ (P)
To weep, to cry	بَكَى/ يَبْكِى/ بُكَاءً
To refuse	رَفَضَ/ يَرْفُضُ/ رَفْضًا
To meet (a demand or request)	لَبَّى/ يُلَبِّى/ تَلْبِيَةً
To call	دَعَا/ يَدْعُو/ دَعْوَةً
To come	قَدِمَ/ يَقْدَمُ/ قُدُومًا
To ask (about)	سَأَلَ/ يَسْأَلُ/ سُؤَالاً (عن)
Reason	سَبَبٌ (SM) أَسْبَابٌ (P)
To give	أَعْطَى/ يُعْطِى/ إِعْطَاءً
To carry	حَمَلَ/ يَحْمِلُ/ حَمْلاً
To do (s. th.) excessively	أَكْثَرَ/ يُكْثِرُ/ إِكْثارًا
To cause	سَبَّبَ/ يُسَبِّبُ/ تَسْبِيبًا
Pimple	دُمَّلٌ (SM) دَمَامِلُ (P)
To understand	فَهِمَ/ يَفْهَمُ/ فَهْماً
Advice	نَصِيحَةٌ (SF) نَصَائِحُ (P)
To accept	قَبِلَ/ يَقْبَلُ/ قُبُولاً
Greed	طَمَعٌ (SM) أَطْمَاعٌ (P)
Happiness	سَعادةٌ (NF)

The Relative Pronoun
الاسم الموصول

One Sunday I got up	فى يَومِ أحدٍ قُمْتُ
from my sleep early .	مِنْ نَوْمِى مُبَكِّرًا.
I lit the lamp which was placed	أَضَأْتُ السِّرَاجَ الذى كانَ مَوْضُوْعًا
on the side table and searched	عَلَى الطَّاوِلَةِ الصَّغِيْرِةِ وبَحثْتُ
for my watch	عَنْ سَاعَتِى
which I had put under my pillow	الَّتِى كُنْتُ وَضَعْتُها تَحتَ وِسَادَتِى
before sleeping.	قَبْلَ النَّومِ.
I saw the time, it was	رأَيْتُ الوَقْتَ، كَانَتِ السَّاعَةُ
five almost.	السَّاعَةَ الخَامِسَةَ تَقْرِيْباً.
I tried to sleep again	حَاوَلْتُ النَّومَ مَرَّةً أُخرَى
but the sleep did not come to me.	ولكِنْ لَمْ يأتِنِى النَّومُ.
I left my bed and went to	تَرَكْتُ سَرِيْرِى و ذَهَبْتُ الَى الحمَّامِ.
the bathroom. I cleaned my teeth	نَظَّفْتُ أسنانى
and washed my face.	و غَسَلْتُ وَجْهِى.
Then I changed my clothes	ثُمَّ غَيَّرتُ مَلابِسِى
and decided to go out for walking	وقَرَّرتُ عَلَى الخُرُوجِ للمَشْى
and inhaling fresh air.	وللتَّنفُّس الهواءَ الجَدِيْدَ.
I came out and walked	خَرَجْتُ وَ مَشَيْتُ
and saw a scene which	وَ رأيتُ مَشْهَدًا
I had not seen all my life.	مَا كُنْتُ رأَيتُه طُولَ حَيَاتِى.
The weather was pleasant	كانَ الجَوُّ لَطِيْفًا
and the breeze was cool and tender.	وَ الهَوَاءُ بَارِدًا وَ نَعِيْمًا.

I walked and walked till I reached	مَشَيْتُ و مَشَيْتُ حَتَّى وَصَلْتُ
the garden of the area.	حَدِيقَةَ الْمِنْطِقَةِ.
The flowers were blossoming	كَانَتِ الأَزْهَارُ تَتَفَتَّحُ
and the birds were sitting	وَكَانَتِ الْعَصَافِيرُ جَالِسَةً
on the trees and chirping.	عَلَى الأَشْجَارِ وَ هِيَ تُزَقْزِقُ.
I also saw people sitting	وَأَيْضًا رَأَيْتُ النَّاسَ جَالِسِينَ
in groups on the green grass	فى زُرَافَاتٍ على العُشْبِ الأَخْضَرِ
beside the flower-beds or walking	بِجَانِبِ سَرَائِرِ الأزهارِ أَو مَاشِيْنَ
on the grass bare-footed.	على العُشْبِ عُرَاةَ الأَقْدامِ.
Everyone was inhaling the fresh air	كَانَ كُلُّ شَخصٍ يَتَنَسَّمُ الهَوَاءَ الطَّلْقَ
which was free from any pollution.	الذى خَلا مِن اىِّ تَلَوُّثٍ.
I also sat in a corner which	أَنَا أَيْضًا جَلَسْتُ فى زاوِيَةٍ
was away from these people	كَانَتْ بَعِيدَةً عَن هَؤُلاءِ النَّاسِ
whom I did not know.	الَّذِينَ لَمْ أَعْرِفْهُم.
I became lost in this beauty which	إسَتَغْرَقْتُ فى هَذا الجَمالِ الَّذى
surrounded me from all sides	أَحَاطَنِى مِن جَمِيع الجَوانِبِ وَنَسِيْتُ
and I forgot everything so much so	كُلَّ شَىءٍ الَى حَدٍّ
that I did not feel the passage of time.	أَنَّنِى لَمْ اَشعُرْ بِمُضِيِّ الوقتِ.
When I felt the pinch of the sun	عِندما شَعرتُ بِلَسْعَةِ الشَّمْسِ
I recovered from my dreams	أَفَقْتُ مِنْ أَحْلاَمِى
and cast a look around me.	وَ أَلْقَيْتُ نَظرةً حَولِى.
I found that those who were sitting	وَجَدْتُ أَنَّ الَّذِينَ كانُوا جَالِسينَ
there had returned.	هُناك قَدْ عَادُوا.
I also prepared to return and decided that I	أَنَا أيضًا إسَتعددتُ لِلعَودَةِ وَ قَرَّرْتُ أنِّى
would get up from sleep	سَأقُومُ مِن النَّومِ
at an early hour of every morning	فى وقتٍ مُبَكِّرٍ كُلَّ صَباح
in order to enjoy myself	حَتَّى أتمتَّعَ

the beauty of Nature and make

good health.

بِجَمالِ الطَّبِيعَةِ وأَبْنِيَ صِحَّةً جِيِّدَةً.

Grammar:

Beside a few other words used as the relative pronouns in Arabic الذى and التى and their different forms for duals and plurals are considered to be the regular relative pronouns. الذى is used for singular masculine and it is considered to be مبنى i.e. indeclinable. Its dual form is اللذان . It is declinable in the sense that while اللذان is used in the nominative case اللَّذَيْنِ is used in the accusative and genitive cases. الذين is the plural form which is also مبنى i.e. indeclinable. Similarly the word التى is used for the singular feminine and it is مبنى or indeclinable . Its dual form is اللَّتَان in the nominative case while اللتين is used in the accusative and the genitive cases. اللاتى or اللواتى or اللائى is the plural of التى and this plural form is treated as مبنى i.e. indeclinable.

Any of the foregoing relative pronouns is used more or less as adjective for the noun it qualifies and this relative pronoun has to be necessarily followed by a pronoun—external or latent, explaining further the noun it qualifies. For example:

I saw the man whose son I beat. رأيتُ الرَّجُلَ الذى ضربتُ ابنَه

In the foregoing sentence it would be seen that the relative pronoun الذى is used here to qualify the noun الرَّجُل and it is followed by the external pronoun which is attached to ابن in إبنه and it further explains the noun الرجل. Without this pronoun which is called in Arabic الضمير الراجع or the returner pronoun in English, the sentence in Arabic will be considered incomplete and its meaning will not be clear.

In the case of an indefinite or common noun this relative pronoun is necessarily omitted, however , the returner pronoun has to be mentioned. For example:

I saw a man whose son I beat.   رَأَيْتُ رَجُلاً ضَرَبْتُ ابنه

In this sentence رَجُلاً (رجل) is used which is an indefnite or common noun. Hence, the relative pronoun الذى can not be used . However, the pronoun ه which explains the common noun رَجُلاً is used.

This rule as explained above is applied to all the changing forms of the relative pronouns for masculine and feminine. For example we would say:

I saw the men whose sons I beat.   رَأَيْتُ الرِّجَالَ الَّذِيْنَ ضَرَبْتُ أَبْنَاءَ هُم.

I saw the woman whose son I beat.   رَأَيْتُ الْمَرْأَةَ الَّتِى ضَرَبْتُ ابْنَهَا

I saw (some) men whose sons I beat.   رَأَيْتُ رِجَالاً ضَرَبْتُ أَبْنَاءَ هُم

I saw a woman whose son I beat.   رَأَيْتُ امْرَأَةً ضَرَبْتُ ابْنَهَا

This pronoun or الضمير الراجع may be clearly written or spoken as we find in the foregoing sentences or it may be hidden (مستتر) in the verb. For example:

رأيت الرجل الذى قتل اسدًا I saw the man who killed a lion.

In the foregoing sentence الذى qualifies the definite noun الرجل followed by the verb قتل which includes the الضمير الراجع المستتر and it is هُو and it would mean to say:

رَأَيْتُ الرَّجُلَ الَّذِى (هُوَ) قَتَلَ أَسَدًا

Exercises:

1) Translate into Arabic:

Strange things happen in this life. There are people who feign friendship and there are people who are not impostors but they can be good friends and very helpful. There is no bar of sex and creed. I remember those were my early days of service. I was young and inexperienced. When I joined the office I was received warmly by all the colleagues who organised a small tea-party. Gradually I took fancy to a colleague who appeared to be sincere from the days of early association. Those who knew him well did tell me about him but I thought it was only the colleguel jealousy. Two colleagues who probably had suffered at his hands earlier advised me to take care, however, I did not pay heed to their advice. Our lady colleague who usually appeared to be a very serious person also advised me but her advice too went waste on me. Gradually, I kept on drifting away from other colleagues who, I realise now, were my true friends. With the passage of time we two became very thick friends and one day I came to realise my folly when I got involved in a serious matter. Some of the important documents which were in my custody were missing from my table. I was afraid that our officer who had tremendous faith on me will be very unhappy when he gets to know that loss. There were indications that my colleague who feigned friendship, was involved in the removal of those papers. Finding myself in a tight corner I approached that kind elderly lady who always kept herself away from others in the office and specially she hardly spoke to this colleague and who had advised me in all sincerity to keep away from this colleague. This kind lady gave me a patient hearing and consulted two other elderly colleagues who in their turn spoke to the office chief. The office chief who is a kind person and who knew my honesty and sincerity, also understood where the problem was.

2) Translate into English:

قبلَ أيام لَدى عَودَتى منَ المحْكَمةِ القَضائيَّةِ ضَيَّعْتُ حَقيبَةَ أوراقى فى السَّيَّارةِ العُمُوميَّةِ الَّتى رَكِبْتُهَا إلى كَنَّاتْ بليس. كانَتِ السَّيَّارةُ مُزْدَحِمَةً و لَمْ يَكُنْ فيها مَقْعَدٌ خالٍ أجْلسُ عَلَيه. فَبَقيتُ وَاقِفاً. فى نَفسِ الوَقْتِ رَأَتْنى امرأةٌ مُسِنَّةٌ كانَتْ جالِسَةً و عَرَضَتْ أَنْ تُساعِدَنى فَوَضَعْتُ لَدَيها حَقيبَتى. إسْتَمَرَّتِ السَّيَّارةُ فى السَّيْرِ حَتَّى وَصَلْتُ مَوْقِفى و نَزَلْتُ. نَسيتُ أن آخِذَ حَقيبَتى. بَعْدَ الوُصُولِ الَى الْمَنْزِلِ ادرَكْتُ بالضِّيَاع وَبَدَأَتْ أَتَصَبَّبُ عَرَقًا وَلكِنْ وُجدَلى الأمَلُ أنَّ المَرأةَ الَّتى كُنْتُ وَضَعْتُ لَدَيها سَتَقْدَمُ لِتَرجيع الْحَقيبَةِ. مَضى يَومان و لَمْ يَقْدَمْ أَحَدٌ وخَابَتْ آمَالى. بَعدَ ثَلاثَةِ أَيَّام أَوْ قُلْ فى اليَوم الرَّابِعِ عِندَ مَا كُنْتُ يَئِسْتُ مِنْ عَودَةِ أوراقى إلىَّ و كُنْتُ أُفَكِّرُ فى إتِّخاذِ الإجرَاءَ اتِ و أَنْ أَضَعَ إعْلاَنًا فى الْجَرَائدِ بِهذا الشَّأنِ إذ دُقَّ جرَسُ الباب. فَتَحْتُ البَابَ و رأيتُ فَتَاتَيْن واقِفَتَيْن أَمَامَ الباب فقالَتَا نَحْنُ قَادِمتان مِن كَذا و كَذَا مكان وَنَبْحَثُ عَنْ فُلان و فُلان. فقُلْتُ: أنا هُوَ، و لكِنْ مَا ذَا تُرِيدان. قَالَتَا بَعَثَتْنَا وَالِدَتُنَا لِنَبْحَثَ عَنْك. هَل تَذْكُرُ أَنَّك تَرَكْتَ حَقيبَتَك فى سَيَّارةٍ عُمُوميَّةٍ مَعَ إمرَأةٍ فَسُرِرْتُ كَثيرًا لِسَمَاع هَذِهِ الْكَلِمَاتِ. فَقَالَتَا: وَالِدَتُنَا

مَوْجُودَةٌ فِى سَيَّارَةِ أُجْرَةٍ خَارِجَ الزُّقَاقِ وَالحَقِيبَةُ مَعَهَا فَخَرَجْتُ مَعَ هَاتَيْنِ الفَتَاتَيْنِ اللَّتَيْنِ جَاءَ تَانِى بِهَذَالخَبَرِ وَ تَوَجَّهْتُ مَعَهُمَا إِلَى سَيَّارَةِ الأُجْرَةِ. رَأَيْتُ المَرْأَةَ الَّتِى كُنْتُ وَضَعْتُ حَقِيبَتِى مَعَهَا جَالِسَةً فِى السَّيَّارَةِ فَعَرَفَتْنِى فَوْراً وَ اسْتَقْبَلَتْنِى بِابْتِسَامَةٍ. سَلَّمْتُ عَلَيْهَا وَهِىَ سَلَّمَتْ لِى حَقِيبَتِى وَبَعْدَ حَدِيثٍ رَسْمِىٍّ وَجِيزٍ عَرَضْتُ عَلَيْهَا أَنْ اَدْفَعَ أُجْرَةَ السَّيَّارَةِ وَلَكِنَّهَا رَفَضَتْ. إِنَّ هَذِهِ الوَاقِعَةَ لَنْ أَنْسَاهَا أَبَداً وَ كَذَلِكَ لَنْ أَنْسَ هَؤُلاءِ النِّسَاءَ اللَّوَاتِى جِئْنَ لِإِعَادَةِ حَقِيبَتِى بِدُونِ أَيَّةِمَعْرِفَةٍ سَابِقَةٍ وَذَلِكَ أَيْضاً عَلَى حِسَابِهِنَّ.

(3) Write a paragraph using the relative pronouns in all the three cases i.e. each relative pronoun should be used in nominative, accusative and genitive cases. You should also keep in mind that appropriate returning pronouns shall also have to be used as explained in the foregoing lesson.

Glossary	الكلمات العسيرة
To light	أضاءَ/ يُضِىُّ/ إِضَاءَةً
Lamp	سِرَاجٌ (SM) سُرُجٌ (P)
To look for, to search for	بَحَثَ/يَبْحَثُ/ بَحْثًا (عن)
To put/ to place	وَضَعَ/ يَضَعُ/ وَضْعًا
Pillow	وِسَادَةٌ (SF) وَسَائِدُ (P)
To try	حَاوَلَ/ يُحَاوِلُ/ مُحَاوَلَةً
Bed	سَرِيرٌ (SM) سُرُرٌ (P)
To clean	نَظَّفَ/ يُنَظِّفُ/ تَنْظِيفًا
To wash	غَسَلَ/ يَغْسِلُ/ غُسْلًا
Face	وَجْهٌ (SM) وُجُوهٌ (P)
To change	غَيَّرَ/يُغَيِّرُ/ تَغْيِيرًا
To decide	قَرَّرَ/ يُقَرِّرُ/تَقْرِيرًا
To breathe	تَنَفَّسَ/ يَتَنَفَّسُ/ تَنَفُّسًا

Sight, scenery	مَشْهَدٌ(SM) مَشَاهدُ(P)
Tender, smooth	نَعِيمٌ (Adj. SM)
To chirp	زَقْزَقَ / يُزَقْزِقُ / زَقْزَقَةً
Group	زُرَافَةٌ (SF) زُرَافَاتٌ (P)
Grass	عُشْبٌ (SM)
Herb	عُشْبٌ (SM) أَعْشَابٌ (P)
Bare, naked	عَارٍ(Adj. SM) عُرَاةٌ
Bearefooted	عُرَاةُ الأَقْدَام
To inhale (air)	تَنَسَّمَ / يَتَنَسَّمُ / تَنَسُّمًا
Fresh air	هِرَاءٌ طَلْقٌ
To be free	خَلا / يَخْلُو / خُلُوًّا
To be polluted	تَلَوَّثَ / يَتَلَوَّثُ / تَلَوُّثًا
To last	إِسْتَغْرَقَ / يَسْتَغْرِقُ / إِسْتِغْرَاقًا
To surround	أَحَاطَ / يُحِيطُ / إِحَاطَةً
Side	جَانِبٌ (SM) جَوَانِبُ (P)
To forget	نَسِيَ / بَنْسَى / نِسْيَانًا
To feel	شَعَرَ / يَشْعُرُ / شُعُورًا
To pass	مَضَى / يَمْضِى / مُضِيًّا
Sting	لَسْعَةٌ (SF) لَسْعَاتٌ (P)
To recover (sense)	أَفَاقَ / يُفِيقُ / إِفَاقَةً
To return	عَادَ / يَعُودُ / عَوْدَةً
To happen	حَدَثَ / يَحْدُثُ / حُدُوثًا
To feign	تَصَانَعَ / يَتَصَانَعُ / تَصَانُعًا
Impostor	مُحْتَالٌ(SM) مُحْتَالُونَ (P)
Bar, impediment	مَانِعٌ (SM) مَوَانِعُ (P)
Sex	جِنْسٌ (SM)

Creed, faith	دِيَانَةٌ (SF) دِيَانَاتٌ (P)
Inexperienced	عِدِيمُ الْخِبْرَةِ
Warmly	بِحَرَارَةٍ
Small tea party	حفلةُ شايٍ صَغيرةٌ
Gradually	رُوَيْدًا رُوَيْدًا
To take fancy (to)	أُعْجِبَ / يُعْجَبُ (ب) إعْجَابًا
To appear	بَدَا / يَبْدُو / بَدْوًا
To think	فَكَّرَ / يُفَكِّرُ / تَفْكِيرًا
Collegueal jealousy	حَسَدُ الزُّمَلَاءِ
To advise	نَصَحَ / يَنْصَحُ / نَصْحًا
To suffer (loss etc.)	تَضَرَّرَ / يَتَضَرَّرُ / تَضَرُّرًا
Advice	نَصِيحَةٌ (SF) نَصَائِحُ (P)
To go waste	ضَاعَ / يَضِيعُ / ضِيَاعًا
To drift away	إبْتَعَدَ / يَبْتَعِدُ / إبْتِعَادًا
To realise	أَدْرَكَ / يُدْرِكُ / إدْرَاكًا
Thick (friend)	حَمِيمٌ (Adj. SM) حَمِيمُونَ / أَحِمَّاءُ (P)
Folly	حَمَاقَةٌ (SF) حَمَاقَاتٌ (P)
To get involved	تَوَرَّطَ / يَتَوَرَّطُ / تَوَرُّطًا
Serious/ dangerous	خَطِيرٌ (Adj. SM)
Custody/ possession	حَوزَةٌ (NF)
To be missing	تَغَيَّبَ / يَتَغَيَّبُ / تَغَيُّبًا
To be afraid	خَافَ / يَخَافُ / خَوْفًا
Tremendous, great	هَائِلٌ (Adj. SM)
To be unhappy, to be angry	إغْتَاظَ / يَغْتَاظُ / إغْتِيَاظًا
Loss	خَسَارَةٌ (SF) خَسَائِرُ (P)
Tight corner	مَوْقِفٌ حَرِجٌ

To approach, to contact	إتَّصَلَ / يَتَّصِلُ / إتِّصَالًا (ب)
Hardly	قَلَّمَا
To consult, to take advice	إسْتَشَارَ / يَسْتَشِيرُ / إسْتِشَارَةً
He heard patiently, to give a patient hearing	سَمِعَ بِهُدُوءٍ
Office chief, boss	رَئِيسُ الْمَكْتَبِ
Honesty	أَمَانَةٌ (NF)
Court of law	مَحْكَمَةٌ قَضَائِيَّةٌ
To lose	ضَيَّعَ / يُضَيِّعُ / تَضْيِيعًا
Bus	سَيَّارَةٌ عُمُومِيَّةٌ
Connought Place	كنات بليس
Seat	مَقْعَدٌ (SM) مَقَاعِدُ (P)
Empty/ free	خَالٍ (خَالِى)
Aged	مُسِنٌّ (Adj. SM)
To ooze	تَصَبَّبَ / يَتَصَبَّبُ / تَصَبُّبًا
To sweat, to perspire	تَصَبَّبَ عَرَقًا
Hope	أَمَلٌ (SM) آمَالٌ (P)
To offer	عَرَضَ / يَعْرِضُ / عَرْضًا
To return	رَجَّعَ / يُرَجِّعُ / تَرْجِيعًا
To disappoint	خَابَ / يَخِيبُ / خَيْبَةً
Hopes fell	خَابَتِ الآمَالُ
To lose hope, to be disappointed	يَئِسَ / يَيْئَسُ / يَأْسًا
To take (measure)	إتَّخَذَ / يَتَّخِذُ / إتِّخَاذًا، (إجْرَاءً)
Advertisement, announcement	إعْلانٌ (SM) إعْلانَاتٌ (P)
In this regard, in this matter	بِهَذَا الشَّأنِ
Young woman, young lady	فَتَاةٌ (SF) فَتَيَاتٌ (P)
To be happy	سُرَّ / يُسَرُّ / سُرُورًا

To head (towards)	تَوَجَّهَ/ يَتَوَجَّهَ/ تَوَجُّهًا (إِلَى)
To recognise, to know	عَرَفَ/ يَعْرِفُ/ عِرْفَانًا
To receive	إِسْتَقْبَلَ/ يَسْتَقْبِلُ/ إِسْتِقْبَالاً
To receive with a smile	إِسْتَقْبَلَ بِإِبْتِسَامَةٍ
Smile	إِبْتِسَامَةٌ (SF) إِبْتِسَامَاتٌ (P)
To greet	سَلَّمَ/ يُسَلِّمُ/ تَسْلِيْمًا (عَلَى)
To handover	سَلَّمَ/ يُسَلِّمُ/ تَسْلِيْمًا (لِ)
Taxi	سَيَّارَةُ الأُجْرَةِ
Talk, conversation	حَدِيْثٌ(SM) أَحَادِيْثُ(P)
Brief	وَجِيْزٌ (Adj. SM)
To refuse, to deny	رَفَضَ/ يَرْفُضُ/ رَفْضًا
Incident	وَاقِعَةٌ (SF) وَاقِعَاتٌ (P)

LESSON — 35

الدرس — ٣٥

The Conditional Sentence الجملة الشرطية

Hamid was looking	كَانَ حَامِد يبحث
for his money purse	عن كِيس نقوده
here and there.	هُنَا وهُنَاك .
When he did not find it, he called his wife	فَلَمَّا لَمْ يَجِدْهُ نَادىٰ زَوجَتَهُ
and asked her about the purse.	وَ سَأَلَهَا عَنِ الْكِيسِ.
She said: I saw your purse	قَالَتْ: رَأَيْتُ كِيْسَك
in the table's drawer.	فِى دُرْجِ الطَّاوِلَةِ.
Open the table's drawer,	إفْتَحْ دُرْجَ الطَّاوِلَةِ
you will find in it your purse.	تَجِدْفيه كِيْسَك
Hamid opened the drawer	فَتَحَ حَامِدٌ الدُّرْجَ
and found his purse.	وَ وَجَدَ كِيْسَهُ.
Hamid said to his wife:	قَالَ حَامِد لِزَوْجَتِهِ:
You were saying	كُنْتِ تَقُولِيْنَ
that you would go today's (this) evening	إنَّكِ تَذْهَبِيْنَ مَسَاءَ الْيَوم
to your friend's house,	إلَى بَيْتِ صَدِيْقَتِكِ،
then, what is your programme?	فَمَا هُوَ بَرْنَامَجُكِ؟
She said: If you return from your office	قَالَتْ: إنْ رَجَعْتَ مِنْ مَكْتَبِك
early I would go.	مُبَكِّرًا ذَهَبْتُ.
He said: Would you go	قَالَ: هَلْ تَذْهَبِيْنَ
to the market also?	إلَى السُّوقِ أَيْضًا؟
She said: If you accompany me	قَالَتْ إنْ تُرَافِقْنِى
I would go, otherwise not.	أَذْهَبْ إلَّا فَلَا.

He said: I will accompany you on
قَالَ: أُرَافِقُكِ عَلَى

the condition that you'll not prolong stay
شَرْطِ أَنْ لَا تُطِيلِي الْمُكُوثَ

in your friend's house,
فِي بَيْتِ صَدِيقَتِكِ

because if you prolong stay
لِأَنَّهُ إِنْ أَطَلْتِ الْمُكُوثَ

the market would close
تَنْغَلِقِ السُّوقُ

and when the market is closed
وَمَتَى تَنْغَلِقِ السُّوقُ

our going there will not be useful.
لَا يُفِدْنَا الذِّهَابُ إِلَيْهَا.

When Hamid was talking
عِنْدَمَا كَانَ حَامِد يَتَكَلَّمُ

to his wife,
مَعَ زَوْجَتِهِ

their daughter came and (she) said:
جَاءَتْ ابْنَتُهُمَا وَقَالَتْ:

I don't have a pen to write with.
مَا عِنْدِى قَلَمٌ أَكْتُبُ بِهِ.

I dropped my pen and spoiled its nib.
أَسْقَطْتُ قَلَمِى وَأَفْسَدْتُ سِنَّهُ.

Hamid took out his pen
أَخْرَجَ حَامِد قَلَمَهُ

and gave it to her saying:
وَأَعْطَاهَا لَهَا قَائِلًا:

Guard it from (against) falling.
حَافِظِى عَلَيْهِ مِنَ السُّقُوطِ.

If you guard it, it will be with you
إِنْ تُحَافِظِى عَلَيْهِ يَكُنْ مَعَكِ

and you will write
وَسَتَكْتُبِينَ

in beautiful handwriting always.
بِخَطٍّ جَمِيلٍ دَائِمًا.

And if you drop it, you will spoil its nib.
وَمَتَى تُسْقِطِيهِ تُفْسِدِى سِنَّهُ.

The girl took the pen from her father
أَخَذَتِ الْبِنْتُ الْقَلَمَ مِنْ أَبِيهَا

and thanked him and left for the school.
وَشَكَرَتْهُ وَخَرَجَتْ لِلْمَدْرَسَةِ.

When Hamid returned (to) home
عِنْدَمَا رَجَعَ حَامِد إِلَى الْبَيْتِ

in the evening, his son Khalid showed him
فِى الْمَسَاءِ أَرَاهُ وَلَدُه خَالِد

the school report.
التَّقْرِيرَ الْمَدْرَسِىَّ

The report was not satisfactory.
لَمْ يَكُنِ التَّقْرِيرُ مُرْضِيًا.

Khalid had failed in two subjects.
كَانَ خَالِد قَدْ رَسَبَ فِى مَادَّتَيْنِ.

The father said to his son:	قَالَ الْأَبُ لِوَلَدِهِ:
It seems that you don't work hard	يَبْدُو أَنَّكَ لَاتَجْتَهِدُ
in your lessons (classes).	فِىْ دُرُوسِكَ .
You (must) know that he who works hard,	إِعْلَمْ أَنَّ مَنْ يَجْتَهِدْ
passes in the examination.	يَنْجَحْ فِى الْإِمْتِحَانِ
And he who passes in the school examination,	وَمَنْ يَنْجَحْ فِى إِمْتِحَانِ الْمَدرَسَةِ
succeeds in life.	يَنْجَحْ فِى الْحَيَاةِ.
And he who succeeds in life,	وَمَنْ يَنْجَحْ فِى الْحَيَاةِ
the world respects him.	تُكْرِمْهُ الدُّنْيَا.
The boy said: I understood that	قَالَ الْوَلَدُ: فَهِمْتُ مَا
you (have) said, o' my father.	قُلْتَهُ يَاأَبِى.
I will work harder than before and pass	أَجْتَهِدُ أَكْثَرَ مِنْ قَبْلُ وَأَنْجَحُ
in the final examination with the rank	فِى الْإِمْتِحَانِ النِّهَائِى بِدَرْجَةِ
"distinction".	"إِمْتِيَازْ"

Grammar:

There are a few particles which are used for obtaining the conditinal sentences. They are known as particles which silence two present tense verbs to obtain this meaning. Some of these particles are as follows:

إِنْ, مَتَى and مَنْ . In such kind of sentence the first clause or part is called شَرْط i.e. condition (which portion in English is known as protasis) and the second clause or part is called جَوَاب الشرط i.e. answer of the condition or the result of the condition (which portion in English is known as apodosis).

In the case of particles as above and few more similar particles, there may be four alternative ways of obtaining conditional sentences and they are as follows:

(1) إِنْ رَجَعْتَ مِنْ مَكْتَبِكَ مُبَكِّرًا ذَهَبْتُ

(2) إِنْ تَرْجِعْ مِنْ مَكْتَبِكَ مُبَكِّرًا ذَهَبْتُ

(3) إِنْ رَجَعْتَ مِنْ مَكْتَبِكَ مُبَكِّرًا أَذْهَبْ

(4) إِنْ تَرْجِعْ مِنْ مَكْتَبِكَ مُبَكِّرًا أَذْهَبْ

All the four sentences above would mean:

"If you return from your office early, I would go."

Now, let us examine the four sentences above. In sentence no. 1 both the verbs رَجَعْتَ and ذَهَبْتُ are in the past tense. In sentence no. 2 the first verb تَرْجِعْ is in present jussive mood and the second verb ذَهَبْتُ is in the past tense. In sentence no. 3 the first verb رَجَعْتَ is in the past tense while the second verb أَذْهَبْ is in the present jussive mood. And finally, in the fourth sentence both the verbs تَرْجِعْ and أَذْهَبْ are in the present jussive mood and it is from this usage that we say that particle إِنْ and similar other particles silence the last letters of two present tense verbs—the first verb which poses conditon and the second verb which constitutes answer to the condition and hence the Arabic terminology شَرط andجَوَاب . However, it may be noted very carefully and once for all that all the four foregoing ways are tenable for this kind of conditional sentences.

In case of a sentence which consists of one imperative verb and the other in the present jussive mood, though it is often taken by beginners as شَرط and جواب الشرط, however, in Arabic grammar terminology we call it طَلَب and جَوَاب الطَلَب i.e. demand and answer to demand, e.g.

Open the table's drawer, you will find in it your purse.   إِفْتَحْ دُرْجَ الطَّاوِلَةِ تَجِدْ فِيهِ كِيْسَك

In the foregoing sentence the first verb إِفْتَحْ (open) is in the imperative mood and the second verb تَجِدْ (you'll find) is in the present jussive mood and hence, the first verبإِفْتَحْ is the demand (order/ request) i.e. طَلَب and تَجِدْ is the answer to the demand (order/ request) and the sentence falls in the category of جَوَاب and طَلَب and جَوَاب الطَلَب as very distinct from the شَرط and الشرط.

In some cases, in the conditional sentences that begin with إِنْ the answer to the condition begins with فَ, e.g. If he gives you food, then you should eat it. إِنْ قَدَّمَ لَكَ الطَّعَامَ فَتَأْكُلُهُ

In the sentence above فَ has been translated as 'then'. It is often so.

It may also be noted here that an unlikely condition is obtained by using the particle لَو often followed byل, e.g

If I were present,
لَوْ كُنْتُ مَوْجُودًا

I would have done justice to you.
لأَنْصَفْتُك

If you had come five minuts before, you would have met your friend.
لَوْ كُنْتَ حَضَرْتَ قَبْلَ خَمْسِ دَقَائِق لَقَابَلْتَ صَدِيْقَك

However, there are always simpler ways to give expression to these kinds of meanings that you would learn with the passage of time.

Exercises:

(1) Translate into Arabic:

Last Sunday, in the morning at about 9.00 am, I was all set to go out that my phone rang. I took the call. It was my friend and classmate Rizwan. After formal enquiries about health and family Rizwan said: Ravi you know, our examinations are fast approaching. My father has told me: If you pass I will give you a new watch and if you fail I will stop your monthly pocket allowance for the year. I thought we should make a programme for combined studies. Why don't you come to Joseph's house in the afternoon. If we meet, we can make our future programme of studies. I said: If you come there , I will also come about 3.00 PM. I said: I wish shyam were not ill these days. If he were with us, we would have solved maths problems easily. He is really good. Rizwan said: Don't worry! He will soon be all right. When he returns home from the hospital, we will contact him and take his help. He said: Good, we will meet at Joseph's place (house) at 3.00 PM and till then bye! I said: Good bye. In the meantime my mother entered the room and I told her about our programme for studies, she was happy. She said: Work hard. This time you should get first division. If you get first division, I will give you money to buy your cricket set. I said: Please give me ten rupees now for transport. She said: Open the drawer, you'll find money.

(2) Translate into Englsih:

أَنَا وَلَدٌ يُطْلَقُ عَلَيَّ وَلَدٌ كَسْلَان حَيْثُ أَنَّنِى دَائِمًا أُوَجِّلُ عَمَلِى إِلَى وَقْتٍ آخَر. لَا أَوَدُّ أَدَاءَ وَاجِبِى فِى وَقْتِهِ وَ حَتَّى لِلْمَدْرَسَةِ أَتَأَخَّرُ فِى كُلِّ يَوم تَقْرِيبًا. وَبِالنَّتِيجَةِ يَفُوتُنِى بَعْضُ الدُّرُوسِ وَلَا أَجْتَازُ فَصْلاً فِى أَقَلَّ مِنْ عَامَيْنِ. دَائِمًا أَتَكَاسَلُ حَتَّى فِى الْقِيَامِ مِنَ النَّوم وَقَلَّمَا أَتَحَمَّمُ قَبْلَ الذَّهَابِ إِلَى الْمَدْرَسَةِ. لَقَد سَئِمَ مِنِّى كُلُّ شَخصٍ فِى الْبَيْتِ وَكَذَلِك فِى المَدْرَسَةِ. وَلَكِنَّنى هَذِهِ الْمَرَّةَ قَبْلَ أُسْبُوعٍ أَوثَلَاثَةِ أَسَابِيعَ مَرِضْتُ وَأَخَذُونِى لِلْمَشْفَى وَأَدْخَلُونِى فِيهِ. قَدِمَ الدَّكَاتِرَةُ لِمُعَايَنَتِى وَوَجَدُونِى وَسِخًا. وَقَالُوا رُبَّمَا هُوَ السَّبَبُ وَالْكَسَلُ أَخَذَ ثَمَنَهُ فِى صِحَّتِى. قَالُوا لِى: يَنْبَغِى أَنْ تُغَيِّرَ عَادَاتِك. يَلْزَمُ أَنْ تَسْتَيْقِظَ مُبَكِّرًا وَ تَخْرُجَ لِلنُّزْهَةِ لِأَنَّك إِذَا خَرَجْتَ فِى الصَّبَاح الْبَاكِر تَسْتَنْشِقْ الْهَوَاءَ الصَّافِى الْخَالِى مِنَ التَّلَوُّثِ وَيَلْزَمُ أَنْ تَتَحَمَّمَ كُلَّ صَبَاح قَبْلَ الذَّهَابِ إِلَى الْمَدْرَسَةِ. إِنْ فَعَلْتَ ذَلِك يُحِبُّك الزُّمَلَاءُ والاسَاتِذَةُ وَمَتَى يُحِبُّك الزُّمَلَاءُ يَعْتَنُوا بِك أَكْثَرَ وَيُسَاعِدُوك فِى إِتْمَامِ الْوَاجِبِ الْمَدْرَسِى. وَمَنْ يُتِمِم الْوَاجِبَ المَدْرَسِى يَنْجَحْ فِى الإِمْتِحَان وَ مَنْ يَنْجَحْ فِى الإِمْتِحَان يَكُنْ مُسْتَقْبَلُهُ حَسَنًا. فَعَرَفْتُ أَنَّ السَّبَبَ فَشَلِى يَكْمُنُ فِى كَسَلِى. لَو لَمْ يَكُنْ كَسَلِى لَمَا ضَيَّعْتُ سِنِينَ. شَعَرْتُ بِالنَّدَمِ فَقَالَ لِى وَالِدِى: لَا بَأْسَ. إِفْتَحْ بَابًا جَدِيدًا فِى الْحَيَاةِ مِنَ الْيَوم تَنْجَحْ فِى الْحَيَاةِ وَ تَسْعَد.

(3) Use all the particles of condition you have known in sentences/ paragraph/s of your own.

Glossary	الكلمات العسيرة
To search, to look for	بَحَثَ / يَبْحَثُ / بَحْثًا (عَنْ)
Purse, bag	كِيسٌ (SM) أَكْيَاسٌ (P)
Money	نَقْدٌ (SM) نُقُودٌ (P)
To call	نَادَى / يُنَادِى / مُنَادَاةً
Drawer (of table etc.)	دُرْجٌ (SM) أَدْرَاجٌ (P)
To accompany	رَافَقَ / يُرَافِقُ / مُرَافَقَةً
Early	مُبَكِّرًا (Adv.)
To Prolong	أَطَالَ / يُطِيلُ / إِطَالَةً

To stay	مَكَثَ / يَمْكُثُ / مُكُوثًا
To be closed	إِنْغَلَقَ / يَنْغَلِقُ / إِنْغِلَاقًا
To be useful, to benefit	أَفَادَ / يُفِيْدُ / إِفَادَةً
To drop	أَسْقَطَ / يُسْقِطُ / إِسْقَاطًا
To spoil	أَفْسَدَ / يُفْسِدُ / إِفْسَادًا
Nib	سِنٌّ (SF) أَسْنَانٌ (P)
To take out	أَخْرَجَ / يُخْرِجُ / إِخْرَاجًا
To guard, to protect	حَافَظَ / يُحَافِظُ / مُحَافَظَةً (عَلَى)
Handwriting	خَطٌّ (SM)
To thank	شَكَرَ / يَشْكُرُ / شُكْرًا
To show	أَرَى / يُرِى / إِرَاءَةً
Report	تَقْرِيْرٌ (SM) تَقَارِيْرُ (P)
School report	التَّقْرِيْرُ الْمَدْرَسِى
Satisfactory, pleasing	مُرْضٍ (مُرْضِى) (Adj. SM)
To fail	رَسَبَ / يَرْسُبُ / رُسُوبًا
Subject (in school)	مَادَّةٌ (SF) مَوَادُّ (P)
To appear	بَدَا / يَبْدُو / بِدَايَةً
To work hard	إِجْتَهَدَ / يَجْتَهِدُ / إِجْتِهَادًا
To pass, to be successful	نَجَحَ / يَنْجَحُ / نَجَاحًا
To respect	أَكْرَمَ / يُكْرِمُ / إِكْرَامًا
To understand	فَهِمَ / يَفْهَمُ / فَهْمًا
Division, rank	دَرَجَةٌ (SF) دَرَجَاتٌ (P)
Distinction	إِمْتِيَازٌ
To offer, to give	قَدَّمَ / يُقَدِّمُ / تَقْدِيْمًا
To do justice	أَنْصَفَ / يُنْصِفُ / إِنْصَافًا

To be all set, to be ready	اسْتَعَدَّ/ يَسْتَعِدُّ/ اسْتِعْدَادًا
All set, ready	مُسْتَعِدٌّ (Adj. SM)
To go out	خَرَجَ/ يَخْرُجُ/ خُرُوجًا
To ring (bell/telephone)	رَنَّ/ يَرِنُّ/ رَنِينًا
Telephone	تِلِفُونٌ (SM)
Classmate, colleague	زَمِيلٌ (SM) زُمَلَاءُ(P)
Formal	رَسْمِيٌّ (Adj. SM)
Enquiries	إسْتِعْلَامٌ (SM) إسْتِعْلَامَاتٌ (P)
To approach	اِقْتَرَبَ/ يَقْتَرِبُ/ اِقْتِرَابًا
To stop (s. o.)	وَقَّفَ/ يُوَقِّفُ/ تَوْقِيفًا
Pocket money	مَصْرُوفُ الْجَيْبِ
To think	اِفْتَكَرَ / يَفْتَكِرُ/ اِفْتِكَارًا
To fail	رَسَبَ/يَرْسُبُ/ رُسُوبًا
Monthly	شَهْرِىٌّ (Adj. SM)
Programme	بَرْنَامَجٌ (SM) بَرَامِجُ (P)
To make programme	إعْدَادُ الْبَرْنَامَج/ وَضْعُ الْبَرنَامَج
To prepare (s. th.)	أَعَدَّ/ يُعِدُّ/ إعْدَادًا
To lay out, to put	وَضَعَ/ يَضَعُ/ وَضْعًا
Combined, joint	مُشْتَرَكٌ (VN/ Adj. SM)
Future i.e. Pertaining to future	مُسْتَقْبَلِىٌّ (Adj. SM)
I wish	يَا لَيْتَ
To want, to wish	وَدَّ/ يَوَدُّ/ وَدًّا
To solve	حَلَّ/ يَحُلُّ/ حَلًّا
Problem	مُشْكِلَةٌ (SF) مَشَاكِلُ (P)
Mathematical/ pertaining to mathematics	رِيَاضِىٌّ (Adj. SM)

Mathematics/maths	عِلْمُ الرِّيَاضِيَّات
Good	جَيِّدٌ (Adj. SM)
Really	حَقًّا (.Adv) / فِى الْوَاقِع
To worry	قَلِقَ / يَقْلَقُ / قَلَقًا
To be right, to improve	تَحَسَّنَ / يَتَحَسَّنُ / تَحَسُّنًا
To return	رَجَعَ / يَرْجِعُ / رُجُوعًا
To return	عَادَ / يَعُودُ / عَوْدَةً
Hospital	مَشْفَى (SM) مَشَافِى (مَشَافٍ) (P)
To contact	إِتَّصَلَ / يَتَّصِلُ بِ / إِتِّصَالاً
To take help	إِسْتَعَانَ / يَسْتَعِيْنُ / إِسْتِعَانَةً
We will take his help.	نَأْخُذُ مُسَاعَدَتَهُ
To meet, to assemble	إِجْتَمَعَ / يَجْتَمِعُ / إِجْتِمَاعًا
Bye	مَعَ السَّلَامَةِ
In the meantime	فِى نَفْسِ الْوَقْتِ
Study	دِرَاسَةٌ (SF) دِرَاسَاتٌ (P)
Revision (of lesson)	مُذَاكَرَةٌ (SF)
Happy	سَعِيْدٌ (Adj. SM) سُعَدَاءُ (P)
First division	جَيِّد جِدًّا / الدَّرَجَةُ الْأُوْلَى
Second division	جَيِّد / الدَّرْجَةُ الثَّانِيَةُ
Third division	مَقْبُولٌ / الدَّرْجَةُ الثَّالِثَةُ
Cricket set	أَدَوَاتُ الْكَرِيكِيت
Money, fils	فِلْسٌ (SM) فُلُوسٌ (P)
Rupee/Rs.	رُوبِيَةٌ (SF) رُوبِيَاتٌ (P)
Transport	نَقْلٌ

For transport	لِلنَّقْلِ
To call	أَطْلَقَ / يُطْلِقُ عَلَى
Lazy	كَسْلَانُ (Adj. SM) كُسَالَى(P)
As, because	حَيْثُ
Always	دَائِمًا
To postpone	أَجَّلَ / يُؤَجِّلُ / تَأْجِيلًا
Performance	أَدَاءً
Duty; assignment	وَاجِبٌ (SM) وَاجِبَاتٌ (P)
Almost	تَقْرِيبًا
As a result	بِالنَّتِيجَةِ
To miss	فَاتَ / يَفُوتُ / فَوَاتًا
I miss some lesson	يَفُوتُنِي بَعْضُ الدُّرُوسِ
To Pass	إِجْتَازَ / يَجْتَازُ / إِجْتِيَازًا
Class	فَصْلٌ (SM) فُصُولٌ (P)
To be lazy	تَكَاسَلَ / يَتَكَاسَلُ / تَكَاسُلًا
Hardly	قَلَّمَا
To take bath	تَحَمَّمَ / يَتَحَمَّمُ / تَحَمُّمًا
To be sick with, to be tired with	سَئِمَ / يَسْأَمُ / سَآمَةً
To fall sick	مَرِضَ / يَمْرَضُ / مَرَضًا
To admit	أَدْخَلَ / يُدْخِلُ / إِدْخَالًا
Doctor	دُكْتُورٌ (SM) دَكَاتِرَةُ(P)
Doctor	طَبِيبٌ (SM) أَطِبَّاء (P)
To see, to check	عَايَنَ / يُعَايِنُ / مُعَايَنَةً
Dirty	وَسِخٌ (Adj. SM)

Perhaps	رُبَّمَا
Has taken its toll in my health	أَخَذَ ثَمَنَه فِى صِحَّتِى
To breathe	إِسْتَنْشَقَ / يَسْتَنْشِقُ / إِسْتِنْشَاقًا
Pure air	الهَوَاءُ الصَّافِى
Devoid of	خَالِى (خَالٍ) مِنْ (Adj. SM)
Pollution	تَلَوُّثٌ
To be necessary, must	لَزِمَ / يَلْزَمُ / لُزُومًا
To care for, to take care of	إِعْتَنَى / يَعْتَنِى / إِعْتِنَاءً ب
To complete, to finish	أَتَمَّ / يُتِمُّ / إِتْمَامًا
Future	مُسْتَقْبَلٌ
Good	حَسَنٌ
Failure	فَشْلٌ / رُسُوبٌ
Laziness	كَسَلٌ
To be hidden, to hide	كَمَنَ / يَكْمُنُ / كُمُونًا
To waste	ضَيَّعَ / يُضَيِّعُ / تَضْيِيعًا
Year	سَنَةٌ (SF) سِنُونٌ / سَنَوَاتٌ (P)
To feel	شَعَرَ / يَشْعُرُ

Grammar At Finger Tips

Things to remember

Arabic Verb:

As Mentioned earlier, majority of Arabic verbs are triliteral. It is from these triliteral verbs that a variety of derived verbs is extracted by doubling the second letter of the verb, or by prefixing or interfixing one, two or three letters. Let us take for example فَعَلَ.

فَعَلَ as can be seen is a triliteral verb i.e. a verb which consists of three original letters. Hereinbelow a list of derived forms of verbs is provided:

Form I: فَعَلَ original verb.

Form II: فَعَّلَ 2nd letter is doubled.

Form III: فَاعَلَ Alif is interfixed after the first letter.

Form IV: أَفْعَلَ Alif is prefixed i.e. placed before the first letter.

Form V: تَفَعَّلَ Ta is prefixed i.e. placed before the first letter and the second original letter is doubled.

Form VI: تَفَاعَلَ Ta is prefixed i.e. placed before the first letter and alif is interfixed after the first original letter.

Form VII: إنفَعَلَ Alif and noon are prefixed i.e. placed before the first letter.

Form VIII: إفْتَعَلَ Alif is prefixed i.e. placed before the first letter and Ta is interfixed after the first letter.

Form IX: إفْعَلَّ Alif is prefixed i.e. placed before the first letter and last letter is doubled.

Form X: إسْتَفْعَلَ Alif, Seen and Ta are prefixed i.e. placed before the first letter.

Notes:

(1) Practically, we can not extract all the derived forms from any given triliteral verb.

(2) Each derived form has a semantic charactersitic or two attached to it.

General features of derived forms of verbs:

Form II: Allocates the meaning to transitive e.g.

To tear مَزَّقَ / يُمَزِّقُ / تَمْزِيْقًا

Form III: Allocates the meaning to do something together, e.g.

To fight some one قَاتَلَ / يُقَاتِلُ / مُقَاتَلَةً

Form IV: Allocates the meaning to causative, e.g.

To seat, to cause to sit أَجْلَسَ / يُجْلِسُ / إِجْلَاسًا

Form VI Allocates the meaning to mutuality of action, e.g.

To fight one another تَقَاتَلَ / يَتَقَاتَلُ / تَقَاتُلًا

Form VII: Allocates the verb to reflexive meaning, e.g.

To be broken اِنْكَسَرَ / يَنْكَسِرُ / اِنْكِسَارًا

Form VIII: Allocates the meaning to intransitive or reflexive, e.g.

To abstain اِمْتَنَعَ / يَمْتَنِعُ / اِمْتِنَاعًا

Form IX : Allocates the meaning to colour or physical defect, e.g.

To turn red اِحْمَرَّ / يَحْمَرُّ / اِحْمِرَارًا

Form X: Allocates the meaning to asking, e.g.

To ask s. o. to come. اِسْتَقْدَمَ / يَسْتَقْدِمُ / اِسْتِقْدَامًا

These are only the general features of the derived forms of the verbs. Dictionary should be consulted to know the right meaning/s of the verb.

Some Small Grammar Points:

* بَيْنَ is basically a preposition which means 'between' and among etc. It also causes kasrah to the last letter of a noun it preceds thus placing the noun in the genitive case, e.g.

(1)   I entered the room and stood between the teacher and the blackboard

دَخلتُ الفَصْلَ وَ وَقَفْتُ بَيْنَ المُدَرِّسِ وَالسَّبُّورَةِ

(2)   I sowed discord between the father and his son

زَرَعْتُ الخِلَافَ بَيْنَ الوَالِدِ وَوَلَدِهِ

(3)   I sat between the two friends   جَلَسْتُ بَيْنَ الصَّدِيْقَيْنِ

(4)   There was long distance between me and my brother

كَانَتِ الْمَسَافَةُ طَوِيْلَةً بَيْنِى و بَيْنَ أخِى

(5)   Who was sitting between you and her in the church?

مَنْ كَانَ جَالِسًا بَيْنَكَ و بَيْنَهَا فِى الكَنِيْسَةِ؟

Note carefully that when بَيْنَ is followed by a personal attached pronoun indicating your, his etc, then in that case بَيْنَ is repeated as you can see in sentences 4 & 5 and when بَيْنَ is used with nouns, it is not repeated as is the case with sentences 1, 2 & 3. بَيْنَ is indeclinable.

*   كُلٌّ is a noun which means among other things 'all' and 'each'. It also functions like a preposition and invariably places the noun it precedes in the genitive case. When it has to be used to mean 'each', it is placed in construct position before a singular noun without the definite article الـ and it would also decline normally according to the case, e.g.

(1) Each student came for the class.   قَدِمَ كُلُّ طَالِبٍ لِلْفَصْلِ

(2) I spoke to each student in the class   كَلَّمْتُ كُلَّ طَالِبٍ فِى الفَصْلِ

(3) I advised each student in the class   أَشَرْتُ عَلَى كُلِّ طَالِبٍ فِى الفَصْلِ

In the meaning of 'all' كُلَّ is placed before a plural noun bedecked with the definite article الـ or before a plural pronoun, or the noun that may be ascribed to another noun and thus defined, e.g.

(1) All the students attended the class   حَضَرَ كُلُّ الطُّلَّابِ الفَصْلَ

(2) All the students of the class attended   حَضَرَ كُلُّ طُلَّابِ الفَصْلِ

      the prize distribution function   حَفْلَةَ تَوْزِيْعِ الجَوَائِزِ

(3) I saw all of them eating their lunch   رَأَيْتُ كُلَّهُم يَأْكُلُونَ غَدَائَهُم

(4) I went to all of them one by one   ذَهَبْتُ إِلَى كُلِّهِم وَاحِدًا وَاحِدًا

* كِلَا and كِلْتَا are nouns meaning both for masculine & feminine respectively. They fall in the category of indeclinable nouns i.e. to say that their terminal alifs don't change in any of the three cases i.e. كِلَا & كِلْتَا remain unchanged in the nominative, accusative & genitive cases. For example:

A.   (1) Both the boys came   الف :   قَدِمَ كِلَا الوَلَدَيْنِ

     (2) I saw both the boys   رَأَيْتُ كِلَا الوَلَدَيْنِ

     (3) I sat with both the boys   جَلَسْتُ مَعَ كِلَا الوَلَدَيْنِ

B.   (1) Both the girls came   ب :   قَدِمَتْ كِلْتَا البِنْتَيْنِ

     (2) I saw both the girls   رَأَيْتُ كِلْتَا البِنْتَيْنِ

     (3) I sat with both the girls   جَلَسْتُ مَعَ كِلْتَا البِنْتَيْنِ

Note that the alifs of كِلَا and كِلْتَا have not changed. Note also that كِلَا and كِلْتَا are always placed in construct position with a dual noun.

Note also that alifs of كِلَا and كِلْتَا remain unchanged only when they are ascribed to nouns as shown above. However, when كِلَا and كِلْتَا are ascribed to dual possessor personal pronouns, they decline as follows:

A.   (1) Both of them (M. D.) came   الف :   قَدِمَ كِلَاهُما

     (2) I saw both of them (M.D.)   رَأَيْتُ كِلَيْهِمَا

     (3) I sat with both of them (M.D.)   جَلَسْتُ مَعَ كِلَيْهِمَا

B.   (1) Both of them (F.D.) came   ب :   قَدِمَتْ كِلْتَاهُمَا

     (2) I saw both of them (F.D.)   رَأَيْتُ كِلْتَيْهِمَا

     (3) I sat with both of them (F.D)   جَلَسْتُ مَعَ كِلْتَيْهِمَا

The predicate or verb that follows كِلَا and كِلْتَا for some reason may be dual as generally maintained or singular. For example:

Both of them are present   كِلَاهُمَا مَوْجُودَانِ or مَوْجُودٌ

Both the boys attended the class.   كِلَا الوَلَدَيْنِ حَضَرَا الفَضْلَ or حَضَرَ الفَضْلَ

Same rule applies to كِلْتَا .

* كَمْ is a particle used as an interrogative and exclamative as follows:

A.   When used as interrogative كَمْ is followed by a singular noun in the
     accusative case, e.g.

(1) How many books do you have?   كَمْ كِتَابًا عِنْدَكَ؟

(2) How many teachers are there   كَمْ مُدَرِّسًا
     in the university?   فِى الْجَامِعَةِ

In its capacity as interrogative particle كَمْ may be followed by مِنْ and in
this case the noun will be plural bedecked with الـ and in the genitive case,
e.g.

(1) How many books do you have?   كَمْ مِنَ الْكُتُبِ عِندَكَ

(2) How many teachers are there in the   كَمْ مِنَ الْمُدَرِّسِيْنَ
     university   فِى الْجَامِعَةِ

B.   When used as exclamative particle كَمْ is followed by a singular noun in
     the genitive case, e.g.

You have so many books!   كَمْ كِتَابٍ عِنْدَكَ!

There are so many teachers in the university!   كَمْ مُدَرِّسٍ فِى الْجَامِعَةِ!

* سـ defines the meaning of present imperfect in the near future and سَوفَ
  defines the meaning of the present imperfect in the (distant) future, e.g.

(1) I go to the school   أَذْهَبُ اِلَى الْمَدْرَسَةِ

(2) I will soon go to the school   سَأَذْهَبُ إِلَى الْمَدْرَسَةِ

(3) I will go to the school   سَوفَ أَذْهَبُ إِلَى الْمَدْرَسَةِ

* أَخَذَ (and similar verbs) followed by the present indefinite verb modifies
  the meaning 'to begin' and the meaning of the verb that follows أَخَذَ e.g.

He began to eat   أَخَذَ يَأْكُلُ

He began to write   أَخَذَ يَكْتُبُ

* يَتِمُّ followed by the infinitive form of verb changes the meaning to
  passive in present and future as follows:

(1) Goats are slaughtered for eating   يَتِمُّ ذِنْحُ الشِّيَاةِ لِلْأَكْلِ

(2) The students will be sent   سَوفَ يَتِمُّ إِرْسالُ الطَّلَبَةِ

    to London next month.   إلى لُنَدُنْ فى الشَّهرِ القَادِم

(3) The restrictions shall be removed in   سَتِتِمُّ إِزَالَةُ القُيُودِ

    the near future.   فى القَرِيْبِ العَاجِلِ

تَمَّ followed by infintive modifies the meaning in the past passive voice e.g.

(1) The goats were slaughtered for the feast.   تَمَّ ذَبحُ الشِّيَاةِ لِلْوَلِيْمَةِ

(2) Yes, all the mistakes have been removed.   نَعَمْ، تَمَّتْ إِزَالَةُ كُلِّ الأَخْطَاءِ

* فَعَّالٌ pattern is generally used for indicating that the person does some work as his profession, e.g. while from خَاطَ he stitched or sewed خَائطٌ would mean some one who stitches, but خَيَّاطٌ would mean some one who stitches necessarily as a professional. Nouns for all professionals will be drawn or cast on this pattern.

* We have talked about imperative verbs and how they are made from trilitiral and derived forms of verbs. We have also known that imperative is made only from the second person verbs. It may also be noted that imperative is also used as request and surely when it is modified by using مِنْ فَضْلِك or some other such expression, e.g.

    (1) Go or please go   إذْهَبْ

    (2) Please go   إذْهَبْ مِنْ فَضْلِك

In some way or other we also convey our order or request or intention to the III & the I persons, e.g. we might say: let him do this & let me eat. To achieve this meaning in Arabic we use ل with kasrah and term this ل as ل of imperative i.e. لَام الأَمْرِ. This ل causes all those alterations to the verb that obtain in imperative e.g.

    (1) Let him go to the calss.   ١. لِيَذْهَبْ إلَى الْفَصْلِ

    (2) Let them (2-men) go to the class.   ٢. لِيَذْهَبَا إلَى الْفَصْلِ

    (3) Let them (all men) go to the class.   ٣. لِيَذْهَبُوا إلَى الْفَصْلِ

    (4) Let her go to the class.   ٤. لِتَذْهَبْ إلَى الْفَصْلِ

(5) Let them (2-women) go to the class.   ٥. لِتَذْهَبَا إِلَى الفَصْلِ

(6) Let them (all women) go to the class.   ٦. لِيَذْهَبْنَ إِلَى الفَصْلِ

(7) Let me go to the class.   ٧. لِأَذْهَبْ إِلَى الفَصْلِ

(8) Let us go to the class.   ٨. لِنَذْهَبْ إِلَى الْفَصْلِ

This ل of imperative can also similarly be used with the verbs of the second person, e.g.

You go or let you go لِتَذْهَبْ

All you (women) go or Let you all (women) go لِتَذْهَبْنَ

Often this ل is preceded by ف with Faṭhah without prejudice to the meaning, e.g. فَلْيَذْهَبْ. In this case ل is silenced.

* ل with kasrah is also used to modify the meaning of the present indefinite to infinitive. In this case it causes Faṭhah to the terminal letter of the present indefinite verbs. It also causes all the noons i.e. ن to drop except in the case of II & III persons plural feminine, e.g.

(1)   He came to attend the meeting.   ١. قَدِمَ لِيَحْضُرَ الإِجْتِمَاعَ.

(2)   They (2-men) came to attend.   ٢. قَدِمَا لِيَحْضُرَا الإِجْتِمَاعَ.
      the meeting

(3)   They (all men) came to   ٣. قَدِمُوا لِيَحْضُرُوا الإِجْتِمَاعَ.
      attend the meeting.

(4)   She came to attend the meeting   ٤. قَدِمَتْ لِتَحْضُرَ الإِجْتِمَاعَ.

(5)   They (2-women) came to attend the   ٥. قَدِمَتَا لِتَحْضُرَا الإِجْتِمَاعَ
      meeting

(6)   They (all women) came to attend   ٦. قَدِمْنَ لِيَحْضُرْنَ الإِجْتِمَاعَ
      the meeting

(7)   You (1 man) came to attend the   ٧. قَدِمْتَ لِتَحْضُرَ الإِجْتِمَاعَ
      meeting

(8)   You (2men) came to attend the   ٨. قَدِمْتُمَا لِتَحْضُرَا الْإِجْتِمَاعَ
      meeting

(9) You (all men) came to attend the meeting

٩. قَدِمْتُمْ لِتَحْضُرُوا الإِجْتِمَاعَ

(10) You (1 woman) came to attend the meeting

١٠. قَدِمْتِ لِتَحْضُرِى الإِجْتِمَاعَ

(11) You (2 women) came to attend the meeting

١١. قَدِمْتُمَا لِتَحْضُرَا الإِجْتِمَاعَ

(12) You (all women) came to attend the meeting

١٢. قَدِمْتُنَّ لِتَحْضُرْنَ الإِجْتِمَاعَ

(13) I came to attend the meeting

١٣. قَدِمْتُ لأَحْضُرَ الإِجْتِمَاعَ

(14) We came to attend the meeting.

١٤. قَدِمْنَا لِنَحْضُرَ الإِجْتِمَاعَ

We also known this ل as ل of cause or causative ل. There are few more particles that modify the verb similarly e.g. لِكَى / كَىْ / حَتَّى / أَنْ. At times the verbs thus modified may be translated as 'so that', 'in order to' etc. e.g.

(1) I came so that I can attend or I came in order to attend

قَدِمْتُ لأَحْضُرَ

(2) I came so that I can attend

قَدِمْتُ حَتَّى أَحْضُرَ

The particle لَنْ modifies the verb as the ل of imperative and its sisters and the meaning in future negative emphatic, e.g.

(1) I will never attend the meeting

لَنْ أَحْضُرَ الإِجْتِمَاعَ

(2) They (men) will never attend the meeting

لَنْ يَحْضُرُوا الإِجْتِمَاعَ

(3) You (women) will never attend the meeting

لَنْ تَحْضُرْنَ الإِجْتِمَاعَ

* The particle مَا in addition to its other uses as mentioned earlier, is also used to indicate exclamation while at the same time it places the adjective of the comparative degree and the noun qualified by this adjective in the accusative case, e.g.

(1) How handsome the boy is!

مَا أَحْسَنَ الوَلَدَ!

(2) How difficult the game is!

مَاأَصْعَبَ اللُّعْبَةَ!

(3) How intelligent the teachers are!

مَا أَذكى الأَسَاتِذَةَ!

(4) How beautiful the girls are!

مَا أَجْمَلَ البَنَاتِ !

* Remember that the sound plural feminine takes only kasrah in the accusative case also.

* There is a term in Arabic grammar known as بَدَل مُبْدَل مِنْه (Badal Mobdal Minho) i.e. a second noun substituting the first noun. In this case the case of the بَدَل i.e. the substituting noun shall be the same as that of the noun which is substituted, e.g.

(1) The peon came nis son i.e. the   قَدِمَ الْفَرَّاشُ وَلَدُه
    peon's son came

(2) I saw the peon his son i.e.   رَأَيْتُ الْفَرَّاشَ وَلَدَه
    I saw the peon's son

It may be بَدَلُ الكُلِّ i.e. one whole substituting the noun as above and it may be a part substituting a whole and thus known as بَدَلُ الْجُزْءِ or the partitive substitute, e.g.

I wounded the boy his eye i.e.   جَرَحْتُ الوَلَدَ عَيْنَه
I wounded the boy's eye

* Particle إمَّا followed by أَوْ is used in the meaning of 'either—or, e.g.

Either you will stay with us in London   إمَّا تُقِيم عِندَنَا فِى لُنْدُن
or I will not visit you next month.   او لَنْ اُزُورك فِى الشَّهرِ القَادِمِ.

Generally in the spoken Arabic إمَّا , may be followed by إمَّا to mean either—or

* إنَّ، أَنَّ، كَأَنَّ، لَيْتَ، لكِنَّ and لَعَلَّ are particles that place the nouns that follow them in the accusative case, e.g.

(1) The teacher is present in the class   إنَّ المُدَرِّسَ مَوجُودٌ فِى الْفَصْلِ

(2) He informed me in writing   بَلَّغَنِى كِنَابَةً
    that his father is sick/unwell   أَنَّ وَالِدَهُ مَرِيضٌ

(3) It seems as if the student will not be   يَبْدُو كَأَنَّ الطَّالِبَ لا
    successful in the examination   يَنْجَحُ فِى الإمْتِحَان

(4) I wish his father were present   لَيْتَ وَالِدَه مَوجُودٌ

(5) The boy is short but the girl is tall   الوَلَدُ قَصِيرٌ وَلكِنَّ البِنْتَ طَوِيلَةٌ

(6) Perhaps the teacher will not   لَعَلَّ المُدَرِّسِينَ
    come tommorrow.   لَايَحْضُرُونَ غَدًا

* Slogans like 'long live the king', and wishing good or bad are expressed vide past tense verbs though this may not be considered unflinching rule, e.g.

(1) Long live the president!   عَاشَ الرَّئِيسُ!

(2) Death on the wrongdoer!   مَاتَ عَامِلُ السُّوءِ!

(3) May Allah bless (you)!   بَارَكَ اللّٰه

(4) May Allah help you!   كَانَ اللّٰه فِى عَونِك

However, present indefinite tense verb may also be used some times, e.g.

(5) May Allah destroy your house!   اللّٰه يُخَرِّبُ بَيْتَكَ
    or May you be doomed!

* مَبْنِى i.e. indeclinable is a word that carries a certain (short) vowel which never chages in any case. e.g. أَمْس is an indeclinable noun and this kasrah does not change, come what may. Similary, there are other nouns and verbs etc., which remain static even when they are preceded by a causative that should ordinarily change the case-terminal.

* As opposed to مَبْنِى words which are not many when compared to the corpus of Arabic words, the rest are مُعْرَب which change case terminal when it is so required for a reason, e.g. , وَلَدٌ

A boy came   قَدِمَ وَلَدٌ

I saw a boy   رَأَيْتُ وَلَدًا

I sat with a boy   جَلَسْتُ مَعَ وَلَدٍ

These معرب words include nouns and present tense verbs. Of these the nouns are also categorised as triptotical i.e. words or nouns that inflect fully according to the case. Some of the words or nouns which do not inflect fully are categorised as untriptotical or غَيْرُ مُنْصَرِفٌ These nouns are those which do not admit nunnation & Kasrah in the genitive case, e.g. مَسَاجِدُ the plural of مَسْجِدٌ.

(1) These are mosques   هٰذه مَسَاجِدُ

(2) I saw the mosques   رأَيْتُ مَسَاجِدَ

(3) I went to the mosques   ذَهَبْتُ إِلَى مَسَاجِدَ

Beside some other specified nouns, all plural nouns having alif as third
letter followed by kasrah, are untriptotical. However, when these plurals are
defined either by the definite article الـ or when placed in construct position,
then in that case they accept Kasrah also, e.g.

(1) I went to the mosques   ذَهَبْتُ إِلَى الْمَساجِد

(2) I went to the mosques of the city   ذَهَبْتُ إِلَى مَسَاجِدِ الْمَدِيْنَةِ

Additionly, adjective of comparative degree is treated as untriptotical. All
adjectives of colour and physical defect on the pattern of أَفْعَل are treated as
untriptotical.

* In Arabic all nouns are divided into two categories i.e. (1) Masculine &
  (2) feminine. There is no neutral gender. All nouns may be considerd as
  masculine gender nouns unless they specifically denote female objects.
  All nouns terminating with ta ة marboota are feminine gender nouns
  unless they are specifically used for masculine objects.

* Originally, Arabic did not have vowels or diacritical marks like we
  know them now as Dammah, Fathah and Kasrah, because it was
  restricted to the native speakers in the Arabian peninsula. However, with
  the arrival and spread of Islam when Arabic also came out of its
  enclosure and travelled to other neighbouring and far off countries
  where Islam was accepted as faith, it came to be learnt by 'unnatural
  speakers', who often committed serious mistakes in reading religious
  texts. This necessitated that Arabic should evolve a system to enable
  learners to handle it correctly and thus grammar was created which may
  rightly be called 'the constitution of the language', and the vowel or
  diacritical marks were determined as they are known today. They are
  Dammah—an open stomached coma above a letter, Fathah—a diagonal
  mark above a letter and kasrah a diagonal mark under a letter. When
  these marks are placed in twos, then they are called تنوين Tanween thus
  giving a terminal nunnation sound. When placed above or below the
  terminal letter of a noun, these very same vowel points are known as
  Raf'a, Nasb and Jarr, thus indicating cases—nominative, accusative and
  genitive respectively. A small circle 'ο' above a letter is known as سُكُون

sokoon, and when placed above the terminal letter then it is known as جَزْم Jazm and the word/noun is considered to be in the apocopate form. The function of this vowel is to create a stop, thus becoming a part of the syllable preceding it.

* There are words in Arabic which contain a letter twice. In this case that letter is written only once but read twice with the help of شَدَّة Shadda which symbol is represented by a sign consisting of three teeth (ّ) .

* All 28 letters of Arabic are known as consonants. However, و, ١ and ى function as (semi) elongative vowels while preceded by a letter carrying a vowel point representing that sound, e.g. بَا, بُو and بِى. In case of elongative الف sound it is supposed that alif is followed by another alif, thus ١ + ١ and hence it is written as آ or ١. It may be noted that this elongated الف obtains only in the beginning of a word.

* When these two semi vowels i.e. و, & ى are preceded by a letter carrying a fathah, then it is called dipthong, e.g. بَوْنٌ i.e. و preceded by fathah and thus causing a sound as in 'bowler' and بَيْنَ as in 'by' when ى is preceded by fathah.

* It has always been considered very difficult to handle correctly the prepositions in any language and it is specially difficult to handle them correctly and accurately if it is the acquired language of the user. In Arabic also it is difficult for the given reasons and due to regional differences. For example it may be فى that is used in the meaning of 'at' in certain meaning in certain countries while على might replace it in some other countries or regions. It is suggested that the preposition ب is used to mean 'in' in the context of cities, e.g. بِدِلْهِى i.e. in Delhi and فى is used to mean 'in' in the context of countries, e.g. فِى الهِنْد. i.e. in India. However, it is not a very hard and fast rule. These two prepositions may be used inversely in the said context. Generally, learners and scholars alike confuse the use of عَلَى and فُوقَ. عَلَى means 'on', and فُوقَ means 'above'. Thus neither of them would replace the other.

* In Arabic there are three numbers—singular, dual and plural. As explained, dual is obtained from a singular noun by adding ان at the end of a singular noun. For example وَلَدٌ would become وَلَد+ان = وَلَدَانِ. This

form is known as dual in the nominative case. In the accusative and genitive cases ان is replaced with يَنِ i.e. وَلَدَيْنِ.

(1) Two boys came (nominative case)   قَدِمَ وَلَدَانِ

(2) I saw two boys (accusative case)   رَأَيْتُ وَلَدَيْنِ

(3) I sat with two boys (genitive case)   جَلَسْتُ مَعَ وَلَدَيْنِ

In case of nouns terminating with Ta ة Marboota, the ta is written as stretched ta and joined to the alif or Ya of the dual , e.g.

Nominative case   مُدَرِّسَةٌ + ان = مُدَرِّسَتَانِ

Accusative & Genitive cases   مُدَرِّسَتَيْنِ

* About the plurals, there are two kinds fo plural nouns—(1) broken plural and (2) sound plural.

(1) Broken plural is the one in which case the order of the singular word is changed and a letter or more may also have to be added anywhere in the body of the singular word, e.g. قَلَمٌ means a pen while أَقْلَامٌ is pens. Note that one alif is added in the beginning and another after the second original letter. كُتُبٌ is books. Its singular is كِتَابٌ. Note that in this case original alif after the second letter is elided and the vowel marks are changed.These are broken plurals. There are preordained patterns to mould plurals, from singular nouns, however, they are many. I consider it much easier for learners to consult dictionary/teacher to know the plural.

(2) Sound plurals are generally made from certain specified singular nouns.

(a) For masculine gender—generally all verbal nouns of active and passive voices i.e. إسم المفعول and إسم الفاعل, denoting human beings are moulded into plural by suffixing to them ون i.e. 'waw' and 'noon' preceded by ḍammah in the nominative case and ين i.e. 'ya' and 'noon' preceded by kasrah in the accusative and the genitive cases. For example: ظَالِمٌ 'a cruel man' is a verbal noun of active voice from triliteral verb ظَلَمَ to be cruel. Now the plural is wrought as follows:

nominative case   ظَالِمٌ + وُنَ = ظَالِمُونَ

accusative & genitive cases ظَالِمٌ + ى نَ =ظَالِمِيْنَ

(1) Torturers came	(١) قَدِمَ ظَالِمُونَ
from Central Asia	مِنْ آسِيَا الوُسطَى
(2) I saw torturers	(٢) رَأَيْتُ ظَالِمِيْنَ
from Central Asia	مِنْ آسِيَا الوُسطَى
(3) I accompanied torturers from	(٣) إصْطَحَبْتُ ظَالِمِيْنَ
Central Asia	مِنْ آسِيَا الوُسطَى

مَظْلُومٌ is a verbal noun of passive voice. It means 'a tortured one' i.e. 'downtrodden'.

nominative case مَظْلُومٌ +وْنَ=مَظْلُومُونَ

accusative & genitive cases مَظْلُومٌ + ى نَ=مَظْلُومِيْنَ

(1) The downtrodden came	(١) قَدِمَ المَظْلُومُونَ
with their complaint	بِشَكْوَاهُم
(2) I saw the downtrodden	(٢) رَأَيْتُ المَظْلُومِينَ
in the room	فى الغُرْفَةِ
(3) I sat with the downtrodden	(٣) جَلَسْتُ مَعَ المَظْلُومِينَ
in the room	فى الغُرْفَةِ

* In case of verbs consisting of four or more letters, the verbal noun of active voice is wrought from its present indefinite form of III person masculine singular by eliding the symbol of present indefinite and prefixing to it meem i.e. م with dammah and the penultimate i.e. last but one letter shall invariably have/be given a kasrah, e.g.

to travel	سَافَرَ / يُسَافِرُ
traveller	مُ=سَافِرٌ = مُسَافِرٌ
nominative case	مُسَافِرٌ + وْنَ= مُسَافِرُونَ
accusative & genitive cases	مُسَافِرٌ + ى نَ = مُسَافِرِيْنَ

In the case of the verbal noun of passive voice the penultimate letter is invariably given a fathah, e.g.

the one who is made to travel مُسَافَرٌ

Theoretically, verbal nouns of active and passive voices can be made from all verbs, however, practically it does not obtain.

Regarding use of verbal nouns, all rules apply as mentioned above.

(b) As regards sound plural feminine, it is generally wrought from infinite forms of verbs and feminine nouns that end with ta ة marboota, e.g.

<table>
<tr><td>To be safe</td><td>سَلِمَ / يَسْلَمُ / سَلَامًا
سَلَامٌ = ات = سَلَامَاتٌ</td></tr>
<tr><td>To give over, to handover,</td><td>سَلَّمَ / يُسَلِّمُ / تَسْلِيمًا
تَسْلِيمٌ + ات = تَسْلِيمَاتٌ</td></tr>
<tr><td>To receive</td><td>تَسَلَّمَ / يَتَسَلَّمُ / تَسَلُّمًا
تَسَلُّمٌ + ات= تَسَلُّمَاتٌ</td></tr>
</table>

From nouns ending in Ta ة marboota sound plural feminine is wrought by eliding the ta ة and suffixing to the remainder ات as follows:

$$كُرَّاسَةٌ + ات = كُرَّاسَاتٌ$$
$$مُدَرِّسَةٌ + ات = مُدَرِّسَاتٌ$$

In the nominative case the ت takes dammah and in the accusative & genitive cases the ت terminates only in Kasrah, e.g.

(1) The (lady) teachers came from New Delhi.	(١) قَدِمَتِ الْمُدَرِّسَاتُ مِنْ نِيودَلْهِى
(2) I saw the (lady) teacher in the lobby.	(٢) رَأَيْتُ الْمُدَرِّسَاتِ فِى الرَّدْهَةِ
(3) I discussed the topic with (lady) teachers.	(٣) نَاقَشْتُ الْمَوْضُوعَ مَعَ الْمُدَرِّسَاتِ

Nouns/ adjectival nouns terminating with a soft ya ى (i.e. which is not مُضَاعَفْ as in كُرْسِىٌّ) preceded by Kasrah is wrought into plural on the pattern of فُعَاةٌ, e.g.

قُضَاةٌ i.e. judge will group in قَاضِى or سُعَاةٌ i.e. courrier will group in سَاعِى etc.

* Please note the following:

To fulfil (promise)	وَفَى / يَفِى / وَفَاءً

To guard	وَقَى / يَقِى / وَقْيًا
To be of the opinion	إِرْتَأَى / يَرْتَئِى / إِرْتِيَاءً
To recount, to narrate	رَوَى / يَرْوِى / رِوَايَةً

Verbs like in the foregoing are not many and they are not generally used because there are many other simple-lettered verbs to replace them. They are sparingly used and in any case all the fourteen patterns of conjugation are not used. Forms of such verbs which do occur in writing are generally mentioned in every good dictionary. Therefore, it is best learnt from the dictionaries.

* It may be noted that occasionally in written Arabic and generally in spoken Arabic verbal nouns of active & passive voices function as verbs, thus affecting the nouns that follow them exactly like a verb. For example, we say:

(1) I am going to the college now.   (١) أنا ذاهِبٌ الى الكُلِّيَّةِ الآن

or   (أَنَا) أَذْهَبُ إلى الكُلِّيَّةِ الآنَ

(2) I 'll be heading to the office at the train's arrival time.   (٢) أَكُونُ مُتَوَجِّهًا إِلَى المَكْتَبِ وَقْتَ وُصُولِ القِطَارِ

or   سَوفَ أَتَوَجَّهُ إِلَى المَكْتَبِ وَقْتَ وُصُولِ القِطَارِ

(3) I present (am presenting) to you this book   أَنَا مُقَدِّمٌ لَك هَذا الْكِتَابَ

or   (أَنَا) أُقَدِّمُ لَك هَذا الكِتَابَ

* La of absolute denial i.e. لَا نَفْى الجِنْسِ causes *fathah* to the noun that follows it, e.g.

There is none in the house	لَا رَجُلَ فِى الدَّارِ
I have no power to solve the problem	لَا حَولَ لِى لِحَلِّ المُشْكِلَة

However, when this La لَا of absolute denial is repeated then in that case it may be allowed to retain its characteristic, e.g.

There is no power and no strength except with (in) Allah.	لَاحَولَ وَلَا قُوَّةَ إِلَّا بِاللّه

However, generally it is used devoid of its characteristic or as it might please the user or suit the placement in writing, e.g.

لَا حَولٌ ولا قُوَّةٌ إلا بالله

لَا حَولَ ولا قُوَّةٌ إلا بالله

لَا حَولٌ ولا قُوَّةَ إلا بالله

* Though there are designated patterns for forming nouns of place, time and instrument etc, however, they are better learnt with the passage of time and the progress in readings. Arabic dictionaries generally provide host of derived forms of words from a basic 3-lettered or 4-lettered or 5-lettered original Arabic verb. Therefore, we should rather concentrate on early and accurate use of Arabic-English dictionary to enrich our vocabulary and enhance our ability to use the Arabic language. Here are some tips to use Arabic dictionary:

Good Arabic-English dictionaries are alphabetical in a restricted way. It means that only the root letters i.e. 3 or 4 or 5 lettered verbs are entered alphabetically into Arabic- English dictionaries followed by a host of derived forms of words to the great advantage of the learner. These words are arranged systematically in order of categories of words beginning with forms of a verb generally in use followed by nouns in order of increase of number of letters except those which forms have preordained meaning derived from the verb, e.g. the active & passive participles i.e. the verbal nouns of active & passive voices may not be mentioned in the list of words under the root letters unless they have meanings different from their preordained meanings. For example فَاتِحٌ , مَفْتُوحٌ , مُقَدِّمٌ , مُقَدَّمٌ , مُسْتَسْلِمٌ may not be mentioned in the dictionary. However, if active and passive participles have some specific or special or extension meaning, then only such nouns/ words find mention in the dictionaries. For example مُسْتَقْبِلٌ which would mean beside the regular meaning of active participle the additional meaning of (radio) receiver or مُسْتَقْبَلٌ would mean the facade or the front part of something or the future.

* In view of above it is very necessary for a learner to acquire the ability of recognising the basic root letters of a word that he would come across during his reading. On the face of it, this thing appears to be difficult.

However, if one can learn the derived forms of verbs, he may not face serious difficulty in overcoming this problem. فَعَلَ or ف, ع & ل are generally considered to be the basic lettering of a triliteral verb, e.g. in the case of ضَرَبَ or ض, ر & ب the first letter ض is said to be ف, ر is considered as ع and ب is called ل because they replace ف, ع & ل respectively of فَعَلَ which is considered to be the measurement of the triliteral basic Arabic verb. Beside the original form of the triliteral verb which may be considered as form I, the other derived forms are as follows:

Form II is obtained by doubling the second i.e. ع letter of the verb, e.g. فَعَّلَ.

Form III is obtained by inserting one elongative alif ا after the first i.e. ف letter of the verb, e.g. فَاعَلَ.

Form IV is obtained by adding one consonant alif ا (which is known as Hamza also) with a *fathah* before the first i.e. the ف letter of the verb, e.g. أفْعَلَ.

Form V is obtained by adding a ta ت with *fathah* before the first i.e. the ف letter of the verb and the second i.e. ع letter is doubled, e.g. تَفَعَّلَ.

Form VI is obtained by adding ta ت with *fathah* before the first i.e. ف letter and an elongative alif ا after the first i.e. ف letter, e.g. تَفَاعَلَ.

Form VII is obtained by adding a consonant alif ا (which is known as Hamza also) with kasrah and noon i.e. ن before the first i.e. ف letter of the verb, e.g. إنفَعَلَ.

Form VIII is obtained by adding a consonant alif ا with kasrah before the first i.e. ف letter and ta ت after the first i.e. ف letter, e.g. إفْتَعَلَ .

Form IX is obtained by adding a consonant alif with kasrah and doubling the third i.e. the last letter i.e. la ل letter of the verb, e.g. إفْعَلَّ.

Form X is obtained by adding a consonant alif ا with kasrah and ت & س before the first i.e. ف letter of the verb, e.g. إسْتَفْعَلَ.

These are the most often used forms of the verbs. There are other forms which are so rarely used that they are almost non-entities. These are forms consisting of four and five original letters and their derivatives. They will be easy to handle by scholars with passage of time and as indicated above, their frequency is not much and in certain cases nil.

Words of foreign origin if assimilated or easy to assimilate and somehow co-related to a triliteral verb etc., then that word is mentioned under that root word otherwise it is mentioned in 'general' alphabetical order. For example the French word كلسون (i.e. calecon) i.e. a pair of men's drawers may be entered under كلس which means in form II to whitewash. The foreign word كَلَبْش meaning "handcuffs" is entered under general alphabetical order after كلب.

It may not be difficult to find the root letters of a word which consists of full number of letters as it requires and which does not consist of a weak letter or two or which has not dropped a letter or two for some grammatical/ etymological reasons. For example ذَاهِبٌ may be measured on فَاعِلٌ and ذ، ه & ب rightly deduced to be the original or root letters or مُذَهَّبٌ may be measurd on مُفَعَّلٌ or مُسْتَخْدَمٌ may be measured on مُسْتَفْعَلٌ etc. and right root letters may be found. However, words consisting of doubled letters at the terminal position may cause some difficulty in deciphering the original letters of a verb/ word. For example, مَقَرٌّ i.e. headquarters or مُسْتَمَدٌّ i.e. extracted or فِرَّ i.e. run (imperative). However, they would pose no difficulty if you remember to unfold the terminal doubled letter i.e. مَقَرٌّ is in reality مَقْرَرٌ, or مُسْتَمَدٌّ is مُسْتَمْدَدٌ and فِرَّ is إِفْرِرْ and hence you can see that after banishing the additional letters you would have (مَدَّ) مَدَدَ, (قَرَّ) قَرَرَ and (فَرَّ) فَرَرَ). The real difficulty is faced only in case of words which consist of some weak letter/s and/or in which case for some grammatical reasons, a letter or two are either dropped or replaced by some other/s.

For example, حَائِطٌ i.e. wall, in which case Hamza ء has actually replaced waw و. This word has been extracted from حوط. Similarly, إِذَّكَرَ or اِذْدَكَرَ or اِذَّكَرَ i.e. to remember, which word has been cast on إِفْتَعَلَ pattern, however, for some morphological reasons it has been 'mutilated' as above. The imperative verb قِ i.e. guard, might cause some difficulty to find original letters as for some morphological reasons 2-3 letters have been dropped here. However, in most of such cases some clue can always be found to reach the right original letters of the word. For example, in case of اِذْدَكَرَ or

إِذَّكَرَ, you may have to look for it in the dictionary under أَذْكَرَ , أَكَرَ ,ذَكَّرَ, and finally you may be led to ذَكَرَ. Similarly, in case of إِضْطِرَابٌ i.e. disturbance or disorder, one might initially face some difficulty because in this case ط *ṭa* has actually replaced ta ت as follows:

$$إِفْتِعَالٌ / إِضْتِرَابٌ = إِضْطِرَابٌ$$

In such cases a little exercise shall have to be done to find the original letters of the words and we may have to look up two or three options to reach the right word mentioned as above.

Most importantly, we should know here that these morphological problems shall get solved if we are informed on this aspect of the language. Generally, conjugations of irregular verbs and/ or verbs consisting of one or two weak letters or Hamza, shall be helpful.

* Eearlier in a lesson we have dealt with adjective— what it is and the formulae of making it etc. In certain cases adjective is also wrought by suffixing doubled ya ي i.e. ya ي with *shaddah* preceded by kasrah, e.g. مِصْرُ i.e. Egypt and مِصْرِىٌّ i.e. Egyptian. This ya ي is known as ya ي of نِسبة or the ya ي of attribution.

* مِنْ is a preposition which generally means 'from' as in أَنَا مِنْ دِلْهِى i.e. I am from Delhi. However, it has an extension meaning "of" in expressions like "made of" e.g. 'this ring is made of gold', i.e. هَذَا الخَاتَمُ مَصْنُوعٌ مِنْ الذَّهَبِ. We may also say that in the sentence above the word مَصْنُوعٌ i.e. 'made' is taken away for reason of frequent use. It may be true. However, generally such meaning is expressed without using the word مَصْنُوعٌ and the meaning is straight and adequate. The word مَصْنُوعٌ can also be used and ignored as per context and need.

* Some tips on irregular verbs:

* Conjugation of regular verbs consisting of sound letters is easy to acquire and similarly it is also easy to decipher the original letters. However, verbs consisting of one or two (semi) vowels occuring anywhere in the verb do create some problem/s even for experienced people. For example verbs like وَقَى & وَلَى, وَعَى,خَافَ, عَدَا, وَعَدَ, مَشَى, بَقِيَ etc. and many more do have irregular conjugations, though in a restricted sense. You must have observed these irregularities in the

conjugations of such sample verbs. The real problem surfaces in verbs—derived forms, where certain letter is replaced by another letter for reason that these two consecutive letters are not compatible in sound, and hence the difficulty to say them correctly. For example ضَرَبَ when cast on افتعل pattern, then this ت is changed to ط because the sound of ض is not compatible to ت whereas the sound of ط is compatible and therefore ت inإضتَرَبَ and its likes shall be replaced by ط and thus written as إضطَرَبَ. Verbs like ذكر when cast on افتعل pattern, in that case ت of اذتكر may be changed to د and written اذذكر or this original ذ may be doubled and written إذَّكَر or this original ذ may be merged in the د that replaced ت and written this إدَّكَر. Similary, some noun forms derived from these kinds of irregular verbs may also have to undergo some changes, For example مُضتَرِبٌ shall be replaced by مُضْطَرِبٌ and مُدتِثرٌ shall be replaced by مُدَّثِرٌ. These are morphological changes that have to be acquired.

* In order to liason a silent letter i.e. a letter with sokoon to its following, the sokoon is replaced by kasrah, e.g. when قَالَتْ [(She) said] shall have to be liasoned to its following then it will be said/ read thus:قَالَتِ امْرَأَةٌ A woman said or قَالَتِ الْبَنَاتُ The girls said. In our lessons generally in such cases we have indicated this kind of liaisoning thus: قَالَتِ الْبَنَاتُ and قَالَتِ امْرَأَةٌ etc.

* Elongative Alif, Yaa and Waw (Serving as semi vowels) are necessarily preceded by an even vowel i.e. Alif is preceded by fathah, Yaa is preceded by kasrah and Waw is preceded by dammah and in this case these three vowels are supposed to be carrying sokoon i.e. ـْ which may not necessarily be placed above them, though generally we have mentioned it in our lessons. Elongative Alif preceded by Fathah sounds 'aa' as in 'bar'. Elongative Yaa preceded by kasrah sounds 'ee' as in 'eel'. Elongative waw preceded by Dammah sounds 'oo' as in 'booze'. Similarly, in dipthong waw and Yaa both are preceded by Fathah and waw and Yaa are supposed to be carrying sokoon. In dipthong waw preceded by Fathah sounds 'ow' as in 'owl' and Yaa preceded by Fathah sounds 'ay' as in 'day' in Australian pronunciation.

* There is a kind of noun which is called collective noun. This noun infact

refers to a variety of things as a whole, e.g. مَوز mawz i.e. bananas or
تُفَّاح toffaah, i.e. apples, or بَيْض bayḍ i.e. eggs etc. To obtain a word to
indicate a single piece of such items, a ta marboota i.e. ة in generally
suffixed to such a noun. For example to say one banana we would say in
Arabic مَوزَةٌ mawzaton, one apple would be تُفاحة toffahaton, and بَيْضَة
bayḍaton would mean one egg, and so on so forth.

* In terms of influence of the verbs, they are generally divided in two
categories i.e. (1) tranitive verbs which take at the minimum one subject
i.e. the doer of the action and one object i.e. receiver of the action. It is
known as مُتعدى in Arabic and (2) intransitive verbs which do not take
object i.e. the receiver of action. This variety of verbs is known as لازم
in Arabic.

* Like in any other language, in Arabic also there are a few particles/
words which are used to connect two/ more parts of the sentence. They
are known as حُرُوف العطف i.e. connectives or conjunctives like وَ wa & أو
etc. 'wa' means 'and', and 'aw' means 'or'. It may be noted that after
these connectives the case terminal of a noun shall be the same as that of
the one preceding it. For example:

أَكَلَتُ الْعِنَبَ وَالْمَوْزَ وَالْبُرْتُقَالَ

* Please note that the noun after أَكَلَتُ and those after the connective 'wa'
serve as objects for أَكَلَتُ i.e. I ate grapes, bananas and oranges.

Note also that in Arabic connetives are frequently used while in English we
use 'comma/s' and only at the final stage connective is used.

* Generally parts of the body which are in 'twos' are used as feminine.
For example يَد hand , عَيْنٌ eye etc. Parts of body which are not in pairs
are generally treated as masculine.

* In Arabic generally verb has to be in consonance with its subject in
gender i.e. masculine verb for masculine subject and feminine verb for
feminine subject, however, if there is a particle/ word between the verb
and the feminine subject then rules permit to use masculine verb. For
example:

Some girls came to me قَدِمَ إِلَيَّ بَنَاتٌ

* Undefined plural nouns include the meaning (some) as above.

* In the case of a mixed subject i.e. where men & women together constitute a subject, then the masculine verb is used. For example:

قَدِمَ الرِّجَالُ وَالنِّسَاءُ لِحُضُورِ الْحَفْلَةِ i.e. the men & women came to attend the function.

* In simple nominal sentence a common noun can not be placed at no. 1. If a common noun has to play necessarily the subject i.e Mobtada مُبتدأ , then it has to be placed at no. 2, that is to say khabar خبر i.e. predicate shall be placed at no. 1 followed by the Mubtada i.e. subject. For example if there is need to say that "A boy is in the room" then this can be rendered in Arabic as follows:

Fil ghor fa ti (In the room) فِى الْغُرْفَةِ

wa la don (is a boy) وَلَدٌ

i.e. A boy is in the room.

or

Ho naa ka (There is) هُنَاكَ

wa la don (a boy) وَلَدٌ

fil ghorfati (in the room) فِى الْغُرْفَةِ

* The imperative verb دَعْ (from وَدَعَ) and its declensions i.e. different changing forms are used to satisfy the meaning of 'let' as in 'let me go'. To obtain this specific meaning دَعْ perecedes the second verb in its required form i.e. to match the number and gender of the subject. For example دَعْنِى أَذْهَبُ would mean 'let me go'. Different forms of دَعْ shall be handled exactly like imperative.

* To obtain the meaning 'begin to' we shall have to prefix أخذ and its declensions to suit the number & gender of the subject. For example 'he began to read', would be rendered in Arabic thus: أَخَذَ يَقْرَأُ while أَخَذْتُ أَقْرَأُ would mean ' I began to read'. To obtain similar meaning in future/ peresent tense we shall use the present tense form of the verb followed by the infinitive form of the verb. For example:

عِنْدَمَا يَرَانِى يَأْخُذُ فِى الْقِرَاءةِ   i.e. when he sees me, he begins to read.

Beside أخذ there are a few more words in Arabic which are used similarly to obtain the meaning as mentioned in the foregoing, like طَفِقَ, بَدَأ and شَرَعَ etc.

Meaning of 'yet' as in 'he has not come yet' is obtained by using لَمْ and/ or لَمَّا before the present tense verb as follows:

(1) Khalid has not come yet.   لَمْ يَقْدَمْ خَالِدٌ بَعْدُ

or

(1) Khalid has not come yet.   لَمَّا يَقْدَمُ خَالد

It may be noted that when we use لم we will also use بعد to obtain the meaning of yet, however, in the case of لَمَّا the word بَعْدُ is not used.

Diminutive noun in Arabic is used for both, endearment and dislike. There are given patterns to make them from triliteral words and others. They are better learnt with the passage of time from the dictionaries.

*   Emphatic meaning of a verb is generally obtained by using the infinitive form of the verb after the required form of the verb. For example:

I beat him severely   ضَرَبْتُهُ ضَرْبًا

In this case the infinitive form of the verb is always منصوب i.e. in the accusative case and it is called مفعول مطلق. Beside this, there are four more expressions which are categorised as مفعول (plural مفاعيل). They are: (1) مفعول به i.e. a noun which is used as object of the transitive verb, e.g. ضَرَبَ حامدٌ كلبًا Hamid beat a dog. In this sentence كلبًا serves as object of the verb 'beat' and hence it is مفعول به. (2) مفعول له or مفعول لاجله, it is generally an infinitive form of verb in the accusative case used to indicate reason or cause for performing some action, e.g.

I bowed to him out of respect.   أنحَنَيْتُ لَه احْتِرَامًا

In the sentence above احتراما is the مفعول له or مفعول لاجله.

*   This مفعول له covers two more subtitles known as (1) حال i.e. state and تمييز i.e. specification. In these two cases also the noun used shall be in the accusative case, e.g.

(١) حال : دَخَلَ الْوَلَدُ الصّفَّ لَاهِثًا   The boy entered the class panting
(for breath)

Be good in intention   (٢) تمييز : طِبْ نِيّةً

(3) There is another مفعول in Arabic called مَفْعُول مَعَه i.e. the مفعول of
accompaniment. In this case the noun in the accusative case is preceded
by a waw و which is also termed as واو الْمَعَيَّة i.e. the waw of
accompaniment and hence the name مفعول معه . It is rarely used as follows
in the meaning of 'by', 'with' and similar kinds of words:

I travelled by the night.   سَافرتُ وَاللَّيْلَ

(4) مفعول فيه is a second name for adverb of time at which some action
takes place and /or adverb of place where some action takes place.
Such مفعول or adverb carries fatḥah, e.g.

I went out for walk in the morning.   خَرَجْتُ لِلنُّزْهَةِ صَبَاحًا

I travelled by land   سَافرْتُ بَرًّا

It may be noted that such meaning is often expressed by the genitive clause
i.e. the relevant noun is generally preceded by the preposition فى and hence
the nomenclature مفعول فيه , e.g

I went out for walk in the morning   خَرَجْتُ لِلنُّزْهَةِ فِى الصَّبَاحِ

These مَفَاعِيل are known in Arabic grammar terminology as الْمَفَاعِيل الْخَمْسَة .
There are other simple ways to express such meaning as indicated above
under each category. They are better learnt with the passage of time and the
increasing studies in the Arabic language.

* There is a noun known as اسم الآلة i.e. noun of instrument. They may be
wrought from triliteral verbs on the patterns of فَعَّالة, or مِفْعَال or مِفْعَل e.g.
مِرْجَل cauldron, مِنْظَار telescope/ magnifying glass and خَلَّاطَة mixer. There
are many more patterns and different ways of making nouns of
instrument from words consisting of more than three basic letters. Please
note that they are nouns that would be better learnt and their plurals
from dictionary with the increasing readings of the Arabic texts.

* There are many ways of expressing that some one or some thing is good
or bad or some one or some thing is good or bad in specific capacity.

For example we want to say: this man is good or bad as a teacher. This
expression can be rendered in Arabic as follows:

This man is good as teacher.   هَذَا الرَّجُلُ جَيِّدٌ كَا لُمُدَرِّس

This man is not good as teacher.   هَذا الرَّجُلُ لَيْسَ جَيِّدًا كَالْمُدَرِّس

However, there are two specific words نِعْمَ and بِئْسَ which mean respectively
good & bad. They are always used in III person in past tense only as نِعْمَ &
نِعْمَتْ and بِئْسَ & بِئْسَتْ and the noun that follows them is invariably in the
nominative case, e.g. نِعْمَ الرَّجُلُ مُدَرِّسًا i.e. The man is a good teacher.

*   The expression لا سِيَّمَا i.e. 'especially' is considered to be a kind of
    exceptive which in all cases is followed by a noun in the nominative
    case. For example:

I was annoyed with the students,   زَعَلْتُ مِنَ الطَّلَبَةِ

especially their monitor.   لا سِيَّمَا عَرِيفُهُمْ

*   Meaning of 'already' in expressions like 'I have already read this novel'
    is expressed by using the verb سَبَقَ followed by the relevant form of the
    relevant verb preceded by أَنْ , e.g.

I have already read this novel.   سَبَقَ أَنْ قَرَأْتُ هَذِهِ الرِّوَايَةَ

*   Meaning of 'will have' or 'would have' & similar expressions is
    expressed by using the relevant form of the verb يَكُونُ followed by the
    relevant form of the relevant verb in the past tense. For example:

I would have eaten   أَكُونُ قَدْ أَكَلْتُ

my breakfast before you rise   فُطُورِى قَبْلَ قِيَامِك

from the sleep.   مِنَ النَّومِ

*   Punctuation as we know presently is a relatively new phenomenon in the
    Arabic language. These commas, semicolons, colons & full stops etc.,
    were non-existant in the Arabic language of the yore. It was after the
    arrival of Islam and subsequent upon its acceptance by the non-arabs, a
    pressing need was felt to dot the words and invent diacritical marks to
    enable the non-arabs to pronounce the Arabic words correctly and
    similarly punctuation marks permeated into it. Herein below a list of

names of Arabic punctuation marks is provided with their English equivalents:

(1) Full Stop	.	نُقْطَة
(2) Comma	،	الفاصلة/ الشَّولَة
(3) Colon	:	نُقْطَتان
(4) Semi Colon	؛	الشَّولَة المَنْقُوطَة or
		الفَاصِلَةُ المَنْقُوطَة
(5) Question Mark	؟	عَلَامَةُ الاسْتِفْهَام
(6) Exclamation Mark	!	عَلَامَةُ التَّعَجُّب
(7) Oblique or slash	/	الخط المَائِل
(8) Dash	—	شُرْطَة
(9) Between Brackets	( )	بَيْن قَوسَيْن
(10) Quotation Marks	« »	عَلامتا الاقتباس
(11) Suspension Points	...	عَلامَةُ الْحَذْف

It may be noted that all the punctuation marks are not as frequently used in Arabic as in English. They are religiously used by translators, though. Even in todays Arabic all 'commas' are generally replaced by the conjunctive waw و or Aw او etc as the case my be.

* An attempt has been made to represent all patterns of verbs — those consisting of all sound letters and/ or one, two or more weak letters, in the list or appendix of conjugations. However, there may be patterns which are not represented or adequately explained or so it might appear for the learners. It may be noted that no language can ever fully be explained and /or taught through written word. We learn more and beyond the written word with the passage of time and with the increasing exprience – theoretical and practical. Surely all books are important as each one might provide that the other did not. As a matter of fact conjugation of sound verbs, Hamzated verbs and other verbs consisting of one or two or more weak letters and other morphological changes in the formation of Arabic words, is an independent and detailed branch of Arabic grammar which we intend to present in a separate book.

* In written Arabic some times elongaive alif is represanted by an alif ا mark above a letter. For example: الرّحْمٰن

* It may be that generally the meaning of 'a few' or 'some' is part of a plural common noun i.e. a plural noun without al الـ. For example:

Some girls came to me قَدِمَتْ إِلَىَّ بَنَاتٌ
A few girls came to me

* There are two varieties of Hamza viz (1) همزة الوصل i.e. the Hamza that disappears when the preceding word is read/said in conjunction with it. For example:

جَلَسْتُ فِى انْتِظَارِك

This Hamza may be called the conjunctive or linkable Hamza. Linkable Hamza occurs in many other words.

(2) The second variety of Hamza is called همزة القطع . This Hamza may be called the separable or the disjunctive Hamza. No preceding word can be read in conjunction with it. Reading has to be stopped at the last letter of the word preceding this Hamza and the word beginning with this Hamza has to be distinctively read with full and clear sound of Hamza. For example:

قَدِمَ الأُسْتَاذُ وَأَخْرَجَ الْكِتَابَ

In this sentence above Hamza of أَخْرَجَ is disjunctive.

Names of some Spices   أسماء بهارات

Coriander	كُزْبَرَة
Turmeric	كُرْكُمْ
A variety of pepper, chilly	شطة
Black pepper	فلفل اسود
White pepper	فلفل ابيض
Powder	مسحوق
Cardamom	حبّهان، حبّهال، حَيْهل
Clove	قرنفل
Cumin	كمّون
Spices	توابل
Spices	بهارات
Sesame	سمسم
Ginger	زنجيل
Mustard	خردل
Cinnamon	قَرْفَةْ
Aniseed	ينسون

Names of some flowers   أسماء زُهُور

Forget me-not	لاَتنسَنِى / زَهْرَة آذان الْفَأْر
Lotus	لُوطَس / عَرائِسُ الْبَحْر
Magnolia	مَغْنُوليَا / مَنُوليا
Jasmine	يَاسْمِيْن
Marigold	آذَرْيُون
Rose	وَرْد
Dahalia	دَالْيَا
Celery	كَرْنَس
Asparagus	هَلْيُون

Names of some vegetables:

Brinjal	بَاذَنْجَان
Lettuce	خَسّ
Green chilly	فِلْفِل أَخْضَر
Coriander leaf or green coriander	كُزْبُرَة خَضْرَاء
Mint	نَعْنَاع
Ladies fingers	بَامْيَا
Cabbage	مَلْفُوف
Cauliflower	قَرْنَبِيط
Turnip	لِفْت/شَلْجَم
Beetroot	شَمَنْدَر
Potato	بَطَاطِس
Sweet potato	بَطَاطَا
Carrot	جَزَر
Radish	فِجْل
Spinach	اسْبَانِخ
Mushroom	فُطْر/عِشُّ الغراب
Head of maize/ corncob	كوز الذرة
Peas	بِزِلَّا/بِسِلَّا
Cowpea	لُوبِيا
Purslane	رِجْلَة/بَقْلَة حَمْقَاء
Egyptian or black bean	بَقْلَة باردة/ لبلاب
Tomato	طَمَاطَم
Onion	بَصَل
Garlic	ثُوم

Bottlegourd	قَرَع
Pumpkin	يَقْطِين
Parsley	بَقْدونِس
Leek	كَرَّات
Parsnip	جَزَر ابَيَض
Colocasia	قِلْقَاس
Lemon	لَيْمُون
Zucchini	كُوسة
Green fenugreek or fenugreek leaf	اورَاق حِلْبَة
Dill	شبد /شبث
Jews mallow	ملوخية

Names of some fruits: أَسْمَاءُ فَوَاكِه:

Mango	انْبَج /مَنْجَة
Orange	بُرْتَقَال
Watermelon	بِطِّيخ
Melon	شَمَّام
Plum	بُرْقُوق
Peach	خَوخٌ
Pear	كُمَّثْرَى
Apple	تُفَّاح
Grapes	عِنَبٌ
Banana	مَوز
Apricot	مِشْمِش
Cherry	كَرَزٌ /كُرِيزٌ
Papaya	بَابَايَا

Pineapple	اَنَانَاس
Mulberries	تُوت
Strawberry	فَرَاوِلَة
Guava	جُوَافَه
Fig	تِيْن
Rasberry	تُوتُ الأَرْض/فِرِيز
Almond	لَوز
Currant	كِشْمِش
Raisin	زَبِيب
Walnut	عَيْنُ الْجَمَل
Pistachio	فُسْتُق
Coconut (dry)	جَوزُ الْهِنْد (مُجَفَّف)
Date	بَلَح
Date (dry)	بلح (مُجَفَّف)
Pulp (of seeds), kernel	لب (البُذور)
Cashew	كَاتِشُو
Dry fruits	يَامِيش/نُقْلٌ

Names of some cereals	أسماء نباتات حُبوبية
Sorghum	سَرْغُوم
Oats	هُرطُمَان/شونان
Wheat	حِنْطَة/قَمْح
Rice	أُرُز
Lentil	عَدَس
Horsebean	فول
Peanuts	فول سوداني

Chickpea	حُمُّص
Barley	شَعِير
Maize	ذرة
Millet, dukhn	دُخْنّ

Names of some Animals: أسماء حيوانات

Chicken	فَرْخ / فِرَاخ
Cock	دِيْك / دُيُوك
Hen	دَجَاجَةً
Chameleon	حَرْباء
Scorpion	عَقْرَب / عَقارِب
Frog	ضِفْدَع / ضَفَادِع
Shrimp	جَمْبَرى
Walrus	فِيْلُ الْبَحْرِ
Dragon fly	يَعْسُوب
Wasp	زَنْبُور / زَنَابِير
Locust	جَراد
Bat	وَطْوَاط
Giraffe	زَرَافَة / زَرَافَاتٌ
Zebra	حِمَارُ الزَّرْد
Hoopoe	هُدْهُد
Hippopotamus	كركدن
Elephant	فيل / فيلة
Wildgoat	تَيْس
Antelope	وَعْلّ / وُعُول
Fox	ثَعْلَب / ثَعَالِب

Crocodile	تِمْسَاح / تَمَاسِيْح
Fish	سَمَك / أَسْمَاك
Eel	ثُعْبَانُ الْمَاء
Butterfly	فَرَاشَة / فَرَاشَات
Shellfish	صَدَف / أَصْدَاف
Spider	عَنْكَبُوت / عَنَاكِب
Stork	لَقْلَق / لَقَالِق
Duck	بَطَّة / بَطُّ
Jackal	اِبْنُ آوَى / اَبْنَاء آوَى
Peacock	طَاؤُوْس / طَوَاوِيْس
Quail	سُمَّان / سَلْوَى
Sparrow	عُصْفُور / عَصَافِير
Bear	دُبُّ / دِبَبَة
Monkey	قِرْدُ / قِرَدَة
Orangutan	إِنْسَانُ الْغَاب
Fly	ذُبَاب / ذُبَّان
Mosquito	بَعُوض
Honeybee	نَحْل
Horse	حِصَان / أَحْصِنَة
Mare / horse	فَرَس / اَفْرَاس
Snake	ثُعْبان / ثَعَابِين
Lizard	سِحْلِيَّة / سَحَالِى
Deer	ظَبْى / ظِبَاء
Hare, rabbit	أَرْنَب / أَرَانِب
Goat	شَأَة / شِياة

Ram	حَمَلٌ
Camel	جَمَلٌ / جِمَالٌ
Cow	بَقَرٌ
Buffalo	جَامُوسٌ

Days of the week	ايام الاسبوع
Day (of twenty four hours)	يَوْمٌ
Day (time from dawn to dusk)	نَهَارٌ
Night (time from dusk to dawn)	لَيْلٌ
Week	أُسْبُوعٌ
Saturday	يَوْمُ السَّبْتِ
Sunday	يَوْمُ الأَحَدِ
Monday	يَوْمُ الإِثْنَيْنِ
Tuesday	يَوْمُ الثُّلاثاء
Wednesday	يَوْمُ الاربعاء
Thursday	يَوْمُ الخَمِيسِ
Friday	يَوْمُ الجُمْعَةِ

Names of months: أسماء الشهور

Christian	Arabic	Islamic	
يَنَايِر	كَانُون الثَّانى	مُحَرَّمُ الْحَرَام	١
فِبْرَايِر	شُبَاط	صَفَرُ الْمُظَفَّر	٢
مارِس	آذَار	رَبِيْعُ الأَوَّل	٣
اِبْرِيْل	نِيْسَان	رَبِيْعُ الثَّانى	٤
مَايُو	أَيَّار	جُمَادَى الأُوْلَى،	٥

٦	جُمَادَى الآخِرَة	حَزِيْرَان	يُونْيُو
٧	رَجَب الْمُرَجَّب	تَمُّوز	يُولْيُو
٨	شَعْبَان الْمُعَظَّم	آب	أغُسْطُس
٩	رَمَضَان الْمُبَارَك	أَيْلُول	سِبْتِمْبر
١٠	شَوَّال المُكَرَّم	تِشْرِين الاوَّل	نُوفِمْبر
١١	ذُوالْقَعْدَة	تِشْرِين الثَّانى	أُكْتُوبر
١٢	ذُوالْحِجَّة	كَانُون الاوَّل	دِيْسِمْبر

Appendix
(Conjugation Patterns)

APPENDIX (CONJUGATION PATTERNS)

Active voice conjugation-triliteral verbs-past tense

	فعل	ذهب	مدّ	قال	خاف	صار	نال	وعد	عدا	مشى	بقي
III P SM	فَعَلَ	ذَهَبَ	مَدَّ	قَالَ	خَافَ	صَارَ	نَالَ	وَعَدَ	عَدَا	مَشَى	بَقِيَ
III P DM	فَعَلَا	ذَهَبَا	مَدَّا	قَالَا	خَافَا	صَارَا	نَالَا	وَعَدَا	عَدَوَا	مَشَيَا	بَقِيَا
III P PM	فَعَلُوا	ذَهَبُوا	مَدُّوا	قَالُوا	خَافُوا	صَارُوا	نَالُوا	وَعَدُوا	عَدَوْا	مَشَوْا	بَقُوا
III P SF	فَعَلَتْ	ذَهَبَتْ	مَدَّتْ	قَالَتْ	خَافَتْ	صَارَتْ	نَالَتْ	وَعَدَتْ	عَدَتْ	مَشَتْ	بَقِيَتْ
III P DF	فَعَلَتَا	ذَهَبَتَا	مَدَّتَا	قَالَتَا	خَافَتَا	صَارَتَا	نَالَتَا	وَعَدَتَا	عَدَتَا	مَشَتَا	بَقِيَتَا
III P PF	فَعَلْنَ	ذَهَبْنَ	مَدَدْنَ	قُلْنَ	خِفْنَ	صِرْنَ	نِلْنَ	وَعَدْنَ	عَدَوْنَ	مَشَيْنَ	بَقِينَ
II P SM	فَعَلْتَ	ذَهَبْتَ	مَدَدْتَ	قُلْتَ	خِفْتَ	صِرْتَ	نِلْتَ	وَعَدْتَ	عَدَوْتَ	مَشَيْتَ	بَقِيتَ
II P DM	فَعَلْتُمَا	ذَهَبْتُمَا	مَدَدْتُمَا	قُلْتُمَا	خِفْتُمَا	صِرْتُمَا	نِلْتُمَا	وَعَدْتُمَا	عَدَوْتُمَا	مَشَيْتُمَا	بَقِيتُمَا
II P PM	فَعَلْتُمْ	ذَهَبْتُمْ	مَدَدْتُمْ	قُلْتُمْ	خِفْتُمْ	صِرْتُمْ	نِلْتُمْ	وَعَدْتُمْ	عَدَوْتُمْ	مَشَيْتُمْ	بَقِيتُمْ
II P SF	فَعَلْتِ	ذَهَبْتِ	مَدَدْتِ	قُلْتِ	خِفْتِ	صِرْتِ	نِلْتِ	وَعَدْتِ	عَدَوْتِ	مَشَيْتِ	بَقِيتِ
II P DF	فَعَلْتُمَا	ذَهَبْتُمَا	مَدَدْتُمَا	قُلْتُمَا	خِفْتُمَا	صِرْتُمَا	نِلْتُمَا	وَعَدْتُمَا	عَدَوْتُمَا	مَشَيْتُمَا	بَقِيتُمَا
II P PF	فَعَلْتُنَّ	ذَهَبْتُنَّ	مَدَدْتُنَّ	قُلْتُنَّ	خِفْتُنَّ	صِرْتُنَّ	نِلْتُنَّ	وَعَدْتُنَّ	عَدَوْتُنَّ	مَشَيْتُنَّ	بَقِيتُنَّ
I P SMF	فَعَلْتُ	ذَهَبْتُ	مَدَدْتُ	قُلْتُ	خِفْتُ	صِرْتُ	نِلْتُ	وَعَدْتُ	عَدَوْتُ	مَشَيْتُ	بَقِيتُ
I PD PMF	فَعَلْنَا	ذَهَبْنَا	مَدَدْنَا	قُلْنَا	خِفْنَا	صِرْنَا	نِلْنَا	وَعَدْنَا	عَدَوْنَا	مَشَيْنَا	بَقِينَا

Active voice conjugation-triliteral verbs-present tense

	فعل	ذهب	مدّ	قال	خاف	سار	نال	بعد	غدو	مشي	بقي
IIIP SM	يَفْعَلُ	يَذْهَبُ	يَمُدُّ	يَقُولُ	يَخَافُ	يَسِيرُ	يَنَالُ	يَبْعُدُ	يَغْدُو	يَمْشِي	يَبْقَى
IIIP DM	يَفْعَلَانِ	يَذْهَبَانِ	يَمُدَّانِ	يَقُولَانِ	يَخَافَانِ	يَسِيرَانِ	يَنَالَانِ	يَبْعُدَانِ	يَغْدُوَانِ	يَمْشِيَانِ	يَبْقَيَانِ
IIIP PM	يَفْعَلُونَ	يَذْهَبُونَ	يَمُدُّونَ	يَقُولُونَ	يَخَافُونَ	يَسِيرُونَ	يَنَالُونَ	يَبْعُدُونَ	يَغْدُونَ	يَمْشُونَ	يَبْقَوْنَ
IIIP SF	تَفْعَلُ	تَذْهَبُ	تَمُدُّ	تَقُولُ	تَخَافُ	تَسِيرُ	تَنَالُ	تَبْعُدُ	تَغْدُو	تَمْشِي	تَبْقَى
IIIP DF	تَفْعَلَانِ	تَذْهَبَانِ	تَمُدَّانِ	تَقُولَانِ	تَخَافَانِ	تَسِيرَانِ	تَنَالَانِ	تَبْعُدَانِ	تَغْدُوَانِ	تَمْشِيَانِ	تَبْقَيَانِ
IIIP PF	يَفْعَلْنَ	يَذْهَبْنَ	يَمْدُدْنَ	يَقُلْنَ	يَخَفْنَ	يَسِرْنَ	يَنَلْنَ	يَبْعُدْنَ	يَغْدُونَ	يَمْشِينَ	يَبْقَيْنَ
IIP SM	تَفْعَلُ	تَذْهَبُ	تَمُدُّ	تَقُولُ	تَخَافُ	تَسِيرُ	تَنَالُ	تَبْعُدُ	تَغْدُو	تَمْشِي	تَبْقَى
IIP DM	تَفْعَلَانِ	تَذْهَبَانِ	تَمُدَّانِ	تَقُولَانِ	تَخَافَانِ	تَسِيرَانِ	تَنَالَانِ	تَبْعُدَانِ	تَغْدُوَانِ	تَمْشِيَانِ	تَبْقَيَانِ
IIP PM	تَفْعَلُونَ	تَذْهَبُونَ	تَمُدُّونَ	تَقُولُونَ	تَخَافُونَ	تَسِيرُونَ	تَنَالُونَ	تَبْعُدُونَ	تَغْدُونَ	تَمْشُونَ	تَبْقَوْنَ
IIP SF	تَفْعَلِينَ	تَذْهَبِينَ	تَمُدِّينَ	تَقُولِينَ	تَخَافِينَ	تَسِيرِينَ	تَنَالِينَ	تَبْعُدِينَ	تَغْدِينَ	تَمْشِينَ	تَبْقَيْنَ
IIP DF	تَفْعَلَانِ	تَذْهَبَانِ	تَمُدَّانِ	تَقُولَانِ	تَخَافَانِ	تَسِيرَانِ	تَنَالَانِ	تَبْعُدَانِ	تَغْدُوَانِ	تَمْشِيَانِ	تَبْقَيَانِ
IIP PF	تَفْعَلْنَ	تَذْهَبْنَ	تَمْدُدْنَ	تَقُلْنَ	تَخَفْنَ	تَسِرْنَ	تَنَلْنَ	تَبْعُدْنَ	تَغْدُونَ	تَمْشِينَ	تَبْقَيْنَ
IP SMF	أَفْعَلُ	أَذْهَبُ	أَمُدُّ	أَقُولُ	أَخَافُ	أَسِيرُ	أَنَالُ	أَبْعُدُ	أَغْدُو	أَمْشِي	أَبْقَى
IP DPMF	نَفْعَلُ	نَذْهَبُ	نَمُدُّ	نَقُولُ	نَخَافُ	نَسِيرُ	نَنَالُ	نَبْعُدُ	نَغْدُو	نَمْشِي	نَبْقَى

APPENDIX (CONJUGATION PATTERNS)

Active voice conjugation—triliteral verbs—past tense

III PSM	يَئِسَ	سَأَلَ	وَعَدَ	رَأَى	قَوِيَ
III PDM	يَئِسَا	سَأَلَا	وَعَدَا	رَأَيَا	قَوِيَا
IIIPPM	يَئِسُوا	سَأَلُوا	وَعَدُوا	رَأَوْا	قَوُوا
IIIPSF	يَئِسَتْ	سَأَلَتْ	وَعَدَتْ	رَأَتْ	قَوِيَتْ
IIIPDF	يَئِسَتَا	سَأَلَتَا	وَعَدَتَا	رَأَتَا	قَوِيَتَا
IIIPPF	يَئِسْنَ	سَأَلْنَ	وَعَدْنَ	رَأَيْنَ	قَوِينَ
IIPSM	يَئِسْتَ	سَأَلْتَ	وَعَدْتَ	رَأَيْتَ	قَوِيتَ
IIPDM	يَئِسْتُمَا	سَأَلْتُمَا	وَعَدْتُمَا	رَأَيْتُمَا	قَوِيتُمَا
IIPPM	يَئِسْتُمْ	سَأَلْتُمْ	وَعَدْتُمْ	رَأَيْتُمْ	قَوِيتُمْ
IIPSF	يَئِسْتِ	سَأَلْتِ	وَعَدْتِ	رَأَيْتِ	قَوِيتِ
IIPDF	يَئِسْتُمَا	سَأَلْتُمَا	وَعَدْتُمَا	رَأَيْتُمَا	قَوِيتُمَا
IIPPF	يَئِسْتُنَّ	سَأَلْتُنَّ	وَعَدْتُنَّ	رَأَيْتُنَّ	قَوِيتُنَّ
IPSMF	يَئِسْتُ	سَأَلْتُ	وَعَدْتُ	رَأَيْتُ	قَوِيتُ
IPDPMF	يَئِسْنَا	سَأَلْنَا	وَعَدْنَا	رَأَيْنَا	قَوِينَا

TEACH YOURSELF ARABIC

Active Voice Conjugation-Triliteral verbs-present tense

III PSM		نَرَى	يَبُلُّ	يَنالُ	يَبِيعُ	يأخُذُ
III PDM		يَرَيانِ	يَبُلّانِ	يَنالانِ	يَبِيعانِ	يأخُذانِ
III PPM		يَرَوْنَ	يَبُلّونَ	يَنالونَ	يَبيعونَ	يأخُذونَ
III PSF		تَرَى	تَبُلُّ	تَنالُ	تَبِيعُ	تأخُذُ
III PDF		تَرَيانِ	تَبُلّانِ	تَنالانِ	تَبيعانِ	تأخُذانِ
III PPF		يَرَيْنَ	يَبْلُلْنَ	يَنَلْنَ	يَبِعْنَ	يأخُذْنَ
II PSM		تَرَى	تَبُلُّ	تَنالُ	تَبِيعُ	تأخُذُ
II PDM		تَرَيانِ	تَبُلّانِ	تَنالانِ	تَبيعانِ	تأخُذانِ
II PPM		تَرَوْنَ	تَبُلّونَ	تَنالونَ	تَبيعونَ	تأخُذونَ
II PSF		تَرَيْنَ	تَبُلّينَ	تَنالينَ	تَبيعينَ	تأخُذينَ
II PDF		تَرَيانِ	تَبُلّانِ	تَنالانِ	تَبيعانِ	تأخُذانِ
II PPF		تَرَيْنَ	تَبْلُلْنَ	تَنَلْنَ	تَبِعْنَ	تأخُذْنَ
I PSMF		أرَى	أبُلُّ	أنالُ	أبِيعُ	آخُذُ
I PDPMF		نَرَى	نَبُلُّ	نَنالُ	نَبِيعُ	نأخُذُ

قتَلَ / يَقْتُلُ / قَتْلاً To kill

ماضي معروف	ماضي مجهول	مضارع معروف	مضارع مجهول	فعل الأمر	فعل النهي	اسم الفاعل	اسم المفعول
قَتَلَ	قُتِلَ	يَقْتُلُ	يُقْتَلُ	اُقْتُلْ	لاَ تَقْتُلْ	قَاتِلٌ	مَقْتُولٌ
قَتَلاَ	قُتِلاَ	يَقْتُلاَنِ	يُقْتَلاَنِ	اُقْتُلاَ	لاَ تَقْتُلاَ	قَاتِلاَنِ	مَقْتُولاَنِ
قَتَلُوا	قُتِلُوا	يَقْتُلُونَ	يُقْتَلُونَ	اُقْتُلُوا	لاَ تَقْتُلُوا	قَاتِلُونَ	مَقْتُولُونَ
قَتَلَتْ	قُتِلَتْ	تَقْتُلُ	تُقْتَلُ	اُقْتُلِي	لاَ تَقْتُلِي	قَاتِلَةٌ	مَقْتُولَةٌ
قَتَلَتاَ	قُتِلَتاَ	تَقْتُلاَنِ	تُقْتَلاَنِ	اُقْتُلْنَ	لاَ تَقْتُلْنَ	قَاتِلَتاَنِ	مَقْتُولَتاَنِ
قَتَلْنَ	قُتِلْنَ	يَقْتُلْنَ	يُقْتَلْنَ			قَاتِلاَتٌ	مَقْتُولاَتٌ
قَتَلْتَ	قُتِلْتَ	تَقْتُلُ	تُقْتَلُ				
قَتَلْتُماَ	قُتِلْتُماَ	تَقْتُلاَنِ	تُقْتَلاَنِ				
قَتَلْتُمْ	قُتِلْتُمْ	تَقْتُلُونَ	تُقْتَلُونَ				
قَتَلْتِ	قُتِلْتِ	تَقْتُلِينَ	تُقْتَلِينَ				
قَتَلْتُماَ	قُتِلْتُماَ	تَقْتُلاَنِ	تُقْتَلاَنِ				
قَتَلْتُنَّ	قُتِلْتُنَّ	تَقْتُلْنَ	تُقْتَلْنَ				
قَتَلْتُ	قُتِلْتُ	أَقْتُلُ	أُقْتَلُ				
قَتَلْناَ	قُتِلْناَ	نَقْتُلُ	نُقْتَلُ				

To beat   ضَرَبَ / يَضْرِبُ ، ضَرْبًا

اسم المفعول	اسم الفاعل	فعل النهي	فعل الأمر	مضارع مجهول	مضارع معروف	ماضي مجهول	ماضي معروف
مَضْرُوبٌ	ضارِبٌ	لا تَضْرِبْ	اِضْرِبْ	يُضْرَبُ	يَضْرِبُ	ضُرِبَ	ضَرَبَ
مَضْرُوبانِ	ضارِبانِ	لا تَضْرِبا	اِضْرِبا	يُضْرَبانِ	يَضْرِبانِ	ضُرِبا	ضَرَبا
مَضْرُوبونَ	ضارِبونَ	لا تَضْرِبوا	اِضْرِبوا	يُضْرَبونَ	يَضْرِبونَ	ضُرِبوا	ضَرَبوا
				تُضْرَبُ	تَضْرِبُ	ضُرِبَتْ	ضَرَبَتْ
				تُضْرَبانِ	تَضْرِبانِ	ضُرِبَتا	ضَرَبَتا
				يُضْرَبْنَ	يَضْرِبْنَ	ضُرِبْنَ	ضَرَبْنَ
				تُضْرَبُ	تَضْرِبُ	ضُرِبْتَ	ضَرَبْتَ
				تُضْرَبانِ	تَضْرِبانِ	ضُرِبْتُما	ضَرَبْتُما
				تُضْرَبونَ	تَضْرِبونَ	ضُرِبْتُمْ	ضَرَبْتُمْ
				تُضْرَبينَ	تَضْرِبينَ	ضُرِبْتِ	ضَرَبْتِ
				تُضْرَبْنَ	تَضْرِبْنَ	ضُرِبْتُنَّ	ضَرَبْتُنَّ
				أُضْرَبُ	أَضْرِبُ	ضُرِبْتُ	ضَرَبْتُ
				نُضْرَبُ	نَضْرِبُ	ضُرِبْنا	ضَرَبْنا

To hear, to listen   سمِعَ / يسْمَع

اسم المفعول	اسم الفاعل	فعل النهي	فعل الأمر	مضارع مجهول	مضارع معروف	ماضي مجهول	ماضي معروف
مَسْمُوعٌ	سامِعٌ	لا تَسْمَعْ	اِسْمَعْ	يُسْمَعُ	يَسْمَعُ	سُمِعَ	سَمِعَ
مَسْمُوعان	سامِعان	لا تَسْمَعا	اِسْمَعا	يُسْمَعان	يَسْمَعان	سُمِعا	سَمِعا
مَسْمُوعُونَ	سامِعُونَ	لا تَسْمَعُوا	اِسْمَعُوا	يُسْمَعُونَ	يَسْمَعُونَ	سُمِعُوا	سَمِعُوا
مَسْمُوعَةٌ	سامِعَةٌ	لا تَسْمَعِي	اِسْمَعِي	تُسْمَعُ	تَسْمَعُ	سُمِعَتْ	سَمِعَتْ
مَسْمُوعَتان	سامِعَتان	لا تَسْمَعْنَ	اِسْمَعْنَ	تُسْمَعان	تَسْمَعان	سُمِعَتا	سَمِعَتا
مَسْمُوعات	سامِعات			يُسْمَعْنَ	يَسْمَعْنَ	سُمِعْنَ	سَمِعْنَ
				تُسْمَعُ	تَسْمَعُ	سُمِعْتَ	سَمِعْتَ
				تُسْمَعان	تَسْمَعان	سُمِعْتُما	سَمِعْتُما
				تُسْمَعُونَ	تَسْمَعُونَ	سُمِعْتُمْ	سَمِعْتُمْ
				تُسْمَعِينَ	تَسْمَعِينَ	سُمِعْتِ	سَمِعْتِ
				تُسْمَعْنَ	تَسْمَعْنَ	سُمِعْتُنَّ	سَمِعْتُنَّ
				أُسْمَعُ	أَسْمَعُ	سُمِعْتُ	سَمِعْتُ
				نُسْمَعُ	نَسْمَعُ	سُمِعْنا	سَمِعْنا

TEACH YOURSELF ARABIC

To take أَخَذَ يَأْخُذُ أَخْذٌ

ماضي معروف	ماضي مجهول	مضارع معروف	مضارع مجهول	فعل الأمر	فعل النهي	اسم الفاعل	اسم المفعول
أَخَذَ	أُخِذَ	يَأْخُذُ	يُؤْخَذُ	خُذْ	لا تَأْخُذْ	آخِذٌ	مَأْخُوذٌ
أَخَذَا	أُخِذَا	يَأْخُذَانِ	يُؤْخَذَانِ	خُذَا	لا تَأْخُذَا	آخِذَانِ	مَأْخُوذَانِ
أَخَذُوا	أُخِذُوا	يَأْخُذُونَ	يُؤْخَذُونَ	خُذُوا	لا تَأْخُذُوا	آخِذُونَ	مَأْخُوذُونَ
أَخَذَتْ	أُخِذَتْ	تَأْخُذُ	تُؤْخَذُ	خُذِي	لا تَأْخُذِي	آخِذَةٌ	مَأْخُوذَةٌ
أَخَذَتَا	أُخِذَتَا	تَأْخُذَانِ	تُؤْخَذَانِ			آخِذَتَانِ	مَأْخُوذَتَانِ
أَخَذْنَ	أُخِذْنَ	يَأْخُذْنَ	يُؤْخَذْنَ	or		آخِذَاتٌ	مَأْخُوذَاتٌ
أَخَذْتَ	أُخِذْتَ	تَأْخُذُ	تُؤْخَذُ	اأْخُذْ			
أَخَذْتُمَا	أُخِذْتُمَا	تَأْخُذَانِ	تُؤْخَذَانِ	اأْخُذُوا			
أَخَذْتُمْ	أُخِذْتُمْ	تَأْخُذُونَ	تُؤْخَذُونَ	اأْخُذِي			
أَخَذْتِ	أُخِذْتِ	تَأْخُذِينَ	تُؤْخَذِينَ	اأْخُذْنَ			
أَخَذْتُمَا	أُخِذْتُمَا	تَأْخُذَانِ	تُؤْخَذَانِ				
أَخَذْتُنَّ	أُخِذْتُنَّ	تَأْخُذْنَ	تُؤْخَذْنَ				
أَخَذْتُ	أُخِذْتُ	آخُذُ	أُوخَذُ				
أَخَذْنَا	أُخِذْنَا	نَأْخُذُ	نُؤْخَذُ				

To question, to ask سَأَلَ يَسْأَلُ سُؤَال الإِسْ

اسم المفعول	اسم الفاعل	فعل النهي	فعل الأمر	مضارع مجهول	مضارع معروف	ماضي مجهول	ماضي معروف
مَسْؤُول	سَائِل	لا تُسْأَلْ	اِسْأَلْ	يُسْأَلُ	يَسْأَلُ	سُئِلَ	سَأَلَ
مَسْؤُولانِ	سَائِلانِ	لا تُسْأَلا	اِسْأَلا	يُسْأَلانِ	يَسْأَلانِ	سُئِلا	سَأَلا
مَسْؤُولُونَ	سَائِلُونَ	لا تُسْأَلُوا	اِسْأَلُوا	يُسْأَلُونَ	يَسْأَلُونَ	سُئِلُوا	سَأَلُوا
مَسْؤُولَةٌ	سَائِلَةٌ	لا تُسْأَلي		تُسْأَلُ	تَسْأَلُ	سُئِلَتْ	سَأَلَتْ
مَسْؤُولَتانِ	سَائِلَتانِ	لا تُسْأَلْنَ		تُسْأَلانِ	تَسْأَلانِ	سُئِلَتا	سَأَلَتا
مَسْؤُولاتٌ	سَائِلاتٌ			يُسْأَلْنَ	يَسْأَلْنَ	سُئِلْنَ	سَأَلْنَ
			اِسْأَلْ	تُسْأَلُ	تَسْأَلُ	سُئِلْتَ	سَأَلْتَ
			اِسْأَلا	تُسْأَلانِ	تَسْأَلانِ	سُئِلْتُما	سَأَلْتُما
			اِسْأَلُوا	تُسْأَلُونَ	تَسْأَلُونَ	سُئِلْتُمْ	سَأَلْتُمْ
			اِسْأَلي	تُسْأَلِينَ	تَسْأَلِينَ	سُئِلْتِ	سَأَلْتِ
				تُسْأَلانِ	تَسْأَلانِ	سُئِلْتُما	سَأَلْتُما
				تُسْأَلْنَ	تَسْأَلْنَ	سُئِلْتُنَّ	سَأَلْتُنَّ
				أُسْأَلُ	أَسْأَلُ	سُئِلْتُ	سَأَلْتُ
				نُسْأَلُ	نَسْأَلُ	سُئِلْنا	سَأَلْنا

To read قَرَأَ / يَقْرَأُ / قِرَاءَةٌ

ماضي معروف	ماضي مجهول	مضارع معروف	مضارع مجهول	فعل الأمر	فعل النهي	اسم الفاعل	اسم المفعول
قَرَأْتُ	قُرِئْتُ	أَقْرَأُ	أُقْرَأُ	اقْرَأْ	لا تَقْرَأْ	قَارِئٌ	مَقْرُوءٌ
قَرَأْتَ	قُرِئْتَ	تَقْرَأُ	تُقْرَأُ	اقْرَئِي	لا تَقْرَئِي	قَارِئَةٌ	مَقْرُوءَةٌ
قَرَأَتْ	قُرِئَتْ	تَقْرَأُ	تُقْرَأُ	اقْرَءُوا	لا تَقْرَءُوا	قَارِئَانِ	مَقْرُوءَانِ
قَرَأَ	قُرِئَ	يَقْرَأُ	يُقْرَأُ	اقْرَئِي	لا تَقْرَئِي	قَارِئَتَانِ	مَقْرُوءَتَانِ
قَرَأْنَا	قُرِئْنَا	نَقْرَأُ	نُقْرَأُ	اقْرَآنِ		قَارِئُونَ	مَقْرُوءُونَ
قَرَأْتُمَا	قُرِئْتُمَا	تَقْرَآنِ	تُقْرَآنِ				
قَرَأْتُنَّ	قُرِئْتُنَّ	تَقْرَأْنَ	تُقْرَأْنَ				
قَرَآ	قُرِئَا	يَقْرَآنِ	يُقْرَآنِ				
قَرَأَتَا	قُرِئَتَا	تَقْرَآنِ	تُقْرَآنِ				
قَرَأُوا	قُرِئُوا	يَقْرَءُونَ	يُقْرَءُونَ				
قَرَأْنَ	قُرِئْنَ	يَقْرَأْنَ	يُقْرَأْنَ				
قَرَأْتُمْ	قُرِئْتُمْ	تَقْرَءُونَ	تُقْرَءُونَ				

To promise وَعَدَ / يَعِدُ وَعْدًا

اسم المفعول	اسم الفاعل	فعل النهي	فعل الأمر	مضارع مجهول	مضارع معروف	ماضي مجهول	ماضي معروف
مَوْعُودٌ	وَاعِدٌ	لَا تَعِدْ	عِدْ	يُوعَدُ	يَعِدُ	وُعِدَ	وَعَدَ
مَوْعُودَانِ	وَاعِدَانِ	لَا تَعِدَا	عِدَا	يُوعَدَانِ	يَعِدَانِ	وُعِدَا	وَعَدَا
مَوْعُودُونَ	وَاعِدُونَ	لَا تَعِدُوا	عِدُوا	يُوعَدُونَ	يَعِدُونَ	وُعِدُوا	وَعَدُوا
مَوْعُودَةٌ	وَاعِدَةٌ	لَا تَعِدِي	عِدِي	تُوعَدُ	تَعِدُ	وُعِدَتْ	وَعَدَتْ
مَوْعُودَتَانِ	وَاعِدَتَانِ	لَا تَعِدَا	عِدَا	تُوعَدَانِ	تَعِدَانِ	وُعِدَتَا	وَعَدَتَا
		لَا تَعِدْنَ	عِدْنَ	يُوعَدْنَ	يَعِدْنَ	وُعِدْنَ	وَعَدْنَ
				تُوعَدُ	تَعِدُ	وُعِدْتَ	وَعَدْتَ
				تُوعَدَانِ	تَعِدَانِ	وُعِدْتُمَا	وَعَدْتُمَا
				تُوعَدُونَ	تَعِدُونَ	وُعِدْتُمْ	وَعَدْتُمْ
				تُوعَدِينَ	تَعِدِينَ	وُعِدْتِ	وَعَدْتِ
				تُوعَدَانِ	تَعِدَانِ	وُعِدْتُمَا	وَعَدْتُمَا
				تُوعَدْنَ	تَعِدْنَ	وُعِدْتُنَّ	وَعَدْتُنَّ
				أُوعَدُ	أَعِدُ	وُعِدْتُ	وَعَدْتُ
				نُوعَدُ	نَعِدُ	وُعِدْنَا	وَعَدْنَا

To run غدا يغدو غدو

ماضي معروف	مضارع معروف	فعل الأمر	فعل النهي
غدا	يغدو		
غدوا	يغدوان		
غدوا	يغدون		
غدت	تغدو		
غدتا	تغدوان		
غدون	يغدون		
غدونا	تغدو		
غدوتَ	تغدوان	اغدُ	لا تَغدُ
غدوتما	تغدون	اغدوا	لا تَغدوا
غدوتم	تغدين	اغدوا	لا تَغدوا
غدوتما	تغدو	اغدي	لا تغدي
غدوتن	تغدوان	اغدوا	لا تَغدوا
غدوتِ	تغدين	اغدينَ	لا تغدينَ
غدوت	نغدو		

APPENDIX (CONJUGATION PATTERNS)

To be disappointed — يَئِسَ يَيْئَسُ يَأْسًا

ماضي معروف

يَئِسَ
يَئِسَا
يَئِسُوا
يَئِسَتْ
يَئِسَتَا
يَئِسْنَ
يَئِسْتَ
يَئِسْتُمَا
يَئِسْتُمْ
يَئِسْتِ
يَئِسْتُمَا
يَئِسْتُنَّ
يَئِسْتُ
يَئِسْنَا

مضارع معروف

يَيْئَسُ
يَيْئَسَانِ
يَيْئَسُونَ
تَيْئَسُ
تَيْئَسَانِ
يَيْئَسْنَ
تَيْئَسُ
تَيْئَسَانِ
تَيْئَسُونَ
تَيْئَسِينَ
تَيْئَسَانِ
تَيْئَسْنَ
أَيْئَسُ
نَيْئَسُ

فعل الأمر

اِيْئَسْ
اِيْئَسَا
اِيْئَسُوا
اِيْئَسِي
اِيْئَسْنَ

فعل النهي

لَا تَيْئَسْ
لَا تَيْئَسَا
لَا تَيْئَسُوا
لَا تَيْئَسِي
لَا تَيْئَسْنَ

اسم الفاعل

يَائِسٌ
يَائِسَانِ
يَائِسُونَ
يَائِسَةٌ
يَائِسَتَانِ
يَائِسَاتٌ

اسم المفعول

مَيْئُوسٌ
مَيْئُوسَانِ
مَيْئُوسُونَ
مَيْئُوسَةٌ
مَيْئُوسَتَانِ
مَيْئُوسَاتٌ

To gaurd, to protect — رَقِيَ يَقِي وُقِيَ

اسم الفاعل	فعل النهي	فعل الأمر	مضارع معروف	ماضي معروف
واقٍ / رَاقٍ			يَقِي	رَقِيَ
وَاقِيانِ	لا تَقِ	قِ		
وَاقُونَ	لا تَقِيا	قِيا		
وَاقِيانِ	لا تَقُوا	قُوا		

APPENDIX (CONJUGATION PATTERNS)

To walk — مشى يمشي مشياً

ماضي معروف	مضارع معروف	فعل الأمر	فعل النهي	اسم الفاعل
مَشى	يَمشي		لا يَمشي	ماشٍ
مَشَيا	يَمشيانِ		لا يَمشيانِ	ماشِيانِ
مَشَوا	يَمشونَ		لا يَمشونَ	ماشونَ
مَشَتْ	تَمشي		لا تَمشي	ماشِيَةٌ
مَشَتا	تَمشيانِ		لا تَمشيانِ	ماشِيَتانِ
مَشَينَ	يَمشينَ		لا يَمشينَ	ماشِياتٌ
مَشَيتَ	تَمشي	اِمشِ	لا تَمشِ	
مَشَيتُما	تَمشيانِ	اِمشِيا	لا تَمشِيا	
مَشَيتُم	تَمشونَ	اِمشوا	لا تَمشوا	
مَشَيتِ	تَمشينَ	اِمشي	لا تَمشي	
مَشَيتُما	تَمشيانِ	اِمشِيا	لا تَمشِيا	
مَشَيتُنَّ	تَمشينَ	اِمشينَ	لا تَمشينَ	
مَشَيتُ	أَمشي		لا أَمشي	
مَشَينا	نَمشي		لا نَمشي	

To remain, to stay   بَقِيَ يَبْقَى بَقاءً

اسم الفاعل	فعل النهي	فعل الامر	مضارع معروف	ماضي معروف
			يَبْقَى	بَقِيَ
			يَبْقَيانِ	بَقِيا
			يَبْقَوْنَ	بَقَوْا
			تَبْقَى	بَقِيَتْ
			تَبْقَيانِ	بَقِيَتا
			يَبْقَيْنَ	بَقِينَ
	لا تَبْقَ	اِبْقَ	تَبْقَى	بَقِيتَ
	لا تَبْقَيا	اِبْقَيا	تَبْقَيانِ	بَقِيتُما
	لا تَبْقَوْا	اِبْقَوْا	تَبْقَوْنَ	بَقِيتُمْ
	لا تَبْقَيْ	اِبْقَيْ	تَبْقَيْنَ	بَقِيتِ
باقٍ			تَبْقَيانِ	بَقِيتُما
باقِيانِ			تَبْقَيْنَ	بَقِيتُنَّ
باقُونَ	لا تَبْقَيْنَ	اِبْقَيْنَ	أَبْقَى	بَقِيتُ
باقِيَةٌ			نَبْقَى	بَقِينا

APPENDIX (CONJUGATION PATTERNS)

To help (مَدَّ یَمُدُّ مَدًّا یعنی) مَدَّ یَمُدُّ مَدًّا

ماضی معروف	ماضی مجہول	مضارع معروف	مضارع مجہول	فعل الامر	فعل النہی	اسم الفاعل	اسم المفعول
مَدَّ	مُدَّ	یَمُدُّ	یُمَدُّ	مُدَّ/اُمْدُدْ	لَاتَمُدَّ/لَاتَمْدُدْ	مَادٌّ/مَادِدٌ	مَمْدُودٌ
مَدَّا	مُدَّا	یَمُدَّانِ	یُمَدَّانِ	مُدَّا/اُمْدُدَا	لَاتَمُدَّا/لَاتَمْدُدَا	مَادَّانِ/مَادِدَانِ	مَمْدُودَانِ
مَدُّوا	مُدُّوا	یَمُدُّونَ	یُمَدُّونَ	مُدُّوا/اُمْدُدُوا	لَاتَمُدُّوا/لَاتَمْدُدُوا	مَادُّونَ/مَادِدُونَ	مَمْدُودُونَ
مَدَّتْ	مُدَّتْ	تَمُدُّ	تُمَدُّ	مُدِّي/اُمْدُدِي	لَاتَمُدِّي/لَاتَمْدُدِي	مَادَّةٌ/مَادِدَةٌ	مَمْدُودَةٌ
مَدَّتَا	مُدَّتَا	تَمُدَّانِ	تُمَدَّانِ	مُدَّا/اُمْدُدَا	لَاتَمُدَّا/لَاتَمْدُدَا	مَادَّتَانِ/مَادِدَتَانِ	مَمْدُودَتَانِ
مَدَدْنَ	مُدِدْنَ	یَمْدُدْنَ	یُمْدَدْنَ	اُمْدُدْنَ	لَاتَمْدُدْنَ/لَاتَمْدُدْنَ	مَادَّاتٌ/مَادِدَاتٌ	مَمْدُودَاتٌ

قدّم يُقَدِّمُ تَقْدِيماً — To present, to offer

اسم المفعول	اسم الفاعل	فعل النهي	فعل الأمر	مضارع مجهول	مضارع معروف	ماضي مجهول	ماضي معروف
مُقَدَّمٌ	مُقَدِّمٌ	لا تُقَدَّمْ	قَدِّمْ	أُقَدَّمُ	أُقَدِّمُ	قُدِّمْتُ	قَدَّمْتُ
مُقَدَّمانِ	مُقَدِّمانِ	لا تُقَدِّمْ	قَدِّمْ	تُقَدَّمُ	تُقَدِّمُ	قُدِّمْتَ	قَدَّمْتَ
مُقَدَّمونَ	مُقَدِّمونَ	لا تُقَدِّمي	قَدِّمي	تُقَدَّمينَ	تُقَدِّمينَ	قُدِّمْتِ	قَدَّمْتِ
مُقَدَّمَةٌ	مُقَدِّمَةٌ	لا تُقَدَّما	قَدِّما	يُقَدَّمُ	يُقَدِّمُ	قُدِّمَ	قَدَّمَ
مُقَدَّمَتانِ	مُقَدِّمَتانِ	لا تُقَدِّمْنَ	قَدِّمْنَ	تُقَدَّمُ	تُقَدِّمُ	قُدِّمَتْ	قَدَّمَتْ
مُقَدَّماتٌ	مُقَدِّماتٌ			تُقَدَّمانِ	تُقَدِّمانِ	قُدِّمْتُما	قَدَّمْتُما
				يُقَدَّمانِ	يُقَدِّمانِ	قُدِّما	قَدَّما
				تُقَدَّمانِ	تُقَدِّمانِ	قُدِّمَتا	قَدَّمَتا
				نُقَدَّمُ	نُقَدِّمُ	قُدِّمْنا	قَدَّمْنا
				تُقَدَّمونَ	تُقَدِّمونَ	قُدِّمْتُم	قَدَّمْتُم
				تُقَدَّمْنَ	تُقَدِّمْنَ	قُدِّمْتُنَّ	قَدَّمْتُنَّ
				يُقَدَّمونَ	يُقَدِّمونَ	قُدِّمُوا	قَدَّمُوا
				يُقَدَّمْنَ	يُقَدِّمْنَ	قُدِّمْنَ	قَدَّمْنَ

APPENDIX (CONJUGATION PATTERNS)

To help   ساعدَ يُساعدُ مُساعدةً

اسم المفعول	اسم الفاعل	فعل النهي	فعل الأمر	مضارع مجهول	مضارع معروف	ماضي مجهول	ماضي معروف
مُساعَد	مُساعِد	لا تُساعَد	ساعِد	يُساعَد	يُساعِد	سوعِد	ساعَد
مُساعَدان	مُساعِدان	لا تُساعَدا	ساعِدا	يُساعَدان	يُساعِدان	سوعِدا	ساعَدا
مُساعَدون	مُساعِدون	لا تُساعَدوا	ساعِدوا	يُساعَدون	يُساعِدون	سوعِدوا	ساعَدوا
مُساعَدة	مُساعِدة	لا تُساعَدي	ساعِدي	تُساعَد	تُساعِد	سوعِدت	ساعَدت
مُساعَدتان	مُساعِدتان	لا تُساعَدن	ساعِدن	تُساعَدان	تُساعِدان	سوعِدتا	ساعَدتا
مُساعَدات	مُساعِدات			يُساعَدن	يُساعِدن	سوعِدن	ساعَدن
				تُساعَد	تُساعِد	سوعِدت	ساعَدت
				تُساعَدان	تُساعِدان	سوعِدتما	ساعَدتما
				تُساعَدون	تُساعِدون	سوعِدتم	ساعَدتم
				تُساعَدين	تُساعِدين	سوعِدت	ساعَدت
				تُساعَدان	تُساعِدان	سوعِدتما	ساعَدتما
				تُساعَدن	تُساعِدن	سوعِدتن	ساعَدتن
				أُساعَد	أُساعِد	سوعِدت	ساعَدت
				نُساعَد	نُساعِد	سوعِدنا	ساعَدنا

أَجْلَسَ يُجْلِسُ إِجْلَاساً

To seat

ماضي معروف	ماضي مجهول	مضارع معروف	مضارع مجهول	فعل الأمر	فعل النهي	اسم الفاعل	اسم المفعول
أَجْلَسَ	أُجْلِسَ	يُجْلِسُ	يُجْلَسُ	أَجْلِسْ	لَا تُجْلِسْ	مُجْلِسٌ	مُجْلَسٌ
أَجْلَسَا	أُجْلِسَا	يُجْلِسَانِ	يُجْلَسَانِ	أَجْلِسَا	لَا تُجْلِسَا	مُجْلِسَانِ	مُجْلَسَانِ
أَجْلَسُوا	أُجْلِسُوا	يُجْلِسُونَ	يُجْلَسُونَ	أَجْلِسُوا	لَا تُجْلِسُوا	مُجْلِسُونَ	مُجْلَسُونَ
أَجْلَسَتْ	أُجْلِسَتْ	تُجْلِسُ	تُجْلَسُ			مُجْلِسَةٌ	مُجْلَسَةٌ
أَجْلَسَتَا	أُجْلِسَتَا	تُجْلِسَانِ	تُجْلَسَانِ			مُجْلِسَتَانِ	مُجْلَسَتَانِ
أَجْلَسْنَ	أُجْلِسْنَ	يُجْلِسْنَ	يُجْلَسْنَ			مُجْلِسَاتٌ	مُجْلَسَاتٌ
أَجْلَسْتَ	أُجْلِسْتَ	تُجْلِسُ	تُجْلَسُ				
أَجْلَسْتُمَا	أُجْلِسْتُمَا	تُجْلِسَانِ	تُجْلَسَانِ				
أَجْلَسْتُمْ	أُجْلِسْتُمْ	تُجْلِسُونَ	تُجْلَسُونَ				
أَجْلَسْتِ	أُجْلِسْتِ	تُجْلِسِينَ	تُجْلَسِينَ				
أَجْلَسْتُمَا	أُجْلِسْتُمَا	تُجْلِسَانِ	تُجْلَسَانِ				
أَجْلَسْتُنَّ	أُجْلِسْتُنَّ	تُجْلِسْنَ	تُجْلَسْنَ				
أَجْلَسْتُ	أُجْلِسْتُ	أُجْلِسُ	أُجْلَسُ				
أَجْلَسْنَا	أُجْلِسْنَا	نُجْلِسُ	نُجْلَسُ				

To speak , to talk
تكلّم، يتكلّم، تكلّمًا

اسم المفعول	اسم الفاعل	فعل النهي	فعل الامر	مضارع مجهول	مضارع معروف	ماضي مجهول	ماضي معروف
مُتَكَلَّمٌ	مُتَكَلِّمٌ	لا تَتَكَلَّمْ	تَكَلَّمْ	يُتَكَلَّمُ	يَتَكَلَّمُ	تُكُلِّمَ	تَكَلَّمَ
مُتَكَلَّمانِ	مُتَكَلِّمانِ	لا تَتَكَلَّما	تَكَلَّما	يُتَكَلَّمانِ	يَتَكَلَّمانِ	تُكُلِّما	تَكَلَّما
مُتَكَلَّمونَ	مُتَكَلِّمونَ	لا تَتَكَلَّموا	تَكَلَّموا	يُتَكَلَّمونَ	يَتَكَلَّمونَ	تُكُلِّموا	تَكَلَّموا
مُتَكَلَّمَةٌ	مُتَكَلِّمَةٌ	لا تَتَكَلَّمي	تَكَلَّمي	تُتَكَلَّمُ	تَتَكَلَّمُ	تُكُلِّمَتْ	تَكَلَّمَتْ
مُتَكَلَّماتٌ	مُتَكَلِّماتٌ	لا تَتَكَلَّمْنَ		تُتَكَلَّمانِ	تَتَكَلَّمانِ	تُكُلِّمَتا	تَكَلَّمَتا
				يُتَكَلَّمْنَ	يَتَكَلَّمْنَ	تُكُلِّمْنَ	تَكَلَّمْنَ
				تُتَكَلَّمُ	تَتَكَلَّمُ	تُكُلِّمْتَ	تَكَلَّمْتَ
				تُتَكَلَّمانِ	تَتَكَلَّمانِ	تُكُلِّمْتُما	تَكَلَّمْتُما
				تُتَكَلَّمونَ	تَتَكَلَّمونَ	تُكُلِّمْتُمْ	تَكَلَّمْتُمْ
				تُتَكَلَّمْنَ	تَتَكَلَّمْنَ	تُكُلِّمْتُنَّ	تَكَلَّمْتُنَّ
				أُتَكَلَّمُ	أَتَكَلَّمُ	تُكُلِّمْتُ	تَكَلَّمْتُ
				نُتَكَلَّمُ	نَتَكَلَّمُ	تُكُلِّمْنا	تَكَلَّمْنا

TEACH YOURSELF ARABIC

To fight one another قاتَلَ يُقاتِلُ تَقاتَلَ

ماضي معروف	ماضي مجهول	مضارع معروف	مضارع مجهول	فعل الأمر	فعل النهي	اسم الفاعل	اسم المفعول
قاتَلَ	قُوتِلَ	يُقاتِلُ	يُقاتَلُ	قاتِلْ	لا تُقاتِلْ	مُقاتِلٌ	مُقاتَلٌ
قاتَلَا	قُوتِلَا	يُقاتِلانِ	يُقاتَلانِ	قاتِلا	لا تُقاتِلا	مُقاتِلانِ	مُقاتَلانِ
قاتَلُوا	قُوتِلُوا	يُقاتِلُونَ	يُقاتَلُونَ	قاتِلُوا	لا تُقاتِلُوا	مُقاتِلُونَ	مُقاتَلُونَ
قاتَلَتْ	قُوتِلَتْ	تُقاتِلُ	تُقاتَلُ	قاتِلِي	لا تُقاتِلِي	مُقاتِلَةٌ	مُقاتَلَةٌ
قاتَلَتَا	قُوتِلَتَا	تُقاتِلانِ	تُقاتَلانِ	قاتِلا	لا تُقاتِلا	مُقاتِلَتانِ	مُقاتَلَتانِ
قاتَلْنَ	قُوتِلْنَ	يُقاتِلْنَ	يُقاتَلْنَ	قاتِلْنَ	لا تُقاتِلْنَ	مُقاتِلاتٌ	مُقاتَلاتٌ
قاتَلْتَ	قُوتِلْتَ	تُقاتِلُ	تُقاتَلُ				
قاتَلْتُمَا	قُوتِلْتُمَا	تُقاتِلانِ	تُقاتَلانِ				
قاتَلْتُمْ	قُوتِلْتُمْ	تُقاتِلُونَ	تُقاتَلُونَ				
قاتَلْتِ	قُوتِلْتِ	تُقاتِلِينَ	تُقاتَلِينَ				
قاتَلْتُمَا	قُوتِلْتُمَا	تُقاتِلانِ	تُقاتَلانِ				
قاتَلْتُنَّ	قُوتِلْتُنَّ	تُقاتِلْنَ	تُقاتَلْنَ				
قاتَلْتُ	قُوتِلْتُ	أُقاتِلُ	أُقاتَلُ				
قاتَلْنَا	قُوتِلْنَا	نُقاتِلُ	نُقاتَلُ				

To be broken, to break (by itself) اِنْكَسَرَ يَنْكَسِرُ اِنْكِسَاراً

اسم الفاعل	فعل النهي	فعل الأمر	مضارع معروف	ماضي معروف
مُنْكَسِرٌ	لَا تَنْكَسِرْ	اِنْكَسِرْ	يَنْكَسِرُ	اِنْكَسَرَ
مُنْكَسِرَانِ	لَا تَنْكَسِرَا	اِنْكَسِرَا	يَنْكَسِرَانِ	اِنْكَسَرَا
مُنْكَسِرُونَ	لَا تَنْكَسِرُوا	اِنْكَسِرُوا	يَنْكَسِرُونَ	اِنْكَسَرُوا
مُنْكَسِرَةٌ	لَا تَنْكَسِرِي	اِنْكَسِرِي	تَنْكَسِرُ	اِنْكَسَرَتْ
مُنْكَسِرَتَانِ	لَا تَنْكَسِرْنَ	اِنْكَسِرْنَ	تَنْكَسِرَانِ	اِنْكَسَرَتَا
مُنْكَسِرَاتٌ			يَنْكَسِرْنَ	اِنْكَسَرْنَ
			تَنْكَسِرُ	اِنْكَسَرْتَ
			تَنْكَسِرَانِ	اِنْكَسَرْتُمَا
			تَنْكَسِرُونَ	اِنْكَسَرْتُمْ
			تَنْكَسِرِينَ	اِنْكَسَرْتِ
			تَنْكَسِرَانِ	اِنْكَسَرْتُمَا
			تَنْكَسِرْنَ	اِنْكَسَرْتُنَّ
			أَنْكَسِرُ	اِنْكَسَرْتُ
			نَنْكَسِرُ	اِنْكَسَرْنَا

إِنْتَخَبَ يَنْتَخِبُ اِنْتِخاب

To elect, to select

اسم المفعول	اسم الفاعل	فعل النهي	فعل الأمر	مضارع مجهول	مضارع معروف	ماضي مجهول	ماضي معروف
مُنْتَخَب	مُنْتَخِب			يُنْتَخَبُ	يَنْتَخِبُ	اُنْتُخِبَ	اِنْتَخَبَ
مُنْتَخَبانِ	مُنْتَخِبانِ	لا يَنْتَخِبْ	اِنْتَخِبْ	يُنْتَخَبانِ	يَنْتَخِبانِ	اُنْتُخِبا	اِنْتَخَبا
مُنْتَخَبونَ	مُنْتَخِبونَ	لا يَنْتَخِبا	اِنْتَخِبا	يُنْتَخَبونَ	يَنْتَخِبونَ	اُنْتُخِبوا	اِنْتَخَبوا
مُنْتَخَبَة	مُنْتَخِبَة	لا يَنْتَخِبوا	اِنْتَخِبوا	يُنْتَخَبْنَ	يَنْتَخِبْنَ	اُنْتُخِبَتْ	اِنْتَخَبَتْ
مُنْتَخَبَتانِ	مُنْتَخِبَتانِ	لا تَنْتَخِبي	اِنْتَخِبي	تُنْتَخَبُ	تَنْتَخِبُ	اُنْتُخِبَتا	اِنْتَخَبَتا
مُنْتَخَباتٌ	مُنْتَخِباتٌ	لا يَنْتَخِبْنَ		تُنْتَخَبانِ	تَنْتَخِبانِ	اُنْتُخِبْنَ	اِنْتَخَبْنَ
				تُنْتَخَبْنَ	تَنْتَخِبْنَ	اُنْتُخِبْتَ	اِنْتَخَبْتَ
				تُنْتَخَبانِ	تَنْتَخِبانِ	اُنْتُخِبْتُما	اِنْتَخَبْتُما
				تُنْتَخَبونَ	تَنْتَخِبونَ	اُنْتُخِبْتُمْ	اِنْتَخَبْتُمْ
				تُنْتَخَبينَ	تَنْتَخِبينَ	اُنْتُخِبْتِ	اِنْتَخَبْتِ
				تُنْتَخَبانِ	تَنْتَخِبانِ	اُنْتُخِبْتُما	اِنْتَخَبْتُما
				تُنْتَخَبْنَ	تَنْتَخِبْنَ	اُنْتُخِبْتُنَّ	اِنْتَخَبْتُنَّ
				اُنْتَخَبُ	أَنْتَخِبُ	اُنْتُخِبْتُ	اِنْتَخَبْتُ
				نُنْتَخَبُ	نَنْتَخِبُ	اُنْتُخِبْنا	اِنْتَخَبْنا

اِحْمَرَّ يَحْمَرُّ اِحْمِرَارٌ

To become red اِحْمَرَّ

فعل النهي	فعل الأمر	مضارع معروف	ماضي معروف
لَا تَحْمَرَّ	اِحْمَرَّ	يَحْمَرُّ	اِحْمَرَّ
لَا تَحْمَرَّا	اِحْمَرَّا	يَحْمَرَّانِ	اِحْمَرَّا
لَا تَحْمَرُّوا	اِحْمَرُّوا	يَحْمَرُّونَ	اِحْمَرُّوا
لَا تَحْمَرِّي	اِحْمَرِّي	تَحْمَرُّ	اِحْمَرَّتْ
لَا تَحْمَرِرْنَ	اِحْمَرِرْنَ	تَحْمَرَّانِ	اِحْمَرَّتَا
		يَحْمَرِرْنَ	اِحْمَرَرْنَ
		تَحْمَرُّ	اِحْمَرَرْتَ
		تَحْمَرَّانِ	اِحْمَرَرْتُمَا
		تَحْمَرُّونَ	اِحْمَرَرْتُمْ
		تَحْمَرِّينَ	اِحْمَرَرْتِ
		تَحْمَرَّانِ	اِحْمَرَرْتُمَا
		تَحْمَرِرْنَ	اِحْمَرَرْتُنَّ
		أَحْمَرُّ	اِحْمَرَرْتُ
		نَحْمَرُّ	اِحْمَرَرْنَا

TEACH YOURSELF ARABIC

To employ, to use — استخدم يستخدم استخداماً

ماضي معروف	ماضي مجهول	مضارع معروف	مضارع مجهول	فعل الأمر	فعل النهي	اسم الفاعل	اسم المفعول
استخدمَ	استُخدِمَ	يستخدمُ	يُستخدَمُ	استخدمْ	لا تستخدمْ	مُستخدِمٌ	مُستخدَمٌ
استخدمَا	استُخدِمَا	يستخدمانِ	يُستخدَمانِ	استخدمَا	لا تستخدمَا	مُستخدِمانِ	مُستخدَمانِ
استخدمُوا	استُخدِمُوا	يستخدمونَ	يُستخدَمونَ	استخدمُوا	لا تستخدمُوا	مُستخدِمونَ	مُستخدَمونَ
استخدمَتْ	استُخدِمَتْ	تستخدمُ	تُستخدَمُ			مُستخدِمةٌ	مُستخدَمةٌ
استخدمَتَا	استُخدِمَتَا	تستخدمانِ	تُستخدَمانِ			مُستخدِمتانِ	مُستخدَمتانِ
استخدمْنَ	استُخدِمْنَ	يستخدمْنَ	يُستخدَمْنَ			مُستخدِماتٌ	مُستخدَماتٌ
استخدمْتَ	استُخدِمْتَ	تستخدمُ	تُستخدَمُ	استخدمْ	لا تستخدمْ		
استخدمْتُما	استُخدِمْتُما	تستخدمانِ	تُستخدَمانِ	استخدمَا	لا تستخدمَا		
استخدمْتُم	استُخدِمْتُم	تستخدمونَ	تُستخدَمونَ	استخدمُوا	لا تستخدمُوا		
استخدمْتِ	استُخدِمْتِ	تستخدمينَ	تُستخدَمينَ	استخدمِي	لا تستخدمِي		
استخدمْتُنَّ	استُخدِمْتُنَّ	تستخدمْنَ	تُستخدَمْنَ	استخدمْنَ	لا تستخدمْنَ		
استخدمْتُ	استُخدِمْتُ	أستخدمُ	أُستخدَمُ				
استخدمْنا	استُخدِمْنا	نستخدمُ	نُستخدَمُ				

Translation Exercises
English-Arabic
With Glossary

Demonstrative Pronouns
(Simple nominal sentences)

1. This is a room.	2. This is a table.
3. This is a chair.	4. This is a pen.
5. This is a car.	6. This is a house.
7. This is a boy.	8. This is a girl.
9. This is a woman.	10. This is a man.
11. This is a tree.	12. This is a garden.
13. This is a flower.	14. This is an ashtray.
15. This is a sofa.	16. This is a radio.
17. This is a cup.	18. This is a door.
19. This is a door-keeper.	20. This is an airhostess.
21. This is a window.	22. This is a servant.
23. This is a clerk.	24. This is a typist.
25. This is an office.	26. This is a postman.
27. This is a driver.	28. This is a stenographer.
29. This is a library.	30. This is a University.
31. This is a college.	32. This is a school.
33. This is a primary school.	34. This is a Higher Secondary School.
35. This is a jug.	36. This is a tumbler.
37. This is a receptionist.	38. This is a Public Relations Officer.
39. This is a building.	40. This is an Engineer.
41. This is a city.	42. This is a village.
43. This is a student.	44. This is a teacher.

45. This is a blackboard.

46. This is a chalk piece.

47. This is a book.

48. This is a note-book.

49. This is a pencil.

50. This is a dictionary

☆☆ ☆

1. That is a cow.

2. That is a camel.

3. That is a horse.

4. That is a mare.

5. That is a bird.

6. That is a sparrow.

7. That is an elephant.

8. That is a lion.

9. That is a man.

10. That is a woman

11. That is a girl.

12. That is a boy.

13. That is a student.

14. That is a fan.

15. That is a lamp.

16. That is a door.

17. That is a house.

18. That is a bi-cycle.

19. That is an umberella.

20. That is a box.

21. That is a mirror.

22. That is a bureau.

23. That is a wardrobe.

24. That is a goat.

25. That is a lamb.

26. That is a dog.

27. That is a magazine.

28. That is a newspaper.

29. That is an envelope.

30. That is an ink-pot.

31. That is a basket.

32. That is a heater.

33. That is a cooler.

34. That is a refrigerator.

35. That is a pin.

36. That is a shelf.

37. That is a grocer.

38. That is a tailor.

39. That is a box.

40. That is a plant.

41. That is a workshop.

42. That is a technician.

43. That is a shirt.

44. That is a hut.

45. That is a pen-stand.

46. That is a calendar.

47. That is a lock.

48. That is a key.

49. That is a curtain.

50. That is a cat.

☆ ☆ ☆

1. These are men.
2. These are women.
3. These are girls.
4. These are boys.
5. These are students.
6. These are servants.
7. These are airhostesses.
8. These are dictionaries.
9. These are drivers.
10. These are tailors.
11. These are tables.
12. These are chairs.
13. These are doors.
14. These are cars.
15. These are offices
16. These are libraries.
17. These are books.
18. These are notebooks.
19. These are pens.
20. These are ashtrays.
21. These are spectacles.
22. These are shoes.
23. These are lions.
24. These are elephants.
25. These are goggles.
26. These are buildings.
27. These are houses.
28. These are locks.
29. These are keys.
30. These are birds.
31. These are gardens.
32. These are trees.
33. These are clerks.
34. These are boxes.
35. These are windows.
36. These are bureaus.
37. These are sofas.
38. These are vegetables.
39. These are rooms.
40. These are grocers.
41. These are baskets.
42. These are fans.
43. These are lamps.
44. These are pins.
45. These are calendars.
46. These are trains.
47. These are aeroplanes.
48. These are pilots.
49. These are officers.
50. These are sentences.

☆ ☆☆

1. Those are men.
2. Those are women.
3. Those are students.
4. Those are teachers.

5. Those are boys.

6. Those are girls.

7. Those are drivers.

8. Those are door-keepers.

9. Those are airhostesses.

10. Those are servants.

11. Those are fans.

12. Those are lamps.

13. Those are houses.

14. Those are huts.

15. Those are refrigerators.

16. Those are coolers.

17. Those are heaters.

18. Those are stones.

19. Those are animals.

20. Those are dogs.

21. Those are cats.

22. Those are radiosets.

23. Those are mirrors.

24. Those are tables.

25. Those are chairs.

26. Those are books.

27. Those are trees.

28. Those are watches

29. Those are notebooks.

30. Those are cities.

31. Those are villages.

32. Those are villagers.

33. Those are pictures.

34. Those are statues.

35. Those are paintings.

36. Those are bicycles.

37. Those are doors.

38. Those are buildings.

39. Those are officers.

40. Those are offices.

41. Those are windows.

42. Those are fields.

43. Those are watchmen.

44. Those are balls.

45. Those are Universities.

46. Those are colleges.

47. Those are schools.

48. Those are jugs.

49. Those are tumblers.

50. Those are cups.

☆ ☆ ☆

1. That man is tall.

2. That woman is tall.

3. That boy is short.

4. That girl is short.

5. That boy is handsome.

6. That girl is beautiful.

7. That man is ugly.

8. That woman is ugly.

9. That man is a teacher.
10. That woman is a teacher.
11. That man is a driver.
12. That woman is a tailor.
13. That teacher is good.
14. That lady teacher is good.
15. This girl is a student.
16. This boy is a student.
17. This pen is costly.
18. This table is cheap.
19. This chair is durable.
20. This ashtray is beautiful.
21. Those buildings are beautiful.
22. Those rooms are locked.
23. Those are books.
24. Those fans are old.
25. Those note-books are on the table.
26. Those dogs are behind the door.
27. These pens are cheap.
28. These stories are interesting.
29. These refrigerators are costly.
30. These shirts are cheap.
31. These bicycles are new.
32. These sentences are easy.
33. These words are difficult.
34. Those clerks are present.
35. Those teachers are available.
36. These rooms are spacious.
37. These streets are narrow.
38. These roads are wide.
39. These buildings are old.
40. These servants are faithful.
41. These cars are fast.
42. These trains are slow.
43. These doctors are experts.
44. Those men are thieves.
45. These students are industrious.
46. These boys are lazy.
47. These workers are active.
48. That bird is a crow.
49. That animal is a lion.
50. This man is a tailor.

1. This is a room. This is a big room. There are in it (it has) one door and one window. There is (it has) a black-board also. Now the teacher is sitting on a chair. He has a book in his hand. Now he is standing infront of the blackboard. He is writing on the black-board.

2. This is a garden. This is my garden. This garden is big. The trees are tall. There are flowers in my garden. These flowers are beautiful. My garden is in Delhi.

3. This is a house. This house is big. This is my house. It has four rooms: one sleeping-room, one dining-room, one drawing-room and one study-room. It has a kitchen and a bath-room also. This is the sleeping room. This room is big. This is the dining room. This room is small. This is the drawing-room. This room is beautiful. This is the study-room. There are books in this room.

4. This is an office. This is my office. There are a peon & a clerk in the office. The clerk is absent. The peon is present.

Interrogative Pronouns

1. What is this?	This is a pen.
2. What is this?	This is a dog.
3. What is that?	That is a bicycle.
4. What is that?	That is a cow.
5. What are those?	Those are dogs.
6. What are these?	These are tables.
7. What are these?	These are cows.
8. What is this?	This is a house.
9. What is this?	This is a cage.
10. What is that?	That is a window.
11. What is that?	That is a hare.
12. What are these?	These are books.
13. What are these?	These are dogs.
14. What are those?	Those are cages.
15. What are those?	Those are lions.
16. Is this a pen?	Yes, this is a pen.
17. Is this a bed?	No, this is a sofa.
18. Is this a boy?	Yes, this is a boy.
19. Is this an elephant?	Yes, this is an elephant.

20. Is that a table?	No, that is a chair.
21. Is that a cat?	No, that is a dog.
22. Is that a girl?	No, that is a boy.
23. Are these men?	Yes these are men.
24. Are these cars?	Yes, these are cars.
25. Are these cows?	No, these are buffaloes.
26. Are those women?	No, those are men.
27. Are those aeroplanes?	Yes, those are aeroplanes.
28. Are those birds?	Yes, those are birds.
29. Are these girls?	No, these are boys.
30. Are these (boy) students?	No, these are (men) teachers.

Pronouns

(Simple Nominal Sentences)

He is a boy. She is a girl. They are men. They are women. Is he a student?
Yes he is a student. Is she a student? Yes, she is a student. Are you (S. M.)
a teacher? Yes, I am a teacher. Are (S.F.) you a clerk? Yes, I am a clerk.
Are you (P.M.) teachers? Yes, we are teachers. Are you (P.F.) clerks? No,
we are officers. I (S.M.) am a pilot. I (S.F.) am an airhostess.

Who is he? He is a driver.

Who is she? She is a typist.

Who are they (P.F.)? They are typists.

Who are you (S.M.)? I am a teacher.

Who are you (P.M.)? We are tailors.

Who are you (P.F.)? We are students.

The boy is sitting. The girl is standing.

Is the boy sitting? Is the girl standing?

Where are you going now?

Are you going to the University now?

The teachers are present in the School.

The students are present in the class.

Are the teachers present in the school?

Are the students present in the class?

1) Now I am going to the University. I am going to the University library. I am now sitting in the library on a chair. In my hand is a newspaper. The magazine is infornt of me on the table. My friend Zainab is sitting on a chair. She is writing. The pen is new and the handwriting is beautiful.

2) The teacher is going to the class. The students are in the class. There are fans and lamps in the class. There is a blackboard also. Now the teacher is in the class. He is standing infront of the blackboard.

3) She is a girl. She is my sister. She is going to the market. She has a basket in her hand. She is now standing at the bus stop. The bus is coming. My sister is in the bus. Now she is in the market.

Construct Phrases

(Possessed and possessor)

This is a book. This is Mr. Shahid. This is Shahid's book. These are books. This is Mr. Adil. These are Adil's books. This is a room. These are Shahid, Adil and Tara. This is the room of Shahid, Adil and Tara. This is the University. This is the library. This is the University library. This is the college. This is the canteen. This is the college canteen. This is the teacher. This is the book. This is his book. These are his books. This is her book. These are her books. This is their (men) book. This is their (women) book. This is your (S.F.) book. This is your (S.M.) book. This is your (P.M.) book. This is my (M.F.) book. This is our (MF) book. This is a class room. This is my classroom. There are many students in my class. They are my classmates. My classmates are present in the class. This is a shop. This is the shop of a grocer. The grocer is an old man. The grocer is sitting on his chair. This is the shop of a tailor. There are many tailors in the shop. The shop is big. This tailor is famous. This is a lighter. This lighter is of the teacher. This lighter is costly.

☆ ☆ ☆

He is Mr. Anis. He is our teacher. He teaches us Arabic. Our teacher is present in the class. His book is in his hand. The books of the students are infront of them. The teacher is reading from his book. The students are reading from their books. The teacher is writing difficult words on the blackboard with his chalk. The students are writing in their notebooks with their pens. The teacher asks: where is your book, Nihad? Nihad : My book is infront of me, Sir. Teacher: Where is your pen, Rashid? Rashid: My pen is in my pocket, Sir. Teacher: Students, bring your new book tomorrow.

Whose book is this?	Whose house is this?
Whose car is this?	Whose books are these?
Whose houses are these?	Whose cars are these?
Whose child is this?	Whose children are these?
Whose shirt is this?	Whose shirts are these?
This chair is made of wood.	This is a wooden chair.
This door is made fo iron.	This is an iron door.
This building is made of red stone.	This necklace is made of gold.
This necklace is made of silver.	This tumbler is made of glass.

Colours and Physical Defects

What colour is your pen?	It is red. The colour of my pen is red.
His shirt is red. Her shirt is green.	His car is red. Her car is green.
This pen is black.	This flower is yellow.
This pen is yellow.	He is brown.
She is brown.	They are brown.
These shirts are black.	These cars are black.
These pens are black.	Is your shirt red?

Yes, my shirt is red.

No, my shirt is green.

He is blind.

She is blind.

He is squint.

She is squint.

Is he lame?

Yes, he is lame.

They are blind.

They are squint.

Is that girl dumb?

Are they dumb?

Past Tense

The boy went to school.

The boy wrote a letter.

The boy read a lesson.

The boy killed a mouse.

The boy opened the door.

The girl went to school.

The girls wrote a letter.

The girls read a lesson.

The girl read a lesson.

The girl killed a mouse.

The girl opened the door.

The boys went to school.

The boys wrote these letters.

The boys read their lessons.

These boys killed the mice.

These boys opened the doors.

These girls went to school.

These girls wrote these letters.

The girls read their lessons.

These girls killed these mice.

The girls opened the doors.

You (S.M.) opened the doors.

You (S.M.) went to school yesterday.

You wrote a letter yesterday.

You read a lesson yesterday.

You killed a mouse yesterday.

You opened the door.

You (S. F.) went to school.

You wrote a letter.

You read a lesson.

You killed a mouse.

You opened the door.

You (P.M.) went to school.

You wrote letters.

You read lessons.

You killed these mice.

You opened the doors.

You (P.F.) went to school.

You wrote letters.

You read lessons.

You opened the door.

I wrote a letter.

I killed a mouse.

We (P. M. & F.) went to school.

We read our lessons.

We opened the doors.

Did the boy close the door?

Did the boys go to school?

Did you kill a mouse?

The boy did not write the letter?

I did not open the door.

Did you not open the door?

Did the boys not kill the mice?

You killed the mice.

I (S.M. and F.) went to school.

I read a lesson.

I opened the door.

We wrote letters.

We killed mice.

Did the boy open the door?

Did the boy write a letter?

Did the girls go to school?

Did you read the letter?

The girls did not go to school.

Did he not go to school?

Did the girl not read the lesson?

Did we not write letters?

☆ ☆ ☆

Mr. Rashid went to the market. He went on foot. He went to the butcher's shop. He bought some meat and returned to his hostel.

What do you have in your hand? This is a magazine. Have you read it? No, I have not read it.

The girls sat in the garden. They ate their lunch. Did you go to the hospital? Yes, I went to the hospital yesterday.

Hello! How are you Miss Zainab? Where is your friend Miss Fatima? Did you go to the theatre yesterday?

Hello! Mr. Rashid, where are you going now? Are you going to the market. Are you going by car. Yes, I am going by car. Where is your driver? My driver is sick.

☆ ☆ ☆

Who are you? I am a student. My name is Rashid. Where are you from? I am from Kashmir. When did you come to Delhi? I came to Delhi last month. Where are you staying in Delhi? I am staying in a hostel. Are you a student of this University? Yes, I am a student of this University. I am studying the Arabic language in this University.

☆ ☆ ☆

Yesterday evening I visited my friend in his house. I sat with him in his drawing-room. We drank tea. After that we left his house and went to the market. I bought books, note-books and papers. I also bought apples, grapes, bananas and oranges.

When I came back home, my wife saw my friend with me. She asked me: who is he? I told her: He is my friend. His name is Mr. Shahid. Then she saw these things in my hands. She asked me: What are these things in your hands? I told her: These are fruits and books. She said: When did you go to the market? I said: I went to the market this evening with my friend.

☆ ☆ ☆

Present Tense

(Present & Future)

1. He goes to office.
2. She goes to office.
3. They (men) go to office.
4. They (women) go to office.
5. You (S.M.) go to office.
6. You (S.F.) go to office.
7. You (P.M.) go to office.
8. You (P.F.) go to office.
9. I (S.M.F.) go to office.
10. We (P.M. F.) go to office.
11. Does he go to office?
12. Does she go to office.
13. Do they (men) go to office?
14. Do they (women) go to office.
15. Do you go to office?
16. She does not go to office.
17. They (men) do not go to office.
18. They (women) do not go to office.
19. You do not go to office.
20. I do not go to office.
21. We do not go to office.
22. Does he not go to office?
23. Does she not go to office?
24. Do they (men) not go to office?

25. Do they (women) not go to   26. Do you (S.F.) not go to office?
    office?

27. Do I not go to office.   28. Do we not go to office.

The name of our teacher is Mr. Anis. He works in the University. He has a room. We go to his room every day for lesson. Yesterday also we went to his room. We knocked at the door. We opened the door. We entered the room. We read a lesson and returned to our rooms.

☆ ☆ ☆

1. He will go to school tomorrow.

2. She will go to school tomorrow.

3. They (men) will go to school tomorrow.

4. They (women) will go to school tomorrow.

5. You (S.M.) will go to school tomorrow.

7. You (P.M.) will go to school tomorrow.

8. You (P.F.) will go to school tomorrow.

9. I (M.F.) will go to school tomorrow.

10. We (M.F.) will go to school tomorrow.

11. Will he go to school tomorrow?

12. Will she go to school tomorrow?

13. Will you (S.M.) go to school tomorrow?

14. He will not go to school tomorrow.

15. She will not go to school tomorrow.

16. I shall not go to school tomorrow.

17 . Will he not go to school tomorrow?

18. Will she not go to school tomorrow?

19. Will they (women) not go to school tomorrow?

20. Shall we not go to school tomorrow?

This is my elder brother. His name is Mr. Anwar. He works in an office in Delhi. He goes to his office every day in the morning. He gets up from his sleep in the early morning. He goes to the bathroom, cleans his teeth and takes bath. He puts on clean clothes and then eats his breakfast. At 9.00 O'clock he takes his bag and leaves for his office. He works in the office till 4.30 P.M. and returns home at 5.00 P.M.

☆ ☆ ☆

The policeman is a government employee. He wears an official uniform. He always has a stick in his hand. He moves from one place to another. He catches thieves, gamblers, drunkards and all bad persons. Bad persons are afraid of him. His salary is small but his work is tiresome.

☆ ☆ ☆

Agra is a small city. It is in North India. This city is small but is very famous. It is famous all over the world for a beautiful tomb. It is called Taj Mahal. It was built by the Mughal Emperor, Shah Jahan many years ago. Thousands of workers built it in twenty years. People come to see this historical monument from all corners of the world.

☆ ☆ ☆

My friend shahid came to me yesterday evening. I was very happy to see him. I received him with all cheerfulness and seated him in the drawing room. Shahid asked me: will you be busy during the coming week? I said: No, why do you ask me this question? Shahid: I and Tara will go to Nainital during the next week. Will you accompany us? I said: It is a nice idea. Now-a-days it is hot in Delhi. It will be nice if we go to Nainital. How long shall we stay in Nainital? Shahid: we will stay there for two weeks. I: That is nice too. When we come back to Delhi after two weeks, it will not be very hot in Delhi. Shahid: fine, then get ready to leave tomorrow morning. We shall go by bus.

Simple Past Tense

1. He was a student.
2. She was a student.
3. They (men) were students.
4. They (women) were students.
5. You (S.F.) were a student.
6. You (P.M.) were students.
7. You (P.F.) were students.
8. I (M) was a student.
9. I (F) was a student.
10. We (P.M.) were students.
11. We (F) were students.
12. He was not a student.
13. She was not a student.
14. They (M), were not students.
15. They (F), were not students.
16. You (S.M.) were not a student.
17. You (S.F.) were not a student.
18. You (P.M.) were not students.
29. You (P.F.) were not students.
20. I (M) was not a student.
21. I (F) was not a student.
22. We (M) were not students.
23. Was he a student?
24. Was she a student?
25. Were they (F) students?
26. Were you (S.M.) a student?
27. Was he not a student?
28. Were we (M) not students?

☆ ☆ ☆

I was free yesterday. I went to Shahid's house to see him. He was (present) at home. He was very happy to see me. He seated me in the drawing room. His servant was absent yesterday. His sitster was also not (present) at home. He went to the kitchen and prepared tea for us. Then we drank tea and talked about many things. After tea we went to Tara's house. Tara was not (present) at home. It was evening. We returned to our houses.

Comparative & Superlative

This house is beautiful.

This house is more beautiful than that house.

This is the most beautiful house.

Is this house more beautiful than that house?

Is this the most beautiful house?

This room is more spacious than that room.

This film is more interesting than the novel.

This lesson is more difficult than that lesson.

This boy is taller than that boy.

This man is shorter than my brother .

This woman is more beautiful than his sister.

This film is lengthier than that film.

Those stories are more interesting than that story.

Those pens are cheaper than that pen.

This boy is taller than that girl.

My car is costlier than her car.

Those cars are cheaper than my car.

This is the most interesting film.

That is the most interesting story.

This is the cheapest car.

He is the most intelligent student.

She is the most beautiful woman.

This is the most difficult lesson.

This is the most spacious room.

Is he the most intelligent boy?

Is this the costliest car?

Is he the most senior officer.

Is her voice the sweetest of all voices.

Is your house more spacious than that of your friend's?

Is your daughter older than my son?

Are your servants more hardworking than my servant?

Numerals

I have one book.

My friend has two books.

She has one note-book.

There are two tables in my room.

There are three books and four note-books in her bag.

I bought five pens, and six note-books from the market yesterday evening.

Shahid has eleven books and twelve note-books.

Tara bought fifteen forks and sixteen spoons.

I have one hundred rupees.

He has two hundred books.

Subjunctive

I want to read this novel.

Do you want to see this film?

I request you to visit me someday.

Can you lend me your bicycle?

I cannot go to London next month.

I pray to God to give me knowledge.

Adjectival phrases

He is a tall boy.	They are tall boys.
She is a tall girl.	They are tall women.
You (S.M.) are a tall boy.	You (P.M.) are tall boys.
You (S.F.) are a tall girl.	You (P.F.) are tall girls.
I am a tall girl.	We are tall boys.
We are tall girls.	Is he a tall boy?
Are you a tall boy?	A tall boy came to me.

A tall girl came to me.

Tall girls came to me.

That tall girl came to me.

Those tall girls came to me

Is this your new shirt?

Is she your younger sister?

This is a new car.

These are new cars.

This is a costly pen.

Tall boys came to me.

That tall boy came to me.

Those tall boys came to me.

Where is your new pen.

Is he your older brother?

My new car is parked in front of my office.

This is an old table.

These are old tables.

These are costly pens.

☆ ☆ ☆

Mr. Adil: Mr. Rashid, are you free tomorrow?

Mr. Rashid: When?

Mr. Adil: In the morning.

Mr. Rashid: No, I am sorry, I will go to see an old friend of mine tomorrow morning. His eldest son is sick.

Mr. Adil: And evening?

Mr. Rashid: I am sorry again, my dear friend this evening too I am busy. I will go to Delhi International Airport. An old friend of mine is coming with his old (aged) mother.

Mr. Adil: When can I see you tomorrow?

Mr. Rashid: You can come to see me in the afternoon at 3 O' clock.

Mr. Adil: fine, thank you.

☆ ☆ ☆

The President of Egypt received the President of India yesterday. They held talks about improving the bilateral relations between the two countries.

☆ ☆ ☆

An official source stated that the Ambassador of Pakistan conveyed to the

President of India a verbal message of the President of Pakistan regarding the bilateral relations between India an Pakistan.

☆ ☆ ☆

The Israeli Prime Minister reached London yesterday afternoon on a six day official visit to Britain. The Israeli Prime Minister will hold talks with the British Prime Minister regarding a peaceful solution to the Middle East problem.

☆ ☆ ☆

Mr. Yasser Arafat, Chairman of the Palestinian Liberation Organisation reached Cairo last night on a five-day visit to Egypt. He will hold talks with top officials regarding the Palestinian problem and the current situation in the region.

☆ ☆ ☆

State Minister for foreign affairs will leave here for Vienna on an official visit to Hungary. He will hold talks with the Hungarian authorities aiming at strengthening bilateral relations between the United Arab Emirates and Hungary.

☆ ☆ ☆

The President of Tunisia received yesterday a member of executive committee of the Palestinian Liberation Organisation. A meeting was held in Kartaj Palace. Present at the meeting were: the Foreign Minister, the Home Minister and the PLO representative in Tunisia.

☆ ☆ ☆

The Prime Minister of India went to Egypt last month. He met the president of Egypt. He was with him for one hour. After the meeting he told the pressmen that he discussed with the president relations between the two countries.

The Foreign Minister of Egypt visited India last week. The Indian foreign minister and some senior officers of the foreign ministry received him at the airport. The foreign minister of Egypt said at the airport: I will stay in India for three days. I will discuss with the Prime Minister and the foreign minister of India bi-lateral relations. We want to improve our relations with India.

☆ ☆ ☆

The Prime Minister called an urgent meeting of the cabinet. He discussed with them some important matters. He also informed his colleagues that his discussions with the president of America were successful.

☆ ☆ ☆

The Home Minister of India met the Prime Minister last night. He was with him for nearly one hour. The Home Minister later informed the pressmen that he did not discuss with the Prime Minister any official matter. It was a purely friendly meeting.

☆ ☆ ☆

The Prime Minister of India received yesterday evening in his office, the Public Works Minister of Syria. Their meeting lasted for one hour. Sources say that Public Works Minister of Syria delivered a verbal message from the Syrian President to the Prime Minister of India.

☆ ☆ ☆

The present Chairman of the Organisation of Arab Unity has launched efforts with non-oil producing Arab and African countries to meet the "Natural Consequences" of next year's oil price rise, Foreign Affairs Under Secretary said yesterday.

☆ ☆ ☆

The Prime Minister today appealed to the people to take the message of family planning to every house to ensure satisfactory living standards to all especially, the weaker sections.

In a message over Radio and Television he said the country's prosperity depended on small families. "We have been making efforts to develop our country so that we are able to give employment to every person and to give a satisfactory living from that employment," he said.

☆ ☆ ☆

Iraq and India have signed a joint minutes for bilateral economic, trade and technical co-operation. The two countries will explore means of consolidating ties of co-operation in technical, culrural, trade, industry, transport, communication, agriculture and irrigation fields.

☆ ☆ ☆

The PM will pay a three day visit to Nepal from December 9. This will be his first visit to a neighouring country since he assumed office this year.

☆ ☆ ☆

Glossary

الكلمات العسيرة

Cup (for tea/coffee)	فِنْجَانٌ / فَنَاجِينُ
Cup/tumbler	كُوبٌ / أَكْوَابٌ
Flower	زَهْرٌ / أَزْهَارٌ / زَهْرَةٌ .N.U. F)
Ashtray	مِنْفَضَةٌ / مَنَافِضُ
Sofa	أَرِيكَةٌ / أَرَائِكُ
Radio	رَادِيو
Radio-set	جِهَاز رَادِيو
Radio-sets	أَجْهِزَةُ رَادِيو
Doorkeeper	بَوَّابٌ / بَوَّابُونَ
Airhostess	مُضِيْفَةٌ / مُضِيْفَاتٌ
Typist (girl)	كَاتِبَةٌ / كَاتِبَاتٌ (عَلَى الآلَة)
Clerk	كَاتِبٌ / كَتَبَةٌ
Stenographer (man)	كَاتِبُ الإِخْتِزَالِ
Postman	سَاعِى البَرِيْدِ
Postmen	سُعَاةُ البَرِيْدِ
Primary school	مَدْرَسَةٌ إِبْتِدَائِيَّةٌ
Secondary School	مَدْرَسَةٌ ثَانَوِيَّةٌ
Jug	إِبْرِيْقٌ / أَبَارِيْقُ
Chalk (piece/ stick)	طَبَاشِيْرُ
Receptionist (man)	ضَابِطُ الإِسْتِقْبَالِ
Receptionists (men)	ضُبَّاطُ الإِسْتِقْبَالِ
Public Relations Officer (man)	ضَابِطُ العَلاَقَاتِ العَامَّةِ
Public Relations Officers (men)	ضُبَّاطُ العَلاَقَاتِ العَامَّةِ

Pencil	قَلَمُ الرَّصَاصِ
Blackboard	سَبُّورَةٌ/ سَبُّورَاتٌ
Camel	جَمَلٌ / جِمَالٌ
Cow	بَقَرَةٌ/ بَقَرَاتٌ
Horse	حِصَانٌ / أَحْصِنَةٌ
Mare/horse	فَرَسٌ / أَفْرَاسٌ
Fan	مِرْوَحَةٌ/ مَرَاوِحُ
Lion	أَسَدٌ/ أُسُودٌ
Sparrow	عُصْفُورَةٌ/ عَصَافِيْرُ
Bird	طَائِرٌ/ طُيُورٌ
Lamp	مِصْبَاحٌ/ مَصَابِيْحُ
Bi-cycle	دَرَّاجَةٌ/ دَرَّاجَاتٌ
Umbrella	مِظَلَّةٌ/ مِظَلَّاتٌ
Box	صُنْدُوقٌ/ صَنَادِيقُ
Bureau (writing desk)	مِنْضَدَةٌ/ مَنَاضِدُ
Mirror	مِرْآةٌ / مَرَايا
Wardrobe	دُولَابٌ/دَوَالِيْبُ
Goat	شَاةٌ/ شِيَاةٌ
Lamb	حَمَلٌ/ حُمْلَانٌ
Magazine	مَجَلَّةٌ/مَجَلَّاتٌ
Newspaper	صَحِيفَةٌ/ صُحُفٌ
Envelope	ظَرْفٌ/ ظُرُوفٌ
Inkpot	دَوَاةٌ/دَوَيَاتٌ
Basket	سَلَّةٌ/ سِلَالٌ
Heater	سَخَّانَةٌ/ سَخَّانَاتٌ
Cooler (water cooler)	مُبَرِّدُ المَاءِ
Air (room) cooler	مُبَرِّدُ الهَوَاء
Pin	دَبُّوسٌ / دَبَابِيسُ

Shelf	رَفٌّ / رُفُوفٌ
Grocer	بَقَّالٌ / بَقَّالُونَ
Green grocer, vegetable seller	خُضْرَوَاتِى
Plant	نَبْتَةٌ / نَبْتَاتٌ
Workshop	وِرْشَةٌ / وِرَشٌ ، مَصْنَعٌ / مَصَانِعُ
Technician	فَنِّىٌّ / فَنِّيُّونَ
Calendar	تَقْوِيمٌ / تَقَاوِيمُ
Hut	كُوخٌ / أَكْوَاخٌ
Penstand	مِقْلَمٌ / مَقَالِمُ
Lock	قُفْلٌ / أَقْفَالٌ
Key	مِفْتَاحٌ / مَفَاتِيحُ
Curtain	سِتَارَةٌ / سَتَائِرُ
Building	عِمَارَةٌ / عِمَارَاتٌ
Vegetable/s	خُضَارٌ
Spectacles/glasses	نَظَّارَاتٌ
Goggles, Sunglasses	نَظَّارَاتٌ شَمْسِيَّةٌ
Shoe	حِذَاءٌ / أَحْذِيَةٌ
Train	قِطَارٌ / قِطَارَاتٌ
Pilot	طَيَّارٌ / طَيَّارُونَ
Stone	حَجَرٌ / أَحْجَارٌ
Aeroplane	طَائِرَةٌ / طَائِرَاتٌ
Official, officer	مُوَظَّفٌ / مُوَظَّفُونَ
Refrigerator	ثَلَّاجَةٌ / ثَلَّاجَاتٌ
City	مَدِينَةٌ / مُدُنٌ
Picture	صُورَةٌ / صُوَرٌ
Statue	تِمْثَالٌ / تَمَاثِيلُ
Field	مَيْدَانٌ / مَيَادِينُ
Beautiful/handsome	جَمِيلٌ

Tailor	خَيَّاطٌ، خَيَّاطُونَ
Tall/long	طَوِيلٌ
Short	قَصِيرٌ
University	جَامِعَةٌ، جَامِعَاتٌ
Painting	لَوحَةٌ، لَوحَاتٌ
Costly, expensive	ثَمِينٌ
Cheap	رَخِيصٌ
Durable	مَتِينٌ
Interesting	مُمْتِعٌ
Open	مَفْتُوحٌ
Locked	مُقْفَلٌ
Behind	وَرَاءَ
Easy	سَهْلٌ
Difficult	صَعْبٌ
Story	قِصَّةٌ، قِصَصٌ
Present	حَاضِرٌ، مَوجُودٌ
Spacious	وَاسِعٌ
Fast	سَرِيعٌ
Slow	بَطِيءٌ
Thief, robber	لِصٌّ، لُصُوصٌ
Shirt	قَمِيصٌ، قُمْصَانٌ
Loyal/faithful	وَفِيٌّ، أَوْفِيَاءُ
Lazy	كَسْلَانٌ، كُسَالَى
Hardworking, industrious	مُجْتَهِدٌ، مُجْتَهِدُونَ
Expert	مَاهِرٌ، مَاهِرُونَ، خَبِيرٌ، خُبَرَاءُ
Old	قَدِيمٌ، قُدَامَى
Narrow	ضَيِّقٌ
Worker	عَامِلٌ، عُمَّالٌ

Crow	غُرَابٌ / غِرْبَانٌ
Animal	حَيَوَانٌ / حَيَوَانَاتٌ
Door	بَابٌ / أَبْوَابٌ
Window	شُبَّاكٌ / شَبَابِيكُ
In his hand, he has	فِى يَدِهِ
Garden	حَدِيقَةٌ / حَدَائِقُ
Room	غُرْفَةٌ / غُرَفٌ
Sleeping room, bedroom	غُرْفَةُ النَّومِ
Dining room	غُرْفَةُ الطَّعَامِ
Drawing room	غُرْفَةُ الاسْتِقْبَالِ
Study room	غُرْفَةُ الدِّرَاسَةِ
Kitchen	مَطْبَخٌ / مَطَابِخُ
Bathroom	حَمَّامٌ / حَمَامَاتٌ
Office	مَكْتَبٌ / مَكَاتِبُ
Peon	فَرَّاشٌ / فَرَّاشُونَ
Absent	غَائِبٌ
Pen	قَلَمٌ / أَقْلَامٌ
Dog	كَلْبٌ / كِلَابٌ
Table	طَاوِلَةٌ / طَاوِلَاتٌ
House	بَيْتٌ / بُيُوتٌ
Hare, rabbit	أَرْنَبٌ / أَرَانِبُ
Elephant	فِيلٌ / أَفْيَالٌ
Girl	بِنْتٌ / بَنَاتٌ
Boy	وَلَدٌ / أَوْلَادٌ
Man	رَجُلٌ / رِجَالٌ
Driver	سَوَّاقٌ / سَوَّاقُونَ
Class/classroom	فَصْلٌ / فُصُولٌ
Library	مَكْتَبَةٌ / مَكْتَبَاتٌ

Infront of	أَمَامَ
Sister	أُخْتٌ ⁄ أَخَوَاتٌ
Bus-stop	مَوقِفُ البَصِ (مَواقِفُ)
Market	سُوقٌ ⁄ أسوَاقٌ
Word	كَلِمَةٌ ⁄ كَلِمَاتٌ
Difficult words, Glossary	كَلِمَاتٌ عَسِيرَةٌ
To bring	جَاءَ ⁄ يَجِيُّ ⁄ جَيْئَةً (ب)
Pocket	جَيْبٌ ⁄ جُيُوبٌ
Child	طِفْلٌ ⁄ أطْفَالٌ
From/ made of	مِنْ
Made of wood	مِنَ الخَشَبِ
Iron	حَدِيدٌ
Red stone/sand stone	الحَجَرُ الأَحْمَرُ
Gold	ذَهَبٌ
Silver	فِضَّةٌ
Necklace	قِلادَةٌ ⁄ قَلائِدٌ
Anklet	خَلْخَالٌ ⁄ خَلاخِيلُ
Defect	عَيْبٌ ⁄ عُيُوبٌ
Physical defects	عُيُوبٌ بَدَنِيَّةٌ
Squint	أعْوَرُ ⁄ عَورَاءُ ⁄ عُورٌ
Blind	أعْمَى ⁄ عَمْيَاءُ ⁄ عُمْيٌ
Lame	أعْرَجُ ⁄ عَرْجَاءُ ⁄ عُرْجٌ
Dumb	أخْرَسُ ⁄ خَوْسَاءُ ⁄ خُرْسٌ
To write	كَتَبَ ⁄ يَكْتُبُ ⁄ كِتَابَةً
To read	قَرَأَ ⁄ يَقْرَأُ ⁄ قِرَاءَةً
To go	ذَهَبَ ⁄ يَذْهَبُ ⁄ ذَهَابًا
To kill	قَتَلَ ⁄ يَقْتُلُ ⁄ قَتْلاً

To open	فَتَحَ / يَفْتَحُ / فَتْحًا
Mouse	فَأْرٌ / فِئرَانٌ (فَأْرَةٌ NUF)
Butcher	جَزَّارٌ / جَزَّارُونَ
Meat	لَحْمٌ
Hostel	دَاخِلِيَّةٌ / دَاخِلِيَّاتٌ
Hostel	دَارُ الإِقَامَةِ / دُورٌ
To eat	أَكَلَ / يَأْكُلُ / أَكْلاً
Hospital	مُسْتَشْفًى / مُسْتَشْفَيَاتٌ
To sit	جَلَسَ / يَجْلِسُ / جُلُوسًا
Lunch	غَدَاءٌ
Dinner	عَشَاءٌ
Breakfast	فُطُورٌ
Yesterday	أَمْسِ
Tomorrow	غَدًا
Today	اَلْيَومَ
To visit	زَارَ / يَزُورُ / زِيَارَةً
Friend	صَدِيقٌ / أَصْدِقَاءُ
To leave	غَادَرَ / يُغَادِرُ / مُغَادَرَةً
After	بَعْدَ
After that	بَعْدَ ذَلِك
Also	أَيْضًا
To buy	إِشْتَرَى / يَشْتَرِى / إِشْتِرَاءً
Apple	تُفَّاحٌ (تُفَّاحَةٌ N.U.)
Banana	مَوْزٌ (مَوزَةٌ N.U.)

Grapes	عِنَبٌ (عِنَبَةٌ. N.U)
Oranges	بُرْتَقَالٌ (بُرْتَقَالَةٌ. N.U)
To return, to come back	عَادَ/ يَعُودُ/ عَوْدَةً
Wife	زَوجَةٌ/زَوْجَاتٌ
To see	رَأَى/ يَرَى/ رُؤْيَةٌ
To ask	سَأَلَ/ يَسْأَلُ/ سُؤَالاً
To tell, to say (to)	قَالَ/يَقُولُ/ قَوْلاً (لِ)
Thing	شَىءٌ / أَشْيَاءُ
Then	ثُمَّ
Fruit	فَاكِهَةٌ/ فَوَاكِهُ
When	مَتَى
Where	أَيْنَ
What	مَا
Who	مَنْ
Is, are, am? (interrogative)	هَلْ/أ
To work	إِشْتَغَلَ/ يَشْتَغِلُ/إِشْتِغَالاً
To work	عَمِلَ/ يَعْمَلُ/ عَمَلاً
Every day	كُلَّ يَوْمٍ
To knock (at)	دَقَّ/ يَدُقُّ/ دَقًّا (عَلَى)
To enter	دَخَلَ/ يَدْخُلُ/ دُخُولاً
Lesson	دَرْسٌ/ دُرُوسٌ
Brother	أَخٌ/ إِخْوَةٌ/ إِخْوَانٌ
Name	إِسْمٌ/ أَسْمَاء
To wake up, to get up	إِسْتَيْقَظَ/ يَسْتَيْقِظُ/ إِسْتِيقَاظًا
Sleep	نَوْمٌ
Early morning	صَبَاحٌ بَاكِرٌ
To clean	نَظَّفَ/ يُنَظِّفُ/ تَنْظِيفًا
Tooth, Teeth	سِنٌّ/ أَسْنَانٌ

To take bath	تَحَمَّمَ / يَتَحَمَّمُ / تَحَمُّمًا
To wear, to put on	إِرتَدَى / يَرْتَدِى / إِرْتِدَاءً
To put on, to wear	لَبِسَ / يَلْبَسُ / لُبْسًا
Clean	نَظِيفٌ
Clothes	مَلْبَسٌ / مَلَابِسُ
At 9.00 O'clock	فى السَّاعَةِ التَّاسِعَةِ
A.M., in the morning	صَبَاحًا / فى الصَّبَاحِ
P.M., in the evening	مَسَاءً / فى الْمَسَاءِ
Bag	حَقِيبَةٌ / حَقَائِبُ
Till	حَتَّى
At 4:30	فِى السَّاعَةِ الرَّابِعَةِ والنِّصْفِ
Policeman	شُرْطِىٌّ / شُرْطِيُّونَ
Policeman/soldier	عَسْكَرِىٌّ / عَسَاكِرُ
Police	شُرْطَةٌ
Government	حُكُومَةٌ / حُكُومَاتٌ
Government official	مُوَظَّفٌ حُكُومِىٌّ
Uniform	زِىٌّ / أَزْيَاءٌ
Official uniform	زِىٌّ رَسْمِىٌّ
Always	دَائِمًا
Stick	عَصًا / عِصِىٌّ
To move	إِنْتَقَلَ / يَنْتَقِلُ / إِنْتِقَالًا
To hold, to catch	أَمْسَكَ / يُمْسِكُ / إِمْسَاكًا
To arrest, to catch (s. o.)	أَلْقَى / يُلْقِى الْقَبْضَ على
Gambler	مُقَامِرٌ / مُقَامِرُونَ
Drunkard	مُسْكِرٌ / مُسْكِرُونَ
Bad people/ persons	أَصْحَابُ السُّوءِ
To fear from	خَافَ / يَخَافُ / خَوْفًا مِنْ
Afraid of	خَائِفٌ / خَائِفُونَ مِنْ

Salary	مُرَتَّبٌ / مُرَتَّبَاتٌ
Tiresome, tiring	مُتْعِبٌ
Agra	آجرَا / آكْرَا
North India	شِمَالُ الهند
North	شِمَالٌ
South	جُنُوبٌ
East	مَشرِقٌ
West	مَغرِبٌ
But	لكِن
Famous	مَشْهُورٌ / شَهِيرٌ
All over/around the world	حَولَ العَالَم
Tomb	مَقْبَرَةٌ / مَقَابِرُ
To build	بَنى / يَبْنِى / بِنَاءً
To be built	بُنِىَ / يُبْنَى / بِنَاءً
Emperor	إِمْبِرَاطُورٌ / أَبَاطِرَةُ
The Mughal Emperor	الإمْبِرَاطُورُ المُغُولِى
Ago, Before	قَبْلَ
Thousand	أَلْفٌ / أُلُوفٌ
Monument	أَثَرٌ / آثَارٌ
Historical monument	أَثَرٌ تَارِيْخِىٌّ
Corner	نَحْوٌ / أَنْحَاءٌ
World	دُنْيَا
World	عَالَمٌ
Happy	سَعِيْدٌ / سُعَدَاءُ
To receive	إِسْتَقْبَلَ / يَسْتَقْبِلُ / إِسْتِقْبَالاً
Cheerfulness	بَشَاشَةٌ
To seat, to offer a seat	أَجلَسَ / يُجلِسُ / إِجْلَاسًا
Busy	مَشْغُولٌ

Weak	أُسْبُوعٌ / أَسَابِيعُ
Next weak	الأُسْبُوع القَادِم
Why	لِمَاذا
Question	سُؤَالٌ / أَسْئِلَةٌ
During	خِلالَ
To accompany	رَافَقَ / يُرَافِقُ / مُرَافَقَةً
Idea, thought	فِكْرَةٌ / فِكَرٌ
Good idea, nice idea	فِكْرَةٌ جَمِيْلَةٌ
Now-a-days, these days	فِى هَذِهِ الأيَّام
Heat	حَرَارَةٌ
It is hot, it is live	هُنَاك حَرارَةٌ
It will be nice	يَكُونُ حَسَنًا
How long, till when	حَتَّى مَتَى
To stay	أقَامَ / يُقِيْمُ / إقَامَةً
To return, to come back	رَجَعَ / يَرْجِعُ / رُجُوعًا
When	عِنْدَمَا
When we come back	عِنْدَمَا نَعُودُ / نَرْجِعُ
Fine, good	طَيِّبٌ
To prepare, to get ready	إسْتَعَدَّ / يَسْتَعِدُّ / إسْتِعْدَادًا
To ge ready	أخَذَ / يَأْخُذُ (الإِسْتِعْدَادَ)
By bus	بالبَاص / بالبَص
To be	كَانَ / يَكُونُ / كَوْنًا
He was	كَانَ
He was not	مَا كَانَ / لَمْ يَكُنْ
Was he	هَلْ كَانَ / أكَانَ
Free, unoccupied	فَاضِى / خَالِى
To prepare s.th.	أعَدَّ / يُعِدُّ / إِعْدَادًا
To drink	شَرِبَ / يَشْرَبُ / شُرْبًا

To talk	تَحَدَّثَ / يَتَحَدَّثُ / تَحَدُّثًا
Many, much	كَثِيرٌ
Many things	أَشْيَاءُ كَثِيرَةٌ
About	حَوْلَ / عَنْ
Comparative/ superlative noun (adjectival)	إِسْمُ التَفْضِيلِ
More spacious	أَوْسَعُ
Bulkier, thicker	أَضْخَمُ
More beautiful	أَجْمَلُ
More interesting	مُمْتِعٌ أَكْثَرُ
More difficult	أَصْعَبُ
Taller, lengthier	أَطْوَلُ
Shorter	أَقْصَرُ
Cheaper	أَرْخَصُ
Costlier	أَغْلَى
More intelligent	أَذْكَى
Senior, older	أَقْدَمُ / أَكْبَرُ
Sweeter	أَحْلَى
Voice, sound	صَوْتٌ / أَصْوَاتٌ
More hardworking	مُجْتَهِدٌ أَكْثَرُ
Servant	خَادِمٌ / خَدَمٌ
Rupee	رُوْبِيَةٌ / رُوبِيَاتٌ
One hundred rupees	مِئَةُ رُوبِيَةٍ
I want to read	أَوَدُّ أَنْ أَقْرَأَ
Do you want to see	هَلْ تُرِيدُ أَنْ تَرَى
I request you to visit	أَرْجُو أَنْ تَزُورَ
I can not go	لَا يُمْكِنُ لِي أَنْ أَذْهَبَ
I pray to God to give me	أَدْعُوا إِلَى الله أَنْ يُعْطِينِى
To come	قَدِمَ / يَقْدَمُ / قُدُومًا

Elder	أَكْبَرُ
Is he?	هَلْ هُوَ؟ أَهُوَ؟
Younger	أَصْغَرُ
Parked	وَاقِفَةٌ
New	جَدِيدٌ
Old	قَدِيمٌ
Sorry (I am)	آسِفٌ
Sick/ unwell	مَرِيضٌ / مَرْضَى
My dear friend	صَدِيقِى الْعَزِيزُ
Airport	مَطَارٌ / مَطَارَاتٌ
Delhi International Airport	مَطَارُ دِلْهِى الدَّوَلِى
Old, aged	مُسِنٌّ
To be able, can	أَمْكَنَ / يُمْكِنُ / إِمْكَانًا
In the afternoon	عَصْرًا / فِى الْعَصْرِ
Thanks, Thank you	شُكْرًا
Journalism	صَحَافَةٌ
Daily newspaper	صَحِيفَةٌ
Journalistic; journalist	صُحُفِىٌّ
Presiden, head, chief, chairman	رَئِيسٌ / رُؤَسَاءُ
Egypt	مِصْرُ
India	الْهِنْدُ
To hold (talks)	أَجْرَى / يُجْرِى / إِجْرَاءً (مُحَادَثَاتٍ)
To improve	حَسَّنَ / يُحَسِّنُ / تَحْسِينًا
Relation/s	رَابِطَةٌ / رَوَابِطُ، عَلَاقَةٌ / عَلَاقَاتٌ
Bilateral relations	عَلَاقَاتٌ ثُنَائِيَّةٌ
Between	بَيْنَ
Source	مَصْدَرٌ / مَصَادِرُ
Official source	مَصْدَرٌ رَسْمِىٌّ

Ambassador	سَفِيرٌ / سُفَرَاءُ
To convey	بَلَّغَ / يُبَلِّغُ / تَبْلِيغًا
Message	رِسَالَةٌ / رِسَالَاتٌ
Verbal message	رِسَالَة شَفَهِيَّة
Written message	رِسَالَة خَطِّيَّة
Regarding	حَوْلَ / عَنْ
Prime Minister	رئيسُ الوُزَرَاءِ
To reach, to arrive (at)	وَصَلَ / يَصِلُ / (إلَى) وُصُولًا
London	لُنْدُن
Pakistan	بَاكِسْتَان
Israel	إسْرَائيل
Afternoon	بَعْدَ الظُّهْرِ / ظُهْرًا
Britain	بريطَانِيَا
Visit	زِيَارَةٌ / زِيَارَاتٌ
Official visit	زِيَارَةٌ رَسْمِيَّةٌ
Six-day (long)	تَسْتَغْرِقُ سِتَّةَ أَيَّام
Solution	حَلٌّ / حُلُولٌ
Peaceful	سِلْمِيٌّ
Problem	مُشْكِلَةٌ / مَشَاكِلُ
Middle East	الشَّرْقُ الأَوسَطُ
PLO=Palestinian Liberation Organisation	مُنَظَّمَةُ التَّحْرِيرِ الفِلَسْطِينِيَّة
Cairo	القَاهِرَةُ
Last night	البَارِحَة
Top officials	كِبَارُ المُوَظَّفِينَ
Situation	وَضْعٌ / أَوْضَاعٌ
Current situation	الْوَضْعُ الرَّاهِنُ
Region	إقْلِيمٌ / أَقَالِيمُ

Minister	وَزِيرٌ / وُزَرَاءُ
Minister of state	وَزِيرُ الدَّوْلَةِ
Foreign Affairs	الشُّؤُونُ الخارِجِيَّةُ
Vienna	فِيِينا
Hungary	المَجَر
Authorities	سُلْطَةٌ / سُلُطَاتٌ
Aiming (at), To aim at	هَدَفَ / يَهدِفُ / هَدَفًا (إلى)
To strengthen	عَزَّزَ / يُعَزِّزُ / تَعْزِيزًا
United Arab Emirates (UAE)	الإمَارَاتُ العَرَبِيَّةِ المُتَّحِدَةُ
Tunisia	تُونس
Member	عُضوٌ / أعْضَاءُ
Committee	لَجْنَةٌ / لِجَانٌ
Executive Committee	اللَّجْنَةُ التَّنْفِيذِيَّةُ
To hold (meeting)	عَقَدَ / يَعقِدُ / عَقْدًا
Meeting	إجْتِمَاعٌ / إجْتِمَاعَاتٌ
Palace	قَصْرٌ / قُصُورٌ
Kartaj Palace	قَصْرُ قَرطَاج
Present at the meeting were...	حَضَرَ الإجْتِمَاعَ
Foreign Minister	وَزِيرُ الخارِجِيّةِ
Home Minister	وَزِيرُ الدَّاخِلِيَّةِ
Representative	مُمَثِّلٌ / مُمَثِّلُونَ
Last month	فِى الشَّهرِ المَاضِى
To meet	قَابَلَ / يُقَابِلُ / مُقَابَلَةً
He was with him	كَانَ مَعَه
Hour; watch, clock	سَاعَةٌ / سَاعَاتٌ
For one hour	لِسَاعَةٍ
Pressmen	رِجَالُ الصَّحَافَةِ
To discuss	بَحَثَ / يَبْحَثُ / بَحْثًا

Last week (in the)	فى الأُسْبُوعِ المَاضِى
Public Works Minister	وَزِيْرُ الأَشْغَالِ العَامَّةِ
Syria	سُورِيَة
Syrian	سُورِىٌّ
To last	إسْتَغْرَق / يَسْتَغْرِقُ / إسْتِغْرَاقًا
Only	فَقَطْ
Minute	دَقِيْقَةٌ / دَقَائِقُ
Report	تَقْرِيْرٌ / تَقَارِيْرُ
Pressreports	التَّقَارِيْرُ الصُّحُفِيَّةُ
Present Chairman	الرَّئِيْسُ الحَالِى
Organisation of Arab Unity	مُنَظَّمَةُ الإتِّحَادِ العَرَبِى
Effort, attempt	مُحَاوَلَةٌ / مُحَاوَلَاتٌ
Oil producing countries	الدُّوَلُ المُنْتِجَةُ للبِتْرُول
Non-oil producing countries	الدُّولُ غَيْرُ المُنْتِجَةِ للبترُولِ
Arab countries	الدُّوَلُ العَرَبِيَّةُ
African countries	الدُّوَلُ الإفْرِيْقِيَّةُ
Result, consequence	نَتِيجَةٌ / نَتَائِجُ
Natrural consequences	النَّتَائِجُ الطَّبِيعِيَّةُ
Price, rate	سِعْرٌ / أَسْعَارٌ
Under Secretary	وَكِيْلُ الوِزَارَةِ
To appeal, to urge	نَاشَدَ / يُنَاشِدُ / مُنَاشَدَةً
People	شَعْبٌ / شُعُوبٌ
Family planning	تَنْظِيمُ الأُسْرَةِ
To ensure	لِضَمان ١
To assure, to guarantee	ضَمَنَ / يَضْمُنُ / ضَمَانًا
Standard	مِعْيَارٌ / مَعَايِيرُ
Standard of living	مِعْيَارُ المَعِيْشَةِ
Satisfactory	مُرْضٍ / مُرْضِى

For/to all	لِلْجَمِيعِ
Especially	خَاصَّةً / بِخَاصَّةٍ
Weaker sections	الطَّبَقَاتُ المَحْدُودَةُ الدَّخْلِ
Radio	إِذَاعَةٌ
Television	تِلِفِزْيُون
Prosperity	رَفَاهِيَّةٌ
To depend (on)	إِعْتَمَدَ / يَعْتَمِدُ / إِعْتِمَادًا (عَلى)
Family	أُسْرَةٌ / أُسَرٌ
We have been making efforts	نَبْذُلُ مَجْهُودَاتٍ
To develop	طَوَّرَ / يُطَوِّرُ / تَطْوِيرًا
To develop	نَمَّى / يُنَمِّى / تَنمِيَةً
Employment, work	وَظِيفَةٌ / وَظَائِفُ
Iraq	العِراق
To sign	وَقَّعَ / يُوَقِّعُ (عَلى) / تَوْقِيعًا
Minutes (of meeting)	مَحْضَرٌ / مَحَاضِرُ
Joint Minutes	مَحْضَرٌ مُشْتَرَكٌ
Cooperation	تَعَاوُنٌ
Economic cooperation	التَّعَاوُنُ الإِقْتِصَادِيُّ
Trade cooperation	التَّعَاوُنُ التِّجَارِيُّ
Technical cooperation	التَّعَاوُنُ الفَنِّيُّ
Cultural cooperation	التَّعَاوُنُ الثَّقَافِيُّ
Industrial cooperation	التَّعَاوُنُ الصِّنَاعِيُّ
To explore	نَقَّبَ / يُنَقِّبُ / تَنْقِيبًا (عَنْ)
Means, path, pathway	سَبِيلٌ / سُبُلٌ
Way, route	طَرِيقٌ / طُرُقٌ
To consolidate	كَثَّفَ / يُكَثِّفُ / تَكْثِيفًا
Tie; relation	رَابِطَةٌ / رَوَابِطُ
Industry	صِنَاعَةٌ / صِنَاعَاتٌ

Agriculture	زِرَاعَةٌ
Cultrue	ثَقَافَةٌ / ثَقَافَاتٌ
Transport	نَقْلٌ
Nepal	النيبال
Neighbour	جَارٌ / جِيْرَانٌ
Country, state	دَوْلَةٌ / دُوَلٌ
Neighbouring country	دولَةٌ جَارَةٌ
To assume (office)	تَقَلَّدَ / يَتَقَلَّدُ / تَقَلُّدًا (المَنْصِبَ)
Standing	وَاقِفٌ / وَاقِفُونَ
Sitting	جَالِسٌ / جَالِسُونَ
Teacher, instructor	مُعَلِّمٌ / مُعَلِّمُونَ
Tamiya i.e. a fried stuff resembling pakora	طَعْمِيَّةٌ
i.e. a piece of some vegetable covered	
with chick-pea flour and deep fried	
Together	سَوِيًّا
Day time (from sunrise to sunset)	نَهَارٌ / أَنْهُرٌ
Room	غُرْفَةٌ / غُرَفٌ / غُرُفَاتٌ
To find	وَجَدَ / يَجِدُ / وُجُوْدًا
Specialist	مُتَخَصِّصٌ / مُتَخَصِّصُونَ
Client	زَبُونٌ / زَبَائِنُ
Crowded	مُزْدَحِمٌ
Counter	كُوَّةٌ / كُوَّاتٌ
Queue	طَابُورٌ / طَوَابِيرُ
To wait	إِنْتَظَرَ / يَنْتَظِرُ / إِنْتِظَارًا
Receipt counter	كُوَّةُ الإِسْتِلَامِ
Payment counter	كُوَّةُ الدَّفْعِ
Dawn, early morning	فَجْرٌ
Toothpaste	مَعْجُونُ الأَسْنَانِ

News	خَبَرٌ / أَخْبَارٌ
Bursh	فُرْشَةٌ / فُرْشَاتٌ
To take bath	إغْتَسَلَ / يَغْتَسِلُ / إغْتِسَالاً
To wear clothes	لَبِسَ / يَلْبَسُ / لُبْسًا
Breakfast	فُطُورٌ
Lunch	غَدَاءٌ
Dinner	عَشَاءٌ
Bread	عَيْشٌ
Egg	بَيْضَةٌ / بَيْضٌ
Butter	زُبْدَةٌ
Milk	لَبَنٌ
Hand bag, vanity bag	حَقِيبَةُ اليَدِ
To go out, to leave	خَرَجَ / يَخْرُجُ / خُرُوجًا
To begin, to start	بَدَأَ / يَبْدَأُ / بَدْءً
Exact	تَمَامًا
At 5:00 O'clock exact	فى السَّاعَةِ الخَامِسَةِ تَمَامًا
Morning Newspaper	جَرِيدَةٌ صَبَاحِيَّةٌ
Intelligent	ذَكِيٌّ / أَذْكِيَاء
Cultured, civilized	مُهَذَّبٌ / مُهَذَّبُونَ
To play	لَعِبَ / يَلْعَبُ / لَعِبًا
To live, to reside	سَكَنَ / يَسْكُنُ / سَكَنًا
Flat, apartment	شُقَّةٌ / شِقَقٌ
Floor	دَوْرٌ / أَدْوَارٌ
Ground floor	الدَّورُ الأَرْضِىُّ
Balcony	شُرْفَةٌ / شُرْفَاتٌ
Father	وَالِدٌ
Mother	وَالِدَةٌ
People, humanbeing	إنْسَانٌ / أُنَاسٌ

Street, road	شَارِعٌ / شَوَارِعُ
Vehicles	عَرَبَةٌ / عَرَبَاتٌ
To sleep	نَامَ / يَنَامُ / نَوْمًا
Comfortable	مُرِيْحٌ
Mattress	مَرْتَبَةٌ / مَرْتَبَاتٌ
Bedsheet	مُلَاءَةٌ / مُلَاءَاتٌ
Quilt	لِحَافٌ / لُحُفٌ
Blanket	بَطَّانِيَّةٌ / بَطَّانِيَّاتٌ
Pillow	وِسَادَةٌ / وَسَائِدُ
Guest	ضَيْفٌ / ضُيُوفٌ
Active	نَشِيْطٌ / نُشَطَاءُ
Beloved	مَحْبُوبٌ / مَحْبُوبُونَ
All	جَمِيعٌ
With all the people	عِندَ جَمِيْعِ النَّاسِ
Ash-coloured, Grey	رَمَادِيٌّ
To hang	عَلَّقَ / يُعَلِّقُ / تَعْلِيقًا
Shoulder	كَتِفٌ / أَكْتَافٌ
To put	وَضَعَ / يَضَعُ / وَضْعًا
Letter	رِسَالَةٌ / رَسَائِلُ
Parcel	طَرْدٌ / طُرُودٌ
In the sun	فِى الشَّمْسِ
Sun	شَمْسٌ / شُمُوسٌ
Rain	مَطَرٌ / أَمْطَارٌ
In the rain	فى المَطَرِ
To perform	أَدَّى / يُؤَدِّى / تَأْدِيَةً
Duty	وَاجِبٌ / وَاجِبَاتٌ
To deliver, to handover	سَلَّمَ / يُسَلِّمُ / تَسْلِيمًا
News, information	نَبَأٌ / أَنْبَاءٌ

Happy	سَارٌّ
Sad	مُحْزِنٌ
To feel	شَعَرَ / يَشْعُرُ / شُعُورًا
Happiness	سُرُورٌ
Person	شَخْصٌ / أشْخَاصٌ
Famous, known	مَعْرُوفٌ / مَعْرُوفُونَ
Respected	مُحْتَرَمٌ / مُحْتَرَمُونَ
Village	قَرْيَةٌ / قُرًى
Villager	قَرَوِيٌّ / قَرَوِيُّونَ
To respect	إحْتَرَمَ / يَحْتَرِمُ / إحْتِرَامًا
To love	أحَبَّ / يُحِبُّ / مَحَبَّةً
Capital (city)	عَاصِمَةٌ / عَوَاصِمُ
Factory, palnt	مَصْنَعٌ / مَصَانِعُ
Station	مَحَطَّةٌ / مَحَطَّاتٌ
Radio station	مَحَطَّةُ الإذَاعَةِ
T.V. station	مَحَطَّةُ التِّلْفَازِ
Parliament House	دَارُ البَرْلَمَانِ
Republic	جُمْهُورِيَةٌ
President of the Republic	رَئِيسُ الجُمْهُورِيَّةِ
Living area, colony	حَارَةٌ / حَارَاتٌ
Inmate, resident	سَاكِنٌ / سُكَّانٌ
Fort	قَلْعَةٌ / قِلَاعٌ
Red Fort	القَلْعَةُ الحَمْرَاءُ
Leader	زَعِيْمٌ / زُعَمَاءُ
National leader	الزَّعِيْمُ الوَطَنِيُّ
Facility, utility, appurtenance	مَرْفِقٌ / مَرَافِقُ
Facilities of life	مَرَافِقُ الحياةِ
Important	هَامٌّ

Like, for example	مِثْل
Mail	بَرِيدٌ
Post Office	مَكْتَبُ الْبَرِيدِ
Centre	مَرْكَزٌ / مَرَاكِزُ
Police Station	مَرْكَزُ الشُّرْطَةِ
First aid centre	مَرْكَزُ الإِسْعَافِ
Fire station	مَرْكَزُ المَطَافِئِ
Railways	السِّكَّةُ الحَدِيدُ
Hospital	مُسْتَشْفَى / مُسْتَشْفَيَاتٌ
Public Hospital	المُسْتَشْفَى العَامُّ
To be situated	وَقَعَ / يَقَعُ / وُقُوعًا
Kilometre	كِلُومِتر
To build	بَنَى / يَبْنِى / بِنَاءً
Memory	تِذْكَارٌ
Marble	مَرْمَر
White marble	المَرْمَرُ الأَبْيَضُ
Platform	مِصطَبَةٌ / مَصَاطِبُ
To appear	ظَهَرَ / يَظْهَرُ / ظُهُورًا
Form, face	شَكْلٌ / أَشْكَالٌ
Bright	لَامِعٌ
Night	لَيْلَةٌ / لَيَالى
Moonlit	مُقْمِرٌ
To come	أَتَى / يَأْتِى / إِتْيَانًا
To watch, to see	شَاهَدَ / يُشَاهِدُ / مُشَاهَدَةً
To be said	قِيلَ / يُقَالُ / قَوْلًا
To cost	كَلَّفَ / يُكَلِّفُ / تَكْلِيفًا
Money, funds, wealth	مَالٌ / أَمْوَالٌ
Fountain	نَافُورَةٌ / نَوَافِيرُ

To sprinkle	رَشَّ / يَرُشُّ / رَشًّا
Sign, symbol	رَمْزٌ / رُمُوزٌ
Glory	مَجْدٌ / أَمْجَادٌ
Proof	دَلِيلٌ / أَدِلَّةٌ
Love	حُبٌّ
Expensive, costly	ثَمِينٌ
Good	طَيِّبٌ / طَيِّبُونَ
Only	فَقَطْ
Earlier	مِنْ قَبْلُ
To move, to run	سَارَ / يَسِيرُ / سَيْرًا
To drag, to pull	جَرَّ / يَجُرُّ / جَرًّا
Benzin, petrol	بِنْزِين
Train	قِطَارٌ / قِطَارَاتٌ
Steam	بُخَارٌ / أَبْخِرَةٌ
To cover	قَطَعَ / يَقْطَعُ / قَطْعًا
Way, passage	طَرِيقٌ / طُرُقٌ
Pedestrian	مَاشِى / مُشَاةٌ
To pass	مَرَّ / يَمُرُّ / مُرُورًا
Wheel	عَجَلَةٌ / عَجَلَاتٌ
Steering wheel	عَجَلَةُ القِيَادةِ
Tyre; frame-work	إِطَارٌ / إِطَارَاتٌ
Mile	مِيلٌ / أَمْيَالٌ
Rubber	مَطَّاطٌ
To cause, to create	أَحْدَثَ / يُحْدِثُ / إِحْدَاثًا
To drive, to lead	قَادَ / يَقُودُ / قِيَادَةً
Information	مَعْلُومَاتٌ
Useful	مُفِيدٌ
To thank	شَكَرَ / يَشْكُرُ / شُكْرًا

Thank you very much, thanks a lot	شُكْرًا جَزِيلًا
Pardon! sorry	عَفْوًا/ العَفْوَ
Success	نَجَاحٌ/ نَجَاحَاتٌ
Examination	إمْتِحَانٌ/ إمْتِحَانَاتٌ
Last	أَخِيرٌ
To help, to assist	سَاعَدَ/ يُسَاعِدُ/ مُسَاعَدَةً
To complete, to carry out	أنجَزَ/ يُنْجِزُ/ إنْجَازًا
To educate, to instruct	عَلَّمَ/ يُعَلِّمُ/ تَعْلِيمًا
To know	عَرَفَ/ يَعْرِفُ/ عِرْفَانًا
Time	زَمَنٌ/ أَزْمَانٌ
Minute	دَقِيقَةٌ/ دَقَائِقُ
To equate, to be equal to	سَاوَى/ يُسَاوِى/ مُسَاوَاةً
Second, 1/60 minute	ثَانِيَةٌ/ ثَوَانِى
Dial; Port, seaport,	مِينَاءٌ/ مِينَاءَاتٌ
Figure	رَقْمٌ/ أَرْقَامٌ
Hand (of a watch)	عَقْرَبٌ/ عَقَارِبُ
To point (to)	أَشَارَ/ يُشِيرُ (إلَى) إشَارَةً
To hold	عَقَدَ/ يَعْقِدُ/ عَقْدًا
Cabinet, council of ministers	الْمَجْلِسُ الوِزَارِىُّ
Soon	عَاجِلًا
Headship, presidentship	رِئَاسَةٌ
To attend	حَضَرَ/ يَحْضُرُ/ حُضُورًا
Number	عَدَدٌ/ أَعْدَادٌ
Issue, problem	مَسْأَلَةٌ/ مَسَائِلُ
To concern	هَمَّ/ يَهُمُّ/ هَمًّا
Finance Minister	وَزِيرُ الْمَالِيَّةِ
Education Minister	وَزِيرُ (التَّعْلِيمِ وَ) التَّرْبِيَةِ
Public Works Minister	وَزِيرُ الثَّقَافَةِ

Home Minister	وَزِيرُ الدَّاخِلِيَّةِ
Foreign Minister	وَزِيرُ الخَارِجِيَّةِ
Minister	وَزِيرٌ / وُزَراءُ
Reason	سَبَبٌ / أَسْبَابٌ
For some reasons	لِأَسْبَابٍ مَا
Cold	بَارِدٌ
Very cold	بَارِدٌ جِدًّا
Class/classroom	صَفٌّ / صُفُوفٌ
Clothe	ثَوْبٌ / ثِيَابٌ
Wool	صُوفٌ / أَصْوَافٌ
Woollen	صُوفِيٌّ
To open	فَتَحَ / يَفْتَحُ / فَتْحًا
To teach	دَرَّسَ / يُدَرِّسُ / تَدْرِيسًا
Obscure/difficult	غَامِضٌ
He began to write	أَخَذَ يَكْتُبُ
Meaning	مَعْنًى / مَعَانِي
Miss (Unmarried girl)	آنِسَةٌ / أَوَانِسُ
Mr./ gentleman	سَيِّدٌ / سَادَةٌ
Mrs./ lady	سَيِّدَةٌ / سَيِّدَاتٌ
O' (each one of these is vocative)	يَا / يَا أَيُّهَا / أَيْ
People, nation	شَعْبٌ / شُعُوبٌ
To love, to like	وَدَّ / يَوَدُّ / وِدَادًا
Link, connection	صِلَةٌ / صِلَاتٌ
Friendly relation	صِلَةٌ وُدِّيَّةٌ
Neighbour	جَارٌ / جِيرَانٌ
Deep heart	صَمِيمُ القَلْبِ
Heart	قَلْبٌ / قُلُوبٌ
To happen	حَدَثَ / يَحْدُثُ / حُدُوثًا

War	حَرْبٌ / حُرُوبٌ
However	عَلَى أَنَّه
Army	جَيْشٌ / جُيُوشٌ
Strong	قَوِيٌّ / أَقْوِيَاءُ
Defence	دِفَاعٌ
Sovereignty	سِيَادَةٌ
Pilot	طَيَّارٌ / طَيَّارُونَ
Seaman, navy man	بَحَّارٌ / بَحَّارُونَ
Artillery man	مِدْفَعِيٌّ / مِدْفَعِيُونَ
To defend	دَافَعَ / يُدَافِعُ / مُدَافَعَةً
Bravery	شَجَاعَةٌ
To protect, to defend	حَمَى / يَحْمِى / حِمَايَةً
Evil	شَرٌّ / أَشْرَارٌ
To ward (off)	رَدَّ / يَرُدُّ (عَن)
Attack, aggression	عُدْوَانٌ
Noon	ظُهْرٌ
Afternoon	بَعْدَ الظُّهْرِ
Scheduled time, Appointment	مَوْعِدٌ / مَوَاعِدُ
Bulletin	نَشْرَةٌ / نَشَرَاتٌ
Second News Bulletin	نَشْرَةُ الأَخْبَارِ الثَّانِيَةُ
End	خِتَامٌ
Commentary	تَعْلِيقٌ / تَعْلِيقَاتٌ
Brief/ headlines	مُوجَزٌ
Session	جَلْسَةٌ / جَلْسَاتٌ
To be completed	تَمَّ / يَتِمُّ / تَمَامًا
Elections	إِنْتِخَابَاتٌ
To send	أَرْسَلَ / يُرْسِلُ / إِرْسَالًا
Security Forces	قُوَّاتُ الأَمْنِ

Country	بَلَدٌ / بُلْدَانٌ
Security Council	مَجْلِسُ الأَمْنِ
United Nations	الأُمَمُ المُتَّحِدَةُ
News	نَبَأٌ / أَنْبَاءٌ
Detail	تَفْصِيلٌ / تَفْصِيلَاتٌ
To hear, to listen	سَمِعَ / يَسْمَعُ / سَمْعًا
Every day three times, thrice in a day	كُلَّ يَوْمٍ ثَلَاثَ مَرَّاتٍ
To broadcast	أَذَاعَ / يُذِيعُ / إِذَاعَةً
Good morning	صَبَاحَ الخَيْرِ
How	كَيْفَ
How do you do?	كَيْفَ الحَالُ
Good	خَيْرٌ
I am good, I am o.k.	أَنَا بِخَيْرٍ
God be praised	اَلْحَمْدُ لِلَّهِ
Engineer	مُهَنْدِسٌ / مُهَنْدِسُونَ
Confrere, colleague (in profession)	زَمِيلِي فِي العَمَلِ
To represent	مَثَّلَ / يُمَثِّلُ / تَمْثِيلًا
Company	شِرْكَةٌ / شِرْكَاتٌ
Project	مَشْرُوعٌ / مَشَارِيعُ
Engineering Projects	اَلْمَشَارِيعُ الهَنْدَسِيَّةُ
Major, main	رَئِيسِيٌّ
To do s. th., to carry out	قَامَ / يَقُومُ / قِيَامًا (ب)
To execute, to implement	نَفَّذَ / يُنَفِّذُ / تَنْفِيذًا
Friendly country	البَلَدُ الصَّدِيقُ
Friendly countries	اَلْبُلْدَانُ الصَّدِيقَةُ
To meet	قَابَلَ / يُقَابِلُ / مُقَابَلَةً
Excellency	مَعَالِي
His Excellency the Minister of Industry	مَعَالِي وَزِيرُ الصِّنَاعَةِ

Any	أَيُّ
For God's sake	بِاللهِ
To be kind	تَكَرَّمَ/ يَتَكَرَّمُ/ تَكَرُّمًا
If	لَو
If you could	لَو تَكَرَّمْتَ
Welcome	أَهْلًا وسَهْلًا
Yes	نَعَمْ
No	لَا
Sir	يَاسَيِّدِى
Married	مُتَزَوِّجٌ/ مُتَزَوِّجُونَ
I am not	أَنَا لَسْتُ
I have	عِندِى
Child	طِفْلٌ/ أَطْفَالٌ
To come	جَاءَ/ يَجِىءُ/ جِيْئَةً
Assignment, mission, work	مُهِمَّةٌ/ مُهِمَّاتٌ
Hotel	فُنْدُقٌ/ فَنَادِقُ
How much	كَمْ
Coffee	قَهْوَةٌ
To want, to wish	أَرَادَ/ يُرِيْدُ/ إِرَادَةً
A bien tot, see you	إِلَى اللِّقَاء
With peace, bye bye	مَعَ السَّلَامَةِ

Translation Exercises
Arabic-English
With Glossary

إِتَّصَلَ الرَّئِيسُ الْأَمْرِيكِيُّ جورج بُوش هاتِفِيًّا لِأَوَّلِ مَرَّةٍ بِالرئيس السُّورِى بَشَّار الْأَسَد.

وَقَالَتْ وكالَةُ الأَنْباء السُّورِيَّةُ الرَّسْمِيَّةُ إنَّ الرَّئِيسَيْنِ أَعْرَبَا خِلالَ الْمُكالَمَةِ عَن رَغْبَتِهِما فِى الْعَمَلِ مِن أَجْلِ التَّوَصُّلِ إِلَى اتِّفاقِ سلام فِى الشَّرق الأَوْسَطِ.

وَذَكَرَتْ الوكالَةُ السُّورِيَّةُ أن الرَّئِيسَ السُّورِىَّ شَدَّدَ عَلَى الْحاجَةِ لِمُعالَجَةِ مَشاكِلِ الْمِنْطَقَةِ بِصُورَةٍ إِيجابِيَّةٍ وَحَيادِيَّةٍ.

☆ ☆ ☆

أَعْلَنَ سفِيرُ الْمَمْلَكَةِ الْعَرَبِيَّةِ السُّعُودِيَّةِ فِى الْكُويت احمد اليحيى أَنَّ الْمَمْلَكَةَ بَدَأَتْ بِتَطْبِيقِ التَّنْظِيمِ الْجَدِيد لِخِدْماتِ الْمُعْتَمِرِينَ وَزُوَّارِ الْمَسْجِدِ النَّبَوِى الشَّرِيفِ وَذلك اعْتِبارًا مِّن غُرَّةِ صَفَرَ الْجارِى.

وأوضَحَ اليحيى أَنَّ التَّنْظِيمَ الْجَدِيدَ الَّذِى يُعْتَبَرُ نَقْلَةً نَوعِيةً فِى الْخِدْماتِ الْمُقَدَّمَةِ لِوُفُودِ الدِّيارِ الْمُقَدَّسَةِ يَعْتَمِدُ عَلَى تَقْدِيمِ الْخِدْماتِ للقادِمِينَ مِنْ خارِجِ الْمَمْلَكَةِ مِنْ قِبَلِ مُؤَسَّساتٍ أَو شَرِكاتٍ سُعُودِيَّةٍ تَحْتَ إِشْرافِ وِزارَةِ الْحَجِّ السُّعُودِيَّةِ.

☆ ☆ ☆

أَعْلَنَ وَزِيرُ التَّرْبِيَةِ وَ التَّعْلِيمِ الْعالِى د.مساعد الهارون أَنَّ وِزارَةَ التَّعْلِيمِ الْعالِى سَتَبْدَأُ الْيَوْمَ الْأَحَدَ فِى اسْتِقْبالِ الرّاغِبِينَ فِى انْشاءِ جَامِعاتٍ خَاصَّةٍ، لِمَلءِ نمُوذَجٍ اوَّلِىٍّ وَاسْتِيفاء الْمَعلومَاتِ الاساسِيَّةِ الْمَطْلُوبَةِ لتقدِيمِ الطَّلَباتِ وَقَالَ الهارُون فِى تَصْرِيحاتٍ أَدَلى بهَا عَقِبَ افْتِتاحِهِ مَعْرَضَ التَّسَوُّقِ الثّانِى وَالعِشْرِينَ فِى كُلِّيَةِ التَّرْبِيَةِ الاساسِيَّةِ أمس أَنَّ مَجْلِسَ الوُزَراءِ سَيُصادِقُ فِى جَلْسَتِهِ الأُسْبُوعِيَّةِ الْيَوْمَ عَلَى قانون مَجْلِسِ الْجَامِعاتِ الْخَاصَّةِ، مضِيفا «اننا بِصَدَدِ انِتْظارِ صُدُورِ الْمَرْسُومِ الاميرى لِقانونِ الجامعاتِ الخاصّة.

☆ ☆ ☆

وَقَعَتْ مَساءَ أمس مُشاجَرَةٌ بَيْنَ مَا يَزِيدُ عَنْ 150 صِينِيا وَعَدَدٍ مِّنْ أَبْناء الْمَمْلَكَةِ الْعَرَبِيَّةِ السُّعُودِيَّةِ الْمُقِيمِينَ فِى الْكُويت لِسَبَبِ إِصْرارِ أَحَدِ السُّعُودِيينَ عَلَى شُرْبِ الْمَاءِ قَبْلَ الْعُمّالِ الصِّينِيِّينَ مَا اثارَ حَفِيظَتهِم فوَقَعَتْ مَعْرَكَةٌ بَيْنَهُم فِى مَكانٍ مُنْعَزِلٍ فِى مَنْطِقَةِ جَلِيب الشيوخ أسفَرَتْ عَن إصابة ثمانية أَشْخاصٍ.

☆ ☆ ☆

إِسْتَقْبَلَ رَئِيسُ مَجْلِسِ الوُزَراءِ رَفِيق الْحَرِيرى أمس فِى السَّراى الْكَبِير الوَزِيرَ الاسْبَقَ مِيشال و إِسْتَعْرَضَ مَعَهُ التَطَوُّراتِ السِّياسِيَّةِ.

ثمَّ اسْتَقْبَلَ الرَّئِيسَ الحَرِيرِى رَئِيسَ إِتِّحادِ غُرَفِ التِّجارَةِ والزِّراعةِ فِى لُبْنان عدنان الَّذى أَطْلَعَهُ عَلَى المَشارِيعِ المُسْتَقْبَلِيَّةِ الَّتِى سَيَقُومُ بِهَا فِى ضَوْءِ إِنْتِخَابِهِ رَئِيسًا لِمَجْلِسِ رِجالِ الأَعْمَالِ اللبنانِيِّينَ و السورِيِّينَ و سُبُلِ تنشِيطِ العَلاقاتِ بَيْنَ القِطاعَيْنِ فِى لُبْنان وَسُورْيا. واسْتَقْبَلَ الرَّئِيسُ الحَرِيرِى ايضًا المُهَنْدِسَ هنرى صفير.

كَمَا الْتَقَى الرَّئِيسُ الحَرِيرِى أمسِ، رَئِيسَ تَحْرِيرِ جَرِيْدَةِ «الشَّرْقِ الأَوسطِ» الزميل عبد الرحمن الرشيد.

☆ ☆ ☆

إِلْتَقَى الأَمِينُ العام لِوِزارةِ الخَارجِيَّةِ السفيرُ زُهَير حمدان سفيرَ الهند آجاي شودرى، الذى نَقَل مَوقِفَ بِلادِهِ الدَّاعِمَ لِلُبنان بشأنِ رَفْضِ التَوطِينِ، وضرورة تَطْبِيقِ القَرارَاتِ الدُّوَلِيَّةِ الَّتِى تقرّ بِحقِّ عَوْدَةِ اللَّاجِئِينَ الفلسطينيين إِلَى دِيارِهِم ولا سِيَّما القرار ١٩٤ .

☆ ☆ ☆

سَوْفَ يَصِلُ رَئِيسُ مَجْلِسِ إدارةِ وِكَالةِ الأَنْباءِ الرُّوسِيَّةِ إِلَى لُبْنان غدًا فِى زِيَارةٍ يَلْتَقِى خِلالَهَا وَزِيرَ الإِعْلامِ اللُّبْنانِيَّ وَغَيْرَهُ مِنَ الشَّخْصِيَات.

وَكانَ قَدْ وَقَّعَ رَئِيسُ مَجْلِسِ إدارةِ وِكَالةِ الأَنْباءِ الرُّوسِيَّةِ وَالمُدِيرُ العَامُّ لِلوِكَالةِ العَرَبِيَّةِ السُّورِيَّةِ لِلْأَنْباءِ إِتِّفاقًا لِلتَّبَادُلِ الأَخْبَارِىّ بَيْنَ الْوِكَالَتَيْنِ فِى دِمَشق اوَّلَ مِن أمسِ وذَلِك فِى إطارِ تَطْوِيرِ العَلاقَاتِ الثُّنائِيَّةِ.

☆ ☆ ☆

إسْتَقْبَلَ السَّيِّدَ الدُّكْتُور مُحَمَّد مُصطَفَى مِيرُو رئِيسَ مَجْلِسِ الوُزَراءِ بَعدَ ظُهْرِ أمسِ السَّيدَ المهندِسَ حاتِمَ الحُلوَانِى وَزِيرَ المِياهِ والرَّىَّ الاردنِيَّ و حَضَرَ اللَّقاءَ السَّيِّدُ طه الأطرَش وزِيرُ الرَّىِّ.

وَ فِى بِدايَةِ اللِّقاءِ نَقَلَ السَّيِّدُ الحُلوَانِى تَحِيَّةَ الْمُهَنْدِسِ عَلِى أَبُو الرَّاغِب رَئِيس مَجْلِسِ الْوُزَراءِ الأُردنِى إِلَى السَّيِّدِ رَئِيسِ مَجْلِسِ الوُزَراءِ فشَكرَهُ عَلَيْهَا وَحَمَّلَهُ تَحِيَّاتِهِ إِلَيْهِ.

وَدارَ الحَدِيثُ خِلالَ اللِّقاءِ حَولَ تَطْوِيرِ عَلاقَاتِ التَّعاوُنِ بَيْنَ سُوريَا والأُرْدن وتَعْزِيزِهَا فِى شَتَّى الْمَجالَاتِ و لَا سِيَّمَا التَّعاوُن فِى مَجَالِ الْمِياهِ والقَضايا الْمَائِيَّةِ الَّتِى تَهُمُّ الْبَلَدَيْنِ.

حَضَرَ اللِّقَاءَ السَّادَةُ الدُّكْتُورُ خَالِد نَائِبُ رَئِيس مَجْلِس الوُزَرَاء لِلشُّئُون الإِقْتِصَادِيَّة وَالدُّكْتُور مُحَمَّد وَزِيرُ الإِقْتِصَاد وَالتِّجَارَة الْخَارِجِيَّة وَالْقَائِم بِأَعْمَال سِفَارَة جُمْهُورِيَّة يُوغُوسْلاَفِيا فى دِمشْق.

☆ ☆ ☆

أَقَامَ السَّيِّدُ حُسَيْن سَفِيرُ الجُمْهُورِيَّة الإِسلامِيَّة الإِيرَانِيَّة بِدِمَشْق حَفْلَ اسْتِقْبَالٍ مَسَاءَ أمس بِمُنَاسَبَة الْعِيد الْوَطَنِي.

حَضَرَ الْحَفْلَ السَّيِّدِ مُصْطَفى نَائِبُ القَائِد الْعَامِّ لِلْجَيْش وَالقُوَّات الْمُسَلَّحَة وَ بَعْض أَعْضاء القِيَادَة الْمَرْكَزِيَّة وَعَدَدٌ مِّنَ السَّادَة الْوُزَرَاء وَعَدَدٌ مِّنْ مُعَاوِنى الوزَراء. كَمَا حَضَرَ الْحَفْلَ عَدَدٌ مِّنْ أعضاء السِّلْك الدِّبْلُومَاسِى الْعَربى وَالْأجْنبى بِدِمَشْق.

☆ ☆ ☆

أَعْلَنَ وَزِيرُ الْخَارِجِيَّة الْأمْرِيكى أنَّهُ يَتَوَقَّعُ مِنَ الزُّعَماء الْعَرَب أَنْ يُشِيدُوا بِأَفْكَارِه الْخَاصَّة بِإِجْرَاء تَغْيِير فِى الْعُقُوبَات الْمَفْرُوضَة عَلَى الْعِرَاق. وَفِى نَفْسِ السِّيَاقِ حَذَّرَت الْأُمَمُ الْمُتَّحِدَة الْعِرَاقَ مِنَ اسْتِلاَم أَىِّ أَمْوَالٍ خَفِيَّةٍ عَلَى بَيْعِ نَفْطِه.

وَقَالَ وَزِيرُ الْخَارِجِيَّة الْأمْرِيكى أوَّلَ مِنْ أمس إِنَّهُ مَا زَالَ مُتَفَائِلاً فِى شَأْن التَّأيِيد الَّذِى تَلَقَّاهُ خِلاَل جَوْلَتِه فِى الشَّرْق الْأَوسَط وَمِنطَقَة الْخَلِيج فِى أوَاخِرِ فِبْرَايِر الْمَاضِى. وَأَضَاف فِى مُؤْتَمَرٍصُحُفِىٍّ مَعَ وَزِير خَارِجِيَّة السُّوِيد "أَعْتَقِدُ أَنَّ التَّأيِيد سَيُصْبِحُ عَلَنِيًّا فِى الْأَيَّام وَالْأَسَابِيع الْمُقْبِلَة عِنْدَمَا يَبْحَثُونَ كَيْفَ سَيُؤَيِّدُونَ المُبَادَرَات الَّتِى سَنَعرِضُها فِى الْأُمَم الْمُتَّحِدَة.

☆ ☆ ☆

تَسَلَّمَ رَئِيسُ الْجُمْهُورِيَّة الْيَمَنِيَّة أوْرَاقَ إِعْتِمَاد عَدَدٍ مِّنْ سُفَرَاء الدُّوَل الشَّقِيقَة وَالصَّدِيقَة لَدَى بِلادِنَا. وَتَسَلَّمَ أوْرَاق إِعْتِمَادِ كُلٍّ مِّنَ السَّفِير الكُويتى وَالسَّفِير الكُوبى وَالسَّفِير الْبَلجِيكى وَالسَّفِير الكُورى.

☆ ☆ ☆

سَادَ التَّوَتُّرُ فِى عَدَدٍ مِّنَ الْمَنَاطِق الفِلَسْطِينِيَّة الْمُحْتَلَّة أمس حَيْثُ حَصَلَت مُوَاجَهَاتٌ بَيْنَ جُنُودِ الإِحْتِلاَل الإِسرَائِيلِيِّ وَ أَبْنَاء الشَّعْب الفِلَسْطِينِيِّ.

فِى هَذَا الصَّدَد ذَكَرَتْ وَكَالَاتُ الأَنْبَاء أَنَّ قُوَّات الاحْتِلاَل عَزَّزَت نَوَاجِدَهَا العَسْكَرِىَّ عَلَى كَافَّة الْمَحَاوِر وَالطُّرُق الْمُؤَدِّيَة إِلَى مَدِينَة الْخَلِيل فِى الوَقْت الَّذِى يُوَاصِلُ فِيه الْمُسْتَوطِنُونَ إِعْتِدَاءَ اتِهِمْ عَلَى الْمُواطِنِيْن خَاصَّةً فِى الْجُزْء الْمُحْتَلِّ مِنَ الْمَدِينَة.

Glossary

الكلمات العسيرة

Companion, friend; comrade	رَفِيقٌ / رُفَقَاءُ
Rafik al Hariri (given name)	رفيق الحريرى
Seraglio	سَرَاى / سَرَايَاتٌ
Al SeraiAl Kabir	السَّرَاى الكَبِير
Former	أَسْبَقُ
Michel	ميشال
Development	تَطَوُّرٌ / تَطَوُّرَاتٌ
Then, after that	ثُمَّ
Union, federation	إتِّحَادٌ / إتِّحَادَاتٌ
Chamber, room	غُرْفَةٌ / غُرَفٌ
Chambers of Commerce & Agriculture	غُرَفُ التِّجَارَةِ والزِّرَاعَةِ
Lebanon	لُبْنَان
Adnan (given name)	عَدْنَان
To inform	أَطْلَعَ / يُطْلِعُ / إطْلاعًا
Project	مَشْرُوعٌ / مَشَارِيعُ
To review	إسْتَعْرَضَ / يَسْتَعْرِضُ / إسْتِعْرَاضًا
Future	مُسْتَقْبَلٌ
Related to future, future	مُسْتَقْبَلِيٌّ
Light	ضَوْءٌ
Employers' Council	مَجْلِسُ رِجَالِ الأَعْمَالِ
Ways, means	سَبِيلٌ / سُبُلٌ
To activate, to invigorate	نَشَّطَ / يُنَشِّطُ / تَنْشِيطًا
Syria	سُورِيَا
Henry Safir (given name)	هنرى صفير
As, also	كما
To meet	إلْتَقَى / يَلْتَقِى / إلْتِقَاءً

Editor/chief editor	رَئِيسُ التَّحْرِيرِ
Colleague, fellow	زَمِيلٌ ، زُمَلَاءُ
Fellowship	زَمَالَةٌ
To transfer, to copy, to convey	نَقَلَ ، يَنْقُلُ ، نَقْلًا
Stand	مَوقِفٌ ، مَوَاقِفُ
His country's stand	مَوقِفُ بِلَادِه
Supportive	دَاعِمٌ
Vis-a-vis, regarding	بِشَأْنِ
To refuse, to reject, to deny	رَفَضَ ، يَرْفُضُ ، رَفْضًا
Settlement	تَوطِينٌ
To make settlement	وَطَّنَ ، يُوَطِّنُ ، تَوطِينًا
To apply	طَبَّقَ ، يُطَبِّقُ ، تَطْبِيقًا
Decision, resolution	قَرَارٌ ، قَرَارَاتٌ
To admit, to approve	أَقَرَّ ، يُقِرُّ ، إِقْرَارًا
Right	حَقٌّ ، حُقُوقٌ
To return	عَادَ ، يَعُودُ ، عَودَةً
Refugee	لَاجِئٌ ، لَاجِئُونَ
House, home	دَارٌ ، دُورٌ ، دِيَارٌ
Specially	لَاسِيَّمَا
Board of directors	مَجْلِسُ الإِدَارَةِ
Russian News Agency	وِكَالَةُ الأَنْبَاءِ الرُّوسِيَّةِ
Minister of Information	وَزِيرُ الإِعْلَامِ
Personalities	شَخْصِيَّةٌ ، شَخْصِيَّاتٌ
Director General	المُدِيرُ الْعَامُّ
Agreement, protocol	إِتِّفَاقٌ ، إِتِّفَاقَاتٌ
Damascus	دِمَشْقُ
Day before yesterday	أَوَّلَ مِن أَمسِ
Framerwork; tyre	إِطَارٌ ، إِطَارَاتٌ

To improve, to better, to develop	طَوَّرَ / يُطَوِّرُ / تَطْوِيرًا
Bilateral relations	عَلاقَاتٌ ثُنَائِيَّةٌ
Noon	ظُهْرٌ
After noon	بَعْدَ الظُّهْرِ
Minister of Water and Irrigation	وَزِيرُ المِيَاهِ والرَّيِّ
Beginning, inception	بِدَايَةٌ / بِدَايَاتٌ
Meeting; interview	لِقَاءٌ / لِقَاءَاتٌ
Greetings, salutations	تَحِيَّةٌ / تَحِيَّاتٌ
To make carry	حَمَّلَ / يُحَمِّلُ / تَحْمِيلًا
To go round	دَارَ / يَدُورُ / دَورَانًا
To have talks	دَارَ الحَدِيثُ
To strengthen	عَزَّزَ / يُعَزِّزُ / تَعْزِيزًا
Different	شَتَّى
Field	مَجَالٌ / مَجَالَاتٌ
Issue, problem	قَضِيَّةٌ / قَضَايَا
To concern	هَمَّ / يَهُمُّ / هَمًّا
Mr.	سَيِّدٌ / سَادَةٌ
Economic affairs	الشُّؤُونُ الإِقْتِصَادِيَّةُ
To hold	أَقَامَ / يُقِيمُ / إِقَامَةً
Function, party	حَفْلٌ / حَفْلَاتٌ
Reception party	حَفْلُ الإِسْتِقْبَالِ
Occasion	مُنَاسَبَةٌ / مُنَاسَبَاتٌ
Festival	عِيدٌ / أَعْيَادٌ
National Day	اَلْعِيدُ الوَطَنِيُّ
Commander, commandant	قَائِدٌ / قُوَّادٌ
Commandant General	الْقَائِدُ العَامُّ
Army	جَيْشٌ / جُيُوشٌ
Armed forces	القُوَّاتُ المُسَلَّحَةُ

Some	بَعْضٌ
Member	عُضوٌ / أَعْضَاءُ
Central leadership	القِيَادَةُ الْمَرْكَزِيَّةُ
Number	عدَدٌ / أَعْدَادٌ
Some of	عَدَدٌ مِنْ
Assistant	مُعَاوِنٌ / مُعَاوِنُونَ
Assistant Minister	مُعَاوِنُ الوَزِيرِ
Diplomatic corps	اَلسِّلْكُ الدِّبْلُومَاسِى
To expect	تَوَقَّعَ / يَتَوَقَّعُ / تَوَقُّعًا
To appreciate, to extol	أَشَادَ / يُشِيْدُ / إِشَادَةً (ب)
Thought, idea	فِكْرٌ / أَفْكَارٌ
Sanction; punishment	عُقُوبَةٌ / عُقُوبَاتٌ
In the same context	فِى نَفْس السِّيَاقِ
To warn	حَذَّرَ / يُحَذِّرُ / تَحْذِيرًا
Money, fund	مَالٌ / أَمْوَالٌ
Secret, unknown	خَفِىٌّ
To sell	بَاعَ / يَبِيْعُ / بَيْعًا
Petroleum	نَفْطٌ
Still, continues	مَا زَالَ
Optimistic	مُتَفَائِلٌ / مُتَفَائِلُونَ
Support	تَأْيِيْدٌ
To receive	تَلَقَّى / يَتَلَقَّى / تَلَقِّيًا
Round, trip	جَوْلَةٌ / جَوْلَاتٌ
Middle East	الشَّرْقُ الأَوْسَطُ
End	آخِرُ / أَوَاخِرُ
To add	أَضَافَ / يُضِيفُ / إِضَافَةً
Conference	مُؤْتَمَرٌ / مُؤْتَمَرَاتٌ
Press Conference	مُؤْتَمَرٌ صُحُفِىٌّ

Sweden	السُّوِيْدُ
To believe	إِعْتَقَدَ / يَعْتَقِدُ / إِعْتِقَادًا
To be, to become	أَصْبَحَ / يُصْبِحُ / إِصْبَاحًا
Public	عَلَنِيٌّ
Coming, next	مُقْبِلٌ
To support	أَيَّدَ / يُؤَيِّدُ / تَأْيِيدًا
Initiative	مُبَادَرَةٌ / مُبَادَرَاتٌ
To present, to place	عَرَضَ / يَعْرِضُ / عَرْضًا
To receive	تَسَلَّمَ / يَتَسَلَّمُ / تَسَلُّمًا
Credentials	أَوْرَاقُ الإِعْتِمَادِ
Each one of	كُلٌّ مِنْ
Cuban	كُوبِى
Korean	كُورِى
Belgian	بَلْجِيكى
To prevail	سَادَ / يَسُودُ / سِيَادَةً
Tension	تَوَتُّرٌ
Area, region, zone	مِنْطَقَةٌ / مَنَاطِقُ
Occupied	مُحْتَلٌّ
To occupy	إِحْتَلَّ / يَحْتَلُّ / إِحْتِلَالاً
Where	حَيْثُ
To happen	حَصَلَ / يَحْصُلُ / حُصُولاً
Encounter	مُوَاجَهَةٌ / مُوَاجَهاتٌ
In this regard	فِى هَذَا الصَّدَدِ
To mention	ذَكَرَ / يَذْكُرُ / ذِكْرًا
Force	قُوَّةٌ / قُوَّاتٌ
Existence, presence	تَوَاجُدٌ
Military presence	التَّوَاجُدُ العَسْكَرِىُّ
All	كَافَّةً

Pivot, centre, axis	مِحْوَرٌ / مَحَاوِرُ
Way, path	طَرِيقٌ / طُرُقٌ
Ways leading to	الطُّرُقُ المُؤَدِّيَةُ
At the time when	فِى الوَقْتِ الَّذِى
To continue	وَاصَلَ / يُوَاصِلُ / مُوَاصَلَةً
Settler	مُسْتَوطِنٌ / مُسْتَوطِنُونَ
To settle, to build up settlement	إسْتَوْطَنَ / يَسْتَوطِنُ / إسْتِيْطَانًا
Portion	جُزْءٌ / أَجْزَاءٌ
To contact	إتَّصَلَ / يَتَّصِلُ / إتِّصَالًا بِ
Telephone	هَاتِفٌ / هَوَاتِفُ
Call (telephonic), talk, conversation	مُكَالَمَةٌ / مُكَالَمَاتٌ
To express	أَغْرَبَ / يُغْرِبُ / إغْرَابًا (عن)
Desire, wish	رَغْبَةٌ / رَغْبَاتٌ
For, for the sake of	مِنْ أَجْلِ
To reach (a decision etc.)	تَوَصَّلَ / يَتَوَصَّلُ / تَوَصُّلًا (إلى)
Peace	سَلَامٌ
To stress (on)	شَدَّدَ / يُشَدِّدُ / تَشْدِيْدًا (على)
Need	حَاجَةٌ / حَاجَاتٌ
To handle, to treat	عَالَجَ / يُعَالِجُ / مُعَالَجَةً
Positive way, positive manner	صُورَةٌ إِيْجَابِيَّةٌ
Neutral way, neutral manner	صُورَةٌ حِيَادِيَّةٌ
Kingdom, empire	مَمْلَكَةٌ / مَمَالِكُ
System, arrangement	تَنْظِيمٌ
Out season pilgrim to Kabah	مُعْتَمِرٌ
To perform out of season pilgrimage to Ka'bah	إعْتَمَرَ / يَعْتَمِرُ / إعْتِمَارًا
Inception, beginning	غُرَّةٌ
To explain	أوضَحَ / يُوضِحُ / إِيْضَاحًا
Shift	نَقْلَةٌ / نَقْلَاتٌ

Qualitative; typical	نَوعِيٌّ
To consider	إغْتَبَرَ / يَعْتَبِرُ / إغْتِبَارًا
Delegate, delegation	وَفْدٌ / وُفُودٌ
By	مِنْ قِبَل
Organisation, body	مُؤَسَّسَةٌ / مُؤَسَّسَاتٌ
Under the aegis of	تَحْتَ إشْرَاف
Ministry of Pilgrimage	وِزَارَةُ الحَجِّ
To establish	أنْشَأَ / يُنْشِئُ / إنْشَاءً
To fill up, to bridge up	مَلأَ / يَمْلأُ / مَلءً
Basic	أسَاسِيٌّ
Statement	تَصْرِيحٌ / تَصْرِيحَاتٌ
To release, give (statement)	أدْلَى / يُدْلِى / إدْلاءً (ب)
Inaugration	إفْتِتَاحٌ
To shop, to do shopping	تَسَوَّقَ / يَتَسَوَّقُ / تَسَوُّقًا
To attest, to certify, to authenticate	صَادَقَ / يُصَادِقُ / مُصَادَقَةً
The royal edict	المَرْسُومُ الأَمِيرِى
Quarrel, fight	مُشَاجَرَةٌ / مُشَاجَرَاتٌ
To insist (on)	أصَرَّ / يُصِرُّ / إصْرَارًا (عَلى)
To raise, to rouse	أثَارَ / يُثِيرُ / إثَارَةً
Anger	حَفِيظَةٌ
Segragated place, lonely place	مَكَانٌ مُنْعَزِلٌ